THE COLOR OF NIGHT

The Color of Night

RACE, RAILROADERS, AND MURDER
IN THE WARTIME WEST

Max G. Geier

Oregon State University Press   Corvallis

The paper in this book meets the guidelines for permanence and durability of the Committee on Production Guidelines for Book Longevity of the Council on Library Resources and the minimum requirements of the American National Standard for Permanence of Paper for Printed Library Materials Z39.48-1984.

Library of Congress Cataloging-in-Publication Data

Geier, Max G.
The color of night : race, railroaders, and murder in the wartime West
  / Max G. Geier.
    pages cm
  Includes bibliographical references and index.
   ISBN 978-0-87071-820-5 (paperback : alkaline paper) – ISBN 978-0-87071-821-2 (ebook)
   1. African American railroad employees–Oregon–Willamette River Valley–Social conditions–20th century. 2. Women, White–Crimes against–Oregon–Willamette River Valley–History–20th century. 3. Murder–Oregon–Willamette River Valley–History–20th century. 4. Folkes, Robert E. Lee, 1923-1945. 5. James, Martha Virginia Brinson, 1921-1943. 6. Trials (Murder)–Oregon–Albany–History–20th century. 7. Racism–Oregon–Willamette River Valley–History–20th century. 8. African Americans–Civil rights–Oregon–Willamette River Valley–History–20th century. 9. Willamette River Valley (Or.)–Race relations–History–20th century. 10. World War, 1939-1945–Social aspects–Oregon–Willamette River Valley.   I. Title.
   HD8039.R12U635 2015
   364.152'3092–dc23

                                     2015030572

First published in 2015 by Oregon State University Press
Printed in the United States of America

Oregon State University Press
121 The Valley Library
Corvallis OR 97331-4501
541-737-3166 • fax 541-737-3170
www.osupress.oregonstate.edu

Contents

Prologue
Workers, Women, and Warriors in an Oregon at War 7

Introduction
Seeing Color, Workers, and Ghosts in Oregon's Willamette Valley 19

Chapter One
Stories of a Snowy Winter's Night in the Willamette Valley 45

Chapter Two
Food Fights for Freedom 77

Chapter Three
The Marine, the Waiter, and the Man in the Pin-Striped Suit 119

Chapter Four
The Trials of Home and Away Lives
in Portland, Albany, and Los Angeles 155

Chapter Five
Men and Women of Conviction 199

Chapter Six
Trials of War and Hopes for Postwar Progress 245

Chapter Seven
Executing Judgment Oregon Style 281

Conclusion
Folkes on the Death Train in Oregon 331

Acknowledgments 349

Notes on Sources 351

Notes 353

Index 367

Prologue
Workers, Women, and Warriors in an Oregon at War

The young woman desperately seeking her missing luggage in blackout conditions at Union Station in Portland, Oregon, late one January night was just one of many college-age men and women aboard the same train, all uprooted from familiar surroundings by the military reorganization of the war. In the disorienting noise and midnight glare on the train platform, Martha Virginia Brinson James stood small and lost. Later descriptions of her said more about those describing her than about the person they noticed. Some remembered her as small, with brownish hair and a tired, anxious look. Others recalled a blonde bombshell confidently carrying off a coat trimmed in leopard fur with matching hat and muff. Others remarked on her pushy demeanor as she demanded assistance carrying her luggage to a forward sleeping compartment. Still others remembered a polite young girl with a sweet southern accent who graciously tipped those who assisted her. Back in her hometown, she was known as "Marti"—an accomplished, alert-looking student, who went to the local university, studied French, joined several campus clubs, and worked on a stage production titled "Women of the Jury." Then, she dropped out of college to marry the man voted "handsomest on campus," just before he was scheduled to leave to train as a navy pilot. Her parents threw the young couple the most lavish impromptu wedding they could muster, including announcements in the local society pages. She accompanied her handsome young navy officer to his first posting in the war—a training base near Bremerton, Washington. A slight woman of less than a hundred pounds, and barely five feet tall, Martha James was just twenty years old when she found herself standing alone on that train platform, far from home in the cold early morning of 23 January 1943.

Martha James' story collided that morning with the lives of three other young people of similar age but wildly different backgrounds. All of them wandered through Union Station in the icy darkness of the late evening and early morning hours and then boarded a train that carried them to an unexpected destination. None of them were from Oregon, but they all lost themselves there, and their passage changed the state. Richard James, Martha's husband, was travelling with his naval air unit from Bremerton to San Diego on routine reassignment to the Pacific theater of war. His background as the son of an Eastern Shore Virginia farmer could hardly have prepared him for what he saw and experienced while travelling through Seattle, Portland, and the Cascade Range as far as Klamath Falls, Oregon. He was equally unprepared for the role he stepped into with his hurried courtship and marriage to a society girl and accomplished undergraduate from Norfolk, Virginia. He and Martha began married life in late September 1942 at a military base on the Puget Sound, disconnected from their families on the Chesapeake. They began their journey south from Bremerton together, taking the ferry to Seattle and then a taxi to the depot. There, Richard James joined his unit on the southbound train, while Martha James, like other military wives, had to travel alone for the first time in her young life. While she wore civilian clothes, her husband travelled in the full dress uniform of a US Navy officer. In the company of other navy fliers, he cut a dashing and romantic figure. Airmen like James were America's best hope for holding the line against the Japanese in the first year of the war in the Pacific, after the naval disaster at Pearl Harbor. Taciturn, reserved, and aloof, James exuded an air of aristocratic authority that belied his farming background and lack of social connections before he married Marti. In late 1942 and early 1943, however, he and other airmen were the toast of the town, enjoying benefits from trainmen and fellow passengers, including free drinks and other favors. Sometime between 10:00 p.m. and midnight on 22 January 1943, just before Martha James struggled with her luggage on the Union Station platform, her husband, with other navy pilots and their wives (possibly including Martha), enjoyed a private drinking party that the dining car steward staged using supplies from the dining car attached to Train 15.

Rank and class differences separated Ensign Richard James from another young man of about the same age who was also travelling aboard Train 15 on military orders from the naval base near Bremerton to a new assignment in San Diego. Private Harold Wilson, like Richard James, was a recent recruit. He had volunteered for duty with the US Marine Corps only a few months earlier. While college-educated Richard James was adjusting to married life and his newfound status as an officer, high school dropout Harold Wilson, a single man, languished in the Bremerton brig, serving time for petty theft and disorderly conduct. The eldest son of a carpenter, Wilson grew up in a small town in southwestern Minnesota. He spent the first two decades of his life within twenty miles of that town and played football for two undistinguished years on the local high school team. His fiancée was a J.C. Penney clerk from the next town. With no connections or social standing, Wilson had few skills, less experience, and poor prospects when he volunteered for the Marines. He waited nearly a year after the war started and nearly three years after he was first eligible to serve before enlisting. Wilson lacked the status of a romantic flyboy, and he boarded Train 15 alone, without his unit or any other companions. Gregarious, outgoing, and ruggedly good-looking, however, he initiated conversations with complete strangers and managed to stand out from the crowd of uniformed servicemen among the other passengers. By some accounts, he talked his way into the steward's exclusive party earlier that evening, and as the train pulled away from Union Station, Wilson was seen chatting with a woman he had just met in one of the chair cars. Somewhere between 2:00 a.m. and 4:30 a.m., as the train rolled south through the mid-Willamette Valley, he got up and found a berth in a Pullman sleeping car.

When the James couple and Wilson stepped onto the train at Union Station, whatever their differences of gender, class, and status, they became simply passengers—unlike Robert E. Lee Folkes, who also arrived on board sometime after 9:30 that evening. The story of how Folkes wound up on Train 15 out of Union Station on that January night illuminates deep fissures of race and class that divided many wartime communities on the West Coast, particularly Portland, Oregon, and Los Angeles, California. Folkes was a twenty-year-old youth who had dropped out of high school at about the same time as Wilson, but for different reasons. The eldest son of a single mother, he found a career-track position with the railroad, working as a dining car cook. His wages supplemented his mother's earnings as a seamstress in the clothing district of downtown Los Angeles, and their combined income supported his two younger siblings. Folkes was born in rural Arkansas, but his mother moved the family to Los Angeles to escape racist pogroms before he was twelve years old. The move transported young Folkes from a rural backwater of prejudiced extremes to an urban center of emergent Jazz Age culture. As an African American growing up in South Central Los Angeles, Folkes attended a multiracial high school and lived in a walking neighborhood of vibrant African American nightclubs, advocacy journalists, writers, labor leaders, and progressive visionaries. When he went to work for the railroad, however, he entered a workplace that was segregated along color lines. African Americans were largely restricted to jobs as porters and dining car workers, or else they worked as redcaps in the Southern Pacific Station at South Central and 12th Street or at the newly constructed Los Angeles Union Station, while White workers mostly found more prestigious and better-paying positions as engineers, conductors, and brakemen. In dining car kitchens, however, Folkes worked in a relatively integrated setting: head cooks were typically White, and lower-ranking cooks were mostly Black. Some lower-ranking Black cooks worked their way up to head cooks, and most head cooks started out as entry-level cooks and worked their way up, even if they were White. Folkes had reached the rank of second cook after working there little more than a year.

At a time when A. Philip Randolph and the Brotherhood of Sleeping Car Porters (BSCP) were staging marches on Washington, DC, demanding fair treatment and living wages on the nation's railroads during the wartime speedup of the early 1940s, Folkes operated in the relatively autonomous world of the dining car cook. Whereas sleeping car porters and dining car waiters relied mostly on tips and were notoriously underpaid, dining car cooks seldom dealt directly with customers. Their wages depended less on obsequious demeanor and more on technical skills related to preparing and cooking meals on a moving platform. In this world, Folkes (apparently a fast learner) excelled at an early age. As second cook, he was known for his quick wit, enjoyed relative workplace autonomy, and mostly worked independent of supervision, at his own pace, to fulfill daily expectations. Whenever he stepped outside the dining car kitchen, however, he entered the segregated world that Randolph was struggling to reform. Dining car workers belonged to a different union, separate from Randolph's Brotherhood, and the Los Angeles local to which Folkes belonged was among the most radical in the Dining Car Workers Union.[1] His role as a dining car employee separated Folkes from higher status White trainmen and also from the brotherhood of porters. Moreover, as a cook, he was relatively isolated from even the dining car waiters. His closest friends and colleagues were other dining car cooks, usually including two or three workers plus the head chef. He belonged to a politically progressive, racially integrated union at a time when Randolph's race-conscious Brotherhood was attracting attention to the legions of Black trainmen who previously went mostly unnoticed by White customers, who routinely called them "George" without regard for their real names, official roles, or faces.

As a dining car cook, Folkes lived half his life on the train and the other half either in the South Central community near his mother or in the temporary housing that the Southern Pacific Railroad (SPRR) reserved for its workers in Portland, Oregon. Housing for Black trainmen was particularly scarce in most Oregon towns, where sundown laws and less formal prohibitions on leasing rooms to Negroes were commonly enforced. As recently as seventeen years earlier, the state constitution had still officially barred African Americans from taking up residence in Oregon—a prohibition commonly invoked to evict those whose behavior attracted attention. In that sense, it was designed to control and intimidate as well as exclude. The exclusion provision was finally revoked in a 1926 referendum that amended the state constitution on that point, and a similar amendment to remove suffrage restrictions for Blacks passed the next year, although literacy restrictions remained. Oregon was notoriously unfriendly to African Americans, and Black trainmen sought safety in numbers in the Portland area, avoiding layovers in outlying towns. Northbound train crews based in Los Angeles typically stayed in downtown Portland hotels that offered short-term accommodations to trainmen awaiting their return assignment home.

These turnaround layovers exposed Folkes to the heightened tensions surrounding race and labor relations in wartime Portland. The Kaiser shipyards recruited and employed African American migrants from southeastern states during the war, and tensions rose in Portland after a contentious gubernatorial campaign ended in November 1942 with the election of the Republican candidate, Earl Snell. As a candidate, Snell promised voters he would prioritize law and order. He particularly singled out the supposed leniency his predecessors had shown in death penalty cases. Snell promised to more strictly uphold convictions and executions in a state where voters had wavered between abolishing and reinstating the death penalty in the first decades of the twentieth century. His candidacy concerned civil rights advocates as well as local labor leaders, who actively opposed his election. Oregon, when Snell took office in early January 1943, was not particularly friendly to organized labor, and even less accommodating to African American workers.

In that tense atmosphere of contentious labor and race relations, Black trainmen discovered Martha Virginia Brinson James bleeding to death in the aisle of a Pullman sleeping car sometime between 4:00 and 5:00 a.m. on 23 January 1943, gasping out her last breath through a slit in her throat while Private Harold Wilson stood over her with his hands covered in blood. Portland-area newspapers immediately seized on the story, and their sensationalized coverage went out over the Associated Press wire services, making front-page headlines around the country. The victim had no Oregon connections, but the story captured the imagination of readers and journalists, whose breathless accounts of the tragic war bride emphasized her youth, beauty, slight stature, and moral purity. Those stories overwhelmed alternative storylines, and police selectively released details that shaped the initial narratives journalists constructed. Using a widely understood euphemism for "rape," early reports incongruously stressed that Martha James had not been "criminally attacked," even while noting that her throat had been slit nearly halfway through, her head lolling back from her shoulders, exposing a gaping hole where her neck should have been. Initial suspicion centered on Wilson, who occupied the berth immediately above the victim and was discovered standing over her after other witnesses heard her terrified screams.

Wilson, however, deflected attention by telling a different story: he claimed he had seen a "dark" man fleeing the sleeper car shortly before he saw Martha James lurch into the aisle. Wilson's tale embraced widely accepted storylines about vulnerable young White women threatened by predatory Black men. Pressed by newsmen hoping to report "breaks" in the case, investigators immediately shifted their focus to a Black waiter named John Funches, who had tried to start up a conversation with several White women travelling alone in a chair car farther toward the head of the train earlier that night. Eyewitnesses, however, who were reliably White, firmly placed Funches far from the crime scene, and he was later released without charge (or apology). Some reports vaguely questioned why Richard James, the husband, would have left his young, helpless wife alone in those circumstances, but investigating officials rushed to shut down that storyline. They explained that Ensign James had actually been on a different train, reserved to military personnel and running about an hour ahead of the one his wife was on, even though it went by the same number. Reporters seemed surprised by that revelation but dutifully reported it as a new wrinkle in the emerging, officially narrated, police story. Speculation briefly centered on the possibility, originating with early police statements, that the assailant had left the train near Tangent, Oregon. Stories of blood in the snow along the tracks near there ended with a story about a farmer with a nosebleed, but not before sparking an official "manhunt," led by Linn County sheriff's deputies, in the nearby countryside. Investigators then refocused on Wilson, interrogating him more intensely for several days while they held him as a "material witness" at the Linn County jail in Albany, Oregon. Records of that interrogation include an elaborate, alternative storyline prosecutors drafted but never released, depicting Wilson as a serial sex fiend. Finally, three days after the murder, the Linn County district attorney announced that the Los Angeles Police Department (LAPD), acting on the DA's request, had arrested Folkes and charged him with murder.

Prosecutors moved swiftly to extradite, indict, try, and convict Folkes. No physical evidence linked the young cook to the murder, no eyewitnesses placed him at the scene of the crime, and investigators never established a credible motive. Even Wilson, whose motives, opportunity, and demeanor made him the most likely suspect, refused to identify Folkes as the man he claimed to have seen fleeing the murder. Los Angeles police detectives, however, told a story about Folkes that resonated with rural Oregonians who lived in a state and a county that actively discouraged Black people from taking up residence. By the end of April, the circuit court in that county empanelled one of the first juries in Oregon to include women jurors in a capital murder case. A young prosecuting attorney from Klamath Falls, himself grieving over the recent loss of his young wife, joined forces with a seasoned prosecutor from Albany, and they read the LAPD's story out loud in front of the jury and into the court record. Eight women and four men from the farm-oriented communities of mostly rural Linn County decided Folkes' fate, agreeing to convict after deliberating for seventeen hours. They found Folkes guilty of first degree murder with extenuating circumstances of aggravated murder sufficient to meet the standard for which state law in Oregon mandated a death sentence.

Between April 1943 and December 1944, lawyers for Folkes tried to tell a new story: a rush to judgment and an orchestrated campaign to cover up the truth, they argued, had convicted their client. Folkes, through his lawyers, appealed the jury's decision, consistently denying his guilt and requesting a new trial. His union leaders led the fight and successfully attracted support from the Portland chapter of the National Association for the Advancement of Colored People (NAACP) and other civil rights advocates in and beyond Oregon, including many from South Central Los Angeles. The Oregon State Supreme Court, however, upheld the conviction in a split decision, and Governor Snell refused to stay the execution, despite a flood of telegrams and letters pleading for clemency. Those appeals included a four-page letter from the young man's mother, Clara Folkes, who tried to remind the governor that her son was a real person, asking Snell to imagine himself as the father of this young man who was at his mercy. On 5 January 1945, less than two years after the murder, the state of Oregon executed Robert E. Lee Folkes in the gas chamber at the Oregon State Penitentiary in Salem.

The Folkes case galvanized the civil rights community in Portland, and clergymen and lawyers from all around Oregon appealed privately and in public for Snell to extend executive clemency. In a state that had pioneered efforts to abolish the death penalty, and where opponents of the death penalty had won a temporary victory only two decades earlier, the case reenergized those committed to ending state-sponsored executions. It was a compelling story that inspired a dramatic dissenting opinion from two of the seven justices on the Oregon State Supreme Court, including the justice who was the most widely known and respected theorist on criminal law in the legal community beyond Oregon. Snell, however, also received many letters urging him to resist such appeals, emphasizing the need to apply the law evenhandedly, regardless of race. Folkes was only the second African American executed by the state of Oregon, and some letter-writers pointed to that statistic as evidence of a sort of reverse discrimination against White convicts. The victim's father, who travelled to Oregon from Virginia to attend the trial and the later execution, met directly with Snell and personally appealed to the governor, demanding justice for his daughter and calling for support through his membership in the Masonic Order, to which the governor, the prosecutor, and the presiding trial judge belonged. NAACP activists in Portland and progressive leaders in South Central Los Angeles joined forces in appealing for nationwide support, arguing that Folkes' case was the West Coast equivalent of the case involving the "Scottsboro boys"—a notorious miscarriage of justice from the Jim Crow South. Progressive labor unions and other activists from around the country subsequently telegrammed Snell, expressing their support for clemency.

In the end, however, the state silenced those appeals by executing Folkes. More than a hundred people crammed into the room housing the gas chamber to witness the execution through portholes in that killing apparatus, their eager faces captured in official photos documenting the condemned man's last thrashing gasps as he strained against his restraints. In the aftermath of the execution, those who had challenged the conviction and death sentence confronted the problem of how to move on. Folkes left behind a mother, brother, and sister in Los Angeles, and an extended family near St. Louis, Missouri. His brother died in the 1970s, his mother lived into the 1980s, and his sister was still living in Los Angeles as late as 2012. Like everyone else, they moved on with their lives. Efforts to save Folkes failed, and with his execution, apart from a few outraged editorials, civil rights advocates shifted their focus to cases involving defendants who were still living and issues where chances of success still survived. The execution of Robert E. Lee Folkes, however, offers a window for understanding how race and labor relations on the West Coast changed during the war, with implications for how communities in the Pacific Northwest would deal with those issues in the postwar period. The fight to save Folkes from Oregon's gas chamber ultimately failed, but it challenged wartime pretensions of unity and forced into the open discussions of race, prejudice, and injustice among Oregonians who survived into the postwar period. NAACP and union activists crowded into an Albany courtroom to witness blatant disregard for fairness under the law. In that courtroom, they sat next to people who cheered the results. In a state where people tried to pretend that race didn't matter, the execution of Robert E. Lee Folkes exposed a more uncomfortable truth.

Racial prejudice was only part of the story that ultimately placed Folkes in Oregon's gas chamber. A perverse sort of bureaucratic inertia propelled the case through the court system and the appeals process, and at each stage, the accumulating weight of previous decisions apparently numbed onlookers, the defendant, and decision-makers such as Snell, who largely abdicated responsibility, citing process and precedent. In the end, the defendant walked calmly to his death, and for his last words, before an audience of over a hundred people, he could only muster the banality, "So long, everybody."

The stories that people told about the case changed during the course of the war in ways that reveal much about how community priorities in Oregon had shifted from the dark, uncertain days of the conflict's early stages. When Folkes was executed, in the last winter of the war, victory seemed likely and discussions focused more on what would come next. Cracks in the façade of wartime solidarity were already apparent. Labor and civil rights voices of dissent were breaking into the open. Folkes, the hardworking young man who dropped out of school to help support his family, was lost in those earlier stories about a young war bride who was murdered as she slept, alone in a Pullman berth, while dutifully following behind her heroic pilot husband.

The young, handsome marine told a story of leaping to her rescue but tragically arriving too late that resonated with a public eager for reassurance that young men in uniform would protect their nation in its darkest hour. Police postured as diligent sleuths, protecting the public from a dark menace they described as an aberrant exhibitionist, and reporters released pictures of the youthful-looking Folkes in a "zoot suit" that he called, simply, a "formal." Newsmen juxtaposed that image of individualistic expression against photos of crisply uniformed young men surrendering their personal lives to the common cause of national defense. The grimly determined prosecutors moved the case through the necessary but inevitable due process, patiently retelling the story in terms that citizen jurors, mostly farm wives, could understand. They introduced those twelve people to an unfathomable and unknowable figure who was from an urban California place and who was alien to their own, assumedly more virtuous, rural landscapes. In the end, prosecutors and most newsmen reassured Oregonians that the system for which they were fighting not only worked, but worked fairly and without regard for race. Folkes, they incredibly argued, should get no special treatment simply because he was Black.

Nearly two years later, in the war's closing stages, Snell's refusal to stay the execution effectively neutralized Folkes, the card-carrying member of a radical labor union, as an emerging symbol of civil rights activism. Snell's banal argument that the decision was already made and out of his hands suggested that the story was no longer about the guilt or innocence of the convicted but rather about the reliability and integrity of Oregon's criminal justice system. Snell's posture of power masquerading as powerlessness previewed the stance of others who would attempt to thwart the dream for more substantial civil rights in the postwar era. Those who criticized the campaign to free Folkes asked rhetorical questions that appealed to the governor's sense of Oregon's unique virtues. Their version of an "Oregon difference" promoted a racially cleansed vision of the state's past and a curious paranoia about the state's standing and respect around the country: What right did people outside the state have to push their "race agenda" on Oregonians? Who was behind the "well-funded" campaign to "overthrow" the system that the people of

Oregon had established? Contrary to that provincialist view, those who criticized the system that had arrested, prosecuted, and convicted Robert E. Lee Folkes included mostly homegrown civil rights activists in Oregon, but as they struggled to expose and assert alternative storylines, the state of Oregon executed the man whose case refocused and reawakened demands for social justice that had been too long deferred. The war, it seems, was won, but the struggle was on.

Introduction

Seeing Color, Workers, and Ghosts in Oregon's Willamette Valley

We live in a world of ghosts that come back to haunt us when we try to fix other people's mistakes.
—Nancy Langston

Nearly seventy years after Governor Snell washed his hands of the Folkes appeal, claiming the decision to execute the young man was out of his hands, another Oregon governor issued a public statement that he would never again approve state-sponsored executions. It was the wrenching, personal statement of a man haunted by his past and other people's mistakes. Oregon governor John Kitzhaber, MD—formerly an emergency room doctor—announced on 22 November 2011 his decision to issue a "temporary reprieve in the case of Gary Haugen." In doing so, Kitzhaber referenced his first stint as governor, when he had allowed two executions to proceed—one in 1996 and the other in 1997. In his 2011 statement, the governor reminded Oregonians of those decisions by default—his passivity and inaction had sealed the deaths of two men. With the words "I allowed those sentences to be carried out," Kitzhaber resorted to passive voice, psychologically distancing himself from the decisions to kill two men. In the next breath, however, he acknowledged he was not entirely successful in avoiding a personal sense of responsibility for what the machinery of state government accomplished when he failed to intervene:

They were the most agonizing and difficult decisions I have made as
Governor and I have revisited and questioned them over and over
again during the past 14 years. I do not believe that those executions
made us safer; and certainly they did not make us nobler as a society.
And I simply cannot participate once again in something I believe to
be morally wrong.[1]

Kitzhaber's statement included a brief overview of the history of capital punishment in the state, where citizens had pioneered efforts to abolish
the death penalty. Oregon's original constitution, adopted in 1859, omitted
any provision for capital punishment, but state officials executed criminals
from 1864 until 1914 under legislative authority, until a statewide voter initiative specifically prohibited the death penalty. Six years later, Oregon voters
reversed that decision, and from 1920 until 1964 executions resumed.

The Folkes case was never just about race—it was ultimately about the death
penalty and militarized notions of authority, morality, and power. Governor
Snell, unlike Kitzhaber, never publicly questioned his own commitment to the
death penalty, but his inaction in the Folkes case galvanized other Oregonians
into action, setting in motion a chain of events that convinced voters to revoke
the death penalty in 1964, nearly two decades later. The Folkes case refocused
attention on the death penalty near the end of the war and linked it with a
resurgent civil rights movement in the state, just as Oregonians shifted their
attention from the war to postwar readjustments. Outraged citizens rallied
behind Folkes in the last full year of the war, petitioning Governor Snell to
extend clemency. Their effort lacked sufficient numbers or influence to sway
the governor, who in any case arched his back against public influence, as if
stubborn determination to execute a man who quite probably was innocent
was somehow a virtue. In their failure to save Folkes, however, seasoned
activists and inexperienced protestors from all over the state joined forces in
a concerted effort focused mostly on the morality of executing an innocent
man. By contrast, those who advocated for his execution more often resorted
to arguments favoring racial intimidation. This latter group included many of
Snell's influential fellows in the Masonic Order.

Snell figuratively washed his hands of the matter, pretending he could
do nothing while other Oregon officials killed Robert E. Lee Folkes, but the
state's execution of the young Black man from South Central Los Angeles

revived public interest in the death penalty and showed how it was linked to systematic abuses of individual civil rights. After Oregon's abolition of the death penalty in 1964, other states followed suit, but that didn't settle the issue in Oregon, where voters reinstated the death penalty in a 1978 state-wide referendum. When Oregon courts struck it down once more, in 1981, the state's voters again mobilized and ultimately reinstated the death penalty in 1984. Kitzhaber's statement of 2011, therefore, gave voice to the anguished uncertainty and public discord that stretched across seven decades, from the unjust execution of Robert E. Lee Folkes in January 1945 to the Haugen case, which lingered, unresolved, well past 2011. Understanding how the state came to execute that young workingman from California during the Second World War, therefore, brings to light the complex ways in which militarization shaped postwar narratives regarding civil rights and tested the boundaries of race, class, age, gender, and rural versus urban values. Central to that process was the stereotypical trajectory of true-crime detective novels that gained popularity during the interwar years of the 1920s and 1930s—reporters, police investigators, and prosecutors fell back on the standard plot devices of that genre, beginning with early reports of the crime and continuing through the trial, sentencing, and appeals process.

TRADITIONS OF STORYTELLING THAT IMPRISONED FOLKES

In retrospect, it is tempting to consider the arrest, trial, and conviction of Robert E. Lee Folkes for the murder of Martha James as just another example of legal lynching—a Black man forced to take the fall in a racially rigged crimi-nal investigation and trial; and certainly, racism was a central factor in a process so deeply compromised by racial bias as to richly deserve the "legal lynching" descriptor. Race, however, is not a sufficient explanation for how and why this particular young workingman was singled out for special treatment during the early stages of the investigation. In fact, lynching of Black men in Oregon, legal or otherwise, was rare—even in an era when it was common in other states—and it was especially unusual for the state of Oregon to execute a Black man. Before the Folkes case, only one other Black man (compared with forty-five White men and two Native American men) had been executed by the state of Oregon between 1904 and 1945, and only one other Black man was executed in Oregon after the Folkes case, before executions were suspended in 1964.[2] The two men whose death warrants Kitzhaber approved in the 1990s—the last two prisoners executed in the state before that governor's unilateral moratorium of 2011—were also both White. In brief, although Black residents of Oregon faced systematic and institutionalized racism, and although person-to-person violence targeting people of color was not uncommon, both formal executions and extralegal lynchings of non-White defendants in Oregon were quite rare.[3] The Folkes case, then, was a significant anomaly in the history of Oregon criminal justice, and what is more, it did not open the floodgates for future abuses; rather, it prompted a critical reconsideration of the death penalty in a reform effort that ultimately blocked executions in the state for most of the latter half of the twentieth century.[4]

Given the rather unusual outcome in the Folkes case, it is perhaps more important to address the question of why a Black man was targeted in this particular case when there was a more likely White suspect—the young marine Harold Wilson. It is not enough to assume, in Oregon, that "of course" the Black man would be blamed because, regardless of the state's unquestionably racist past, at the time of this trial (1943), White men were more commonly blamed for murder than Black men in Oregon. Beyond the broader issues of White versus Black, we need to consider the more specific question of why this *particular* Black man was targeted. The most obvious suspect in the Martha James murder was Wilson, whose odd and agitated behavior attracted the attention of several people on the train in the hours just before the murder and whose movements and actions before, during, and after the discovery of the murder were erratic and suspicious. The fact that he was discovered standing over the body, with his hands covered in blood, and that his story changed many times over the next several months, should have made him a leading suspect, even if investigators were unaware of his prior criminal record. The fact that Wilson had been released from the brig at Bremerton Naval Station the day before the murder, or that his incarceration there had been related to allegations of sexual assault and indecent behavior, should have made him the focus of close scrutiny in a case initially reported with suggestive references to the victim's sexual allure. As a matter of fact, it appears investigators did, initially, consider charging Wilson with the crime. If charged, convicted, and sentenced to death, Wilson would have been just one among many White men executed in the state, and he would not have been the first White serviceman in Oregon charged with or convicted of criminal activity during the war.

Understanding why police targeted Folkes, rather than the more obvious suspect (Wilson), requires a more subtle approach than merely assuming that the investigators were motivated solely by racial bias. In addition to race, labor relations and militarization were major contributing factors shaping how this case played out. Folkes was a relatively skilled worker, a card-carrying member of a left-leaning labor union and the employee of one of the largest railroad corporations in the nation. Wilson, by contrast, was a relatively unskilled, minimally trained, low-ranking serviceman in a nation at war, and he had already alienated his commanding officers, who were in the process of transferring him to one of the least desirable wartime assignments. He was en route, at the time of the murder, to San Diego, reassigned to a unit where he had no prior experience and no friends or protectors, at a time when San Diego was a staging ground for the amphibious, island-hopping campaigns of US forces in the Pacific. Wilson was clearly in a more precarious position than Folkes at the start of the investigation, so the compelling questions are why and how did Folkes lose status relative to Wilson during the course of that inquiry?

To answer these questions, it is important to recognize the networks linking this case to communities and institutions beyond Oregon, including various branches of the US military, the corporations involved in the transport of military personnel and equipment during the war, and the personal affiliations linking local Oregon officials with racially motivated and classist organizations in Los Angeles, California, and Norfolk, Virginia. The melodramatic trial that played out in the Linn County courthouse in Albany, Oregon, ultimately reached the Oregon State Supreme Court on appeal, but the principals in the case (witnesses, suspects, and the murder victim) were all from other states. What tied them together and linked them with the legal process in the mid-Willamette Valley were the accelerated patterns and mechanisms of mobility that introduced extra-regional forces and urban sensibilities to rural residents of the mid-Valley.

Good citizens of Linn County judged and convicted Folkes, but they were just local actors in a machinery of order and control that began beyond the boundaries of their municipality. As local police and prosecutors built their case against Folkes, they borrowed the familiar language and shorthand of racial stereotypes, recognizable throughout the United States, to construct a melodramatic narrative of innocent and virtuous White womanhood threatened by dark and malicious forces of degenerate and impulsive Black manhood. They emphasized the militarized, impersonal (but blandly likeable) façade of the young White marine as a symbol of authority and reliability, and they misrepresented Folkes in the darker tones of dissipate individualism and antisocial behaviors. Racialized identities were visible in the courtroom, but the official court record was inarticulate on this point, as prosecutors and judges hid behind the pretense of color-blind justice. Before they hit upon that strategy, however, investigators considered and then rejected other suspects. These alternative suspects included other Black men, and also Wilson. Prosecutors consciously shifted the focus away from Wilson and looked for someone else who could take the fall. Race was a factor in that decision, but it was not the only contingency that made Folkes a scapegoat in the racialized melodrama that prosecutors staged in that courtroom.

THE RURAL-URBAN DIVIDE AND CONNECTED WORLDS INTERSECTING IN OREGON

The lives of the people central to this case intersected on a train in rural Linn County, and in the Albany courtroom, but their worldviews and frames of reference originated largely outside the state: Norfolk, Virginia (the victim's family and influence); Los Angeles, California (the home of the accused); rural Arkansas (the place where the accused was born and raised, and from which his family fled racist pogroms and genocide); and rural Minnesota (the place where the most likely killer, Wilson, was born and raised). Wartime militarization put three people from those different worlds (Martha Brinson, Robert Folkes, and Harold Wilson) in the same train, and their fate was decided in Oregon: Martha was murdered there, Folkes was tried there, and Wilson evaded criminal charges and escaped battlefield service by involving himself in the murder investigation there. Rural farm women in Linn County decided Folkes' fate, and although the African American and civil rights communities in Portland and beyond mobilized in his defense (belatedly), the state's governor and the state supreme court failed to act, largely as a consequence of the racialized and militarized assumptions that guided the initial investigations and stories. That investigation, and those stories, brought Folkes to trial and convicted him in a Linn County courtroom. Those decisions and actions involved many actors who were far from Oregon but connected through corporate and professional networks (the Pullman Palace Car Company, the Southern Pacific Railroad Corporation, the Masonic Order, and various police and detective agencies) that were national and extra-regional in scope. The process of arresting, trying, convicting, and executing Folkes in Oregon, however, also involved state and local leaders in a process that demonstrates the multiple ways in which even rural people in Oregon's mid-Willamette

Valley were linked into broader networks that extended far beyond local, state, or even regional boundaries during the era of the Second World War.

The original investigation files document how corporate detectives, police, and prosecutors directly colluded in bringing to judgment a Black trainman who they must have known was most likely innocent. In the process, they also collaborated in releasing a White serviceman who was, in all probability, guilty. In exploring those broader networks of linked contingencies, I am concerned with the backgrounds that brought Martha James and Robert Folkes into close proximity on a train ride that destroyed both their lives; the worker radicalism of the Black man local papers referenced only as a "friend" of Folkes, but who was actually William Pollard—a labor organizer and leader of the radically inspired Dining Car Workers Union, headquartered in South Central Los Angeles; the context of South Central Los Angeles as a cultural homeland for an African American diaspora comprising refugees from the pogroms of Arkansas and other southern states—the so-called Great Migration of the interwar years; and the experience of Black trainmen like Folkes, who lived home lives and "away" lives that linked South Central with the heightened racial and labor tensions in Portland, Oregon, during the Second World War. Marginalized voices, especially those of porters who served as witnesses, offer perspectives on mid-Valley cities and communities like Albany, Oregon, but their voices are filtered through the perceptions of Pullman Company and Southern Pacific Railroad agents and investigators who monitored the case and reported, independently, on the trial, back to their corporate headquarters.

The Folkes case serves as a lens for reconsidering the militarized, mobilized, and racialized landscapes of the American West during the period of the Second World War. The case links these issues to an emerging awareness, not only of racial injustice, but especially of the questionable morality of the death penalty. Those who advocated for the execution of Folkes commonly argued that the execution would put the matter to rest and allow Oregonians to focus on more important matters. For many Oregonians who opposed the execution, however, the Folkes case was just the beginning of a longer struggle for justice and civil liberties.

STORIES OF CRIME AND PUNISHMENT THAT SHADOWED FOLKES IN THE COURTROOM

The trial of Robert E. Lee Folkes began long before the Martha James murder case reached the Linn County courtroom. Criminal trials are largely exercises in crafting and telling stories in ways that appeal to a particular group of jurors, under the watchful eye of a presiding judge who interprets the law and what it means to that captive audience. At the Folkes trial, lawyers and prosecutors vied for jurors' attention, encouraging them to focus on particular storylines to the exclusion of others. The jurors who filed into the jury box at the beginning of the Folkes trial in April 1943 were unusual, by Oregon standards, for that era. They were mostly women (eight of twelve plus one alternate), in a state that had effectively excluded women from juries on all capital cases prior to the war. A jury comprising mostly women was still a novelty in Oregon when those jurors were empanelled. Prosecutors and defense attorneys alike were on unfamiliar ground as they looked for ways to reach that novel audience. They borrowed compelling storylines and symbols of virtue and villainy from popular prewar literature, which they hoped might resonate with this jury of mostly middle-aged, reasonably well-off, literate White women. They framed the story around standard plots and stock characters they cribbed from true-crime detective stories and pulp fiction magazines and books, adapting those stories to the wartime setting and to the mostly rural, almost exclusively White context of Linn County's community of farm families.

The process of constructing a storyline, or theory of the case, began during the initial investigation in late January 1943, shortly after the murder, and continued through the trial and appeals process that stretched from 1943 into early 1945. By issuing regular statements to news reporters throughout the investigation, police and prosecutors introduced a credulous and fearful public to an imaginary Folkes, well before Los Angeles police delivered the real person to Albany to stand trial. They linked that character to racialized, gendered, and militarized images of White innocence and female virtue threatened by a leering, degenerate Black man. Using those familiar tropes, police and prosecutors constructed a moralizing melodrama tailored first to the reading public and, finally, to the audience of jurors. Once unleashed, those stories took on a life of their own, adding an aura of inevitability to the legal proceedings. Governor Snell ultimately hid behind that constructed sense of inevitability, refusing to intervene in the matter in a pretense of upholding color-blind justice.

Published narratives of the crime stubbornly followed the formulaic narrative of "whodunit" murder mysteries, focusing on efforts that led police to the supposedly villainous cook, while ignoring actual evidence or contrary details.[5] John R. Brazil, in a thoughtful analysis of why American news outlets found a willing and growing audience for detailed coverage of true-crime murder trials during that period, notes that the genre follows a predictable pattern of plot development. By the end of the interwar period, the most successful news writers on the murder-trial beat worked each story into a stereotypical plotline with easily recognizable characters, situations, phrases, and descriptions. They referred to each new case as a "crime of the century" and described it as "bestial," "shocking," or "horrible." In melodramatic style, investigators "combed the city" until, at some point, they made a "positive identification." Bit players typically included a "little woman," an "aged mother," and an "alleged confession" that was later retracted. At trial, a "grim prosecutor" squared off against an obstructionist defense lawyer who issued "peremptory challenges," claiming the press had made a "fair trial" impossible. Once the jury was empanelled, however, this panel of twelve "average, fair-minded Americans" weighed prosecutorial claims that the "degeneracy" of a "modern" or "jazz-mad generation" had violated some "unwritten law" or the assumed moral virtues of some honored tradition. Ultimately, the "smiling and confident" or cocky demeanor of the defendant or key defense witnesses would break down into stolid indifference, following a broken alibi or "surprise witness" that would reveal the "naked truth," culminating in a series of "impassioned pleas" from prosecuting and defense attorneys.[6]

Courtroom audiences expected a moralizing melodrama of the sort commonly driving the plotlines of the murder-mystery genre, and prosecutors in the Folkes case worked with that expectation. All the standard plot characteristics that Brazil describes featured prominently in the courtroom melodrama that prosecutors presented to jurors in the Martha James murder case, and in the statements that prosecutors and police issued to reporters during and after the investigation and trial. News coverage of the "Lower 13" case, both in mainstream news outlets and in the Hearst chain's graphic dramatization for its weekend insert (as well as other true-crime publications on the pulp-magazine racks), closely followed the formulaic narrative that Brazil considers typical of the period. That narrative, Brazil suggests, focused public attention on a set of circumstances that writers in this genre framed as a test of shared moral values. Readers were presented with a melodramatic spectacle in the public arena of mass media, offering a familiar storyline in which "deviants" posed an indefinite, sinister challenge to some larger, mostly unexamined national consensus on what was virtuous and what was not.[7]

The story that police investigators and prosecutors spun for the benefit of jurors and crime reporters in the Martha James case updated the true-crime genre of the interwar period to suit the mood of a populace still adjusting to the militarization of the Second World War. In the national morality play of true-crime trial dramatizations, the really big stories often revolved around people who were "extraordinary because they were not exceptional." Brazil notes that the reading public apparently wanted "a particular kind of murder, one that involved situations and central figures with whom it could identify." Martha James, her flyboy husband, and the idea of a heroic marine who arrived, tragically, too late to save the young war bride filled the roles that a reading public would have instantly recognized as the new normal for a nation at war.

In an adaptation to wartime militarization, authority figures assumed a more positive role in the Martha James murder case than was common in true-crime detective stories of the interwar period. Before the war, crime reporters and novelists elevated the cool, detached, cynical detective to the status of a cultural icon, immortalizing the type in characters such as Ellery Queen, Perry Mason, and Sam Spade. Writers like Dashiell Hammett famously moved murder "out of the Venetian vase and into the alley," in the words of another practitioner of that effort, Raymond Chandler. In the James murder case, Oregon State Police forensic pathologist Joseph Beeman filled the role of the cool, detached detective, but with more organizational authority and the added aura of scientific methods and precision. Beeman's more sinister role in either extracting or dictating questionable "confessions" in both the Folkes case and in the closely parallel Layton case during the early months of 1943 went largely unexamined in the courtroom record. In a bizarre twist, unexplained or even contradictory elements of the case, rather than raising questions about the validity of the charges, merely made the case seem more believable and a closer parallel to the detective-novel genre. Brazil observes that the interwar years were a period in which Americans found irrationality and ambiguity the rule rather than the exception: "It is a world in which there are lots of loose ends, lots of things one does not or cannot know and at which one can only hazard guesses."[8] The very fact that the evidence did not fit the charges against Folkes, consequently, may have worked against his defense. Jurors steeped in the traditions of interwar true-crime narratives expected nothing less.

The story that police presented as if it were Folkes' confession played to that expectation of unexplained loose ends. That supposed "statement" was particularly vague about motive, suggesting that the murder just sort of happened, in a hazy, vague, numbing, dreamlike sequence of horror that eerily echoed the plot of Theodore Dreiser's interwar crime/detective novel, *An American Tragedy* (1925).[9] Similarly, the "statement" that Los Angeles police attributed to Folkes narrates a comparable sequence of unplanned events. According to the version prosecutors read out loud to jurors, Folkes initially intended to kill Martha, but froze, yet somehow managed to startle and terrify her. When she screamed, he impulsively, savagely, almost instinctively struck out, cut her, and then just ran away. It was a sequence that an inventive police detective might have lifted right out of a true-crime story or detective novel and pasted into the blank spaces of a page that reporters and prosecutors claimed was actually a "confession" in the Lower 13 murder case.

TRUE-CRIME NARRATIVES OF FOLKES IN OREGON

The pattern of news coverage and popular interest in the Martha James murder case more closely followed the model of a true-crime mystery narrative than a southern-style lynching. It was a story that appealed to the popular culture of Oregonians who espoused middle-class pretentions of fair play. Newsmen and commentators proudly boosted the Folkes trial as evidence of the great respect for due process in their state, contrasting with their disdain for the mob mentality they associated with a southern-style lynching. Instead of a frenzied mob hell-bent on lynching the accused Black man, a large crowd of onlookers, largely middle-aged White women, gathered daily in the courtroom to follow the proceedings, and newsmen reported a buzz of conversations in the courtroom hallways during breaks in the proceedings. It was an atmosphere of curiosity, trying to guess the "solution" to the true-crime puzzle: "Who killed Martha James?" This was a far cry from the atmosphere and demeanor of crowds at a typical lynching, as Leon Litwack explains in an essay titled "Hellhounds."[10]

From the 1890s on, Litwack argues, the phenomenon of lynching in the Jim Crow South took on the trappings of a public ritual—a voyeuristic spectacle in which people who participated in this mob violence tortured, dismembered, and mutilated their victim in a prolonged collective experience with the intent of extending the agony of the victim for as long as possible to satisfy the "emotional appetite of the crowd."[11] They acted, moreover, out of disdain for what they considered an ineffectual legal system, and in the belief that immediate action, with prolonged suffering, was preferable to drawn-out courtroom trials, which would have allowed their Black victims the pretense of equality and significance. The most common alleged offenses that motivated lynch mobs to execute Black victims involved minor transgressions that challenged the façade of White supremacy: insulting, disrespectful, or "incendiary" language and "insubordination, impertinence, impudence, or improper demeanor (a sarcastic grin, laughing at the wrong time, a prolonged silence)."[12]

Folkes apparently transgressed all these boundaries of deferential demeanor, if the testimony of his coworkers is to be believed, and that likely prompted his special treatment and possible torture, early in the murder investigation and, especially, at the hands of Southern Pacific railway detectives and the Los Angeles police, but he subsequently endured a drawn-out legal proceeding, not a vicious lynching. The multiweek trial balanced the expectations of the victim's family, from a state (Virginia) where lynchings were relatively common, against the ideals and pretensions of a state whose citizens espoused an "Oregon difference"—a landscape of promise and new opportunities regardless of class or background. The state's motto, "She flies with her own wings," suggested this common ethos of an "Oregon difference," and participants and onlookers at the Folkes trial expected a public ritual worthy of that motto. The guilt or innocence of the accused was less important than the public ritual of discovery. Their focus was on the trial, not the resulting execution. The case that prosecutors assembled played to that expectation, orchestrating a legal lynching in a distinctively Oregon style.

RACE, MILITARIZATION, GENDER, AND DIFFERENCE IN THE OREGON SYSTEM

Differences of personality, self-representation, and attachment to community isolated both Folkes and Wilson from other travelers, but Wilson enjoyed the benefits of a military uniform, White identity, and assertive masculinity that Folkes did not. Those differences proved fatal to Folkes and empowering for Wilson. Travelling alone and detached from all normal constraints on his impulses, Wilson fit the profile of the interwar criminal—as seen both in the popular literature and in the criminology scholarship of the period—more closely than Folkes, but his military persona, more imagined than real, transformed his standing in the eyes of investigators. If Folkes was a mundane, somewhat ordinary figure—one among many Black trainmen on the night of the murder—Wilson was a remarkable and memorable character whose outgoing personality played to the expectations of detectives and prosecutors in Oregon. Most witnesses remembered Folkes more for his location than for his personality, which by most accounts of his coworkers was somewhat reserved (or introverted), although also smart-alecky. By contrast, Wilson was an exuberant extrovert. His boyish eagerness to help detectives "solve the case" apparently charmed onlookers already bedazzled by his marine uniform. In the war-stressed atmosphere of 1943,[13] readers familiar with true-crime narrative conventions wanted an alternative (surprise) suspect, and with the startling disclosure that a smart-aleck cook in the next car admitted that he "dunit," reporters, police, and prosecutors told the more satisfying, militarized story of a heroic, low-ranking marine who, with his take-charge attitude and amateur sleuthing, helped befuddled, inept, and, not coincidentally, Black trainmen organize the search while he tracked down evidence that professional investigators had missed.

Militarization trumped race as a motivating factor in the theory of the crime that prosecutors constructed as they shifted the focus from Wilson to Folkes, further distancing this case from the familiar grounds of "legal lynchings." In shifting the focus from Wilson to Folkes, prosecutors deflated initial suggestions that the crime was sexually motivated. Their early interrogations of Wilson focused closely on his sexual proclivities, but that line of inquiry was relatively insignificant in the questions asked Folkes. Instead, in building the case against Folkes, they stressed the randomness of the attack. The victim's father contributed to that shift, working behind the scenes to block insinuations or evidence that the murdered woman—his young daughter—had been sexually violated, or even that sexual assault was a motive. Prosecutors went to great lengths to emphasize that the victim had not been "criminally attacked," stressing the motiveless impulse behind the attack. The decision to suppress any evidence or suggestion of sexual assault was undisclosed to readers: this Black man would not be accused of raping, or even intending to rape, this White woman. The desexualized, motiveless theory that prosecutors presented ultimately denied readers of this true-crime narrative the salacious tale they might have expected, without allaying their suspicions. Rumors were rife. Judge Lewelling, for example, cryptically ruled to suppress autopsy photos, denying access to them, even for jurors. His ruling, and the "professional" discretion of both Beeman and the Eugene coroner, protected the assumed chastity of the young married victim, shielding photos of her body from prying eyes while asserting that, although her head was nearly severed from her body, she was not "criminally attacked."

The reasons for this shift in prosecutorial theory are clear: the more sex-tinged the case, the more Wilson, and not Folkes, emerged as the obvious suspect. Wilson had a previous record of sexual assault and harassment, having very recently served time in the brig for related charges (he was released on the day he boarded the train that carried the James couple to their fate). Despite unsubstantiated rumors later circulated about Folkes, there was no similar record in his background. If Wilson had remained the suspect, it may have been difficult to secure a conviction without raising that evidence of sexual assault. A jury of White middle-class farm women, drawn from a population familiar with the wartime activities of faceless soldiers who trained nearby at Camp Adair and recreated on off-base leaves in Albany's bars and brothels, would not likely have been surprised that Wilson's sexual impulses broke down his respect for rules, regulations, and common decency. With Folkes, however, no such reference to sexual intent was necessary to convince that same jury that a young Black man of an obviously different, not-military background and not-rural culture might succumb to impulses for unrestrained, violent behavior.

The uniquely virtuous rural communities that Oregonians imagined as their joint heritage conflicted with the disorderly realities of wartime urbanization and industrial transformation that confronted rural residents of the mid-Willamette Valley by 1943. Rural communities in the Valley were distant but not isolated from urban landscapes and issues that absorbed residents of Portland, Oregon, and other cities on the West Coast in 1943, and the story of why the state executed Robert Folkes shows how the war drew those rural and urban worlds closer together. The war made it more difficult for rural residents of the mid-Valley to ignore the changing, more urban structure of race and labor relations in the early to mid-twentieth century. On the surface, Linn County, Oregon, was relatively remote from the wartime dislocations that transformed West Coast urban centers like Portland, Los Angeles, and Seattle during the first years of American involvement in the Second World War, and prosecutors relied on the comparative homogeneousness of that rural populace in framing their case against Folkes. The apparent sameness of that population, however, belied an undercurrent of anxiety afflicting farm folk of the mid-Valley.

The racialized nature of the country's war against Japan, including military zones excluding people of Japanese descent, complicated patterns of racial resentment and prejudice in the mid-Willamette Valley. Oregon, like other states on the West Coast, was a staging area where military personnel prepared for operations in the Pacific. The war accelerated urbanization trends in cities but also brought unfamiliar and uncomfortable changes to the rural economy, most notably the wartime relocation of Japanese nationals and Japanese Americans out of the area—a population that was an important source of agricultural workers for the labor-intensive fruit and vegetable crops of the area. In the aftermath of mandatory relocation, truck-crop farmers in the exclusion zone throughout the Pacific Northwest rallied in support of a related agricultural labor policy known as the Bracero Program.[14] This federal program brought Mexican nationals into the agricultural workforce in 1942 to address a farm-labor crisis brought on by wartime recruitment and the removal of Japanese and Japanese American farmworkers. This transition from ethnic Japanese to ethnic Mexican workers introduced yet another unfamiliar "other" into the supposedly homogeneous landscape of the mid-Valley. It was one more disruption in a landscape undergoing dramatic transformation during the war.

The linked policies of the Bracero Program and the War Relocation Authority (WRA), in combination with wartime recruitment and training programs, disrupted networks through which growers recruited farmworkers they needed to manage and harvest labor-intensive crops in the mid-Valley. As the racialized face of militarization on the West Coast, these two federal initiatives linked rural communities of Willamette Valley growers with national and regional networks of immigration and labor management. Although racism was neither a new nor a unique feature of this rural landscape, the forced mobility and racially segregated camp-town structure of WRA, Bracero, and military cantonments like Camp Adair forced the race issue into open discussion among the overwhelmingly White farm owners and growers of Linn County. Most county residents had deep local roots and were connected in some way with farm-owning White immigrant families that dated back to the nineteenth-century Oregon Trail migration. Before the Second World War, local farm tenancy rates were only about 20 percent. Even in the Depression years of the 1930s, Linn County's tenant farmers were mostly close relatives of those established farm owners. The close-knit farm families in Linn County, however, lived in a rural landscape that was rapidly urbanizing. The county-wide population increased from 24,700 in 1930 to over 30,000 by 1940. Only 8,385 county residents lived in urban places by that year (either in Albany or in nearby Lebanon—the only local towns qualifying as "urban" places in the 1940 census), but by 1950, the urban population grew to nearly 20,000, representing over 40 percent of the county's residents.[15]

The trial of Robert Folkes, in these circumstances, might be understood as a public ritual that focused attention on a simplified version of race relations at a time when wartime mobilization and militarization was redefining, reshading, or complicating previously drawn color lines. The melodramatic trial assigned each character exaggerated, stereotypical roles that substituted for the subtler shades of a multiracial society with more nuanced interests and values. Among other elements, that melodrama exaggerated rural-urban differences at a time when the war was actually blurring many such distinctions. The man prosecutors accused of murdering Martha James was a defendant whose differences from most local young men of the mid-Willamette Valley were obvious and visible: he was a young Black man who favored ostentatious styles of dress, speech, and physical demeanor that were distinctly urban. He was also a member of a relatively radical labor union in a period when A. Philip Randolph's Brotherhood of Sleeping Car Porters (BSCP) and the March on Washington Movement (MOWM) transformed the way White Americans thought about African American trainmen: earlier images of innocuous service attendants were set aside, and in their place, White passengers perceived Black trainmen as threatening and challenging symbols of racial difference.

By the standards of Linn County, Robert E. Lee Folkes appeared suspiciously and threateningly deviant, unlike the young men who frequented Albany entertainment venues from nearby Camp Adair in their reassuring military uniforms and with their (mostly) whiter complexions. Folkes lacked any similar, outwardly apparent, symbols of personal virtue that local residents would have recognized. The positive post-verdict response of urban Oregonians to the rural jury's decision that Folkes was guilty demonstrates, however, that the supposed rural-urban divide between Portland and the mid-Valley was, in important ways, more imagined than real. The views of those Linn County jurors were also widely shared by urban and rural readers well beyond Oregon. The courtroom melodrama in Albany, in other words, had the unintended consequence of breaking down pretenses that rural areas were somehow insulated from urban problems during the war years. There was no rural refuge.

Prosecutors, in their zeal to convict Folkes, demonstrated and highlighted the multiple and serendipitous networks that connected rural Oregonians with urban centers across the United States. The trial drew together stories from the seemingly separate worlds of Minnesota agricultural towns, Virginia port cities, Washington naval centers, and California metropolitan areas. Events in those and other distant locales, rural and urban, had already unleashed powerful forces beyond the control of rural communities in the mid-Valley. Read in this way, the events of the trial were not an isolated criminal case in a remote, mostly rural state in the Pacific Northwest. The issues and context of the case resonated with the aspirations of civil rights and labor advocates from across the American West, and the trial brought national attention to the situation in Oregon, drawing local activists closer to the mainstream of those movements. The letters and appeals that flowed into the governor's office after the jury convicted Folkes demonstrate, in their return addresses, the geographic reach of those broader networks. Writers from across the trans-Mississippi West, and especially the Intermountain West and Pacific Coast states, demanded justice for Folkes. Although they often mentioned "similarities" with instances of southern racism, most notably the Scottsboro case,[16] they emphasized the belief that western communities in places like Oregon, and western governors like Snell, were supposed to be above the extremes of racial violence typically associated with the Jim Crow South. This trail of letters to Oregon collectively expressed the belief that things should work differently in that promised land.

With wartime militarization warping the prewar fabric of rural and urban traditions in Oregon and the greater West, the Folkes trial might be seen as a surrogate discourse that substituted for more difficult conversations about changing community values concealed beneath the enforced patriotism and censorship of those years. The same wartime militarization that drove much of the urban growth in the mid-Valley also fostered a tense situation pitting long-term permanent residents against short-term or transient residents. The nearby Camp Adair (located in adjacent Polk County, between Albany, Corvallis, and Monmouth) had ballooned to a population of over one hundred thousand military personnel by the time Folkes faced trial.[17] Bus service between the camp and Albany regularly filled city streets and hotels with visiting servicemen seeking rest and recreation during short-term leaves. Locals regarded this temporary and transient population with conflicted interest: phalanxes of unfamiliar faces from Camp Adair often challenged local standards of decorum and morality, but they also spent money at local businesses, and their disposable income created opportunities for nonfarm employment in the service economy.

Black trainmen were among the more visible nonmilitary elements of wartime urbanization trends, and they, consequently, were particularly vulnerable as surrogate targets for those who resented wartime disruptions to prewar rural communities. Wartime censorship stifled criticism of militarization trends, but wartime propaganda militarized racial difference, particularly on the West Coast, where paranoia about a Japanese invasion ran high by 1943. Despite the importance of Pullman porters and Southern Pacific dining car employees to the African American community, their treatment in Albany during the trial, their exclusion from local accommodations, and the disregard for their testimony by local White jurors demonstrates the low regard for Black trainmen among White communities, even in railroad towns. Race, if not a sufficient explanation for targeting Folkes, certainly eroded the status and authority of Black witnesses who spoke in his defense.

PORTLAND AND THE URBAN FOUNDATIONS OF AFRICAN AMERICAN COMMUNITY IN OREGON

Even within the established centers of Black community in Portland, trainmen lost status during the war—their job classification, not simply their race, rendered them more vulnerable during the period of rapid militarization. Even though the war created new opportunities for African American employment, those opportunities eroded the relative status of other occupations traditionally reserved for Black workers.[18] Before the war, trainmen were a mainstay of the African American middle class in Portland and other West Coast cities. Regular, reliable, wage-earning work established trainmen as respectable pillars of the Black community in the post-Reconstruction Jim Crow period, when African American workers in other jobs were often the last hired and first fired. Industrial development during the war years of 1942 to 1945, however, offered higher-paying defense-related jobs with reliable, steady hours for the duration of that conflict. Industrialist Henry J. Kaiser, drawing on federal subsidies, constructed three major shipyards in the Portland vicinity—two on the Willamette River near St. Johns Bridge and at Swan Island, and the third on the Vancouver side of the Columbia River, near the bridge to Portland. He also constructed residences sufficient to house over forty thousand workers on the floodplain of the Columbia north of Portland, in a wartime housing project known as Vanport City. The shipyards employed as many as 120,000 workers, and by the end of the war more than a third of Vanport's residents were African Americans.[19] These new Black residents of Portland were mostly employed outside the railway sector, in positions where tips were not an expected or significant component of their income.[20]

Although trainmen enjoyed relatively high standing within African American communities before the war, their status declined during and after the war, even in their home districts.

In Portland, residence patterns and areas of racial congregation also shifted during the war years, as higher-wage industrial workers congregated in Vanport, far north of the rail yards, located nearer the city center in an older warehouse district mostly constructed during the late 1800s. Despite their bland sameness, the progressive-looking, freshly painted façades of Vanport contrasted with the gritty urban landscapes of the rail yard district, where decaying hotels, bars, and restaurants catered to trainmen, often in racially segregated venues. White and Black trainmen mostly spent their turnaround time in different settings, maintaining class differences that were also apparent aboard the trains. The new suburb of Vanport, by contrast, gained cachet among the emergent Black middle class as a more integrated and progressive setting where the new race man and his family could find respectability, opportunity, and good schools for their children. Trainmen, linked with the industrial façades of the aging downtown, and with the obsequious, tip-seeking roles of redcaps, waiters, and porters, seemed hopelessly old-school, even to activists and journalists in the African American community, who sometimes referred to them as an embarrassing link to the past.[21]

Black trainmen like Folkes, during the period between 1941 and 1943, were trapped between two debilitating stereotypes that undermined their personal security and professional identities. On the one hand, their roles in service positions left them individually vulnerable to savage and demeaning treatment in the Jim Crow era. On the other hand, they collectively symbolized upstart labor radicalism, as the uniformed workers who spearheaded a protest movement that aroused the fears of White leaders and passengers. Randolph and the Brotherhood of Sleeping Car Porters responded to the increased pressures of the early war years with the March on Washington Movement, which peaked during the summers of 1941 and 1942. Randolph intended the march as a response to wartime readiness programs that relegated Black workers to service roles as hotel and restaurant workers, janitors, and manual laborers, in positions previously filled by White workers who were finding better jobs in defense-related industries. Just a year before the United States entered the war, Randolph met with President Franklin Roosevelt, T. Arnold Hill of the National Urban League, and Walter White of the NAACP to discuss opportunities for Black Americans in the armed forces

under the new Selective Service Act. During that meeting, Roosevelt reportedly referred to African American men as "boys" and suggested that they were
suited to careers as cooks and musicians in the military. In subsequent public
statements, the president announced the continuation of prewar segregation
policies in the military and implied that Randolph, Hill, and White agreed
with that approach. Randolph subsequently urged White to join him in
developing a language of protest that would "shake up white America." White
America, he argued, needed to see "Negro masses in action." In the winter of
1941, BSCP chapters in New York, Detroit, Los Angeles, and Chicago spearheaded efforts to deliver fifty thousand African Americans to the Capitol in a
mass demonstration scheduled for 1 July 1941. When the Roosevelt administration learned that this March on Washington would likely include over
one hundred thousand people, the president met with Randolph and White
to hear their demands and, in a weeklong process, worked out the draft of
Executive Order 8802, which prohibited discrimination in hiring in defense
industries or the government on the basis of race, creed, color, or national
origin. In return, Randolph cancelled the march and reorganized the March
on Washington Movement as a watchdog organization to monitor enforcement of the executive order. From late summer 1941 through fall 1942, the
MOWM and the Black press struggled to put teeth into the enforcement arm
of the order, the Fair Employment Practices Committee (FEPC).[22]

Randolph's movement opened new opportunities for African Americans
in the government, the military, and defense industries during the war, but
it also eroded the status of trainmen while arousing White fear and resentment against underpaid workers who still depended on passenger tips for a
living wage. In many ways, trainmen were more vulnerable in 1942 than they
had been in 1941 because they were powerless scapegoats who symbolized
the rising power of a race-conscious labor movement. The arrest, indictment,
and trial of Folkes in winter and spring 1943, and the treatment of Pullman
porters and other trainmen in Albany before, during, and after the trial, demonstrate the difficult situation in which Black trainmen found themselves
at the time. Newspapers catering to White Oregonians anxiously noted the
"rapidly growing" population of African American men in the state, especially
Portland, and that outlook colored their early reports of the murder. By comparison with the overall population in the Portland metropolitan area, which
increased by more than 250,000 people during the war years, the number of
Black residents remained relatively small, accounting for less than 10 percent

of that increase. Longer-term residents, however, largely blamed this "new racial element" for apparent increases in crime and violence. More generally, wartime mobilization filled the city with a variety of unfamiliar faces. Union Station was a major transfer point for military personnel relocating from one assignment to another, and those mostly White transients, together with new, longer-term White residents, made the city seem less familiar and more alien to holdovers of any race from the prewar era. Crime rates were rising, in a city of greater anonymity, but Black residents, as a highly visible minority, were more likely scapegoats and victims than perpetrators.

WHITE REFUGE: WARTIME TRAVEL AND THE EROSION OF GENTEEL SPACE

As the climate of fear and racial tensions escalated during the early stages of the war, railroads tried to reassure potential passengers that the nation's railways were safe for White women. This was a particular concern on the West Coast, where the Southern Pacific Railroad supplied nearly 90 percent of the nation's military transport needs. With unprecedented numbers of servicemen moving in military transport trains and in regularly scheduled passenger service, more women were travelling alone, or with children and other female relatives, in an effort to follow their men to their new assignments. These military and civilian passengers strained the capacity of dining cars and Pullman sleeping cars and undermined earlier advertising efforts that had emphasized railway travel as a safe, domesticated genteel experience. The idealized persona of the "genteel" sleeping car porters and conductors, observes historian Amy Richter, was an identity constructed for the explicit purpose of putting White women at ease travelling in the company of an all-Black crew of male attendants.[23] Wartime militarization threatened that carefully constructed genteel space with hordes of all-male passengers travelling in large groups, detached from community ties. The parallel emergence of the BSCP at the head of the MOWM reenergized, among a mostly White populace, fears of racial unrest and threats to the purity and physical safety of White women in the company of Black trainmen.

The demographics of train workers also shifted during the war in ways that eroded previous traditions of reassuringly genteel service from porters and dining car workers. Executive Order 8802 and the FEPC, despite their flaws, pried open job opportunities for African Americans in defense industries and government after July 1941, and many younger Black trainmen left jobs in the dining car division of the Southern Pacific Railroad for positions previously reserved for White workers. Railroads were leading defense contractors, and wartime militarization placed new pressures on sleeping car porters and dining car workers who were pressed into duty to serve military transport trains. Those who remained were overworked, older, and unwilling or unable to adjust to the demands of learning a new job, but they were also less protected in their roles as respected trainmen than before the war. Young, predominantly White military men tended to view all trainmen, Black or White, as little different from servants, but their demands and behavior toward Black railroad workers were particularly demeaning and made those trains a more hostile workplace. Young Black men like Folkes, however, found employment with the dining car division of the Southern Pacific Railroad during the period when Randolph and White were negotiating with FDR, and the shifting demographics opened up avenues for rapid career advancement. As mid-career workers either found other employment in war industries or volunteered for military service, Folkes moved quickly up the career ladder. At the time, a young Black man growing up in South Central Los Angeles would have seen a railroad job in the Southern Pacific's dining car division as a prestigious and promising opportunity. By all reports a diligent, energetic worker, Folkes was able to move up more quickly than might otherwise have been the case. He was not as immersed as his older coworkers, however, in the culture of gentility that the Pullman Company had promoted and that Black trainmen had cultivated as a strategy for coping with the dangers of working on interstate transport under Jim Crow. His was a newer, less subservient approach to a service position, and that sometimes rubbed people—both White customers and Black coworkers—the wrong way.

AN "OREGON DIFFERENCE"?

Prosecutors and the multiagency investigative team orchestrated a public ritual of discovery tailored to the self-congratulatory mood of Oregonians at midcentury. The theory of the crime that they presented, first to the press and then to the courtroom audience, emphasized the scientific precision and incontrovertibility of Beeman's forensic laboratory and investigative techniques. The state that lent its name to the "Oregon System" of citizen government (initiative, referendum, and recall) had linked the progressive ideal of professional expertise with utopian notions of "open" government during the early twentieth century. The Folkes case advanced Beeman's office in the public eye. His supposedly scientific inquiry satisfied public expectations for an open and transparent, formal process—even though the actual performance of Beeman's lab fell ridiculously short of those ideals. Progressive Oregonians did not look too closely into Beeman's methods, even as they congratulated each other on their refusal to accept anonymous nighttime lynch mobs—in their utopian Oregon, the Folkes trial would proceed in the bright light of day, in a modern courtroom well-lit with open windows and orderly citizens crowded into hard wooden seats in a proper visitors gallery. Witnesses, White and Black, paraded through the courtroom, where trial principals played their assigned roles. Everyone knew the story and their roles, which overwhelmed every fact in the case.

The murder of Martha James, coming amid the dislocating changes and rapid mobilization of the early war years in the mid-Willamette Valley, offered local residents, lawmen, and reporters an outlet for the frustrations of a society adjusting to the sudden militarization of its communities. Criminologists of the 1930s and 1940s (including Beeman) were strongly influenced by sociological theories that suggested that mechanisms of rapid mobility (such as trains and automobiles) generated a change of social scale, in which distant networks and organizations transformed human relations and local communities. John Dewey, in 1927, for example, had argued that "the invasion of the community by the new and relatively impersonal and mechanical modes of combined human behavior is the outstanding fact of modern life."[24] The Lower 13 murder combined in one case elements of accelerated mobility, distant networks and organizations, and alien urban elements, and then focused the lens of media attention on the local communities of the mid-Willamette Valley and their racialized and militarized notions of justice and fairness.

In constructing a case against Folkes, prosecutors merged popular notions of guilt and innocence with scholarly notions of progressive social science in the emerging field of criminology. A 1926 textbook on criminology and penology asserted that, since murder, robbery, rape, adultery, and lewdness had increased dramatically after "the War" (the First World War), modern criminal investigators would require nothing less than "the zeal of a prophet, the calmness and patience of a scientist and the relentless perseverance of a Hebrew Jahveh."[25] DA Harlow Weinrick, who headed the prosecution, assigned that role to a young firebrand: L. Orth Sisemore—the Klamath Falls district attorney whom Martha's father hired on private retainer to assist in the case. Sisemore, who was still grieving the recent death of his wife, brought an evangelical zeal to the case that began with his interrogation of Folkes in Klamath Falls on the day of the murder.

All the variables that Brazil described as common to both the true-crime murder-mystery genre and the criminal justice textbooks of the interwar years found their way into the charges that prosecutors leveled at Folkes, with Beeman's help. At the time of the murder, Beeman was struggling to establish and consolidate the reputation of his laboratory as a model of scientific inquiry and efficiency. The Folkes case delivered a regional and national audience for showcasing the accomplishments of Beeman's two-man unit within the relatively new Oregon State Police (OSP) agency, and the forensic pathologist played a key role in delivering supposed "confessions" in several different cases that came under critical scrutiny shortly before and after the Folkes case. In a pretense of scientific methodology, Beeman and the prosecuting team, with the assistance of OSP officers and the sheriff's office, downplayed the importance of race in the Martha James murder case. In retrospect, they were not entirely disingenuous in that assertion. Personality and sociological theories of the interwar period apparently fueled the imagination of detectives with little regard for evidence, no less than their evident racism. They stressed the idea of a criminally deviant and impulsive, or "exhibitionist," suspect, and then they attached those labels to the young Black man from South Central Los Angeles, Robert Folkes. Why they zeroed in on Folkes, rather than Wilson or other possible suspects, is a central concern in this study.

The very ordinariness of Folkes—cooks were a ubiquitous presence aboard passenger trains, often seen but seldom dealt with directly—and the coincidence that his closest friend and his strongest mentor were both out sick apparently worked against him. Criminologists of the interwar years claimed that a nationwide "crimewave" was growing rapidly and that murders were becoming "more atrocious and ruthless." Students of this "crimewave" blamed it on immigration, urbanization, and industrialization, but most importantly, on the breakdown of social order. They argued that, rather than a particular criminal "type," murderers differed little from any other "man on the street," and that, while environmental circumstance might lead someone to criminal behavior, such actions were also instinctual or impulsive, residing in human nature and requiring, therefore, careful enforcement of social constraints and controls. In circumstances where such constraints broke down and where individuals found themselves in a situation of unaccustomed liberty, freed from traditional controls, resulting patterns of "moral confusion, personal disorganization, and social disorientation" would increase the likeli-hood that they would resort to impulsive, criminal behavior.[26]

In Folkes, investigators saw a young man isolated from his usual cowork-ers, and therefore in a situation lacking traditional social controls. At liberty from social constraints, he was also young and Black, and they found his "story" and actions disorganized and his demeanor disoriented. On these characteristics, and no other evidence—in fact, in direct contradiction to other eyewitness testimony and physical evidence—they concluded he was their most likely suspect. Then, because he was Black, they acted with impu-nity in coercing a "confession," knowing full well that their race would shield them from any form of retribution.

Against the backdrop of an industrial landscape of increasingly tense labor and race relations, the case of the Lower 13 murder tapped a vein of popular imagination that was rooted, at least in part, in the mystique of Oregon and its place in the folklore of the American West. The Virginian (Martha Brinson), in the melodramatic storyline that prosecutors fabricated, was a paragon of vir-tue who was murdered by a wild man of the West with a dark visage (Robert Folkes). Re-gendered and racialized to conform with the anxieties of people in the western states during the war in the Pacific, that storyline, concocted by prosecutors without much concern for factual accuracy, blended themes that Owen Wister explored in *The Virginian*—an iconic novel of the western genre that Wister wrote in the early 1900s—with the true-crime detective genre of the interwar years. The same people (prosecutors and the Oregon State Police) who conjured that image of Folkes as a wild man of the West seized on the case as an opportunity to promote the state's progressively efficient, scientific police work, in an overt effort to distinguish themselves from the typically "southern" narrative of racist ignorance. Governor Snell affirmed those values in his terse statement refusing to offer clemency. The trial records and newspaper reports self-consciously and self-servingly emphasized the "fairness" of the trial, stress-ing how that process differed from those in southern states, where, they argued, Folkes would have been summarily lynched without trial. Those same records also document a racial double standard in admitting evidence and applying the law. In many ways, the trial really was a formalized path to the same result as an illegal lynching. It was both public spectacle and community ritual with a moralizing and intimidating purpose, but if it was a legal lynching, it was with a distinctively Oregon difference, and rural folk in Linn County, Oregon, played a central role in shaping prosecutorial strategies in that distinctive effort.

Although neither Martha James nor Robert Folkes was from Oregon, investigators settled on the assumption that the murder happened in Linn County, somewhere between Albany and Tangent, and their construction of a theory of the crime consequently represents their understanding of how local people think about issues of race, class, and gender. The Linn County sheriff and district attorney led the initial investigation and prosecuted the case in the circuit court at the Linn County courthouse. By fixing the place of death within the borders of Linn County, these and other legal officials virtually ensured the case would be tried before an all-White rural jury. As a result, this particular murder offers an opportunity to explore the kinds of arguments and characterizations that those jurors found convincing in 1943, in relation to the race, gender, and social standing of the murder victim and the person accused of that murder. By the time the case wound its way through the appeals process, however, a broader regional audience understood the appeals process as a symbol of resistance and difference in the Pacific Northwest in relation to national issues of race, class, and social justice. Citizen appeals to Governor Snell, for and against the pending execution, emphasized the importance of either staying or following through with the execution, as a test of Oregon's progressive status and autonomy from outside influences. Throughout those discussions, the contending parties constructed and reconstructed the gendered and racialized identities of the victim, and of the accused perpetrator, in ways that demonstrated changing priorities of race and labor relations at a critical stage in the transition from a wartime to a postwar West.

Chapter One
Stories of a Snowy Winter's Night
in the Willamette Valley

At least thirty-six people passed the night of 23 January 1943 within twenty-five feet of death on Train 15 as it headed south through the mid-Willamette Valley in western Oregon, but all we know for sure is that one of them did not live to tell the story. Those who lived through the night on that train left shadowy evidence of their passage in the form of ticket stubs and berth assignments scribbled in porters' pencil in the small hours of the night. Five of them survive only as "unknown" passengers in the oral recollection of the Pullman porter in charge of that car. Others told their stories at least once, sometimes multiple times, to police investigators, railway officials, and reporters. The stories they told mention other passengers in that car who went completely unnoticed in the official record—a baby, or babies, crying in the night; children, sleeping with their parents; a family of at least five crammed into two bunks in one section. Thick Pullman curtains only partially muffled the sounds of crying, sneezing, coughing, and snoring people who slept in eight pairs of double berths only six feet long and four feet wide, with an aisle only two feet wide between the double-tiered bunks. Each passenger came with a personal past invisible to their fellow travelers. In the confined space and time of Car D on Train 15, in that night, each person lived with their particular past in an ever-emerging present. What happened that night, for most of them, was simply inexplicable and beyond their previous experience.

People outside the train first learned what had happened to Martha James from the stories that newspaper reporters wove about the crime, borrowing stock characters and plotlines from popular detective fiction to flesh out a dramatic angle that would hook readers. In weaving those narratives, reporters created the basic fabric of a common public understanding for the case, and that grand narrative gained a symbolic importance disproportionate to the significance of one more death in a world at war. Their combined journalistic efforts transformed the Lower 13 case into a public spectacle that hammered home simplistic moral lessons. Reporters interpreted each new snippet of information in ways that affirmed and extended their emerging grand narrative. In other words, the first news stories about the case influenced how later reporters, investigators, and public audiences understood or recognized new facts and information. The resulting melodrama was a murder mystery in real time that reinforced gendered stereotypes common to the prewar, true-crime literary genre. Journalists assigned moral value to each character they introduced, favoring simplified caricatures of good versus evil over more complex characterizations of morally conflicted human behavior. In the fearful times of the first full winter of American involvement in the war, however, they discarded the well-worn character of the corrupt or ineffective police investigator so common to those detective novels. In a time when censorship boards consciously shaped how people learned about current events, Americans desperately wanted to believe in the virtues of their public officials. In the Lower 13 case, consequently, reporters focused on individually immoral, "deviant" criminals, and they sought heroic figures among the uniformed young men who travelled aboard the same train as the young female victim.

The cramped conditions aboard the "murder car" defied description and largely escaped the imagination of the first reporters, but those conditions should have alerted them to the most important inconsistencies among the eyewitness accounts on which they based their stories. Smells, sounds, and movements overwhelmed and disoriented passengers more than investigators were willing to admit, hindering their ability to recall when or what they experienced or witnessed, and in what order. The thirty-six people who, according to surviving records, were on board Car D that night included sixteen women, fifteen men, and at least five children. They were all crammed into a long, narrow space of less than 450 square feet, with little more than curtains separating them. Those curtains provided the illusion of privacy in an intensely public place. The lurching, rumbling, clattering interior of Car D was a confined environment filled with unfamiliar smells, sounds, and textures. Nearby human bodies emitted gas, gave off odors, and sprayed mucus and spittle into

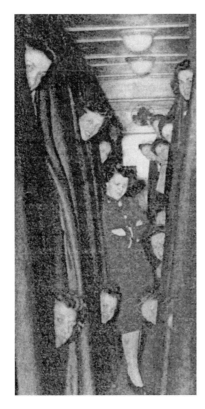

Interior image of a Pullman car (left) with berths made down for sleeping, showing the dimensions of the space where the murder happened. From *SPRR Bulletin* November 1942 (cover at right). Original bulletin located in SPR collection, CSRM Library and Archives. Images courtesy Union Pacific.

the air with each cough, burp, and rumbling of the bowels. Howling babies and whining toddlers taxed the patience of even their devoted parents and assailed the eardrums of nearby passengers, depriving them of sleep and setting nerves on edge. People who trundled aboard in the early morning hours of one of the coldest nights of that winter frantically sought berths in the dimly lit and overcrowded train while wearing heavy winter clothing. In the warm interior of the Pullman car, they sweated profusely from stress and exertion beneath the burden of coats, luggage, and scarves, stomping snow off their boots and wedging steaming wet wool into storage nooks and luggage racks in the cramped semiprivate berths. The interior of Car D was a warm, steaming, humid, dank, and dark environment. Lights flickered on and off as the faulty electrical system alternately drained its storage batteries when the train was stationary and recharged when the car's wheels turned as forward motion resumed. These were challenging conditions, even for seasoned travelers.

Very few passengers could honestly claim they slept soundly, and those who did fall asleep during the long delay before the train left Portland were even more disoriented when they awoke four hours later to find they had gone less than eighty miles since the scheduled departure time. Most passed a fitful night, waking intermittently, sometimes walking up and down the aisles to visit the lavatory, to smoke, to stretch their muscles, to visit with friends in other berths or cars, to request help from the porter, or to otherwise settle their nerves or escape the cramped confines of their berths. Many tossed back and forth in near delirium, suspended between consciousness and unconsciousness, observing the lights flickering, shouting out in their sleep, hearing sounds that they could not identify, and feeling nauseous, uneasy, and fearful. At least one of the women was suffering severe menstrual cramps, and she commiserated with several other women in the lavatory during the early morning hours.

Under such conditions, even an ordinary night may have seemed surreal, but 23 January 1943 was no ordinary night. It was early in the second winter of American involvement in the Second World War, and Train 15 out of Portland, headed toward Los Angeles, was a military transport train in two different sections. The lead section carried servicemen in closely packed quarters. The trailing section was mixed, including military and civilian passengers, some of whom were following family members in the lead section. The train followed blackout protocols, meaning the train windows were covered to prevent light from escaping the interior. This blocked out moonlight, starlight, and even light from passing towns and stations. The cramped interior of the train seemed like a separate world, completely cut off from the outside. Passengers and crew passed the night largely oblivious to where the train was or which stations it had already passed. Those without watches had no way of reckoning time and little knowledge of the passing landscape. Even experienced trainmen, equipped with watches and schedules and with assigned duties at each stop, disagreed in later accounts about what time the train arrived at or left a particular station that night. Fixing the murder within the boundaries of Linn County, therefore, relied on a timeline of events patched together from conflicting eyewitness accounts. Brakemen and engineers familiar with the exterior landscape had virtually no knowledge of what went on inside the passenger cars, whereas conductors and porters had only a sketchy understanding of where the train had been when they first learned of the murder. Moreover, they were uncertain how much time had elapsed between when they learned about the murder and when it had actually happened. Most stories seemed to agree the murder happened after the train left Albany, fixing the northern boundary of the event firmly in Linn County, and most stories also agreed that the train stopped, after the murder, for an extended time in Harrisburg, just within the southern boundary of the county. This latter detail was important because it firmly fixed the murder within the limits of Linn County, rather than Lane County, just to the south of Harrisburg. Residents (and potential jurors) of Lane County, a more urban setting that included the university and commercial-industrial districts of Eugene, Oregon, were, on average, better educated than those in Linn County.

Even those with access to the outside of the train were confused by the unusual appearance of the mid-Valley landscape that night. An unusually cold, icy storm blanketed the mid-Valley, from Portland to Eugene, in over a foot of new-fallen snow. The storm came at the tail end of a severe cold snap, during which the Columbia River reportedly froze over at The Dalles and smaller streams froze solid throughout the Willamette Valley. By 23 January 1943, the cold snap and snowstorm was entering its fourth day, and temperatures at the weather station nearest the location of the murder stood at 12°F that morning.[1]

On cold mornings such as 23 January, the inside and outside worlds of train travelers and workers met in the dining car kitchen. Those whose jobs took them outside the train at stops along the way witnessed an unfamiliar landscape of snow-covered lowlands and ice-blackened waterways. In such circumstances, the dining car took on added significance as a place where passengers and crew sought the warmth of companionship, coffee, and conversation, and for that reason, it was a place where those familiar with the outside world interacted with those confined to interior spaces. Experienced travelers may have previously encountered similarly difficult travelling circumstances, but few on board Car D that night were frequent train travelers, and even fewer had previous experience dealing with train travel amid the stress and confusion of a winter storm. Unusual delays due to snowdrifts and related equipment failures stressed travelers and frustrated crewmembers. In this stressful environment, passengers with colds, flu symptoms, fevers, and coughs struggled through the night as healthier travelers futilely tried to keep their distance in those cramped 450 square feet.

For an event that took place in such a small space filled with so many people under unusual stress, and within such a narrow window of time, a surprising variety of details remain unknown—in fact, the unanswered questions far outnumber the facts that survive in the historical record. Many details that at first appear factual actually contradict other, equally credible evidence. Early on, investigators filtered out eyewitness accounts they could use from those they preferred not to use. The most important filters they applied were race, gender, and military status. All the investigators knew for sure was that someone had murdered Martha Virginia Brinson James on board that train in the early morning hours of 23 January 1943 and that the site of the murder stretched across the aisle from the berths designated Lower 13 to Lower 14 aboard Car D. Martha James died that night, literally within an arm's reach of thirteen other people who occupied the berths immediately adjacent to her own. Of those thirteen people, seven were women and three were children younger than ten years old. Only three of those thirteen people were adult men, and two of those men were the only people from those berths who later admitted to having heard anything alerting them to the fact that a woman sleeping within two feet of them had screamed loudly enough to be heard by witnesses at the other end of the sleeper car, over thirty-six feet away. Of these thirteen people, only two of the three men were eventually called to testify in the murder trial. Both men were White, uniformed marines.

White adult men in military uniform, and the stories they told, enjoyed privileged status throughout the investigation and subsequent trial regardless of factual evidence. Elusive facts scarcely deterred early reports of the murder the day it was discovered. News reports shaped public perceptions of the crime with unsubstantiated theories of how it happened, filling in the blanks with unreliable details gleaned from the few police sources cited, from unnamed passengers or crew, or from the reporters' fertile imaginations. These initial reports manipulated and experimented with different timelines, motives, and details supposedly describing the actual crime. Later reports introduced new details that often contradicted earlier stories, but reporters seldom acknowledged that the story had even changed. The *Corvallis Gazette-Times*, for example, reported in its Saturday edition, the morning of the murder, that state police had identified Mrs. Martha Virginia Brinson James, twenty-one, Seattle, slain "as she lay asleep in her berth" on the southbound Southern Pacific passenger train: "Her throat was cut. Robbery apparently was not the motive, as considerable money was found on her person." The story reported that the body was discovered at Tangent, at about five o'clock that morning, and taken off the train at Eugene. This initial report, appearing in the daily newspaper published closest to the location where the murder presumably took place as the train passed through, indicated that Oregon State Police planned to board the train in northern California and that naval authorities were also investi-gating. It noted that "Ensign Richard James, USN was informed at Klamath Falls that his wife Martha was murdered near Tangent, OR."[2] Many of these details, reported as if they were factual, conflicted with evidence and eyewit-ness accounts that later emerged and gained credibility.

Early news stories unquestioningly reported information from military sources and stressed the innocence and virtue of the victim and her family, and the blamelessness of military authorities. The navy initially claimed the woman was travelling under the protection of her husband, and not alone on the train. The Corvallis paper, in one of the earliest reports, cited the Thirteenth Naval District Headquarters as source for the claim that "Ensign Richard F. James was with his wife when they boarded a south bound train at Portland last night, but . . . they had sleeping space in separate cars." According to this report, navy sources also said that Ensign James "may have been on the train, unaware of the tragedy, at the time his wife was slain." The same news story suggested the couple also knew other people on the train, including a "neighbor" from Seattle who told reporters Martha and Richard James were from Richmond, Virginia.[3] This early version seemed to be reassuring readers that, despite the swirling mass of moving humanity on troop transport trains, the navy was not in the business of separating families and leaving women vulnerable and alone. Somebody else, not the military, must be to blame for the woman's death.

Reporters gradually exoticized the hour and circumstances of the murder. Time was impressively malleable in early versions of the official story, and the earlier the hour, the darker the suspect and the blonder the victim's hair. By the time the afternoon papers went to press, reporters had shifted the time-line for the murder to an hour earlier than first reports, and they introduced new, previously unremarked details about race and color: readers learned that Wilson had seen a "Negro" fleeing the scene. The Albany Democrat-Herald, an afternoon newspaper conveniently located adjacent to the Linn County courthouse housing the Linn County district attorney's office, was one of the first to focus on the appearance of the female victim and the race of the male fugitive. Citing unnamed "police" sources, the Democrat-Herald headlined the story with Wilson's claims: "Knife Wielder Reported Seen Making Getaway," and "Negro Is Suspected as Slayer," and "Marine Sees Killer." Without explain-ing why the timeline had been moved one hour earlier than the time reported earlier that morning in the Corvallis paper, the Albany paper merely claimed, as if the timeline were not at all in question, "Mrs. James, the wife of Ensign Richard F. James, . . . apparently was murdered about 4 a.m., police said, as the train rolled through the Willamette Valley toward Eugene."[4]

Wilson, in the Albany paper's version of the story, assumed the role of a militarized guardian of White female virtue—a surrogate protector filling the role of the absent husband. In this emerging version, Martha shrank in size, becoming more obviously vulnerable and in need of protection but also more chaste and adult. It stressed the watchful vigilance of the marine occupying the bunk immediately above hers, and it described "Mrs. James" as "a tiny brown-haired woman." This report focused more on the heroic, White marine who sprang alertly to her rescue. In doing so, the story unwittingly revealed early evidence that this star witness for the prosecution was an inventive storyteller spinning false yarns. The article gave the first of several inaccurate addresses for Wilson, explaining, "the suspected murder was discovered by a horrified marine private, Harold R. Wilson, [of] San Diego, who was awakened by a commotion in the berth below—No. 13—and peered out in time to see Mrs. James' body sag into the aisle of the swaying car. He told police he was awakened by a stifled scream and as he looked out between the curtains of his upper berth saw a man in a pin-striped suit hurrying down the aisle and out of the darkened car." Without disclosing how reporters came by the information, the same article also informed readers, "Pvt. Wilson told police he believed the man was a negro. Police doubted the assailant remained on board and said he probably left the train at Tangent, some forty miles north of here."[5]

The Linn County sheriff's office initially racialized the investigation by encouraging speculation that a Black assailant had fled the train at Tangent and was heading north through the snow-covered landscape of the mid-Willamette Valley. The Albany newspaper's account of a "Negro" on the loose in rural Linn County fueled race fears among local White residents. At the same time, however, it highlighted Wilson's role as an alert, responsible marine, emphasizing the comforting presence of military officials protecting chaste White womanhood. This inflammatory angle, although it shifted attention away from the train and into the surrounding rural landscape, also linked the murder of a young southern White woman with a furtive Negro fugitive, and that feature eventually shifted the focus back to the train. If no Black fugitive could be found in rural Linn County, then perhaps he never left the train? The Albany paper initially claimed that investigators with the sheriff's office had found "tracks" in the snow near the rail line on the Tangent siding. According to a section headlined "Negro missing," the article concluded, the tracks "may have been those of a trainman, but might, on the other hand, be those of the fugitive, the sheriff said. If the latter theory is correct, the suspect has probably proceeded north [presumably in the direction of African American communities in Portland]." The sheriff, according to this same Albany article, was informed by Southern Pacific officers that one particular "Negro" passenger who had been on the train could not be found when a check was made of train personnel after the crime had been discovered.[6] None of these claims withstood close scrutiny, but the suggestion, not factual evidence, drove the subsequent investigation: officials were on the lookout for a fugitive Black man.

These initial news reports supplied the central plot and characters for the courtroom melodrama that prosecutors eventually presented at trial: a furtive and cowardly Black man viciously attacked a vulnerable, chaste, married, White society woman and then fled into the night, frightened off (albeit too late) by an alert marine, ever-ready to spring to the defense of White womanhood. Portland-area reporters, within a day of the murder, offered additional detail on the background, patriotic sacrifices, and vulnerability of the murdered woman. The Sunday edition of the *Oregon Daily Journal* focused on the couple's ties to the navy, the wife's connections with Norfolk, Virginia, and her photogenic face, including a large photo with the caption, "Mrs. Martha Virginia Brinson James, 21, of Seattle, and formerly of Norfolk Virginia" (no longer Richmond). The photo, which later ran as the standard illustration accompanying most subsequent stories about the Lower 13 murder, was apparently taken from her wedding announcement in the *Norfolk Virginian-Pilot* the previous September, and it clearly established, if there was any lingering doubt, that the victim of the murder was a respectable White woman, while the headlines emphasized the insubstantial (but widely accepted and oft-repeated) theory that the perpetrator was a Black man.[7]

Although the murder took place aboard a Southern Pacific train as it passed through Linn County, Oregon, few other aspects of the case tied it to that locale, and perhaps for that reason, early reports in other newspapers emphasized more universal themes in crafting a narrative that would resonate with urban readers beyond that rural setting. After the first day of coverage, Portland-area dailies (the *Journal* and *Oregonian*) largely drove the storyline, gearing their reporting to a White urban readership increasingly concerned about the disruptions of wartime mobilization. Beyond the immediate Oregon setting, most out-of-state newspapers picked up AP or UPI wire service reports that summarized coverage from the Portland-area dailies. Reporters and editors who initially seemed uncertain about how to approach the story soon settled on a human-interest angle that set the frame for how investigators understood and interrogated subsequent "facts" and witnesses.

The Portland dailies targeted an audience struggling with the social implications of a massive wartime mobilization. Portland's Union Station was a major transfer terminal for military transports on the Southern Pacific Railroad, linking Seattle in the north with Sacramento, San Francisco, Los Angeles, and San Diego to the south, and with Spokane and Salt Lake City to the east. Train 15 boarded at Union Station that night, collecting passengers from northern and northeastern lines and connecting them with the main route through the Willamette Valley then across the Cascades via Oakridge to Klamath Falls and, ultimately, Sacramento and Los Angeles. These railroad networks made Union Station a place where dislocated people from all over the country crossed paths with other transients from all over the western United States and Canada. By late January 1943 Portland residents were accustomed to large contingents of military men and their families travelling through Union Station. The entire city was on a war footing, as wartime workers arrived in large numbers for new jobs in war-related industries. Military personnel who moved into and through the city on transfer orders were shorter-term visitors, but they mixed together with longer-term migrants in a growing confusion of unfamiliar faces. Portland's official population increased by more than 160,000 between 1940 and 1944,[8] and many more were only passing through on their way to someplace else.

Martha James' murder came at the peak of this transition, when the outcome of the war remained in doubt and while war-induced fears of invasion, subversive activities, and aerial attack were still running high. In the Pacific theater, the Guadalcanal campaign was nearing its final stages by January 1943, when the Marines transferred control of the island to the army, after more than four months of intense campaigning to drive out tenacious Japanese defenders. In North Africa, on the morning of the murder, Allied forces compelled German units under Rommel's command to surrender Tripoli, and in Eastern Europe, the Soviet Union gained ground in its efforts to retake Stalingrad, regaining control over the last airfield linking Nazi defenders with resupply from outside the city. Just one week before the murder, Churchill and Roosevelt met at Casablanca to discuss plans for the impending invasion of Italy and an eventual "second front" in western Europe. Later that week, as the

German hold on Stalingrad rapidly deteriorated, Jews in the Warsaw Ghetto rose up against the Nazi occupation. By the end of the month, as the murder investigation gained momentum, the Japanese abandoned Guadalcanal to American forces, and one day later, Field Marshal Friedrich Paulus surrendered the bulk of the German Sixth Army at Stalingrad.[9]

The Lower 13 murder, in other words, gained national attention at a time when breakthrough Allied successes were just beginning to turn the tide of the war. From late January through early May 1943, news of the murder, the investigation, and the eventual trial squeezed onto the front pages of newspapers around the country, sharing headline space with bigger, seemingly more momentous, events. On a global stage of monumental battles, catastrophic loss, deprivation, and genocide, the death of one relatively privileged young woman aboard a night train in Oregon was tragic but not obviously more important or significant than any other death in that month of a world at war. The case is remarkable, therefore, because newsmen and prosecutors approached it as an opportunity to promote a particular moral view of the dangers on the home front at this pivotal point in a war that was just beginning to turn in their favor.

Newspaper coverage of the case latched onto the "hook" of personal sacrifice and innocent virtue counterpoised against callous and amoral, deceitful shirkers. Although initial reports from the sheriff's office in Albany racialized the crime, subsequent news stories shifted the narrative in a more militarized direction. Portland-area newsmen framed the case of Martha James' murder as a melodramatic parable of innocence lost in a wartime society that had not yet adequately embraced the virtues of constant vigilance. The resulting storyline that most reporters embraced, consciously or unconsciously, emphasized militarized themes of virtuous duty and order, and warned the reading public to increase their alertness. At a time when more people were travelling by train each year than ever before, women, especially, increasingly travelled alone, surrounded by strangers and far from home. Melodramatic articles about the Lower 13 murder voiced the gendered and racialized fears of a White populace uprooted from familiar touchstones of morality, order, and personal security, and urged an alternate, military discipline.

In the first weekend after the murder, Portland-area newspapers sketched the outlines of a dominant narrative within which all other evidence must fit or be ignored. The timing of the murder, in the early hours of Saturday morning, lent itself to dramatic reinvention, allowing news editors greater leeway for expanded coverage in Sunday editions that included more photographs

and other images. The prominent story on the front page of the Sunday edition of the *Oregon Daily Journal*, for example, began with the breathless headline "Death of Bride in Lower Berth 13 Starts Hunt" and the sensationalized
subheading "Beautiful Young Woman Gashed as West Coast Limited Speeds
Through Night; Young Husband Is Informed of Tragedy."[10]

The Portland-area dailies remade both Martha James and the assailant
within two days of the attack, exaggerating the woman's golden beauty and
emphasizing the man's hulking size and dark, racialized features. While largely
continuing the race-tinged version of the crime, as presented in the Albany
paper, the *Journal* abandoned that publication's description of Martha as a
"tiny, brown-haired" woman and, instead, eroticized and militarized the story.
The *Journal* lamented "the outrageous murder of beautiful, blonde, 21-year-old
Mrs. Martha Virginia Brinson James," and it stressed Wilson's military credentials, repetitiously identifying him as "Marine Private Harold R. Wilson." The
Journal highlighted the physical description Wilson provided of the "burly"
man he had seen fleeing the scene of the murder, "wearing a pin-stripe suit,
swarthy complexion, or perhaps a Negro." The *Journal* also claimed that
investigators had discovered an open vestibule door and "footprints in snow
between the two S.P. tracks at Tangent," and it quoted the Linn County sheriff
as saying the tracks indicated a man had jumped from the southbound train
and then boarded a northbound train (Train 20) that passed as Train 15 sat
waiting on a siding, shortly after the murder.[11] These new details implied that
the swarthy perpetrator had headed back to Portland, perhaps with the intent
of taking refuge in that city's African American community, thus providing a
Portland-area angle for local readers.

Reporters scrambled to learn more about the victim, focusing on her status, connections, education, good breeding, and responsible choice in a husband—all elements calculated to affirm her status as a virtuous married White
woman of standing and respectability. The *Journal* reprinted information
about Martha Brinson James' wedding and background, with details apparently gleaned from the wedding announcement that her hometown newspaper in Norfolk, Virginia, published the previous September. The *Journal*
described her as "a daughter of Mr. and Mrs. Wilbur G. Brinson, who live on
the fashionable North Shore district of Norfolk. She attended the Norfolk
division of William and Mary College [now Old Dominion University],
and just before her marriage she was a student at Sweet Briar College. Her
Husband is a son of Mr. and Mrs. Harry Mapp James of Nassawadox, Va.

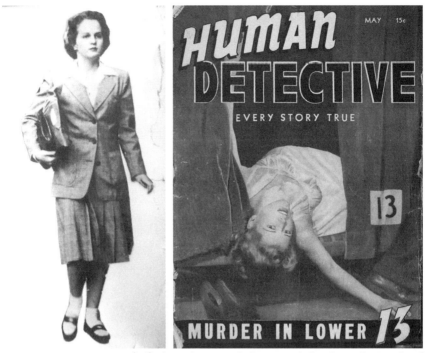

Martha Virginia Brinson James (left). Photo taken in Seattle the morning before the murder. Introduced at trial as State's Exhibit and shown to jurors. Original print located in OSSC case file, Oregon State Archives. Image courtesy Oregon State Archives. *Human Detective* cover (right) with sensationalized story about the Lower 13 murder. Original located in Lower 13 murder file, PPC collection, Newberry Library and Archives. Image courtesy Newberry Library and Archives.

He attended the University of Virginia."[12] The article observed that Martha met her husband, Richard Floyd James, while they were students attending the Norfolk Division of the College of William & Mary, beginning in 1940, asserting (erroneously) that they had each finished a "two-year course of study" at that school before they married in fall 1942.

By emphasizing, even exaggerating, the status and attractiveness of the victim, and juxtaposing that with lingering details about her gruesome death and the "ghastly" nature of her wound, these early reports encouraged public speculation on the deviant character of the assailant: What kind of a person could do such a thing? This storyline played to popular expectations of stereo-typical characters familiar to readers of the true-crime literary genre. Initial reports suggested a brutish, ripping attack. According to the *Journal*, for exam-ple, Coroner Poole of Lane County explained that a "gash five inches deep had been torn in the neck with some *very blunt instrument* [emphasis added] and that the wound was jagged and torn." One officer who viewed the body reportedly speculated that the murder weapon may have been an ordinary screwdriver.[13] Earlier that day, the (morning) *Oregonian* had reported that Martha's throat was "slashed" but went to great lengths to cite an authoritative source: "Dr. John [*sic*] Beeman, state police crime detection expert," the article noted, "disclosed that she had not been attacked otherwise." This evasive statement was clearly an effort to rule out rape as a motive in the crime, and it established a narrative template for later stories: an innocent victim, recently married, separated from her military husband by red tape, murdered while sleeping, but not "otherwise" attacked. Details about the nature of the wound, however, and the likely murder weapon, were dramatically revised over the next several weeks. The initial emphasis on unthinking, brutish, ripping force was an important part of the effort to construct a story that corresponded with what a White audience would more likely believe about a Black assailant than a White attacker.

Uncritical reporting of the police investigation effectively legitimized the racially biased assumptions that framed the initial inquiry, and reporters gradually racialized the description that Wilson provided police. When the police detained two men from the train in Klamath Falls, reporters for the *Oregonian* assumed that dining car waiter John Funches, a thirty-year-old African American man from Oakland, California, was a suspect, and that Wilson was merely a witness. Funches was reportedly "held at Klamath Falls in connection with the case" although he "denied knowledge of the crime and said he was asleep at the time." By contrast, the same article reported that police had detained twenty-one-year-old Wilson "as a material witness." The newspaper printed details of everything Wilson claimed to have witnessed, whereas it only suggested that Funches had denied involvement. Wilson's story, by this second day of reporting, was more elaborate than earlier accounts. The *Oregonian* dutifully paraphrased Wilson's claim that he was "awakened by a woman's scream. He [Wilson] peered from his berth and [as he later reported] '. . . saw a dark heavy-set man get out of lower 13 and run down the aisle toward the train rear. . . . He kind of turned a little sideways, so I could just get the side of his face. . . . It was pretty full. He had on a brown pin-point stripe suit. I think he was about 5 feet 10 inches, and he had short hair. The light was so dim I couldn't tell whether he was a light negro or a dark white man.'" At any rate, reporters concluded, the man was certainly dark, although Wilson would not go on record as claiming the assailant was a Black man. Wilson further reported, "Mrs. James had already fallen out of the berth, already dead, by that time." The story did not bother to report any significant details about Funches and only implied that he was the most likely suspect. Conversely, nothing in the account of Wilson's statement suggested that he was anything more than merely a witness.[14] Racial assumptions by reporters in this way reinforced, legitimized, and normalized the racialized tone of the investigation.

Militarized identities carried greater weight with reporters and the police, who typically viewed military witnesses as more truthful and reliable, possibly better trained as observers. The initial stories of the investigation demonstrated that militarized bias. Reporters misidentified witnesses and revised the timeline for the murder to more closely match the claims Wilson made in his first statements. Curiously, according to early reports, no other witnesses directly corroborated Wilson's account of a swarthy man fleeing the scene of the crime. The *Oregonian*, however, prominently featured the stories of two other "Marines" in nearby berths: William Van Dyke and Eugene W. Norton. Van Dyke and Norton, by this account, both reported they were awake at 4:00 a.m. when they heard a woman exclaim, first, "I can't take this any longer!" Then, after a brief pause, "My God, he's killing me," followed by a scream.[15]

By privileging the stories of these two other "Marines," reporters reinforced the story of military virtue and alert vigilance that Wilson had introduced early in the investigation. The timeline that Norton and Van Dyke provided, according to initial news reports, closely corresponded with the 4:00 a.m. time at which, according to similar stories, Wilson claimed to have first heard the woman's screams. Local news reports also noted that Norton said he may have seen a shape in the corridor after the scream, but that he couldn't distinguish clearly that it was a person, and he concluded, "It might have been a curtain fluttering.'" (He later altered this story at the trial, three months later, claiming to remember seeing the dark shape of a man running out the back of the car.) Both Norton and Van Dyke, however, agreed, according to these initial reports, that when they first looked out into the aisle, they clearly saw Wilson already standing over the body, or holding the body, or lowering the body to the floor, immediately after they heard the scream at around 4:00 a.m. (both witnesses later altered their testimony to correspond more closely to the timeline prosecutors constructed for the murder at the trial, moving the estimated murder time closer to 5:00 a.m.). Norton, by this account (who, as a matter of fact, was not a marine, nor a member of any other branch of the military), reportedly said he saw a marine, in undershirt and trousers, lifting the body of the woman and putting a pillow under her head. Blood was spurting from a wound in the victim's neck and, he said, "it looked to me like the wound was made by a gouge." This statement also seemed to corroborate the "ragged wound" described in other initial accounts of the murder. Van Dyke, who was a disabled marine (walking only with the aid of a cane), reportedly observed that when he heard the woman screaming, he looked out and saw "a partially dressed marine ministering to an injured woman." Neither Norton's nor Van Dyke's observations, as recounted in these initial reports, actually corroborated Wilson's claim that a swarthy man had fled the scene of the murder; nonetheless, multicolumn headlines for this account in the *Oregonian* read, "Woman's Scream Heard" and then "Marine Aids Victim."[16] Reporters apparently accepted the premise that the only person witnesses actually saw at the murder scene—Wilson—was attempting to assist the victim, ignoring the possibility that the witnesses may actually have caught him in the act of committing the crime or attempting to cover up his involvement in it.

The investigation, as reported in these initial accounts, focused from the outset on "Negro" passengers and employees of the Pullman Palace Car Company and Southern Pacific Railroad, and detectives attempted to establish a timeline for interactions involving the victim with African Americans on the train. They questioned passengers and crew on the train and at Union Station, exploring why and how the young navy pilot, variously described as "Ensign" or "Lt." Richard Floyd James, was not travelling with his wife, and why she seemed to be alone in Car D, berth Lower 13, at the time she was murdered. These reports emphasized the tragic circumstances, the beauty of the victim, the shattered, bereaved spouse, and the disposition of the body.[17] The *Oregonian* reported that although Richard James had a sleeping berth on a train from Seattle, and the railcar in which he was travelling was hooked onto the "SP Oregonian train," which left Portland at 1:00 a.m., Martha James, his "bride of four months," had transferred from the Seattle train to the West Coast Limited (Train 15) while it was being made up in Portland, and according to this account, her train did not leave Portland until 1:25 a.m. that Saturday morning (23 January).[18] This narrative confused the issue more than it clarified the circumstances by which the couple was separated, although it seemed to indicate that the husband's train left Portland less than half an hour ahead of Martha's. It did not explain how much time elapsed between the arrival of the train from Seattle and the departure of Richard James' train at 1:00 a.m. That time gap was important to an alternate scenario involving the steward's party and other possible motives for the murder relating to those who attended that party, but none of the articles discussed the significance of the apparently arbitrary nature of the various timeframes that these reliably White military witnesses provided.

Reporters carefully sidestepped the apparent reality that a young White married woman might have travelled on her own all the way from Seattle to Portland on the night of the murder, holding on to the fiction that the navy would not have left the young woman unprotected and alone on a crowded troop train. The most reliable reports, however, suggest that the James couple was separated in Seattle, and that Martha James was travelling, not with her husband, but with her friend, Mrs. Keaton, who was the wife of Ensign G. E. Keaton of Eudora, Arkansas—a close friend and colleague of Ensign James.[19] Most news reports highlighted Martha James' difficulty finding her luggage while waiting to board Train 15 at Union Station, implying that the confusion of Black trainmen at the railway station (and not the militarized travel arrangements) had exposed the "beautiful blonde" woman to licentious scrutiny as she stood alone on the platform.[20] The navy, however, issued a press release from the Thirteenth Naval District Headquarters, claiming that "Ensign Richard F. James *was with his wife* [emphasis added] when they boarded a south bound train at Portland last night, but . . . they had sleeping space in separate cars."[21] This conflicted with later explanations about the two separate trains, and with the account of Mrs. Keaton, who had a sleeping berth all the way from Seattle and said she offered to share it with Martha James on the overnight leg from Portland to Sacramento. Martha, however, decided instead to take a "tourist berth" in the "D" Pullman sleeper car.

Newsmen were so caught up in the grand eroticized narrative they had constructed about a sensual blonde victim that they ignored clear evidence that the Thirteenth Naval District, the two airmen, and the marine (Wilson) were telling mutually contradictory stories. Although other reports, including those from the navy's official representatives, claimed that Martha and her husband failed to connect in Portland, the Keatons contradicted that claim in their public statements to reporters after the murder. "Lt. Keaton," who reportedly was travelling with his friend, Ensign James, claimed that he last saw Martha standing on the platform in Portland at 1:00 a.m. Rather than considering how this claim differed from what both James and the Naval District officials had asserted, the reporter for the *Journal* used Keaton's version to focus on the exotic appeal of the dead woman. Keaton, the *Journal* reporter observed, "emphasized the beauty of Mrs. James" as she stood alone on the platform in Portland at 1:00 a.m. Elsewhere in the same story, the

Journal reported, "Mrs. Keaton told reporters she had been unable to find Mrs. James on the train today [the morning after the murder], that she heard a woman had been killed on the train, but she did not know Mrs. James was the victim until Ensign Keaton informed his wife of the tragedy [when her section of the train reached Klamath Falls, where he was waiting for her]." The Keatons also figured prominently in an alternative storyline involving the steward's party that investigators explored but never publicly reported. The close connection between Mrs. Keaton and Martha James also raised the possibility that the murder victim and her husband had attended that party sometime before the two ensigns left her on the station platform awaiting a berth assignment. Preliminary police interviews with Wilson suggested that he became agitated at the sight of White women drinking in the company of Black men in that setting. These alternative storylines, however prominently they appeared in the police investigation files, never made it into the news reports at the time of the murder investigation.

Rather than pursuing an angle of investigation that might have called into question the virtue and morals of one or more navy men and their spouses, Southern Pacific Railroad detectives considered, instead, the involvement of trainmen, both White and Black, who had staged the illicit "party" using food and drink pilfered from railroad company. That party may have had nothing to do with the murder, but the primary assignment of the railroad detectives was to investigate allegations of theft and misappropriation of company resources, and they were predisposed to suspect dining car crews of graft and corruption. As detectives primarily concerned with property theft and pilfering, they were poorly prepared, in terms of either training or experience, for a murder investigation, but their early involvement focused police attention on the dining car crew on Train 15. Railroad detectives closely questioned all waiters (uniformly middle-aged Black men), dining car cooks (including the White head cook and the Black third and fourth cooks, all of whom were middle-aged workers), and the dining car steward (a middle-aged White man) working Train 15. The youngest man they questioned was Folkes, the twenty-year-old second cook, who was closest in age to the young navy fliers and their wives, and this circumstance apparently attracted attention to him in the early stages of the murder inquiry.

The early focus on Black workers was mostly a fishing expedition, as investigators looked for alternatives to the more obvious suspect, Wilson. Investigation files suggest police detectives actually suspected the marine,

SPRR waiter John Funches (center, with white scarf and no hat) awaiting fingerprinting and inspection in Klamath Falls the morning after the murder. Original caption misidentifies the man being fingerprinted as Robert Folkes. He and the man leaning on the window are apparently dining car workers on Train 15. Original photo located in OSP case file, SPR collection, CSRM Library and Archives. Courtesy of California State Railroad Museum.

but trainmen bore the brunt of their scrutiny. Interrogations of most Black workers on Train 15 began in earnest while lawmen detained it on a siding at Klamath Falls, but the evolving investigation and most of the news stories initially focused on one particular dining car worker—a Black waiter who some passengers reported had been seen talking to White women on the train. There was no indication that investigators singled out Folkes on the first day, but after talking with other trainmen, their attention shifted to him after police in Klamath Falls released the train and allowed it to proceed south. Train 15 reportedly reached Klamath Falls at 3:15 p.m. on 23 January 1943, the afternoon after the murder was first discovered, after other, unscheduled stops at either Harrisburg or Tangent (perhaps both) and after a prolonged delay at Eugene, where Martha's body was removed from the train. When the "murder train" reached Klamath Falls, an interrogation team took statements from passengers and crew for nearly five hours, finally releasing the train at 8:00 p.m. after first cutting out the so-called murder car (Tourist Pullman Car D) and placing it on a siding. Passengers from Car D were transferred either to

From left, Linn County sheriff Shelton, an unidentified deputy sheriff, Private Harold Wilson, and John Funches aboard the train back to Albany the day after the murder. Original photo located in OSP case file, SPR collection, CSRM Library and Archives. Image courtesy of California State Railroad Museum

chair cars or to other Pullman sleeper cars. Oregon State Police sergeant E. W. Tichenor detained Wilson and Funches in Klamath Falls as material witnesses, sending them back to Albany under police escort.[22] With both Wilson and Funches in custody, DA Weinrick reportedly issued a "John Doe warrant" for "a stocky man of dark complexion," and "citizen posses" in the Tangent area of rural Linn County combed the countryside for evidence and suspects.

By the time the train was under way to California, however, it was clear that investigators had failed to identify the culprit. According to the *Oregonian*, police emphasized there was "no evidence to link Funches with the crime" and "no Negro with a brown pin-striped suit such as that described by Private Wilson, a brakeman, and another passenger, was found." The newspaper published a photo of Harold Wilson standing outside near the train at Klamath Falls next to the Klamath Falls county coroner, Dr. George Adler, and another one showing Richard James standing near the train with a state patrolman (Clyde Lowery) and a Southern Pacific investigator (C. W. "Champ" Champlin), "receiving details of the murder." The *Journal* also ran these and other photos from the Klamath Falls venue, including one of "John Preston Funchess [sic], 29, dining car waiter," in its afternoon edition.[23]

By the end of the second day, investigators had taken only two "material witnesses" into custody, and neither of them suited the storyline that police and prosecutors had released to the public in the previous two days of reporting. The photos of Wilson showed him hobnobbing with investigators while attired in the natty dress uniform of a marine. These images reinforced the respect with which police and other investigators publicly embraced Wilson's version of events (even as they skeptically questioned his story in their internal documents). Their public comments, however, had reinforced reporters' initial descriptions of the marine as a heroic military man who leapt to the aid of a woman in distress in an attempt to assist her. Efforts to cast Funches in the role of a dastardly killer initially seemed more promising, given his race and his apparent reputation as something of a ladies' man (a characteristic that internal files suggest Wilson also shared), but White witnesses placed Funches far from the scene of the crime, at the other end of the train, and that happy circumstance protected him from prosecution. With few options, and with the trainload of stunned passengers already trundling toward Sacramento, the investigating team released information suggesting there was a third suspect whom they had not detained at Klamath Falls, even though he was included in the initial round of questioning. The *Democrat-Herald*, in a story that went out on the Associated Press wire on the evening of 25 January, reported that a young "negro dining car cook" named Robert Folkes was arrested in Los Angeles when Train 15 arrived in that city, two days after the murder.[24]

Given the uncritical embrace that investigating authorities publicly accorded Wilson's tale, their inquiry necessarily included Folkes, and he was their refuge from public ridicule. The young trainman was a bit player in the first stories that Wilson told reporters about his own actions after discovering the murder, and Folkes was one of several dining crew members whom authorities had closely questioned in Klamath Falls. With the news that LA police had detained Folkes merely as a "material witness,"[25] Associated Press news service writers began to spin the story as a "bizarre and baffling crime" that had "stumped" Oregon police. They portrayed Oregon investigators as stumbling buffoons who "ran into one blank wall after another" in seeking to learn "who cut the throat of beautiful, blonde Mrs. Martha Virginia Brinson James, twenty-one, bride of a naval officer." That verbal image of inept Oregon lawmen accompanied photos depicting an aristocratic-looking Virginian in a distinguished-looking military uniform—actually the grieving husband, Richard James. Widely distributed news stories claimed Richard James had "prominent" family connections in Norfolk, Virginia (he was actually the son of an Eastern Shore farmer). AP writers embraced a new storyline that inverted common wartime images (with the appeal of a "man bites dog" story): the grieving, patrician navy officer mourning his wife's violent death, and his efforts to claim her body and make arrangements for shipping it back to Norfolk. Amid all the other images of grieving families who had lost their young men who had joined up to fight in the war, it was a story that turned on its head an otherwise familiar, tragic tableau, and in that sense, it was a reporting angle that grabbed the attention of war-weary readers. By Friday, 29 January, the physical remains of Martha Virginia Brinson James were home in Norfolk with her family, and the local newspaper largely avoided mention of the way that she died, presumably respecting the wishes of her grieving family.[26]

As public attention shifted from Oregon to Virginia, the district attorney and Oregon newsmen tried to shift the focus from the frightening reality of an unsolved crime and an escaped killer to a more reassuring story about the inevitable progress of Oregon's professional scientific police work. The investigating team, led by the Linn County district attorney, moved to reassure the public that professional police using scientific methods of crime scene investigation would protect the public by ferreting out clues that would inevitably

Wilbur Brinson (right) and Richard James (left) escort Mrs. Wilbur Brinson to the funeral of her daughter, Martha, in Norfolk, Virginia. Original print located in OSP case file, SPR Collection, CSRM Library and Archives. Image courtesy California State Railroad Museum.

lead detectives to the killer. The Albany paper reported on the evening of 25 January that the "death car" had been "returned" to that city, where it was awaiting "a thorough inspection by Dr. John Beeman, state criminologist." This story indicated, without explanatory details, that R. C. Howard, of the Oregon State Police, who was reportedly "heading the investigation" near Tangent, had "tabled" the theory that the killer left the train there to board a northbound train and was proceeding with "the presumption that the murderer remained with the train until it reached Los Angeles, or until after it left Eugene."[27]

The shift to the theme of scientific expertise and professional sleuthing by Oregon lawmen yielded apparently immediate results. The next morning, one day after the Albany paper's announcement of a $1,000 reward "for information leading to the killer," readers of the *Oregonian* learned that Robert Folkes, second cook on the West Coast Limited, had been "booked on suspicion of murder." The article described Folkes as a trainman whom Wilson encountered in the dining car immediately behind the murder car and noted that he (Folkes) had been "under surveillance by special agents of the railroad aboard the West Coast limited for 36 hours" until he was arrested in LA.[28] Some reporters, however, remained skeptical. Later that day, Portland's evening paper, the *Journal*, detailed police claims about Folkes' alleged role but also noted that the young cook was "steadfast in his denial of knowledge of the slaying" and that "a search of the murder car . . . failed to yield any clues."[29]

The new focus on scientific police work and professional sleuthing included a dramatic recharacterization of the evidence in ways that directly contradicted previous storylines, notably including Wilson's, but the change went unremarked and unexplained. On the day of Folkes' arrest, Weinrick corrected earlier news reports that had suggested the wound was made with a blunt instrument, perhaps a screwdriver, noting, rather, that Martha James' throat was "slit by a sharp knife—possibly a pocket knife—downward in four directions from the back of her left ear to the front of her neck; the knife penetrated so deeply that it reached a bone at the end of the slash." Moreover, Weinrick claimed, the nature of the cut indicated it had been made by a right-handed man, and the position of her body "probably prevented the killer from getting much of her blood on his clothing."[30]

As attention shifted to Folkes—a second cook with regular access to sharp knives in the dining car galley—the official narrative as reported in the local newspapers began to shift in ways that supported police claims that

Folkes was responsible for the murder. Apart from revising police statements describing the nature of the wound and likely murder weapon, Weinrick also corrected two other pieces of information his office had previously released to the press—opportunity and motive—and he closed the book on an early narrative thread that had suggested the slayer fled the train at Tangent. Splotches of blood reportedly found along the tracks in Tangent where Train 15 had supposedly stopped to wait for a passing northbound train, according to Weinrick, "came from a railroad track-walker [a local farmer walking along the track] who had a nose-bleed." Weinrick also suggested he was not ruling out rape as a motive, although police had established "Mrs. James was neither robbed nor raped."[31]

The district attorney's public statements to the press inflamed public opinion and aroused a backlash of popular outrage and protest. Weinrick's announcement set the stage for a sensational murder trial that aroused protests from Black communities across the United States. The fact that the case had "baffled" police until the inexplicable "confession" of a young Black man in police custody at the infamous Central Jail facility in Los Angeles[32] further inflamed public opinion in a racialized response that kept news about the trial on the front pages of newspapers across the country at a time when people were otherwise preoccupied with some of the most intense campaigns of the Second World War.

Once the district attorney settled on Folkes as his primary suspect, he also publicized a theory of the crime that rested on racialized stereotypes. In doing so, Weinrick drew support from representatives of the military and other collaborating law enforcement agencies that met with him in Albany on the same day he sprang the surprising news that Folkes had confessed. Included among the attendees at that Albany meeting was "Marine Corps Major James B. Hardle, from the Portland HQ, [who] arrived to look into the matter, and to give whatever assistance he may toward progress of the investigation."[33] In the victim's hometown, the news reports of Folkes' arrest appeared next to a picture of Ensign Richard James learning of his wife's murder. This juxtaposition of a grieving, uniformed, tall and White young Virginian contrasted with the accompanying narrative description of Folkes as a slight, young, and cocky Black man with a smart mouth in a "zoot suit" who worked as a cook in a railroad dining car, and not in military service.[34] Major Hardle's presence at the DA's summit of investigating agents is just one example of how military concerns—and militarized priorities—shadowed a criminal investigation that might otherwise attract only local interest. Deference to military author-ity was connected with deference to social status in the early stages of the investigation, as the victim's identity influenced the tone and coverage of the evolving case.[35]

Weinrick's office misrepresented facts and exploited racist stereotypes to shape public attitudes about the case in the hours after Los Angeles police arrested Folkes. He reconfigured the timeline for the murder by nearly a full hour, from 4:00 a.m. to just a few minutes before 5:00 a.m., to more closely correspond with what investigators had learned of Folkes' movements on the night of 22–23 January.[36] Detectives and the press, meanwhile, played fast and loose with the spelling of the young cook's name, commonly misspelling it as "Fowkes," "Fokes," and "Fowlkes," much as they had misspelled the name of the previous Black suspect, Funches. By contrast, the same writers fastidi-ously spelled the names of Wilson and the James and Brinson families. The frequent misspellings of "Folkes" conveyed the (erroneous) impression that the young man came from an uneducated family ignorant of how to spell even their own name.[37]

Reporters mostly repeated Wilson's version of events without question, but they edited out, without comment, elements of his story that contradicted the version Weinrick's office was promoting. Once the DA identified Folkes as his chief suspect, for example, newsmen commonly deleted any reference to the supposed assailant's brawn, height, or age, noting only his darkness.[38] Earlier stories had emphasized that the attacker was "burly," over five feet ten inches tall, and in his midthirties. Folkes, however, was a slight youth who stood less than five feet six inches tall and weighed only 140 pounds. He could never have been mistaken for a tall, burly middle-aged man, and so those uncomfortable details simply disappeared from most stories about the murder.

The case ultimately revolved around whether Folkes actually had made a statement amounting to a confession and, if so, under what circumstances Los Angeles police had extracted it. Newspapers in the mid-Willamette Valley were initially cautious in reporting LAPD claims that Folkes had confessed while in custody in their Central Jail facility in downtown Los Angeles. The Albany paper, in a front-page story under a banner headline reading "Negro Cook Held for 'Lower 13' Murder," noted that Folkes "has steadfastly denied his guilt. The prosecutor [Weinrick] reached his decision to file the complaint against Folkes after learning early today that the negro had implicated himself sufficiently to warrant prosecution." This carefully worded story avoided the word "confession," and it also continued the previously reported timeline for the murder.

Skeptical reporting did not prevent reporters from advancing the image of professional and scientific detective work that Weinrick and Beeman jointly tried to promote with this case. Investigating authorities in Albany went to great lengths to detail the professional police work and interagency cooperation within and across state lines that had led to the arrest of their latest suspect. Weinrick claimed that Folkes' arrest had cleared both Funches and Wilson of "all suspicion," and although he had ordered Funches' release, he also named others who "will be detained," including Wilson; H. M. Hughes (Pullman porter in the death car); "Corporal William W. Van Dyke, U.S.M.C.; and R. M. Kelso, U.S. naval chief tender; who were all passengers in car C [*sic*]." Apart from Wilson, however, none of these men were actually in custody. Weinrick emphasized that diligent and exhaustive police work had led to the break in the case. He observed: "We were enabled to sift what we believe to be true facts . . . from the more than 300 statements and reports which we examined, as well as from the scores of additional signed and unsigned letters and telephone calls." He also claimed support from city police departments "from San Diego to Seattle."[39]

Neither the newspaper nor Weinrick seemed comfortable enough with the alleged "confession" to openly argue that the purported statement was sufficient foundation for arresting Folkes. Weinrick, in fact, claimed that he had decided to arrest Folkes based on Wilson's report that he had discovered Folkes in the dining car shortly after the murder. Wilson, however, revealed that he had himself been the focus of the investigation that Weinrick headed and expected to be charged with the crime, right up until the point where he learned that Folkes had "confessed." Upon hearing that news, Wilson reportedly heaved "an obvious sigh of relief: 'Boy, am I glad to hear that.'"[40] Other witnesses elaborated on what he meant, noting, "Wilson was elated . . . when he learned that Folkes had been named in the murder complaint. 'I knew I didn't do it,' Private Wilson said, in full realization that he had been in a 'tough spot.'"[41]

Weinrick also was in a tough spot, politically speaking, until he arrested Folkes. The Brinson family, understandably distraught at the news of their daughter's murder, had turned to their close friend and neighbor, the influential governor of Virginia, seeking his support for quick resolution of the case. One day before Weinrick met with reporters in Albany, Oregon, to explain his reasoning for arresting and charging Folkes with the murder, Governor Earl Snell of Oregon exchanged telegraph messages with Governor Colgate Darden of Virginia, reassuring him, according to the *Norfolk Virginian-Pilot*, that "authorities in Oregon were doing 'everything possible' to bring about the apprehension of the slayer of Mrs. James." Darden lived on the same block of North Shore Drive as the Brinson family, literally across the street, and a Darden youth attended Maury High School with Martha Brinson, graduating one year ahead of the girl whom everyone in that prestigious country club district of Norfolk knew as Marti.[42]

Weinrick's claim that Folkes had admitted guilt came at a politically fortuitous time for the district attorney and was, perhaps, more than coincidental. Less than one day after the police and the district attorney's office were, by all accounts, "baffled" by the case, Darden's inquiries to Snell prompted a positive response from the Oregon governor, immediately followed by Weinrick's surprising announcement. Weinrick apparently faced political pressure from the governor's office to quickly resolve the case, and then he immediately arrested Folkes. From that point on, Weinrick and other investigators set about convincing a credulous group of reporters that the man charged with the crime was, indeed, guilty. Amid police efforts to convince reporters that detectives had used all scientific methods to carefully scrutinize "bloody bed sheets, towels, clothing, and other clues from which they are weaving the tale of tragedy enacted on the morning of January 23 in lower 13," however, a few unusually alert local reporters noticed a troubling lapse in the official narrative: police had produced three different versions of "confessions" that Folkes allegedly made: one a verbal declaration, one in a question-and-answer manner, and a third as a narrative, but "none of these had been signed."[43]

Wilson was another loose end that troubled Weinrick's office right up until the end of the trial. At least one alert reporter observed that the man who breathed an audible sigh of relief upon learning of Folkes' arrest, and whose story of the murder had captured the imagination of Weinrick's investigative team, was not who he claimed to be. Wilson initially claimed to be from San Diego, and then he admitted he was from Buckley, Washington. When a reporter contacted residents of Buckley, however, he discovered that the "identity of Marine Private Harold R. Wilson . . . is proving quite a puzzle to Buckley residents. . . . Nearly everyone here is asking his neighbor, 'Who is Harold R. Wilson?'" When told that school authorities, the chief of police, and the postmaster in Buckley had no record of Wilson ever residing in that city, the marine changed his story again, claiming that his parents moved to Buckley "a short time ago" from Windom, Minnesota.[44] After authorities arrested Folkes, however, Wilson completely dropped all reference to Buckley and admitted Windom, Minnesota, was his hometown. His story of his own past changed with each telling, but except for Archie Watts, who filed the story from Buckley, everyone ignored the fluidity with which this marine private reinvented his own identity.

The inconsistencies in Wilson's personal biography raise questions about the public rationale that Weinrick provided to explain his decision to arrest Folkes. Weinrick claimed Wilson's story was the reason he decided to arrest Folkes, but if Wilson couldn't be trusted to tell the truth about where he was from, then why would prosecutors trust his elaborate version of events from the night of the murder? At the time Weinrick made the announcement, the files Weinrick's office had compiled for the case already contained clear evidence that Wilson was fabricating stories. Weinrick, and the rest of the investigative team, had to have been aware that Wilson was not telling the truth, and yet the district attorney asserted that Wilson's statements were the foundation of his case against Folkes.

Wilson's mercurial past was only one evasive detail among many that investigators willfully buried as they simplified the Lower 13 murder case to portray Folkes as their sole suspect less than a week after discovering the crime. Most police statements and news reports from that first week of the investigation settled on 4:00 a.m. as the time at which the murder was committed, but in order to convict Folkes, prosecutors needed to move the time of the murder closer to 5:00 a.m. Most reports indicated the train was stopped on a siding at Tangent during or shortly after the murder, fixing the time of the murder closer to 4:30 a.m., but other reports indicated the train stopped at Harrisburg. This issue of whether the husband left his spouse on the platform or they simply "became separated" due to "traffic conditions" was a critical detail with the potential to dramatically transform public perceptions of guilt, innocence, and virtue. Who was to blame for leaving a young woman alone and vulnerable? The husband? The navy? The railroad? The woman's friend?

The murder scene itself was also a disputed landscape. As represented in news reports and police statements from the first week of the investigation, Wilson variously described the man he claimed to have seen leaving the

Robert E. Lee Folkes, 20, second from left, manacled to OSP officers Curtis Chambers, left, and Ray Howard, in Salem, outside the state prison, April 26, 1943. (AP Photo/Paul Wagner). Image courtesy the Associated Press.

scene of the crime as a "burly" man about five feet ten inches tall and about thirty years old, "heavy-set," and either running down the aisle or climbing out of Lower 13 when he first saw him. He claimed the man was wearing a "brown pin-point stripe suit," and he said the man was either a light Negro or a dark White man. Wilson claimed that he was awakened by the woman's scream, looked out into the aisle and saw the man running, and then saw the woman slumping into the aisle, and that he pulled on his pants and leaped into the aisle. Norton and Van Dyke, sometimes described as "two marines," said that they heard the woman scream, immediately looked out, and saw Wilson already standing, partially dressed, in the aisle, apparently holding the woman's head while attempting to place a pillow beneath her. The victim was variously described as a tiny, brown-haired woman or as a beautiful blonde war bride, and the wound in her throat was variously described as a jagged and gaping tear made by a dull weapon or even a screwdriver, or as a cut made with an exceptionally sharp blade, in four distinct motions. Most reports emphasized the dim lighting conditions in the car and uncertainties about what people could see in such conditions.

With the arrest of Folkes, investigators and reporters ceased treating the case as a murder mystery and shifted, instead, to the task of constructing a true-crime storyline that would explain and expose how and why Folkes committed the murder. The decision to charge Folkes as the suspected murderer transformed the narrative within which reporters and investigators made sense of these disputed elements of events leading up to the murder and transformed the landscape of the murder itself. Folkes was a young man, only twenty years old at the time of the murder. He was a slight youth who stood five feet six inches tall and weighed only about 130 to 145 pounds. The physical description of the man Wilson claimed to have seen was dramatically different from the surviving images and recorded vital statistics about Folkes. Moreover, despite his youth, Folkes was a worker assigned a particularly responsible and relatively prestigious position for an African American man in the employ of the Southern Pacific Railroad, and he had a specific set of tasks that he was required to accomplish on the morning of the murder—tasks that, if not completed on a specific timeline, would have been obvious evidence of inattention to his duties. Beginning with his arrest and news of his alleged confession, investigators and reporters revised the narrative within which they explored the contours of the murder case, and the narrative that they constructed influenced their interrogation of facts and witnesses in the two months between Folkes' arrest and trial. In none of those stories, however, did they bother to explore the background and history of how and why that young man came to be on that train on that particular day.

Interlude

ONE MORNING AT HOME IN SOUTH CENTRAL LOS ANGELES

Early in the morning on 19 January 1943, thirty-nine-year-old Eddie Dooley shrugged on his brand new, brightly colored, bluish-green overcoat and stepped out the front door of his home on Hooper Street, just south of East 42nd Street in South Central Los Angeles. From there, he caught a streetcar northbound toward the house at 1163½ E. 25th Street, where Robert Folkes lived with his common-law wife, Jesse Taylor Wilson Folkes. The streetcar carried Dooley past Jefferson High School, "Home of the Democrats," at the corner of Hooper and East 41st Street, and after riding another fifteen blocks, he had only a short, two-block walk from the car stop on 26th Street to his friend's house on 25th Street.

Dooley often stopped by early to chat, over coffee, with Folkes' wife, Jesse Wilson, before the two men headed in to work at the Southern Pacific Railroad's commissary for the dining car division, where they were both employed as dining car cooks. Jesse and her husband lived in a small, wood-frame duplex midway between Hooper and South Central Avenue in a street of modest, one- and two-story bungalows. Dooley later observed of his friend Folkes, "The only woman I ever heard him talk about was Jesse." Usually, the two men walked together another eight blocks up the streetcar line to the commissary on the corner of 12th Street and Central Avenue. On this morning, however, Dooley rode the car all the way up from 42nd Street just to tell his friend and coworker he would not be heading in to work that day because he had a bad cold. When Dooley broke the news, Folkes asked to borrow the new coat, because he was assigned to a northbound train and, he said, "yours is heavier than mine, and mine is torn, anyway."

Dooley, a third cook, was nineteen years older than his young friend, whose position as second cook was, nonetheless, more prestigious and responsible in the hierarchy of the dining car division. In less than two years, Folkes had been promoted twice, and at the age of twenty, had already reached the pinnacle of his career for a Black man in the dining cars—only the chef and steward ranked higher, and those positions were customarily reserved for White men, and only very rarely went to Black men, prior to 1943.[45] On the morning of 19 January, their dining crew was assigned to a train heading north from Los Angeles to Portland on a round-trip duty scheduled to last about six days. Dooley had learned from trainmen who had come down the previous day from the Northwest run that a cold winter storm was hammering northern California and Oregon. For that reason, after they walked together to the car stop, Dooley gave Folkes his new overcoat with a joking, "Don't you come back to Los Angeles unless you bring my coat." Then Dooley caught a car headed south, toward home, while his friend, Robert E. Lee Folkes, caught a streetcar heading north, toward the commissary and Oregon.[46]

Chapter Two
Food Fights for Freedom

Don't Waste It: Food Fights for Freedom
—Headline for December (1943) *Southern Pacific
Bulletin*

Despite the many and varied interrogations of Robert E. Lee Folkes, even avid readers of news reports covering the trial and its aftermath would have learned nothing about his life before the night Martha James turned up dead on Train 15. In his twenty years, Folkes faced racial exclusion and persecution, but he also found opportunities as a youth growing up in South Central Los Angeles. His background shaped how Folkes responded when questioned about the murder, and those responses influenced how people in Oregon understood his trial. Folkes did not react in the ways that police or courtroom observers expected, and that worked to his disadvantage as a Black man on trial for murder in Oregon courts. His trial, which prosecutors staged as a public spectacle, built around standard plotlines and stereotypical characters. Prosecutors promoted, with melodramatic flair, racialized notions of moral order that they hoped would resonate with the middle-class White women sitting as jurors. But a broader audience also witnessed that trial from outside the jury box, and many of them drew a lesson opposite from the one prosecutors intended. They empathized with Folkes, recognizing him as one of their own—a young man who frequented local establishments in Portland's African American community before he was unfairly targeted for trial. Folkes was not from Oregon, and he was alien to the Linn County setting where he faced trial, but he was not alien to the Pacific Northwest. He, and men like him, formed the backbone of a prewar African American community centered in Portland. He was not entirely alone in the courtroom, where skeptical civil rights activists monitored the stories prosecutors presented there.

For two years before that trial, Robert Folkes' work experience with SPRR connected him with Pacific Northwest communities. His ties with Oregon were stronger than any of the three other young people whose lives changed that night as a result of the murder. Oregonians were accustomed to seeing Black trainmen like him moving through their towns and cities, spending time in local restaurants, hotels, and public spaces. In Portland, some businesses catered to men like Folkes; others were considerably less welcoming and often blatantly hostile. Exclusionary policies and intimidation tactics in Albany clearly disturbed Black trainmen during the trial, but it did not prevent them, and other members of Portland's African American community, from making the trip to participate in, or simply monitor, those proceedings. Black men and women took the stand as witnesses, sat in silent support as observers, advised defense counsel, and walked together on downtown sidewalks in solidarity with the Folkes family. Joining them were local and regional leaders in the civil rights community, including executive officers from the regional office of the NAACP in Portland, Oregon. If Folkes was not exactly at home in Oregon, neither was he alien there.

As a trainman regularly assigned to work the round-trip route from Los Angeles, Folkes was a frequent visitor who followed accustomed routines on Portland layovers. His home life revolved around South Central LA, but as a railroad cook, he spent more time travelling to and from Portland (his "away" life) than he did in his home community (his home life). His stays in Portland were limited to the time it took train yard workers to make up the southbound return train to LA—typically less than six hours after the northbound train arrived at Union Station. Folkes mostly passed his time in Portland with other trainmen, lingering in downtown businesses catering to their short-term needs—hotels, bars, restaurants, and liquor stores. A few of his coworkers had families in Portland whom they visited for home-cooked meals, but most of his closest friends had home lives centered in South Central. Their earnings, presence, and experiences helped shape the African American community of Portland, where they interacted with Black workers more permanently rooted there. With few exceptions, however, trainmen like Folkes spent most of their time in that city preparing to head back on the road. Portland was just a small part of their "away" life, which mostly involved long hours of travel and only brief releases from their work duties. The murder trial trapped Folkes and his coworkers in that "away" life, forcing them to become more acquainted with the people of the mid-Willamette Valley.

Past experiences shaped the way Folkes presented himself in public, and that influenced how Oregonians reacted to his trial and, ultimately, the trial's significance to the state. His understanding of his own position and vulnerability in Oregon as a Black man suspected of murdering a White southern war bride inevitably built on his own experiences and understanding of racial difference and prejudice as a twenty-year-old Black man. In Folkes' life experience, the American West was an imperfect refuge from persecution and a landscape of uneven promise.[1] His background extended from the southern Midwest, through the Southwest, and into the Pacific Northwest. As a young boy, shortly after the First World War, he and his mother survived the horrors of a racist pogrom in the Arkansas Delta, and they left family and friends to join the Great Migration of African Americans who abandoned the South for urban centers in the North and West during and after the First World War.[2] Like many of those who headed West, they joined a protective community centered in South Central Los Angeles in the early 1930s.

In South Central, Folkes grew up in progressive surroundings, where African American community activists avidly followed the *Chicago Defender* for national news particularly relevant to their concerns. Locally, they subscribed to the *California Eagle*, a race paper published in the core of South Central. In that area, Folkes was surrounded by African American workers who demanded access to better jobs. They joined labor unions and worked to improve conditions in places where they had already gained employment. In the 1930s, as Folkes entered his preteen and teenage years, the best, most secure, career-level jobs available to young Black men in South Central were with the Southern Pacific Railroad, which operated from its headquarters shops and terminal at 12th Street and Central. Those jobs were also the focus of union organizing and labor activism, including efforts by the Dining Car Cooks and Waiters Union—one of the most active of the new labor organizations particularly recruiting Black workers.[3] Worker radicalism was a central component of the world Folkes knew: a community where activists organized self-help efforts with significant but not universal success.

Folkes came of age in the relatively protected environment of South Central, where it was not uncommon for young Black men to mingle in crowds that included young White men and women. He was accustomed to living and working in a racially mixed landscape, but he also lived in an area where African Americans clustered together in a protective enclave of racial solidarity. South Central was not an idyllic or utopian place, but rather a district where African Americans took refuge from systematic segregation and then carved out space for their community. Effectively excluded from other LA neighborhoods by restrictive covenants, they congregated in areas with fewer obstacles, seeking safety together. South Central was not a walled city—its borders were permeable and changing, meaning that Folkes, his mother, and his two younger siblings also lived in a fluid, integrated landscape of evolving rules and norms rather than a static system of racial segregation. Historian Douglas Flamming observes, "The district was neither ghetto nor slum. It was mostly white, with significant numbers of nonwhites. Neither rich nor poor, it was a sort of middling area."[4] The district included a mix of very nice homes but also very poor housing. Residents lived amid apparent wealth adjoining abject poverty, in a place with plenty of urban conveniences, including good streetcar lines, stores, restaurants, churches, theaters, and nightclubs. It was an urban setting where Black people who lived under the heel of racism nonetheless found new opportunities for improving their circumstances. In many cases, it was a landscape of optimism, for people who had every reason to be pessimistic.

As a relatively young man, Folkes brought those sensibilities of self-directed opportunity to Oregon, where he was a jarring reminder to urban and rural residents that their world was changing in ways beyond their immediate control. In manner, style of dress, and self-presentation, Folkes differed from other Black trainmen that White Oregonians were accustomed to seeing in mostly subservient roles. His breezy demeanor and informal manner apparently offended and sometimes impressed local residents who expected a more contrite or perhaps terrified defendant. Folkes, however, was young, and he embodied the demeanor of optimism and individualistic expression common to young people of his generation in South Central. He was out of his element in Linn County, Oregon, but he conducted himself in the fashion that, in his experience, yielded positive results. Self-confidence, good-natured banter, and a responsible work ethic had served him well until his arrest. At trial, he emulated his labor union representative, William Pollard, who stood out from the crowded courtroom galleries of local small-town folk as a serious-minded, educated, urbane professional—a Black man attired in a crisp business suit, taking careful notes on everything in the courtroom, acting as

Robert E. Lee Folkes in the interrogation room at the Linn County courthouse in Albany, Oregon, the day he was extradited from California. Original print located in the OSP case file, SPR collection, CSRM Library and Archives. Image courtesy California State Railroad Museum.

de facto assistant to the White defense attorney, LeRoy Lomax. In appearance and demeanor, taking their places with quiet reserve and businesslike focus, Folkes and Pollard demanded Oregonians sit up and take notice—this Black defendant was not a cowed victim of mob violence; he was a skilled worker and educated citizen demanding due process. It was a publicly expressed identity that challenged the foundations of the case prosecutors had prepared.

CONSTRUCTING IDENTITY: LOCATING FOLKES IN LOS ANGELES BEFORE 1943

Prior to stepping out onto the platform in Los Angeles and into the arms of the LAPD three days after beginning the southward leg of his round-trip duty to and from Portland, nothing in Folkes' prior record seemed to lead in the direction of a criminal conviction in a distant Oregon courtroom. Folkes, in fact, left very few footprints in the records of Los Angeles County, where he attended high school without earning distinction or lasting demerits and then entered the permanent workforce. Writers and commentators at the time of the trial apparently forgot he was still a minor, barely out of his teens. The "Minor's Release" form he filed with the SPRR in December 1941 bore his mother's signature and noted his father was "deceased," giving his birthdate as 20 June 1922 and his Los Angeles address as 1250 E. 20th Street—the same as his mother's. His prior work record was at locations within easy range of her influence. It included three years as "swamper" with Mr. C. Z. Hardy of 4315 Morgan Avenue, from 1937 to December 1940, and another year, from January to December 1941, as a swamper working for Mr. Edward Eckford, of 545 E. 33rd Street. Prior to those positions, he worked for nearly a year as an "attendant" for the Mack Fee Service Station at the corner of Adams and Hooper. These limited records suggest he was an able young man who sought and held regular long-term jobs in his community from the time he was twelve or thirteen years old until the day LAPD officers took him off the train at Union Station. As a twenty-year-old man, he had already accumulated a record of at least seven years of unbroken employment.

This young workingman built a solid reputation as a reliable employee in a close-knit community of businesses and acquaintances, all within easy walking distance of the racially integrated public schools he attended near his mother's house and within earshot of their neighborhood church. He grew up in the public eye, working at locally owned businesses in service jobs that put him in daily contact with customers and other passersby. At each of the jobs he held for a year or more, local residents in that walking neighborhood would have seen him almost daily. His was a recognizable face in a place that valued community and created opportunities for its hardworking young people, and he carried credentials linking him with the mainstream values of that progressive community. When he sought a position at the Southern Pacific Railroad, Folkes provided paperwork confirming his local roots and mainstream values. Adeline Richardson, the "coordinator of guidance" at Jefferson High, confirmed Folkes attended that school in 1936 and 1937, compiling a "satisfactory" record. Neither his name nor his picture appears in school yearbooks, although many other Black, Asian, Hispanic, and White faces appear in the photo galleries.

As a Black youth living and working in South Central, Folkes mostly escaped official notice. The most detailed records about him, from the years before news reports of the Train 15 murder, appear in railroad personnel files. The SPRR Hospital Department, in April 1942, listed his birthplace as Newark, Arkansas, his nationality as Negro, and added the detail that Folkes had injured his left arm three years earlier in a "car accident."

SEEKING REFUGE AND FINDING COMMUNITY IN SOUTH CENTRAL LOS ANGELES

Robert Folkes made few direct marks on the historical record prior to his arrest in January 1943, but like many other migrants into the West, his was a story at once singular and familiar. He was a young man with few connections or prospects trying for a new start on the West Coast, escaping his family's past. He apparently never knew his father, who died before Robert was born. In the first twelve years of his life, Robert and his mother moved around, fleeing the virulent, racist violence that quite likely killed his father. His mother's struggles through this period could not have escaped the attention of her eldest child. In most records involving her son Robert, Clara Folkes merely listed the boy's father as "deceased," but in one case, she listed him as "Robert Folkes [Sr.]." According to some records, a Robert Folkes died in a town listed as Jack, Arkansas, shortly before Robert E. Lee Folkes was born in nearby Newark, Arkansas. Allowing for some confusion in precisely when young Robert was born, this man may be the boy's father.[5]

Robert's mother, Clara, conceived and bore her child during the period of legal maneuvering that followed the peak of racial tensions in the Arkansas Delta, and the farcical legal proceedings that subsequently blamed Black victims for a racist pogrom in that region likely convinced her to relocate her young family. Family folklore about those postwar experiences also likely heightened young Robert's nervousness when investigators targeted him as a suspect in the James murder. His family witnessed racialized violence when White property owners in the Delta region responded to the demands of the Progressive Farmers and Household Union of America,[6] after the 1919 harvest, that landlords pay tenant farmers a fair share of the largest cotton crop in southern history. Landowners, claiming evidence of an organized "uprising," mobilized a militarized response. Nearly fifteen hundred deputies, volunteers, and federal troops equipped with twelve machine guns descended on the countryside, ranging outward in a two-hundred-mile radius from Elaine, Arkansas. Nan Woodruff estimates that, in a series of attacks on unarmed civilians near Helena and Elaine, this force left a bloody trail of "856 dead negro bodies with a wounded list probably five times greater [about six thousand casualties overall]." During that murderous march, the force rounded up another thousand Black people and marched them back to the Helena jail, where they systematically tortured and electrocuted them in order to secure "confessions." In nearby Elaine, jailers reportedly killed another four hundred

Black prisoners in the so-called Elaine Schoolhouse Massacre, coercing conspiracy confessions from survivors by executing other prisoners.[7] Family lore
about these events would have weighed heavily on Robert's mind during his
interrogations at the LAPD's Central Jail, where at least one fellow prisoner
was tortured to death during Folkes' stay. In that context, a false confession
may have seemed like a wise option.

In a bitter twist, acting on the basis of the (false) confessions coerced
from terrified prisoners under extreme duress, Arkansas courts prosecuted
the victims who survived terror and torture at the Elaine Schoolhouse and
the Helena jail, convicting several dozen Black "conspirators" on charges that
they had "murdered" several members of the marauding force of White mili-
tiamen and soldiers. In *Moore v. Dempsey* (1923), however, the US Supreme
Court overturned those convictions, arguing that the only evidence against
the defendants was confessions jailers coerced from desperate, tortured cap-
tives forced to witness the summary execution of their fellow prisoners.[8] The
same trial courts failed to prosecute anyone for the thousands of injured
and murdered Black victims. Somewhere in the aftermath of this explosion
of genocidal violence and systematic terror, Robert Folkes Sr. died in southeastern Arkansas, apparently leaving his wife, Clara, pregnant with his son,
Robert E. Lee Folkes.[9] The parallels between these events and the later accusations against her son could not have escaped Clara's notice.

Events in postwar Arkansas would have become part of family lore as
young Robert Folkes grew up in a single-parent household under the protection of his mother. Clara Folkes would have emerged from these experiences
with a clear understanding that a "confession" was not necessarily evidence
of guilt—a notion with added significance when her son stood trial in 1943.
What her son learned from his family's Arkansas experience is another question. By comparison with the world his father and mother endured, young
Robert Folkes grew up in a relatively secure, progressive environment, thanks
to Clara's hard work and determination. Less than a decade after the horrific
genocide in the rural Delta, Clara Folkes was living as a single Black mother
making her way in the integrated urban landscape of South Central's most
progressive district. Court records indicate she lived in Los Angeles by 1931.
When and how she moved from southeastern Arkansas to South Central Los
Angeles between 1922 and 1931 is uncertain. In leaving Arkansas, she followed
many other Black refugees who fled that state in the wake of the genocidal horror. That experience radicalized many people in southeastern Arkansas who

organized into resistance networks based on fraternal orders, churches, the NAACP, and Marcus Garvey's Universal Negro Improvement Association.

During this period, Robert Folkes and his mother joined one of the largest migrant streams in the so-called Great Migration of Blacks who headed out of the rural South toward northern and western urban centers. Working-class African Americans, formerly sharecroppers, migrated to cities and factories in increasing numbers, fleeing the violence and poverty of rural areas suffering through a decade of collapsing cotton prices. A major flood in 1927 and a catastrophic drought during 1930 and 1931 drove the plantation economy into near collapse, forcing another massive out-migration of former sharecroppers.[10] That trend accelerated during the Great Depression and the Second World War, and African Americans in West Coast cities like Los Angeles, San Francisco, Portland, and Seattle grew in number all through the 1930s and 1940s.

In South Central, Clara Folkes successfully gained a foothold in those decades, and she enjoyed modest upward mobility until 1943, moving her family every few years into marginally better living quarters. Like many other Black residents of the district, she became a more critical participant in local politics, abandoning the Republican Party and embracing a more radical Socialist identity. In 1932, Clara Folkes appears for the first time on voter registration rolls in South Central, where she is listed as a Republican voter living at 1343½ E. 18th Street.[11] Two years later, she had moved farther south in the district, residing at 829½ E. 27th Street, still registered as a Republican. She shared that residence with at least two other women, both registered as "Democrat": Mrs. Bertha Carter and Mrs. Roxie E. Walker.[12] That year, her son Robert was an eleven- or twelve-year-old boy, living with his single mother near the heart of South Central.

His mother's efforts to anchor her family in the progressive community of South Central paid off for Robert Folkes before he entered his teenage years. By the time he got his first job, in 1935, his mother was already a well-respected member of the community. She settled her family in a more long-term residence, in a neighborhood of respectable bungalows, near good integrated schools and social services at the core of South Central. She worked as a "seamstress," residing at 1546 E. Adams Boulevard, and by 1936 had enrolled herself as a Democratic Socialist voter. Only a few blocks down Adams, Robert Folkes secured one of his first jobs at the service station on the corner of Hooper and Adams. Clara's nearest neighbors on Adams were married couples. It was a neighborhood of middle-class aspirations, if not accomplishments. The men worked mostly as laborers or carpenters and the women identified themselves mostly as "housewife." As a single seamstress, Clara Folkes was the only Democratic Socialist in that neighborhood, where registrations shifted heavily from Republican to Democratic Party affiliations (ten of her fourteen nearest neighbors) at the peak of the Great Depression.[13]

In a neighborhood of New Deal Democrats, Clara Folkes showed her Delta region roots by joining a more radical party, and she also stood out from her neighbors in other ways, most notably as a single working woman and family head. During this period of relative stability for his family, Robert attended nearby Jefferson High and worked for several local businesses. By 1938, when he was sixteen, the family still lived at that address—an unbroken period of nearly five years in the same house—and Clara continued to support the family as a seamstress. Around them, their neighbors were relatively prosperous and stable. Most of the same families still lived nearby, but they more commonly listed themselves in skilled trades and occupations (carpenter, merchant, driver), and less commonly described themselves as simply laborers. Women, except for Clara, still mostly self-identified as "housewife." Clara headed an intact family household where the eldest son worked steadily at jobs he held for multiple years. He worked for seven consecutive years for businesses near the neighborhood where his family was well established and respected, and his earnings helped his mother and two siblings enjoy a relatively stable home life through the darkest years of the Great Depression.[14]

When he secured a career-track job with the SPRR dining car division in the early 1940s, Robert Folkes' future, and his family's situation, seemed relatively secure, but the war brought unexpected disruptions and complications to his own and many other families. Shortly before the United States entered the war, Clara Folkes moved her family from their long-term residence on Adams to a smaller house at 1250 E. 20th Street. After the move, which took her out of the close neighborhood of middle-class bungalows where she had made a life, Clara Folkes disappeared from the Los Angeles voting rolls. She did not reappear until she registered for the 1944 elections. In the interim, Robert secured a position with the SPRR, starting as fourth cook and advancing to second cook by the first full year of the war—a period of accelerating turnover in the dining car division. As late as April 1942, Robert Folkes listed his mother's 20th Street address as his home.[15] Even with this move, Clara Folkes situated her family squarely within the core of the

South Central community centered on the YMCA near 25th Street. All the residential addresses for Clara Folkes from 1932 through 1942 were within a radius of about ten blocks from that progressive core, and all her son's jobs, including the SPRR position, were located within that tight circle of close family, neighbors, and employers. Despite the widespread dislocations of the Great Depression, the Folkes family was notable for its decade-long record of geographic stability, modest upward mobility, and deepening roots in a multiracial, community-centered neighborhood.

As eldest son in a family of four headed by a single mother, Robert Folkes shouldered adult responsibilities at an early age, earning solid recommendations from his high school counselor, accolades from his employers, and rapid advancement in his SPRR career. He earned a reputation among his SPRR coworkers and with his immediate superior as a steady, reliable worker, perhaps the hardest worker on the crew. He was known for quick comebacks, for a sarcastic wit, for acting "smart," and for his intellectual curiosity. He spent free time reading newspapers that passengers left behind on the train. In scavenging for reading material, he ignored company rules that required dining car workers to stay in the diner at all times, and he bristled at coworkers who warned him those excursions would get them all in trouble. Folkes occasionally played smart-aleck jokes on his coworkers that apparently confused them. One waiter recalled the time he placed a customer's grill order with Folkes, who told the waiter they were all out of that menu item. The waiter went back to tell the customer, but when he returned with a new order, Folkes had already prepared the original request and placed it on the pass-through shelf from the kitchen, awaiting delivery to the customer. His deadpan delivery of playful jokes seemed to baffle older coworkers, but he was efficient, capable, and reliable, and they spoke fondly of him, universally in positive terms, and would defend him even when detectives encouraged them to be more critical.

FROM BREADWINNER TO MURDER SUSPECT:
UNRAVELING THREADS OF COMMUNITY AND IDENTITY

The offhand comments about Folkes that his coworkers made to investigators after the murder describe a young man accustomed to more personal freedoms than the restricted and segregated world of dining car workers and Pullman porters allowed. He was younger than most of his coworkers by at least a decade, and he grew up in one of the most progressive, culturally assertive communities open to African American families in the 1930s. In a neighborhood otherwise comprising mostly married couples and families with mainstream party affiliations, Folkes had more radical inclinations. By 1942, he had joined a community-oriented union headed by one of the more radical labor activists in South Central. His rapid promotion to second cook spoke well for his ability to work effectively with peers and supervisors, and at the young age of twenty, he held an SPRR job that would have been the envy of most young Black men at his high school. Folkes, in other words, was a remarkable success story, given his difficult family background. By 1942, he had already achieved goals that would have been unrealizable dreams for men like his father, only two decades earlier, back in rural Arkansas.

Despite the family's decade-long climb to social respectability, during which they relied on individual effort, hard work, family values, and community involvement, Clara Folkes and her children lost almost all their hard-won gains within the first few years of American involvement in the Second World War. Between April 1942 and October 1944, records of police interrogations and courtroom testimony sketch only the vaguest hints of how life changed for Robert and his family. By the time of her son's trial in April 1943, Clara Folkes listed her address as 1638 Essex Street—the location of the historic St. Turibius Roman Catholic Church and Catholic School (K–8), located on the corner of 16th Street and Essex, one block off Central Avenue. Her son's common-law wife, Jessie Taylor Wilson Folkes, lived about ten blocks away, at 1163½ E. 25th Street.[16] The family's focus shifted fifteen blocks southward during the trial, closer to an emerging community of trainmen living near the Dining Car Workers Union headquarters, just beyond 40th Street.

Clara Folkes and her family drew vital support—material and emotional—from her son's labor union and from the churchgoing community of South Central as Robert's case proceeded through the Oregon legal system. With her eldest son no longer bringing in a paycheck, and with two other minor children to support, Clara faced severe financial challenges, in addition to the emotional burden and physical demands of her two-year effort to save her son. From early February 1943 through January 1945, she worked tirelessly with William Pollard, the secretary of her son's union local, arranging public meetings, making personal appearances and appeals for assistance, and writing letters and petitions seeking support. Pollard moved during the same period into a residence at 914½ E. 42nd Place, near Dooley's house. In working with Pollard to organize a defense committee for her son, Clara became more closely affiliated with the community of railroad workers in that area, leaving her previous neighborhood of aspiring middle-class tradesmen and moving nearer church leaders and community organizers deeper in South Central. During those years of trial, Clara always listed 1638 Essex—the Catholic Church—as her address. This suggests she may have given up any permanent residence and either roomed with friends or sought sanctuary at that church during the period when she devoted all her available resources to saving her son from the gas chamber.

As the legal struggle to save Robert Folkes' life exhausted virtually all her financial resources, Clara Folkes cashed in her hard-earned social capital. She relied heavily on church networks and the churchgoing community of railroad workers and their families. Churches provided a venue for fundraising efforts, and local trainmen helped her secure more reliable, wage-earning work. Clara told her son's story at church meetings throughout the district, and by the end of the legal struggle, in late 1944, she began working for the SPRR herself, cleaning railcar interiors. About that time, she also moved into a shared residence at 1515 E. Santa Barbara Avenue,[17] close to a longtime acquaintance (Harriet Simpson) from the family's previous neighborhood on Adams. Clara's Santa Barbara Avenue residence also housed two other single women of different surnames and one married couple, Thomas and Mary Hart. Other near neighbors were a minister and his wife (Joseph W. Bircher and Myrtle Mae Bircher). It was a blended household of unrelated individuals, situated in a family neighborhood of relatively prosperous and conservative Republican voters, located just a few blocks from Jefferson High. Most nearby residents were service-industry workers, many with ties to railroad work and others with "defense worker" designations. One next-door neighbor was a married railroad porter, whose wife, like Clara, was also registered as a Democratic Socialist, and that couple also managed the rooming house where Clara lived near the end of her son's appeal process.[18] Clara was clearly gravitating toward those in the community most able to help and support her son's fight for justice, notably including railway workers who formed the backbone of the Black middle class in South Central and the nucleus of a more radical railway workers union movement.

HOME AND "AWAY" LIVES: ONE TRAINMAN'S EXPERIENCE

As a child of South Central who came of age in the late 1930s, Folkes learned an urban style of personal presentation that set him apart from his older coworkers. His home life was a landscape of zoot-suited urban sophisticates whose style of dress and demeanor challenged traditional symbols of author-ity and asserted a newfound individualism and brash self-confidence.[19] His "away" life, however, imposed rules and restrictions on his personal style, lim-iting his personal movements and imposing a demeaning dress code (black and white checkered cook's pants with a white jacket and cook's hat, and a shapeless brown smock for whenever he left the kitchen).

Folkes walked the razor's edge at work, struggling to reconcile two separate worlds in the segregated landscape of railway service. His home life embraced the flamboyant style of nightlife sophisticates who rubbed shoul-ders in clubs and joints along Central Avenue, and he often showed up for work wearing knee-length dark dress-coats with contrasting, pegged trousers, dark shirts, and flashy ties—an ensemble reporters later termed a "zoot suit." He wore his lighter-colored wide-brimmed felt hat pushed back on his head, with decorative feathers tucked into its wide sweatband. Most of his cowork-ers dressed in more conservative suits and hats and openly criticized his more flamboyant style. They quickly learned, however, that he gave as good as he got—he was not mild-mannered or retiring, and he paid no deference to age. They described him as quiet and reserved, but always ready with a quick and pointed comeback, and his slower-witted, older associates consequently avoided verbal jousting matches with the younger and sharper second cook.

Folkes' unwillingness to bow to authority figures ran counter to tra-ditional etiquette on the train, where Pullman porters and dining car wait-ers worked mostly for tips, cultivating habits of respectful deference to the demands of White passengers. He gained a reputation for an edgy demeanor that blended his showy home-life persona with the standoffish reputation of dining car cooks. As compared with the intensely public roles other Black trainmen commonly assumed in their away-life assignments, cooks like Folkes worked in relative seclusion. Rather than working directly with the public, dining car cooks performed assigned tasks in the semiprivate space of the dining car kitchen, and with few exceptions, they served the public only through the intermediary roles of the waitstaff. Perhaps for this reason, Folkes was less obsequious in demeanor than many of his older coworkers—waiters in the dining car. Even among other cooks, his failure to show exaggerated deference to White customers, and his style of dress, marked Folkes as some-thing of a rebel. His (and his mother's) close association with radical labor leader William Pollard before, during, and after the trial also apparently ran-kled PPC and SPRR investigators. In demeanor, style of dress, and political affiliations, Folkes challenged the hegemony of White authority and militarized priorities of conformity, and those habits of individualistic expression apparently inflamed the prejudices of police investigators, prosecutors, and railway officials. He became, in their eyes, a symbol of larger issues beyond the murder.

Even leaders in the African American community openly recoiled at the brash flamboyance with which Folkes and others of his generation and background represented themselves. Many longtime residents in South Central criticized young refugees from southern states (especially Arkansas and Oklahoma) for exhibiting an excess of exuberance in public arenas. Charlotta Bass, the progressive editor of South Central's leading community newspaper, the *California Eagle*, for example, patronizingly suggested that the embarrassingly loud behavior of these new migrants was rooted in the repressive conditions they had experienced in southern states. They enjoyed relative freedoms in Los Angeles, including relaxed standards of deference to White people, that, she reasoned, encouraged their overly exuberant behavior, which embarrassed more established African Americans in that city. As Bass editorialized, "Unseemly loudness in public places by Negroes fresh from the lower strata of Southern life is understandable. At home they were not permitted to enter so-called 'white' theaters and restaurants; it is no wonder that they sometimes revel loudly in the non-segregated freedom of Los Angeles." Other residents worried that these new migrants were "uncommonly aggressive" and "very belligerent" toward Whites. An Urban League researcher in the Little Tokyo district of Los Angeles (a mostly Black neighborhood after the forcible relocation of ethnic Japanese early in the war), observed that the "[Black] newcomers have a freedom they haven't experienced before, and sometimes they become wild." Civil rights activist and vice president of the California Congress of Industrial Organizations (CIO) council Revels Cayton, however, viewed the aggressiveness and determination of the new migrants as a political asset: "They are determined to stay, become integrated in their communities and attain full citizenship. . . . The Negro people are in the forefront of the West Coast progressive movement."[20]

Their biases against rural southern refugees apparently shaped the initial responses from urbane, progressive leaders in South Central's African American community when they first learned of Folkes' arrest. When the LAPD reported that a native of Arkansas had confessed to the murder while in custody at the infamous Central Jail facility, Bass' *Eagle* initially responded with a hand-wringing editorial lamenting how damaging renegades like Folkes were for the future of "the race." The *Eagle* uncritically reported the police version of the alleged confession, observing, "With the race battling hard for equal rights, and subject to new war-time blame and recrimina-tions . . . local leaders had been hoping against hope that inspite of Folkes confession that developments would prove someone of another race had committed the brutal crime. Now they fear repercussions from all over the country, especially from the south. . . . Every race trainmen here in discussing the affair forsees more trouble with travelling southern troops which in far more instances than reach [the public] create trouble with colored train crews or colored passengers" (errors original).[21]

Even in his home community, local leaders who viewed the war as an opportunity for advancing "the race" initially characterized Folkes as an unwelcome embarrassment. Rather than rallying to his defense, they pro-moted other, militarized role models: Black men who had sacrificed their personal lives to military or other public service. The *Eagle*, for example, praised the former UCLA Bruins football-star-turned-police-officer Kenny Washington, marveling at his cleverness and alertness as an interrogator in an unrelated case, in an article headlined "Traps Murderer into Confession." The article detailed, with apparent admiration, the rookie police officer's ability to trick a reluctant witness into confessing, resulting in that person's eventual conviction. In a dismissive display of apparently unintended irony just to the right of that story, the *Eagle* ran a small one-column article headlined "Robert Folkes Says, 'I didn't do it.'"[22] Even at that late date, Bass' newspaper ignored the apparent coerced nature of the Folkes "confession" and made no attempt to link reports of torture and abuse cases at Central Jail with the "confession" police claimed he made while confined there. Confronted with the contra-diction between his denials and police assertions that Folkes "confessed," the Black press followed the *Eagle*'s lead, initially accepted the police narrative, and presumed Folkes guilty.

ZOOT SUITS AND INDIVIDUAL EXPRESSION IN AN ERA OF MILITARIZATION

Even in his home community, the creeping militarization of civil society worked against Folkes. Like many so-called zoot-suiters, Folkes embraced a counter-military youth persona that distanced him from those who viewed the war as an opportunity for the race. He emphasized individualistic expression—loose-fitting high-style suits and hats rather than uniformed conformity; wisecracking sarcasm and informal address rather than the habitual "yes, sir" and "no, sir" of militarized deference; and a civilian job, classified defense-critical, which exempted the otherwise draft-eligible twenty-year-old from military service. While other young men his age either volunteered for military service or responded to draft notices, Folkes cultivated individual skills and work habits that helped him advance rapidly through the ranks of dining car employees. In accepting the police narrative, even the Black press initially ignored early parallels linking police mistreatment of Folkes with other examples of police abuses in a period of rising tensions between military men and ethnic minorities in West Coast cities.

By adopting the manner of dress linking him, at least stylistically, with the zoot-suiters of the early war years, Folkes challenged, perhaps unknowingly, wartime standards of patriotic self-sacrifice and rationing. Historian Kathy Peiss observes that urban youth embraced the zoot-suit style shortly after the United States entered the Second World War, just as the federal government introduced restrictions aimed at conserving woolen textiles for military use. Limitation Order L-73, Peiss notes, "ordered manufacturers to reduce the amount of wool in suits by 25 percent and remove cuffs, pleats, and pocket flaps."[23] Production of wool suits subsequently declined dramatically during the first three years of the war, as more men entered military service and fewer purchased formal wear, but among fashion-conscious urban youth, sales of zoot suits increased after these restrictions were introduced. In October 1942, the War Production Board responded with a new Limitation Order (L-224) that specifically banned "high-rise trousers" and imposed regulations restricting trousers with a thirty-two-inch waist to a circumference at the knee of no more than twenty-two inches of material, and a maximum of eighteen and a half inches at the ankle. They proposed to take the "droop and drape" out of zoot suits. With this measure, the WPB depicted those who continued to drape themselves in the expansive fabric of the zoot suit as "unpatriotic," but it was not illegal to wear one.[24]

During 1942 and 1943, WPB propaganda against the zoot suit unintentionally enhanced its renegade appeal, but for men like Folkes, it was more an emblem of successful manhood. The style, with its profligate use of expensive materials, was far beyond the reach of most lower-income Black men, and many who could afford it lacked the panache to carry it off. Those who could afford it, and who attempted the style, were known as "sharpies"—stylish men who were especially particular about their appearance. Rather than "marginal men," Peiss argues, these were relatively prosperous, successful young consumers who self-consciously emulated prominent entertainers, musicians, and celebrities who embraced the same showy, expensive style.[25] In the world of South Central, his suit identified Folkes as a prosperous young man of means and responsibility, but to rural residents of Oregon, and to news writers seeking a melodramatic storyline, it branded him a nonconforming, antimilitary exhibitionist and truculent urban youth of suspect morals.

In other circumstances, Folkes might have been lionized as the model of progressive promise in South Central. He was not only a person who demonstrated through his actions and through his outward representation of self the belief that he could make himself into whoever he wanted to become, he was also someone who attained relative success while more than a decade younger than most of his coworkers. On the other hand, his outward expression of individualistic self-confidence was not an isolating or dismissive attitude toward those around him. He was affiliated with a community-oriented, left-leaning labor union, and his family embraced left-of-center political traditions. Together, they networked in one of the most politically and socially progressive African American communities in the country. In the militarized context of the early war years, however, even the otherwise progressive *Eagle* ignored Folkes' connections on the labor left and embraced the reactionary arguments of his police interrogators. Lifestyle choices that walked the margins of middle-class respectability further inflamed the prejudices of investigators, police, and legal authorities. The young cook's common-law arrangement with Jessie Folkes, for example, while not particularly unusual, challenged standards of acceptable sexual expression and personal mores in his mother's adoptive neighborhood of middle-class respectability. Investigators demonstrated prurient curiosity about Folkes' sexual habits, even as they emphasized, in public and private records, that no evidence suggested sexual intent in the attack on Martha James.

Whatever status Folkes' style of dress might have conveyed in his home community, in the eyes of White newsmen and lawmen, it indelibly linked him with the racialized violence of the "zoot suit riots" that had shaken San Diego and Los Angeles just a few months earlier. Public awareness of those riots, and the related Sleepy Lagoon murder case, closely paralleled the timeline for the James murder case.[26] Lurid descriptions of the riots, during which US Navy sailors squared off against young men of color attired in flamboyant zoot-suit style, aggravated preexisting White fears of "racial friction." In the immediate aftermath, moreover, navy officials racialized the response and shifted the focus from the Mexican American youths that sailors had targeted to the supposed "Negro problem" and the potential for further racial unrest and violence. Historian Josh Sides observes that Commander Clarence Fogg, senior naval patrol officer in LA, demanded something be done to prevent a "racial outbreak in Los Angeles. . . . The existing local racial situation grows more tense. It appears to spring directly from an aggressive campaign sponsored by local, state, and national representatives of the negro race. Apparently this campaign is founded upon a planned policy of agitation designed to promote unrest and dissatisfaction among the local Negro population." Fogg then proposed a "3 wave" retaliation plan headed by the navy with support from the Marines and the Coast Guard. Amid reports of widespread race rioting in Detroit (Michigan), Harlem (New York), Mobile (Alabama), and Beaumont (Texas) that summer, however, the *California Eagle* reminded its readers that there had been "no mass rioting by Negroes" in Los Angeles, nor any "serious outbreak by the Negro people." Area resident Loren Miller, however, later recalled that when rioting sailors threatened to come down Central Avenue, Blacks sent back a warning to sailors who would "come over here and take somebody's trousers off over here, cut somebody's hair. We'll be ready for them. So they never showed up." Miller had also told the mayor that if any sailors showed up on Central, "somebody was going to get killed, and I didn't think it was going to be Negroes." Sides reports that Miller explained, "The Negroes always felt that Mexicans were far too tame during the riots."[27] In this context, Folkes refused to accept being labeled a "zoot-suiter," even as he adopted the style of a counter-militarist fashion common among Black youth in his home community.

LIVING APART:
THE "AWAY" LIFE AND MILITARIZATION ON THE RAILROAD

The "away" life that trainmen lived on the road changed dramatically during the Second World War, as military mobilization transformed the SPRR into the largest troop transport network in the North American West. It was also a major force driving rapid urbanization in Pacific Coast states such as Oregon, and the Folkes trial brought that reality home to rural folk in the western part of the state. Dooley's streetcar journey through South Central LA passed through the heart of a world that, for residents of the mid-Willamette Valley, was completely beyond their experience. Dining car workers like Folkes and

Dooley lived an "away" life of weeks on the road, serving the never-ending demands of passengers, porters, conductors, chefs, and stewards. Their home life was a more fragmented series of shorter interludes: overnight and multiday layovers with family and friends in South Central. From the time he started working for the railroad, Dooley recalled, he worked every run with Folkes, "except two trips he [Folkes] missed [on] account of his throat, and I missed three."[28] Their "away" life mostly overwhelmed their home life. Working conditions for dining car crews were particularly difficult under the unusual circumstances and relentless rush of wartime travel in trains crammed with military personnel on the move from one staging area to another.

The war years were grinding and exhausting for dining car crews, who often worked for months with no days off and with no private refuge aboard the train. These experiences radicalized workers whom Pollard organized into the Los Angeles local of the Dining Car Workers Union that Folkes joined. At a time when Bass' *Eagle* extolled the virtues of the "new race man," Pollard's union focused more on class issues in a local that organized across color lines. Union organizers under Pollard's leadership capitalized on worker resentment fueled by the pressures of wartime militarization. As the predominant carrier for military forces in the western United States, the SPRR was particularly important for moving troops from the Southeast to the West Coast. The railroad, consequently, overburdened its predominantly Black trainmen on West Coast lines with overcrowded trains filled mostly with White military recruits more accustomed to the segregated accommodations of train travel in the Jim Crow South. Black trainmen, consequently, had to deal with large groups of aggressive racists, but the increased workload, more than the nature of the passengers, concerned organizers like Pollard. The railroad maximized profits during the war by exploiting its service workers, playing up the theme of "sacrifice" to keep wages low while requiring trainmen to work harder and longer hours without respite.[29]

While SPRR propaganda stressed the wartime voluntarism and patriotic spirit of its employees, the company ignored the human toll on workers like Folkes. Police investigators, in their clumsy attempt to portray Folkes as a wartime shirker, actually documented the difficult working conditions he and his fellow employees suffered during the early years of the war. In his daily duty record, the SPRR documented the exhausting and debilitating round of inhuman hours and unremitting labor that broke his health but not his spirit. In the first year of American involvement in the war, Folkes reported for duty on all but 71 days for the 365-day period from December 1941 through December 1942. That means he averaged less than one and a half days off for each workweek that year, but that statistic understates the relentless grind he faced. Most commonly, Folkes worked weeks on end without any days off, interspersed with weeklong periods of involuntary unemployment. His longest layover in Los Angeles, prior to January 1943, lasted ten days, from late June through the Fourth of July weekend of 1942. This extended release came only after a three-month period with no days off (only brief overnights between trains), and upon his return from that ten-day unpaid layoff he worked for two months, from July to September 1942, with no days off. Then, after a five-day layoff, he worked another two solid months until mid-November, when he took another five-day layoff without pay. With few exceptions, the railroad assigned Folkes to serve round-trip runs to and from Portland. His typical assignment on these runs totaled at least five or six days away from South Central. Even for a normal nine-to-five job, this would be a relentless schedule, but as second cook, the hours that Folkes worked each day were more commonly from 3:00 a.m. until past 10:00 p.m.—a shift that lasted nineteen hours or more, leaving fewer than five hours off each day.

The long hours and unbroken periods of service trapped trainmen in an "away" life of inhumane conditions that wore them down and led to high turnover in the dining car division during the war years. Unlike many other employees whose sacrifices the railroad recognized in its published newsletters, and despite Pollard's efforts to represent their concerns, workers in the dining car division, both Black and White, suffered in relative anonymity as the wartime speedup took its toll. In late December 1942 and early January 1943, after a full year of nearly unremitting work, Folkes suffered serious health problems, apparently culminating in tonsillitis. He took an extended layoff for medical reasons (again, without pay) that stretched nearly two weeks, from 7 January until 19 January.[30] This means the Portland run that placed him on the "murder train" was the first time Folkes had worked in nearly two weeks, and it was his first earning opportunity in that time. Not only was he working hard on that train, he was also recovering from a recent, debilitating illness brought on by, among other things, complete and utter exhaustion.

Difficult and worsening working conditions in the SPRR dining car division fueled the unionization movement and worker flight during the war. The daily grind for a dining car cook was a brutal pace for someone trying to recover from a serious illness. Folkes' responsibilities, in his first week back,

Interior of dining car kitchen, showing unidentified chef (front), second cook, third cook. SPRR
dining car, 1945. Original print located in the SPR collection, CSRM Library and Archives. Image
courtesy California State Railroad Museum, and David Perata of David Perata Studios

did not allow for adequate rest, even for a healthy person. A typical workday for
a second or third cook with the SPRR began when he woke up and prepared
to "make watch"—commonly as early as 3:00 a.m. Making watch involved
preparing the kitchen for the morning meal and for the workday. Dooley
observed that as second cook, Folkes had more responsibilities that often

required him to begin earlier than the third cook (Dooley), with whom he alternated days making watch. The first half hour of work, for a cook assigned that duty, involved building a fire in the wood-burning stoves, tending the fireboxes until cooking surfaces and ovens reached a sufficient temperature, and then, in the next thirty to forty minutes, baking muffins while cooking oatmeal or Cream of Wheat and brewing coffee. If the stoves were already clean, heating the fireboxes, according to Dooley, might take only thirty-five or forty minutes, but if full of ashes, getting the stove hot enough for cooking and baking might take an additional fifteen or twenty minutes (totaling an hour of carefully tending and feeding the fires). Meanwhile, stoves heated the cramped galley kitchen to the point where the cook broke a sweat, even on cold winter mornings. The cook's workday continued through three major mealtimes: morning, midday, and evening, lasting into the late hours shortly before midnight. Dining car staff served meals until 10:00 p.m., but during the wartime rush of 1942 and early 1943, they frequently stayed up until midnight finishing their closing duties.[31] This schedule meant that a second cook, making watch on an alternating schedule with the third cook, would get only three hours of sleep every other day, and only five hours of sleep on the intervening days. In a six-day run of 144 hours, Folkes could expect a total of only twenty-four hours of sleep in the makeshift berths the railroad supplied dining car workers. No wonder cooks spent most of their layover time in Portland sleeping three or four to a room in places like the Medley Hotel. The "away" life was mostly unrelenting work on a moving train, with a few precious hours of rest in Portland.

Company efforts to monitor and regulate the on- and off-duty activities of trainmen obliterated any hopes for privacy for the duration of an assigned run. Like other dining car workers of his generation, Folkes lived a tightly circumscribed life aboard the train, from his first waking moments until he nodded off to sleep. He, like other dining car workers, had no personal space and no refuge from supervisory oversight. The kitchen attracted unannounced visits from coworkers and restless passengers seeking a cup of coffee, conversation, or an impromptu snack in the early morning or late evening hours. A dining car cook had no place to hide and nowhere to go without being noticed, but the farm women and rural folk on the jury that convicted Folkes had no experience with the working conditions he faced. Prosecutors relied on that ignorance, claiming Folkes had enough unsupervised time and privacy to commit the murder without anyone noticing he was missing from his work station. Contrary to those claims, however, a tired or ailing worker had no place to rest in private at any time during a six-day run. The dining car crew caught whatever sleep they could each night in makeshift berths that they assembled from the booths and tables where they served the public during the day. By five o'clock each morning, dining car workers had to break down their berths, reconvert the space into dining booths, and hide their personal effects in a hole beneath each seat, then make themselves presentable to the public.

The company's refusal to provide adequate privacy or breaks for workers effectively harnessed peer pressure to enforce speedup conditions. Reconversion from the workday to the off-duty refuge of temporary berths was a race against the clock, and the entire crew lost precious sleeping time if anyone lagged behind. Shirkers could not hide from coworkers. Waiters moved quickly to clean the serving areas and prepare their berths after 10:00 p.m., while kitchen staff finished after-hours duties in the galley. Second and third cooks usually shared the mundane, manual labor of closing down the kitchen, cleaning utensils and food preparation surfaces, cleaning the slats laid over the floor (for clear footing in the event of spills), cleaning the floors under the slats, and picking up dirty linens (towels, clothes, etc.). These cleanup duties took upwards of ninety minutes to complete after the last meal was served at 10:00 p.m. Only after completing these tasks could dining car cooks retire for the night, usually after 11:30 p.m., and they made up their berths long after the waiters had retired. This situation strained relations between cooks and waiters, whose slumber they inevitably disturbed when making up their bunks near midnight. Everyone rushed to finish the workday and snatch what rest they could before beginning again the next morning, but kitchen staff had more to do, worked later into the night, and rose earlier each morning.

In an effort to minimize conflict with waiters, cooks customarily slept closer to the kitchen, and this arrangement placed Folkes closer to the murder scene in Car D than anyone in his work group. At trial, prosecutors portrayed these sleeping arrangements, which protected other workers from the late-night and early morning noise of an exhausted cook trying to make up and break down his bunk, as an opportunity for unsupervised adventuring. In fact, however, the second cook's sleeping berth was closer to his immediate supervisor than anyone else in the kitchen staff. With scarce opportunities for privacy, dining car workers carved out personal space with traditional claims to a particular location for their berth each night. The second cook customarily made up his berth in the first booth on the right-hand side nearest the kitchen (the "back" of the dining car), directly across the aisle from the chef's berth. The third cook slept in the second berth on the left, just ahead of the chef, with the fourth cook immediately ahead of the second cook. Dining car waiters and the steward occupied spaces farther forward, with the steward taking the two booths at the "front" end of the car. With practice, these routines created a sense of home and belonging in the semiprivate setting of the off-duty dining car, but it was a crowded space where fifteen to twenty people lived and worked around the clock.

Dining car cooks were wage-labor employees who functioned as independent artisans with considerable control over their workspace but not the pace or duration of their labor, and Folkes advanced through the ranks at a time when class-conscious unionism was displacing artisanal values. Although their task-based duties separated them from other dining car workers, kitchen crewmen were a mutually supportive group, sharing roles and equipment. Each cook supplied his own set of knives as the tools of his trade. They carried their knives aboard the train in distinctive satchels that marked them as trainmen—a designation that conveyed significant status in the prewar world of South Central—and they arranged those tools in the galley kitchen for the duration of the run. A full kit signified status and longevity in the craft. Dooley's relatively extensive knife kit, for example, included two French knives, one cleaver, three paring knives, one butcher knife, and a sharpening steel. Folkes' kit was relatively spartan—it included only two paring knives and one medium-sized French knife. As a much younger cook, Folkes had not acquired a full set of cutlery like Dooley's. Instead, he supplemented his small kit with knives borrowed from the chef's rack. Chef Clermont Baker's kit included a large French knife, a spatula, a sharpening steel, a boning knife, a can opener, a small slicing knife, and a long-handled fork. Cooks and chefs were separately responsible for sharpening and maintaining their own cutlery, and although most cooks commonly shared knives, a fastidious few, like Dooley, repacked their cutlery each night with their personal effects, bringing them out only when they went back on duty the next day.[32]

The fact that Folkes invested few resources or energy in assembling a complete kit is a clue to how he advanced quickly through the ranks in the early 1940s. These kits, for his older coworkers, were symbols of a cook's status and autonomy—not just tools of the trade. Folkes' minimalist kit and habit of borrowing tools demonstrates a younger, more pragmatic mind-set that disregarded their status significance. Dooley's fastidious concern for his own set of knives suggests he set greater store in them as symbols of his artisanal status. By 1943, however, the wartime speedup favored Folkes' more pragmatic and efficient style, and he advanced to second cook ahead of Dooley, who modeled an earlier, more artisanal approach that stressed meticulous attention to detail and deep knowledge of the craft. The two men were good friends, however, and the cooperative, team-oriented environment of the dining car galley survived this transition from artisanal values to pragmatic efficiency during the war. Folkes apparently commanded respect and loyalty from an experienced man nearly twice his age, despite his unusually rapid advancement to second cook.

SELF-MAKING INDIVIDUALISM AND WORK IN AN ERA OF ENFORCED CONFORMITY

The very qualities that helped Folkes advance up the promotion ladder faster than older, more experienced workers exposed him to close scrutiny and suspicion after the James murder. Unimaginative detectives on the case considered it unusual that Folkes woke up early, before anyone else in the dining car, and they viewed his multitasking efforts to prepare breakfast for an entire train as suspicious behavior. Work itself was grounds for suspicion in the minds of corporate detectives trained to look after the property interests of the SPRR. Thinking ahead, with preplanned shortcuts to maximize efficiency in preparing the morning meal, was even more suspect. Doing his job, and doing it well, without supervision, on the morning of the murder made the young Black man working in the kitchen their primary suspect. Most suspiciously, he managed to take a short break for a smoke, just before the breakfast rush was due to begin. By that time, somewhere around 4:30 a.m., Folkes had been on the job, working alone and without supervision, for roughly ninety minutes. In the militarized context of wartime troop transports, SPRR trains were filled with uniformed men who were organized into units that merely followed orders during a period of enforced leisure en route to someplace else. As a result, the individualized identity and self-directed purpose that Folkes exemplified made him stand out from everyone else on that train in the early morning hours. Moreover, the lack of privacy in his workplace made him obviously visible to anyone who passed by the galley kitchen looking for someone to blame for the murder.

Unfortunately for Folkes, at the time of the murder, dining car managers, especially chefs, stewards, and cooks, were under intense scrutiny by railway detectives in a covert surveillance effort prompted by wartime concerns about misappropriated food. In addition to their regular watch duties, chefs and second cooks were responsible for securing and loading supplies at the beginning of each run. This meant they usually reported to the station about three hours before the train's scheduled departure, secured a hand truck from the loading dock, trundled it over to the depot commissary, and then towed it back to the dining car, where they loaded food, drinks, and other supplies into the pantry and kitchen. They kept fresh meat and fish in secure lockers, with chefs responsible for the keys. In the close camaraderie of the dining car kitchen, however, chefs often delegated responsibility to trusted subordinates—especially the second cook, whose early morning duties, through the midday meal, required access to meat storage lockers.[33]

Wartime rationing made meat supplies an important trust and temptation for anyone with access to the chef's keys. Opportunities for black-market profiteering cropped up at each step of securing, trimming, and cutting retail-sized portions from the chef's well-stocked lockers. Those assigned those tasks were in a position of trust with temptations for private profit. The commissary secured, for each train, fresh fish and meat from local markets, and cooks loaded those into the locked iceboxes. As the crew served breakfast and prepared midday meals, the second cook worked independently and with minimal supervision preparing fish and meat cuts for each subsequent meal. Working with beef, pork, and poultry, he cleaned and prepared whole chickens and turkeys, cut steaks from roasts, and prepared other, larger cuts, according to the requirements of menu offerings.[34] The job required individual initiative, meat-cutting skills, and the ability to work without direct supervision, but it also offered temptations for setting aside portions for personal use and black-market resale. Folkes clearly earned the trust and respect of his superiors, who regularly entrusted him with valuable resources that an unscrupulous man might otherwise convert into personal profit, and comments on his workplace performance were uniformly positive and approving.

Partly because the railroad suspected dining car workers would sell company property for personal profit, especially during wartime rationing, cooks were among the most closely watched people on the train. Their distinctive clothing and uniforms were critical details in the murder investigation. Except for trainmen, few witnesses knew anyone else on the train by name. Investigators, consequently, relied on vague resemblances. By SPRR security policy, cooks and chefs wore uniforms that clearly distinguished them from

other trainmen. No witness claimed to have seen a man dressed as a cook anywhere near the murder scene, although several witnesses variously mentioned
seeing a redcap, a porter, and a conductor in that vicinity at various times
through the night. None of the uniforms for those railroad jobs remotely
resembled a cook's attire. While on watch, chefs and cooks wore white coats,
white cloth caps, and—most distinctively—clown-like checkered trousers.
If they left the kitchen to use the restroom, which required them to go into
an adjacent passenger car (because dining cars had no restrooms), they were
supposed to don brown smocks to cover their white coats—partly for sani-
tary reasons, but mostly to make them more obvious to observers. No one
else on the train wore brown smocks.[35] Either way, the checkered pants were
impossible to miss. No one saw anyone near Martha James' berth wearing
checkered pants before, during, or after the murder.

HOME AND AWAY: CORPORATE TIES, CLASS, RACE, AND PROGRESSIVE COMMUNITY

Partly because they were singled out for special scrutiny, even by other trainmen, dining car chefs and cooks stuck together, on and off duty, and older
workers mentored newer hires, teaching them the ropes and helping them
get along. Chefs and their crews of cooks commonly stayed together as a
functional work unit for periods exceeding a full decade, and in Los Angeles,
they typically lived in close proximity with other cooks and chefs. William
G. Aaron, for example, was a chef with twenty-seven years of experience for
SPRR, and he was also Dooley's near neighbor and crew leader. He lived just
a few blocks away on East 43rd Street in Los Angeles. From the time Folkes
was first hired as fourth cook, in 1941, Aaron mentored him. Under Aaron's
tutelage, Folkes quickly advanced. Although Aaron, a forty-seven-year-old
married man, explained he did not associate with Folkes when they were not
at work, the chef observed of the much younger man, "I always found [him]
to be a good worker and he did his work well. . . . He did not seem to have
much temper."[36]

   Folkes was a fatherless eighteen- or nineteen-year-old when he first
started working for Aaron's cooking crew, and he had never worked for any
other chef before he reported for duty on 19 January 1943. Aaron was the
master craftsman, father figure, and mentor to whom Folkes normally turned
for advice and support at work. That January morning, however, Aaron notified the SPRR commissary he could not report for work because of a family

emergency—the funeral and burial of his son. As a result, for the first time
in his railroad career, Folkes reported to work that day with a chef he did not
know and without his closest workplace friend and constant away-life companion, Eddie Dooley. Worse, railroad detectives were already predisposed
to suspect him, like any second cook, of stealing food for resale. They closely
scrutinized him more than anyone else because that was their normal practice
in dealing with kitchen workers of his rank.

The man who replaced Aaron as chef for the round-trip run to Portland
that day was virtually unknown to any other crew members, and he had never
previously worked with Folkes. Clermont Baker, a thirty-eight-year-old chef
with sixteen years of experience, had worked with the SPRR for only a little
over a year. His previous experience was with the merchant marine.[37] He lived
somewhat removed from most other SPRR chefs and cooks clustered around
42nd Street in South Central, listing his address as 3120 Stanford Avenue.
That address was just a few blocks west of South Central near 32nd Street.
Baker initially tried to excuse himself from assignment to the Portland-bound
train because he preferred to work only military transport trains, generally
avoiding civilian passenger trains. In this case, however, SPRR commissary
dispatchers insisted.[38]

The SPRR promoted a wartime corporate image of employees who all
pulled together to support the war effort, but workers in the Los Angeles
branch of the dining car division embraced a class-conscious community centered on the revitalizing culture of the South Central district. Most members
of the dining car crew working Train 15 the night of the murder had worked
closely with each other for a number of years and had close connections with
the African American community that stretched southward along Central
Avenue from the SPRR depot. Central hubs of community activity clustered
around 23rd Street and 41st Street along Central, spreading east and west of
that north–south arterial. Renowned civil rights attorney Walter L. Gordon
opened his law office in 1937 at 41st Street and Central, in the front offices of
the building housing Charlotte Bass' *California Eagle*. Nearby, at 4015 Central
Avenue, the Dunbar Hotel and the Club Alabam anchored a nightclub scene
that featured Black entertainment for integrated audiences. Farther north,
near the corner of 23rd Street and Central, big-time acts like Sammy Davis Jr.
and Fats Domino headlined shows at the Lincoln Theater.[39]

Beyond the famous nightclubs and performers, however, longtime
residents recalled a family feel to the area during the 1930s and 1940s.

Mendenhall Grocery, at 22nd Street and Hooper, was a local hub of community. Folkes, his wife, Jessie, and his mother, Clara, all lived within a few blocks of that central meeting place. Children in the district attended Jefferson High School—an integrated school where Black and White children stood next to each other for class photos and served together on voluntary student organizations. Joan Moore Williams, whose father, a railroad employee, moved the family from San Antonio to a home near 43rd Street and Hooper in 1921, later remembered that people who lived in the area between 20th Street and 43rd Street, along the Central Avenue axis, felt a "real sense of community." She argued that the neighborhood was "a great place to grow up . . . you belonged." Walter Gordon recalled that most African Americans in that area regularly read Black press newspapers like the *Chicago Defender*, even though, as he recalled, LAPD officers "would stop newsboys and rip up the papers" when they caught them delivering them on the street.[40]

Railway employment provided the economic underpinnings for the South Central community. SPRR's Los Angeles Station stretched from 5th Street to 12th Street along Central Avenue, until it was replaced by Union Station in 1938, and the company's commissary, which stretched several blocks south from 12th Street, was the most important employment hub for area residents from the 1920s through the 1940s. Gordon and Fleming recalled that the Rock Island Hotel, located across the street from South Central Station, contracted with the SPRR to house trainmen otherwise excluded from Whites-only hotels nearer downtown. Gordon observes, however, that the neighborhood bordering 22nd Street, 23rd Street, and Hooper, near Mendenhall Grocery, was the "most progressive" in the district in its political and community involvement. Residents there were relatively isolated from beachfront areas and communities in the northern valleys of LA, but that isolation helped African American people in the district maintain "intact families." He recalls it was a "place to go to be strengthened by the love of your family after you had been knocked down in the outside world." Dion Morrow, however, recalls that despite the emphasis on family units in that area, most local residents never talked about their family's origins. South Central was a place where people thought about the future, and where their children learned optimistic lessons about individual opportunity.[41]

At the heart of the district, centered along the corridor from 12th Street to 42nd Street where trainmen like Dooley and Folkes located their families, African American community leaders fought for more radical change, organizing an activist branch of the NAACP and encouraging other progressive organizations. In NAACP elections of 29 January 1942, members of the Los Angeles chapter "unanimously re-elected" President Thomas L. Griffith and elected four vice presidents: L. G. Robinson, Walter L. Gordon Sr. (who represented Folkes in LA courts), Dr. H. Claude Hudson, and the Reverend E. E. Lightner. Bass urged African Americans, in a 24 September 1942 editorial, to "seize the initiative" during the opening offered by the war, observing: "We must stand in the forefront today in demanding full freedom and full citizenship rights." During the war years, the Los Angeles NAACP grew rapidly, recruiting seven thousand new members in 1943 and registering more than eleven thousand by 1945, making it the fifth-largest chapter in the United States.[42]

Race relations in South Central were complex compared with the overtly segregationist Jim Crow system of the American South, and the neighborhoods where Folkes grew up changed rapidly during the war. Although the district was a refuge for supportive African American families, it was an integrated, multiracial community, not an isolated ghetto, before the war. As wartime migrants from Oklahoma, Arkansas, and Texas flooded into South Central neighborhoods, however, longer-term residents, including earlier refugees from Arkansas like the Folkes family, noted an uptick in overtly racist behaviors. Community activist Floyd Covington referred to the influx of White "Okies" and their resettlement in and near South Central as the "Southernizing of California." He observed, "On all sides can one sense a general change of attitude toward the Negro, due to the impress of the southern influence on almost every activity within the community."[43]

During the war, the tight-knit community Folkes had known as a youth fragmented into zones of relative stability surrounded by transitional neighborhoods on the periphery of respectability, and what outsiders understood about South Central was colored by lurid stories about those marginal districts. New migrants often settled first in slumlord hotels that sprang up in the Little Tokyo district just east of Central Station, where forced removal drove out Japanese families and opened the area for rent-gouging landlords. Migrant Black families of seven or more people crammed into single hotel rooms with so-called kitchenettes that were often little more than a single hotplate, contributing to overcrowded, unsanitary conditions in that district. Those with family connections in Los Angeles often doubled up with relatives in South Central apartments, where family networks eased their transition into the local community. So many migrants, in fact, moved in with their families on South Central that the Southern Pacific Railroad established an "ad-hoc station stop" at 40th Street and Central, three miles south of where trains officially stopped at Union Station.[44]

Lurid stories about vice and corruption in the popular press linked the wartime concentrations of new migrants east and south of downtown Los Angeles with patterns of conspicuous leisure and exhibitionist behavior that worked against Folkes in 1943—a period when militarized notions of patriotism demanded voluntary self-sacrifice. The Black experience in South Central, however, was more complex than the media-fed stereotypes that catered to the prejudices of White readers. Higher levels of employment during the war meant the incomes of Black families in the overcrowded district increased, while housing restrictions elsewhere in the city forced room-sharing in these neighborhoods. As a result, many residents of Little Tokyo and South Central lived in slum conditions, but with much more disposable income than they had previously enjoyed. The nightclub culture later remembered as a characteristic feature of the Avenue consequently built on this foundation. Along Central Avenue, in addition to other venues catering to major headliners, popular nightclubs included the Downbeat Club, the Flame, and the Casablanca, featuring gospel, blues, and R&B acts. The club culture attracted both positive and negative attention. Deputy Mayor Orville Caldwell, who toured the nightclub district one Saturday night in 1943, reportedly was "appalled" at the sight of Negroes with "more money in their pockets than they had before in a year. Many will use it to buy liquor and marihuana."[45]

Black clubs along Central Avenue attracted Hollywood celebrities and other well-to-do revelers and thrill-seekers during the war, including servicemen and war workers. Revelers tagged the district "Bronzeville," and during the war it developed a reputation as a place where drinks were cheap, picking up prostitutes was easy, and police enforcement was lax. The area was notorious for frequent street fights and bar brawls, often across racial lines. Illicit nightlife activity in Bronzeville also fueled popular stereotypes among White Angelenos that Black people were particularly prone to licentious behavior. The sudden growth in the Black population, paired with the sudden surge of (mostly) White servicemen seeking entertainment before they shipped out to distant theaters of war, fueled an upsurge in violent crime. Those trends reinforced already prevalent anti-Black racism among White Angelenos, resulting in a backlash of public and private discrimination, police repression, and harassment in South Central.[46]

Folkes came of age in this milieu, where an emergent African American youth culture of relative affluence rubbed shoulders with the rich and famous but also with thrill-seeking military men who expected to find vice and corruption and whose presence attracted those willing to provide those services. In his leisure time, during extended layovers in the district, Folkes would have stood out from many of the young faces on the Avenue. In a locale where police expected to find criminal degenerates profiting from wartime vice, he was a well-dressed, self-possessed young man who walked with confidence and flair. His money came from honest labor in a career-level railway position, but LAPD officers saw only a racial stereotype: they clearly considered him, and even professional entertainers, as undesirable and degenerate exhibitionists.[47]

By January 1943, the all-embracing community that Folkes had known growing up along Central Avenue was breaking down into fragmented neighborhoods with more overt and frequent racial conflict. The war disrupted previous patterns of racial preference for railroad employment. Work in the dining car division became more attractive to White men seeking draft exemptions, and it became relatively less attractive to Black men and women for whom wartime labor shortages opened better-paying opportunities in other, more prestigious jobs previously off-limits. Baker—the White man who served as chef on Folkes' last duty assignment—was just one example of those who sought new jobs with the dining car division shortly after it was designated a draft-exempt defense sector. Although the merchant marine was similarly exempt, the risk of falling victim to an enemy attack at sea made it less desirable. Railway workers were safer from enemy attack, but many porters and dining car workers moved into other categories of employment that paid better and were less stigmatized as "Negro" jobs. Still others volunteered for service in the military. As a result, turnover in the SPRR dining car division increased during the war, creating unusual opportunities for Folkes. In 1942, second cook with the SPRR was still a relatively prestigious and accomplished position for a young Black man in South Central, but less so than in previous decades.[48]

FIGHTING SPIRIT AND CORPORATE POWER

Long before he was charged with murder, and despite his excellent work record, Folkes posed a problem for the railroad company. He was a union man with strong ties to the progressive prewar South Central community, and he was a self-directed, skilled worker accustomed to autonomy and individual self-expression. These attributes ran counter to the company's approach to wartime mobilization: serving more passengers with fewer workers while driving wages downward to maximize profits from government contracts. In many ways, the murder trial gave the company a chance to challenge the worker activism of Pollard's union, and SPRR detectives helped prosecutors and police construct a negative public image of Folkes grossly at odds with his actual record. Railroad managers responded to worker flight and labor organizing with a propaganda campaign that publicly shamed employees into volunteering support for company goals and profits. Folkes was a member of Pollard's radical union and also his near neighbor in South Central. In taking down Folkes, despite Pollard's personal efforts to defend him, the railroad sent a strong message to union members: dining car workers would pay a price for standing out from the crowd and acting with self-confidence beyond their station.

The SPRR's labor-management strategy during the war included propaganda that tried to link selfless service in defense of the nation with quiet, diligent, compliant labor. The company urged railroad workers to consider their private-sector employment a wartime sacrifice, rather than a job with negotiable wages, working conditions, or hours. It was an unsubtle, anti-union, and antistrike message that rankled many workers. While holding wages down and pressing workers to assume an inhumane workload, SPRR publications nonetheless argued its workers were vital to national defense. Promotional literature and company newsletters emphasized the vital service trainmen provided in moving military personnel. The entire June 1942 issue of the corporate newsletter, *Pacific Lines Southern Pacific Bulletin*, featured stories about war bonds purchased by company employees: "36,000 SP'ers have ALREADY signed to purchase War Bonds through Payroll Allotment. They're in it to WIN IT! HOW ABOUT YOU?"[49]

The SPRR rebranded itself with a militarized identity, seeking privileged status as a private-sector linchpin of the public-sector war effort. The company emphasized in its employee bulletin that SPRR "Victory Trains" carried troops and war materials that should take precedence over all other passenger and freight services.[50] The *Bulletin* devoted its November 1942 issue to problems of "manpower" shortages, emphasizing jobs traditionally reserved for men but increasingly filled with women: steam hammer operators in its shops, refueling workers in Eugene, turntable operators in Dunsmuir, scrap-cutting torch welders in Sacramento, and car-tracking switchyard workers in the Richmond, California, transfer yard. Curiously, SPRR dining car workers and chair car porters remained all-male classifications even though workers in those overwhelmingly African American roles cooked, cleaned, and made up beds—all jobs that, outside the environment of a passenger train, were stereotypically "women's work."[51]

Black men like Folkes worked in segregated, re-gendered jobs in which they were expected to assume subservient, compliant, supplicating roles. While the SPRR emphasized variations on the "Rosie the Riveter" theme of re-gendered labor roles, its policy of racialized labor roles continued, largely without notice except in newspapers aimed at African American readers, such as the *Eagle*.[52] Instead, the company's employee bulletin emphasized the capacity of its workers to "SERVE IN SILENCE," noting the presence of "special agents" ensuring the security and safety of its passengers at all times, in cooperation with federal agents and military officials.[53]

The Martha James murder case was an embarrassment to the company during this crucial phase of rebranding, but the SPRR tried to turn it to the company's advantage by making Folkes a scapegoat for the crime, striking back, through him, at Pollard and the Dining Car Workers Union he represented. Company detectives took the lead in first singling out Folkes and then making an example of him by working with prosecutors to ensure not only a conviction but also a death sentence. The company took this hard line against Folkes just as labor tensions peaked amid contract negotiations with the Dining Car Workers Union. Central to those negotiations were worker concerns about the speedup conditions on Southern Pacific trains as the nation mobilized for war. The union also demanded an across-the-board increase of thirty cents per hour, with a minimum wage of seventy cents per hour. After trying but failing to split White workers (mostly chefs and stewards) from the predominantly Black union leadership, company propagandists turned to a militarized shaming strategy. Telling its employees, "You're in the war, railroader," the SPRR *Bulletin* emphasized the unique responsibilities of personnel employed in a transportation sector that made them "vital parts in your nation's growing war machine."[54]

The company responded to the minimum wage demands from Local 582 in early 1942 by outsourcing. It contracted with the Threlkeld Commissary Company to bring in three hundred Black trainmen recruited and transported from southern states that July (1942), requiring them to sign a yellow-dog contract agreeing to six-day workweeks of at least eight hours per day, sometimes extending to days of nine to ten hours, with straight time paid for the first ten hours at a rate of only forty-six cents per hour (less than two-thirds the minimum that Pollard's union was demanding), and with various mandatory payroll deductions, including a "hospitalization fee" of $1.75 per month, "boarding charges" of $1.29 per day, and "commissary charges" assessed against individual workers' salaries and then paid to the Threlkeld Commissary Company. The workers reportedly brought to LA under these terms were housed in section houses, outfit cars, or tents, to keep them isolated from the radicalized South Central community.[55]

Pollard's union struggled to look after the interests of its members in a period of rapid destabilization and deteriorating working conditions. Mobilization for war nearly overwhelmed the railroad system on the West Coast. In the first seven weeks after the attack on Pearl Harbor, Southern Pacific handled 573 military trains, compared with only 111 in the preceding seven weeks, and transported six hundred thousand military personnel over that period. Most of these travelled in dedicated Pullman sleeping cars, and the railroad established supplemental kitchens in baggage cars to support troops travelling in large units, while smaller groups took meals in regular dining cars.[56]

As one wartime measure, the SPRR moved from a quality-of-service model to a volume-of-service model that eroded worker autonomy. Men like Folkes paid the price. As one example of this shift in emphasis, in an effort to assure "maximum occupancy," the company adopted measures to regulate access to Pullman berths, requiring same-day ticket purchase and travel. This allowed the railroad to fill berths on an as-needed basis, but it created uncertainties for travelers, especially nonmilitary, who lost status relative to high-priority military personnel travelling on military vouchers (such as Wilson). Civilians (such as Martha James) settled for what was left after servicemen, usually officers or troops returning from furlough to rejoin their units, took their pick. Enlisted men travelling with intact units mostly rode troop trains from which civilians were excluded. The heavy overload of civilian and military passengers during the holiday travel period of December 1942 to January 1943, and severe winter storms in the region, forced the company to reschedule trains to allow for delays in long-distance travel. New policies adopted during these months required passengers to load baggage twenty-four hours in advance,[57] further complicating travel for civilians, as Martha James discovered on the platform in Portland. Even experienced trainmen and seasoned travelers found these circumstances unfamiliar and disconcerting.

The South Central community was especially affected by the wartime surge in railway travel. Los Angeles' Union Station handled about one million passengers per month during the first two years of the war (1941–1943) and an average of ten to thirteen trains in and out during each two-hour period. The forty-two-acre facility employed 1,180 workers, not including train crews. Checked bags handled at the facility increased from 92,250 pieces in its first four months of operation (June–September 1939) to 120,000 per month during the first nine months of 1941, "due to increased troop movements" as the nation braced for war.[58] By August 1942, the LA yard handled a previously incomparable peak of 146,875 cars per day.[59]

As the increased traffic on the SPRR severely stressed its workforce, company employees left their jobs for other opportunities. During 1942, nearly ten thousand SPRR employees left the company for service in the armed forces. the SPRR responded by hiring some two thousand "railroadettes" (young women), at lower wages, in an effort to replace those workers, increased the maximum age for employees by fifteen years, and opened schools training young men under the age of eighteen in technical skills they would need for railroad work.[60]

The wartime unionization efforts of the Dining Car Workers Union challenged the public image that the SPRR had carefully cultivated. Company profits actually increased during the war, but antistrike propaganda fueled by patriotic appeals for self-sacrifice and war-related legislation mostly stifled labor organizers and kept wages low. Corporate revenue, meanwhile, increased at the expense of workers who faced exhausting conditions. The company mined the energy of its workforce for unprecedented gains. War-related contracts generated windfall profits for the SPRR transportation system, which realized a 54 percent increase in operating revenues for the first ten months of 1942, while operating expenses increased only 37 percent over the same period, in part because the company froze wages (labor costs) as a "war measure." Net operating revenue for that period totaled $78.2 million— an increase of $25.7 million over the same period in 1941. Net income for the railroad, after deducting dividends and interest on securities and "other fixed charges," totaled $47.6 million, compared with only $27.6 million for the same period in 1941, or nearly a 90 percent increase in net income from the start of the war.[61] Clearly, the SPRR realized a massive increase in revenue streams, yet conditions of employment and wages paid to dining car crews stagnated. Worse, from the perspective of people like Folkes and Dooley, home leaves evaporated even as their workload increased.

The impact of the Folkes trial on worker morale in the SPRR dining car division was immediate and intensely negative. Despite tense labor relations between the company and its waiters and cooks, the dining car division, during the first year of the war, was a stronghold of support for the SPRR's war bond drive.[62] The company pressured employees to demonstrate loyalty by enrolling in its (voluntary) Pay Roll Deduction for War Bonds program. The *Bulletin* posted monthly rates of enlistment in this plan for each of the nineteen divisions in its Pacific Lines department, claiming a company-wide enrollment rate of 76 percent of its workers by November 1942. The 48,496 enrollees from those nineteen divisions included over 91 percent (1,913) of dining car division employees. That participation rate, from a division comprising mostly African American men, was fifth highest among all nineteen of the Pacific Line divisions that the SPRR listed in the report. Most other units ranged from 39 percent to 85 percent, including many departments that disproportionately hired White workers and, increasingly, women (e.g., the superintendent's office staff, dispatchers, clerks, and enginemen).[63] These high levels of participation, however, dropped precipitously with news of Folkes' trial and conviction.

The Folkes trial presented the company an opportunity to reinforce wartime policies that demanded conformity of its workers and were intended to break union organizing efforts. Folkes was a card-carrying member of Local 582 of the Dining Car Waiters and Cooks Union (commonly known as the Dining Car Workers Union), and a near neighbor of its radical secretary, William Pollard. Other workers in the dining car division responded to the company's complicity in pinning the murder on Folkes, despite clear evidence to the contrary, by withdrawing their support from the company's wartime propaganda campaign—most visibly by ceasing to enlist in the war bond drives that the SPRR trumpeted as evidence of its employees' patriotic sacrifice. Shortly after Folkes was arrested in late January 1943, as alternative narratives began to challenge the official story by late February, the mostly Black employees of the dining car division reduced their enrollment to only 82 percent participation—a marked decline from the previous peak. Over the same four-month period, the total number of workers in the division also dropped, from a high of 1,913 workers in December 1942 to 1,874 by March 1943. After the trial, the number of workers in the division fell to

1,816 by May and to only 1,793 by August. Over the same period, participation in the company's war bond drive dropped to only 67 percent among dining car workers.[64] In other words, the total number of workers in the division declined by 6.3 percent during a period of phenomenal increase in the number of passengers they were expected to serve and the scheduled travel times for long-distance passenger trains. These numbers suggest a shift in the demographics of the workforce as well as an adjustment in outlook. That precipitous decline also coincided with widespread publicity about the James murder and the aggressive interrogations targeting Black trainmen, especially Folkes, on the day she was murdered.

Company profits rose, while worker morale collapsed in the wake of the Folkes trial. In the same issue that reported declining enrollments and worsening working conditions for dining car workers, the SPRR *Bulletin* published its annual report for 1942, indicating an increase in net income from all operations of $50.9 million, and an increase in net revenue from railway operations of $106 million over the previous year.[65] Even as company profits increased, SPRR dining crews worked longer hours at stagnant wages in overcrowded conditions with fewer extended layovers and less support from experienced coworkers, many of whom left the company in this period. The dining car workforce, under these circumstances, resisted company pressure to enroll in war bonds, and the division's participation in that program dropped by nearly a quarter (24 percent) in less than eight months.

CONCLUSION: REACTION, RESISTANCE, AND THE COMMITTEE FOR DEFENSE OF ROBERT FOLKES

When SPRR agents persecuted Robert Folkes, they exposed the corporate pretense that its private-sector jobs were the equivalent of military service. Worker alienation escalated as word spread about the company's mistreatment of Black trainmen during the trial in Albany. Between February and June 1943, dining car workers, who faced deteriorating working conditions and stagnant wages, left SPRR employment in droves, preferring to demonstrate their loyalty to the war effort by volunteering for service directly in the US armed forces. In June 1943, the company listed forty-seven workers who left employment with the dining car division for military service over the previous month, compared with sixty-three from all other eighteen divisions of the SPRR's Pacific Lines, combined.[66] One month later, thirty-eight dining car workers enlisted in the armed forces—more than twice as many volunteers as any other division.[67] This pattern of recruitment dramatically reversed recruitment ratios from 1942, when dining car workers were less likely to join the military than employees from any other SPRR division.

In late summer 1943, the company responded to employee flight with a wave of propaganda that emphasized the military contributions of workers in its dining car division. Earlier issues of the company's *Bulletin*, for example, virtually ignored that division's leadership in the voluntary enrollment plan for war bonds, profiling, instead, White workers from other divisions. Previous stories featuring "SP'ers" who joined up for military service also depicted a volunteer corps that was virtually all White. In August 1943, however, a special issue of the *Bulletin* prominently featured an image of dining car cooks posing in front of a sign that read "This Un-usable Grease Is Being Salvaged by the Chefs and Cooks on the Southern Pacific Diners—It Will Be Used By Our Country to Make Explosives to Help Beat OUR ENEMIES— This Is Their Effort to Show Their Comrades Who Are in the Service That They Are Doing Their Bit on the Home Front."[68] The accompanying article credited the idea to chefs and cooks on dining cars operating out of the Los Angeles commissary. The following month, the *Bulletin* featured a photo of Elmer Devereaux—a dining car waiter on Train 15—sharply dressed in military uniform and stylish sunglasses in a gallery depicting "Fighters from LA Division, Shops, and Other LA Departments."[69]

Employee turnover in the ranks of cooks and waiters working for the Southern Pacific after February 1943 was much more severe than the overall decline in numbers of employees might suggest. In early 1944, in a *Bulletin* themed "Food Fights for Freedom," the SPRR reported a particularly high turnover rate in its dining car division for all of 1943. The company hired fifty-two hundred new workers to replace five thousand who left the division that year.[70] Despite this flight of trained labor, however, railroad dining cars served a record 11.7 million meals plus several million box lunches for the year ending in December 1943, compared with only 3.5 million meals in the peacetime year of 1939. "Passenger trains," the report concluded, "were never before so heavily loaded, and the problem of providing meal service for passengers . . . was further complicated by shortage of trained personnel and food rationing." The same issue listed nearly a hundred dining car workers who joined the armed forces in January 1944.[71]

Progressive labor activists in Los Angeles demanded immediate improvements in working conditions for Black trainmen, revitalizing union locals and pressuring NAACP leaders to pay more attention to these traditional sectors of employment. The local chapter responded by asking the SPRR and Union Pacific to move trainmen from lower-ranking service roles into better-paying industrial jobs. Pollard, by contrast, pressed for radical action within the traditional labor sector and then, working with Revels Cayton of the CIO, brought that outlook into the executive committee of the NAACP's Los Angeles chapter. The *California Eagle* increasingly recognized his leadership during the first two years of the war, and in early January 1943, Bass ran a front-page photo in the *Eagle* identifying Pollard as "AFL's militant" and a leading figure in the wartime "Negro Victory Committee."[72]

Pollard, as secretary-treasurer of the AFL-affiliated Dining Car Workers Union Local 582, pursued "progressive labor policies" that, according to the *Eagle*, "have made Local 582 . . . not only a vital part of the lives of working men but of the community as a whole." In 1942, Pollard led a recruitment drive that doubled membership for Local 582. Under his leadership that year, Local 582 opened a new community center in its headquarters at 40th Street and Central. Members of Local 582, Bass reported just a week before authorities arrested Folkes, "participated in every progressive movement in the state during the last year."[73]

As the public face and leading organizer for Local 582, Pollard was already a prominent figure in South Central when he organized, with Clara Folkes, the Robert Folkes Defense Committee (RFDC) in April 1943.[74] He and Cayton had joined fellow labor leaders John E. Hargrove and Fay E. Allen on the executive committee of the Los Angeles NAACP, serving alongside Gordon, Bass, and about seventeen other members. Hargrove, the elected president of the Los Angeles chapter of the Urban League, also represented dining car workers employed with the Union Pacific Railroad, organized into Local 465 of the same union as Pollard's Local 582.[75] Those who followed Oregon newspapers that April could not have missed Pollard in the photos of "trial principals," but they learned nothing at all from those sources about his role as a community activist and union leader. The *Oregon Journal*, for example, referred to him only as "W. E. [*sic*] Pollard . . . [a] Negro friend from Los Angeles" who was "seated with Folkes during the trial."[76] The *Albany Democrat-Herald* was marginally more informative, observing that he was "a friend [of Folkes'] from Los Angeles" who "took copious notes but professed not to be a lawyer."[77] A week later, the *Journal* observed that "Mrs. Clara Folkes [who] attends [the trial] every day, speaks only to W. H. [*sic*] Pollard, friend of Folkes."[78]

Only after the trial did Oregon readers learn that William Pollard had "assisted the defense as a representative of the Los Angeles local of the cooks' and waiters' union to which Folkes belonged."[79] Residents of South Central, however, knew him as the man who organized and facilitated each year, with Hargrove as cohost, the Annual Sermon of the Dining Car Employees Union (Locals 582 and 465) at the First A.M.E. Church at 8th Street and Towne Avenue, followed by an open house at the union headquarters at 4006½ South Central Avenue.[80] They also would have recognized him as a founding member of the Negro Victory Committee (along with Reverend Mansfield Collins, Reverend Clayton D. Russell, Griffith, Bass, and five other community leaders), which later that year petitioned Mayor Fletcher Bowron, demanding "a real city fight against discrimination."[81] Only later did the Black press in Portland raise the possibility that Folkes had been targeted as part of a broader campaign to squelch labor activism in the shipyards and railroad networks of the West Coast.

The persecution and trial of Robert Folkes, as it ultimately unfolded, was a public spectacle that served the purpose of intimidating and discouraging a nascent awakening of labor resistance among dining car workers. The fight to save Folkes consumed Pollard's energies for most of the last three years of the war, and then he faded from prominence. His unionization drive faltered as members abandoned their draft-exempt positions in record numbers during the period of Folkes' arrest and trial in early 1943. The dining car division suffered the heaviest attrition in the company, as waiters and cooks rejected corporate propaganda that their railroad work was a valued contribution to the war effort and volunteered to serve directly in the military. Those workers chose militarization over organization after the legal melodrama of the Folkes trial unjustly sacrificed one of their own. Newsmen ignored their story, focusing instead on the staged melodrama in the Linn County courthouse. Those who avidly followed the "true-crime" story of the Lower 13 murder learned nothing about the meaning that other trainmen took from the experience of Robert Folkes or the labor struggle in which he was involved.

Chapter Three
The Marine, the Waiter, and the Man in the Pin-Striped Suit

Staged melodrama, militarization, the distraction of a leading man, and the excitement of narrating a real-life "whodunit" mystery completely blinded reporters to evidence that railroad detectives intentionally targeted Robert Folkes and then conspired to ignore or conceal information that should have exonerated him. Instead, newsmen gullibly reported, as if true, obviously invented stories detectives fed them about three stock characters: the Marine, the Waiter, and the Man in the Pin-Striped Suit. Then, as those stories unraveled, rather than reconsidering the motives of investigators who leaked that information, newsmen revised their own fanciful reports to fit whatever new stories prosecutors spun. Almost none of this involved facts or evidence, but rather it built on character archetypes and plot devices borrowed from the true-crime pulp fiction genre of the interwar years.

In the fevered atmosphere of wartime reporting, newsmen ignored complicated backstories about labor unrest and collective bargaining, favoring simplistic, melodramatic plots populated with stereotyped characters. Harold R. Wilson, in that context, fit the mold of a photogenic leading man of unremarkable accomplishments—an "everyman" who rose to the occasion with boyish enthusiasm, acting alertly where trained professionals and Black trainmen were relatively inept. In a militarized version of the prewar true-crime genre, reporters portrayed him as an overgrown Scout: a small-town boy in uniform who alertly guarded American womanhood. In doing so, with one exception, they never bothered to check the backstory he invented to conceal his checkered past, and they ignored other voices that questioned both his story and his outward appearance of boyish enthusiasm and small-town normalcy.

In order to accept Wilson's story at face value, investigators, reporters, and jurors had to ignore the observations of other eyewitnesses with status and authority—both Black and White. In doing so, they embraced racial stereotypes regarding the character and perceptiveness of each witness, but they also filtered their conflicting accounts through a military and corporate bias. Wilson was the first to claim he saw a murderer fleeing the crime scene, but he was also the first person other eyewitnesses reported they saw standing over Martha James as she bled to death. The White train conductor (Banks), the Black sleeping car porter (Hughes), and the White military officer (Kelso) all raised concerns that should have alerted authorities to many other possible answers to the question "Who killed Martha James?" Moreover, their stories and the ways they diverge illustrate how this case involved much more than murder: it was about company policy and efforts to control both workers and public perceptions of a major corporation. The SPRR enjoyed windfall profits from government contracts at a time when other Americans were required to sacrifice lives and fortune for the cause. Public and private agents and prosecutors viewed railroad workers, White or Black, with suspicion, and prosecutors even pushed aside military men such as Kelso if their version of events challenged the SPRR's façade of patriotic sacrifice.

Oversimplified plotlines streamlined the task of prosecuting Folkes and complicated his defense. Lomax, Pollard, and the Robert Folkes Defense Committee needed a more compelling story to distract jurors from the stage-managed melodrama prosecutors presented at trial. They concentrated mostly on breaking down the militarized façade of Wilson—the man in Upper 13 who claimed to have seen the murderer running away from James' berth as she fell to the aisle from Lower 13. By focusing on Folkes and Wilson, however, both prosecutors and defense attorneys ignored the slipshod investigative methods of railway detectives, sheriff's deputies, and others. Instead, they reduced a complex case involving many actors and motives to a simple story of binary opposition: both sides in the trial argued that to acquit Folkes, jurors must reject Wilson's story.

Neither side seemed to notice that nothing Wilson had said implicated Folkes in the actual crime. Prosecutors simply established that Folkes, at some point, walked through the sleeping car. Defense counsel countered with simple alibis for Folkes. Both sides obviously expected that White rural jurors would mistrust the motives and impulses of a young urban Black man. Defense counsel, no less than prosecutors, simply ignored the fact that of nearly three hundred passengers on Train 15, investigators questioned only about forty of them before passengers started leaving the train, unquestioned, uncounted, and unnamed. Of all the people on that train, no one was asked to provide as detailed an accounting of their actions as investigators demanded of Folkes—least of all, Harold R. Wilson. Most importantly, for the defense, multiple interrogations of Folkes yielded several police transcripts that prosecutors characterized as "confessions." To defend Folkes, his lawyers needed to challenge the veracity of the railroad's investigative team and the Klamath Falls district attorney who collaborated on the initial stages of the investigation. In doing so, they might have turned to the person who seems to be, in retrospect, the most credible man on the train: Conductor Banks—a resident of northeast Portland.

DISCOUNTING THE OFFICIAL INVESTIGATION BY TRAIN CONDUCTOR BANKS

The railway detectives who collaborated with prosecutors and the Oregon State Police (OSP) in constructing the case against Folkes demonstrated general mistrust of trainmen, and they pointedly ignored and attempted to disappear the official report of the first investigator, Conductor William H. Banks. Southern Pacific detectives were involved, at the time, in a system-wide surveillance of trainmen, seeking to ferret out corruption and black-market profiteering. That primary assignment, based on the assumption that railroad men were not trustworthy, colored their inquiry into the James case. SPRR detectives, in any case, were ill-equipped for investigating murder, but theirs was the first agency to coordinate a comprehensive inquiry aboard the train as it advanced from Eugene to Klamath Falls and, ultimately, Los Angeles. Banks, by contrast, initiated his inquiry as soon as he discovered the murder near Harrisburg. His perspective as the man responsible for ensuring the safety and security of all passengers and crew aboard Train 15 guided his investigation.

Banks' account illustrates how it was possible for a White person in a position of authority to look past the marine's military persona and doubt Wilson's racially suggestive claim that the murderer was a dark-complexioned man in a brown pin-striped suit. The conductor's treatment by SPRR investigators, however, also illustrates how wartime priorities eroded the status of trainmen. As conductor of Train 15, Banks initiated the first official inquiry, questioning witnesses and deciding how to secure the crime scene, evidence, and suspects. Banks questioned Wilson shortly after the murder and reported that the marine was "very excited" (that excited state is obvious in Wilson's first signed statement to police). Banks later provided railroad detectives and police with a detailed account of his own actions after the murder, and his lengthy signed statement detailed discrepancies between the marine's official account and the stories Wilson reportedly told other passengers. Citing those conflicts, Banks questioned Wilson's believability, clearly suggesting he suspected the marine was hiding his own involvement.[1] Despite some indications that detectives did find corroborating evidence supporting Banks' initial suspicions, SPRR detectives quickly dropped that angle of inquiry. They collaborated, instead, with the Linn County district attorney and the relatively new Oregon State Police in deciding to charge Folkes as the sole suspect. From that point, railroad detectives, police, and other investigators all colluded in concealing from the defense and from the broader public any evidence and witness statements that might contradict their claims that Folkes committed the murder.

Police and railway detectives were particularly careful to conceal from public oversight their interrogations of the trainmen, Black and White, whom they detained in Klamath Falls the day after the murder. Publicly, they announced they were holding only Wilson and Funches. Banks, however, along with several other trainmen, actually returned to Union Station in Portland on a northbound train from Klamath Falls on 23 January. Two days after the murder, on 25 January, the OSP interrogated Banks and six other trainmen in a racially mixed group interview conducted in a small third-floor room at Portland's Union Station. In that group interview, they treated Banks, the railway official responsible for securing and ensuring public safety aboard the train, as though he were any other trainman subject to routine questioning. In front of a racially mixed group of six other witnesses, Banks outlined his actions and recollections from the evening of 22 January through the morning of 23 January.

Banks assertively challenged the official story that railroad investigators and lawmen had publicly circulated. He was most concerned with correcting the timeline that he had seen reported in local newspapers, which placed the time of the murder at 4:00 a.m. Banks noted that although he never actually saw James that night, she must have been murdered between 4:25 a.m. and 4:31 a.m. because every passenger he interviewed after the murder said the train was in motion "when they heard the victim scream."[2] The precise timing of the stop at Tangent was the only reliable time reference from that night, and Banks noted he first learned of the murder shortly after the train left that stop.

Banks was directly critical of Wilson's explanation of why he was standing over the dying victim. When OSP sergeant Sheridan asked, "What is your opinion about Wilson, the Marine," the conductor responded with a list of inconsistencies in what Wilson had said: "Heard him say that he went to bed anywhere from 2:30 to 4:00 a.m., a different time each time his story was related. His first statement was made to the Pullman conductor and that was that he went to bed at 4:00 a.m." He noted Wilson claimed the woman's scream woke him, but when other witnesses encountered him at the scene, "He was wide awake. I don't feel that the Marine had ever been asleep." Banks observed that although Wilson claimed he spent two hours riding in a chair car with a passenger named Bernice Ball, she did not confirm his account: "I asked her [Ball] how long she talked with this Marine. [She said,] 'Not any at all, only just to pass the time of day with him.'"

Banks demonstrated significant attention to detail and showed he had given serious thought to how conflicting statements from passengers lined up with the physical evidence. He described to police how the crime scene itself, as well as statements from other witnesses, directly contradicted Wilson's account. The way the blood saturated the scene, Banks argued, meant it was impossible for Martha's body to have been positioned as the marine claimed: "The Marine stated [to Banks] that the lady was in a heap with her left arm under her." This conflicted with the location of the blood, which was mostly in the (vacant) berth 14, not on the floor, where it would have been if Martha were positioned in a heap on the floor, as Wilson initially asserted.[3] Only later, when Banks confronted Wilson with this contradiction, did the marine adjust his story, saying he found her leaning on berth 14. Apart from Banks, none of the investigators noted that discrepancy, either in their reports or at trial. Banks also noted that Wilson's account of when he arrived on the scene directly conflicted with other witness statements. Citing Eugene Norton's first statement the morning of the murder, Banks observed, "Mr. Norton, said he was not asleep. He heard the first scream. She screamed twice. When he looked out the Marine was in the aisle holding her. How could he [the marine] get his pants on and get down before anyone could get there ahead of him out of a berth?"[4]

Banks attempted, during the joint deposition, to retell the story of the murder in terms that would reconcile conflicting statements from the various witnesses, and he did so from the position of a person uniquely responsible for integrating the interior life of the train with the exterior landscape. As conductor, he kept track of where each passenger planned to disembark and notified them when the train reached that station. Based on his notes, Banks reconstructed the timeline of train stops from Salem to Tangent for the night of the murder. By his account, the train left Salem at 3:27 a.m. and stopped at Tangent at 4:36 a.m. for a "block signal," indicating a northbound train. Banks noted that while the train was stopped at Tangent, and before 4:41 a.m. when it pulled out, "the porter [Hughes] came. He exclaimed, 'come Quick, there is the murder of a lady in my car.'" Banks hurried back with Hughes from the conductor's seat in the head coach (near the front of the train). Their route took them through the crowded central aisles of seven overcrowded passenger cars, and through the multiple doors on the connecting vestibules between each car, to Car D.[5] Working back from the time he was first notified of the murder, Banks estimated how long it took Hughes to reach him, rushing forward through those seven passenger cars, and he added on how long it took Hughes, from the time he learned about the murder until the time he made up his mind to rush forward to find Banks. From those calculations, he assured investigators, the murder could not have happened any later than 4:31 a.m. on 23 January, which would place the time and place of the murder about four minutes before the train stopped at Tangent.

In all likelihood, Banks' estimate of the timing of the murder should have been adjusted even earlier than 4:30 a.m. because it relied on Hughes' agility. Hughes was a very large man who wore a size 52 jacket, and he was the first crewman on the murder scene in Car D. He responded to an alarm bell sounded by a passenger in Lower 12, immediately adjacent to Lower 13, who heard Martha James' first scream.[6] When that passenger rang in a panic for the porter, Hughes responded on the run and found Wilson already standing over Martha's body. James was lying on her back in the aisle, still bleeding through a ghastly neck wound. After briefly questioning Wilson, the burly porter rushed forward through seven cars to reach Banks sometime between 4:36 and 4:41 a.m. The time required for a very heavy man to walk hurriedly (as he testified) through seven crowded cars on a moving train, plus the time that elapsed between when the witness called the porter and when Hughes reached the scene, plus the time the porter spoke with Wilson as they stood over the body, results in an estimate for the likely time of murder at between 4:25 and 4:31 a.m., but if Hughes moved more slowly than he claimed (and as his large bulk in the crowded cars might suggest), then the time of the murder was more likely between 4:20 and 4:25 a.m. These time estimates later proved critical at trial because the earlier time frame would have given Folkes a better alibi. Regardless, Banks disputed official statements placing the murder nearer 4:00 a.m. At trial, prosecutors changed that timeline to nearly an hour later—but that, too, was inconsistent with Banks' reconstruction of events.

The reasons SPRR detectives and other investigators disregarded Banks—a White witness with a respectable record who spoke from a position of authority—had more to do with wartime militarization than with racial difference. As conductor, Banks was clearly in a better position to know the train's location and the timeline of stops than anyone else working the inside crew of Train 15, but investigators ignored his calculations, relying instead on other, less informed, accounts that made the charges against Folkes seem more plausible. That misdirection was facilitated by the proliferating number of agencies, public and private, whose agents jumped in to the investigation in Eugene. Control of the crime scene broke down before an onslaught of investigators representing two different county governments, the state government, the federal government (navy), and two major railroad corporations (SPRR and PPC). The Lane County coroner also collected blood evidence and bedding from Lower 13 and Lower 14, and he removed the body and personal effects.[7] This unorganized array of investigators brought conflicting agendas and questionable methods to the case, and they shouldered aside the only person with an integrated knowledge of the train, the chain of events, the people involved, and the crime's immediate aftermath. Instead, they restarted the investigation on the basis of what they learned through informal channels, disregarding the firsthand accounts Banks had compiled. In this case, the word of a White trainman—Banks—failed to convince investigators, who relied instead on several military men who were mere passengers, including one who should have been their chief suspect.

REBOOTING THE INVESTIGATION:
A MILITARIZED PRETENSE OF PROFESSIONALISM

Whereas Banks was predisposed to trust trainmen, regardless of race, the motley crew of "professional" investigators who boarded the train at Eugene were predisposed to trust witnesses who were not employees of the railroad, especially if they were uniformed servicemen. They were especially suspicious of Black trainmen, but also White railroaders like the conductor, the steward, or the chef. They were also more casual about maintaining the integrity of the crime scene, evidence, and witnesses than Banks had been. Banks initially quarantined the train in Harrisburg, where he posted a brakeman, Anders, and a retired hostler named Bill Lawrence as guards assigned to watch both sides of the train to ensure no one attempted to disembark. While these railroad workers guarded the train, Banks instructed the Harrisburg dispatcher to "hold everything, get all authorities at Eugene." He also recruited other trainmen in the station to watch the cars to ensure no one got off. After holding the train there for thirty minutes while he awaited confirmation that lawmen would meet the train in Eugene, Banks authorized the train to proceed. Once in Eugene, however, those lawmen unsealed the train. While the coroner removed the body and other evidence, they allowed Eugene-bound passengers to disembark without taking their statements or even verifying their identities. They allowed new passengers to board, and then they allowed the train to proceed toward Oakridge. All of Banks' care to ensure no one left the train was completely compromised.

The investigators who boarded the train in Eugene were relatively low-ranking officials whose names seldom appear anywhere in court records or in subsequent lists of witnesses, and they made virtually no progress beyond what Banks had already accomplished. They included, according to Banks, a Mr. (J. J.) Hodges (later identified as a Southern Pacific Railroad investigator), a Mr. (John) Huber (also an SPRR investigator), "and two deputy sheriffs," including Lane County deputy sheriff R. B. Southerland and one other, known to the conductor only as "Mr. Sullivan" (apparently OSP officer Mark Sullivan). Banks cooperated with these investigators to facilitate initial interrogations of witnesses who remained on the train while it continued over the Cascades into Klamath Falls. At his own initiative, Banks required the steward for each dining car attached to Train 15 to, one at a time, "account for his special crew being present in the car" before waking them. They found no one missing. After going through each dining car with the investigators, Banks returned to Wilson, posing additional questions for clarification. At this point, as the train neared Oakridge, Banks recalled he specifically asked Wilson whether the man he claimed to have seen fleeing the murder scene was "a black or white man. He [Wilson] replied a white man, about 5'10" tall, 175 or 180 lbs." Later, Banks noted, Wilson changed this to say that it was a "colored man."[8]

At a time when other investigators were clearly inclined to believe a military man over a civilian, Banks was a lone voice challenging that militarized bias. He challenged it both rhetorically and with precise, clear statements detailing his direct observations and his interrogation of firsthand witnesses. In his initial statements to other investigating officials aboard the train, and then two days later in the interview at Portland, Banks sharply criticized the marine's believability and stressed the integrity and professionalism of the nonmilitary trainmen, including Porter Hughes. Banks' own account of Wilson's appearance and demeanor was detailed and specific: after learning of the murder and rushing back through those seven cars to the scene of the crime, Banks recalled that he entered the aisle of the tourist sleeper to observe, "There was no one in there other than one or two heads sticking out of their berths. No one from the lower berths. . . . I seen this sheet laying in the aisle along the side of the berth." When he lifted the sheet to look at the body, Banks recalled, "All of a sudden this Marine was right at my side. . . . [He] had on trousers and undershirt. I don't think his shoes were laced. [He] had considerable blood on both hands and wrists. He was terribly excited. . . . Throughout the questioning he was terribly excited."[9]

Banks was obviously dismayed by the disjointed and amateurish inquiries of the other investigators, but his efforts to put Wilson's inconsistencies on record had unintended consequences. After hearing the marine tell several different versions of his story to investigators, the conductor confronted Wilson with the most glaring discrepancies. Banks noted, however, that Wilson simply changed his story to fit the additional information that he gleaned from the conductor's questions. The marine claimed he jumped down from his berth before Martha slumped to the ground, and that he got there in time to "hold her [Martha] as she clawed her way out of this berth. I got a pillow and held her in my left arm and put her head on the pillow. She was still alive and blood was gushing out of this wound. I hollered and yelled, 'Help! Stop the Train, This is murder, Call the Marines, and Get the Military Police. This is Army Business.'" Banks reported that Wilson then claimed he "followed the fellow that I saw leave the berth and go to the rear." When Banks pressed for details on how far he went in pursuit of the man in the pin-striped suit, Wilson claimed he went all the way to the rear of the train. When Banks asked him how many cars he went through, and whether he saw anyone back there, Wilson reportedly said, "I did not see a soul, there was no one back there." When asked what he meant in saying he went all the way to the rear of the train, Wilson claimed he went "through the dining car and one other car." When Banks told him that there were more than two cars behind Car D,

Wilson then said, "I went further than that, I am pretty sure I went to the rear of the train." When Banks informed him that on his own trip through the back of the train, after rushing back to the murder scene, he encountered a cook in one car, a porter in another car, and a brakeman in a third car, Wilson then admitted, "Well maybe I did not get to the rear of the train."[10]

Banks inadvertently provided Wilson with sufficient detail to shore up his story, and he also provided a list of people Wilson could claim he encountered on his supposed search toward the rear. By listing their occupations, Banks also supplied Wilson with encoded information about the race of each person that he should have encountered if he actually went all the way to the last car: a Black cook in the diner, a Black porter in a sleeping car, and a White brakeman in the next-to-last car. The cook that Banks noted in the diner during his own search to the rear was Robert Folkes, and in addition to alerting Wilson to the cook's presence in the diner, the conductor provided an important observation about Folkes' demeanor on that morning within about fifteen minutes of when Hughes discovered the murder. Folkes, according to Banks, "was tending to his duties 100%. . . . He was working on the fires when I saw him and appeared quite calm."[11]

The brakeman whom Banks encountered in the rear car was Arthur E. Enell, a White man from Klamath Falls. Enell's initial statement stressed that Wilson did not go to the rear of the train, as he claimed to have done. Enell reported that between 2:30 a.m., when Pullman Conductor Bryant came through, and later that morning when Train Conductor Banks rushed through shortly after the murder, no one else entered his car, which at that time was the second from the rear of the train and second car behind the diner (or the third car behind Pullman Tourist Car D, where the murder took place). Enell also reported that Wilson later came into the washroom in his car, carrying a towel with blood on it, and that he laid the towel on a windowsill while pretending to look through the wastebasket, and then picked up the towel and went back toward the front of the train, and he later observed Wilson writing on the towel in "indeligible pencil" in the presence of "officers."[12]

The investigative team grew even more disjointed, unwieldy, and unreliable as the train progressed from Eugene to Klamath Falls and then south to Los Angeles. More investigators boarded the train at Klamath Falls, at Dunsmuir, and in Sacramento. As the number of investigators increased, the coherence of the story dissolved into guesswork completely divorced from the evidence Banks had painstakingly collected. A bewildering array of investigators from different agencies interrogated and reinterrogated witnesses, asking them to repeat their stories numerous times, in semipublic settings, and without isolating them from other witnesses. As a result, the stories began to blur together. In between interrogations, witnesses talked to each other and they began to notice that the authorities were questioning some witnesses more closely than others. In discussing what they had seen and how they were being interrogated, witnesses influenced each other, and some of them apparently altered their stories to match what they thought others saw or heard. As a result, later investigators had a greater number of more homogeneous stories from which they could select details to assemble a coherent story, but those details were increasingly divorced from the real events that witnesses thought they remembered.

FALSE CERTITUDE:
THE UTILITY OF A SINGLE AUTHORITATIVE NARRATIVE

Investigators chose to adopt Wilson's version of events as the framework for their case even though they had full knowledge of the falsehoods Banks had uncovered in the marine's story. They made it the standard by which they evaluated all testimony and evidence. As a result, the case veered almost immediately away from a search for the truth and instead became an opportunity for asserting authority over the railroad's workforce and managing public perceptions. With the narrative Banks provided, and corroborating accounts from Enell and other statements taken on board the train on 23 January, investigators had compelling evidence that Wilson's story was demonstrably false. OSP internal reports and interagency reports between the police division of the SPRR and the OSP, however, show that they largely accepted his account as an authoritative narrative, discounting all others and fixating their attention first on an off-duty dining car waiter and then on the young second cook.

Wilson's version of events, unlike most others, had the utility of being remarkably fluid and adaptable as new facts emerged, and that characteristic made it especially attractive for a case riddled with baffling contradictions. His initial on-train account of 23 January, like those of many other witness accounts in the OSP case file, is unsigned. There is no way of verifying whether it accurately reports what he said, or only what investigators wanted readers to believe he said. It was just one of many third-person narratives describing what passengers in Car D told investigators the morning of the murder. None of these accounts were ever entered into evidence at trial. Wilson, however, had many other opportunities to publicly tell his story, and those subsequent versions reveal a constantly evolving storyline. By the time he finally appeared on the witness stand, Wilson had had nearly three months to reconsider, revise, or otherwise embellish his remarks. As he retold his story to credulous public audiences during those months, he adjusted the narrative according to their reactions and to fit other useful accounts that investigators had turned up. Between 4:30 on the morning of 23 January and when he testified at trial on 23 April, Wilson frequently retold and continually reconstructed his story, polishing it into a compelling narrative that obviously influenced other witnesses. Even more remarkably, except in newspapers specifically targeting African American readers, reporters seemed oblivious to how Wilson's story changed. By the time of the trial, readers and jurors understood Wilson's testimony within the context of a larger racialized, militarized, authoritative narrative that investigators fed to news writers from January through early April. Central to their story was the notion that trainmen, and their representatives, were inherently corrupt and untrustworthy, whereas SPRR detectives, working closely with military authorities in the service of their nation, were reliably looking after the interests and safety of their customers.

MILITARIZED AUTHORITY AND THE PROPAGANDA VALUE OF THE JAMES CASE

Wilson, in his recorded statements and observed actions in the moments, days, and weeks after the murder, assumed the anonymous authority of a military serviceman with a command demeanor that shielded him from closer scrutiny. He explained his actions immediately after the murder as a "military matter," and he combined military mannerisms with vague and contradictory statements that effectively diverted attention from himself and redirected it elsewhere. None of this would have been possible for a private in the US Marines without the support and collusion of those with the authority and power to directly challenge, silence, or simply relocate him beyond public contact. Those authorities, however, chose not to intervene. Instead, they allowed Wilson to repeatedly retell his evolving story. Without naming names or directly implicating any single person in ways that might be factually verified, Wilson shaded descriptions and colored his account just enough to encourage authorities who insisted that a hardworking Black trainman must be convicted of the crime.

Marine private Harold Wilson and
Klamath County coroner George
Adler outside Tourist Pullman Car D
in Klamath Falls. Original photo in
OSP case file, SPR collection, CSRM
Library and Archives. Image courtesy
California State Railroad Museum.

In many ways Wilson remains an enigma, and the elusiveness of his
motives and actions says more about race relations and militarization in
Oregon early in the war than about Wilson. Of the four young people whose
lives intersected on Train 15 that January morning, only Harold R. Wilson survived the war, and in fact, the murder likely saved him from becoming a casu-
alty. Some police and news reports initially misidentified Wilson as "Marine
Private Dave Jones,"[13] but they amplified his voice beyond those of all other
witnesses. Wilson spoke often and freely to passengers and detectives early in
the investigation, and he gave multiple official statements to railway and police
investigators who interrogated him for several days after the murder.

Wilson's various statements and police records of his interrogations
reveal a gregarious storyteller adeptly reading his audience, whose story often
varied from one telling to the next. Photographs of Wilson during the layover in Klamath Falls on 23 January show a rakish, brash, confident player.
He struck jaunty poses with smiling lawmen whose body language suggested
an assumed familiarity and pride of association. They seemed to like and
trust Wilson, at least at first. In his initial statements to police, when interrogated aboard the train the morning after the murder, Wilson's by-the-book
military demeanor diverted attention from gaps in his story. When asked his
name, he began with only slightly more information than name, rank, and
serial number: "Pvt. Harold R. Wilson. I'm being transferred to fleet marine
force, San Diego. 404258 serial No."[14] In follow-up questions, he was polite

and responsive, but careful not to express certainty where ambiguity offered refuge.

The story Wilson told came in two parts: discovery and investigation. In the first part, as related to railway detectives on the day of the murder, he explained how he found himself in a position to discover the body before anyone else. He said he boarded the train in Seattle, secured berth Upper 13, Car D, and went to bed "between 3 and 4." Sometime later (in the stilted vernacular and abbreviations of police notes), his (unsigned) narrative explains, "when the lady screamed I rose up and turned light on leaned over and looked through curtain, . . . seen about half of a man getting out of her berth, still so surprised from that scream kind of glanced at him, he went to rear of car on a run. As he ran he kind of turned little sideways so I could get just side of his face, pretty full, had on brown pin stripe, think about 5' 10" and he had short hair kind pompadour, combed straight back, light so dim I couldn't tell whether light negro or dark white man, then when I glanced down, seen this lady sitting on the floor with her left elbow on the left side of the arm of 14 lower bunk, she was sprawled out with right arm resting on bunk itself." Asked which way she was facing, he said, "Head toward rear of car. And then I was already on deck at that time, put on my trousers and shoes, jumped down and grabbed a pillow from lower 14 placed it in the aisle and with my hands grasped her below her armpits and lowered her to pillow, and I saw the left side of her neck I saw the scar, I stepped back and said this is murder, stop the train, about that time the lights came on the porter [Hughes] came and stopped dead in his tracks and says she is dead. . . . He got a sheet from 14, empty, and placed it over the body. The last I seen of her she was gasping for air and the blood was gushing out of her."[15]

In the second part of his story, Wilson portrayed himself as a man of action who took charge of the situation and directed hapless trainmen on how to do their duty. After realizing the woman was dead, Wilson said he told the porter [Hughes], "You go that way [forward], in the meantime I gave him the description I recalled, and said I'm going this way and I went to the rear, and in doing so, I went to the last car, coming back met this cook in the galley and stopped and asked him how long been working, said he was later than usual, I told him this was military information I have to have, murder committed, he asked me if I'd been drinking I asked if he had seen a man pass with blood on him, gave him description, said he hadn't, then I went on talking about the murder." At this point in Wilson's interrogation, one of the investigating agents asked Wilson to describe conditions of lighting in the car. Wilson responded, "It wasn't pitch black, but sort of dim so I could see what I was doing. When he went got about 5 feet from the door the light was brighter and I distinguished the color of his suit. I imagine he was about five, five ten. . . . Very heavy, about 175 or 185." Later, he added, he took a woman (Bernice Ball) back to see the scene of the crime: "I wanted to show the young lady the berth and [Porter Hughes] wouldn't let me in." Asked whether he'd seen anyone who might be the killer, Wilson replied, "No sir." Asked whether he'd "looked at the colored boys on the train?" Wilson replied, "Yes sir."[16] This last statement reconfirmed that although Wilson did not specify the racial identity of the attacker, he agreed with investigators who assumed they would find the most likely suspect among "colored boys on the train."

ASSERTING CORPORATE CONTROL AND AUTHORITY OVER THE INVESTIGATION

The three SPRR agents who led the investigation aboard Train 15 after Klamath Falls clearly agreed with Wilson's implication that trainmen were less qualified observers than uniformed military servicemen. In ascending rank in the SPRR police division, these three men included Sergeant George Banich, Investigator C. W. "Champ" Champlin, and Special Agent Frederick A. Taylor. These three agents ignored the detailed timelines and narratives that Banks had compiled for their use. Instead, they detained the train in Klamath Falls while a disjointed team of approximately twenty investigative officers sifted through other witnesses and evidence. Boarding the train in Klamath Falls, Taylor and Banich joined the four investigators who took over from Banks in Eugene. Asserting their authority over the investigation, Taylor and Banich filed regular reports to their district supervisor, Mr. D. O'Connell, between 29 January and 31 January 1943, detailing how other investigators had interrogated witnesses while the train was en route to Klamath Falls, while it was held there, and while it proceeded from Klamath Falls to Dunsmuir. Banich apparently learned of the murder from Taylor, whom O'Connell alerted in a phone conversation at least four hours after the crime was first discovered. Taylor then contacted Champlin in the Klamath Falls office, directing him to meet the train when it arrived there and to arrange for the Oregon State Police, the Klamath Falls police, and the Klamath County sheriff's office to do likewise. Taylor then drove north with Banich from Dunsmuir to Klamath Falls, arriving at 12:45 p.m. on 23 January.[17]

The official internal reports of these company men contradicted public statements of police and military authorities who were previously quoted in news stories about the murder. Taylor's first order of business, upon arriving in Klamath Falls, was to meet Train 17 when it arrived at the station at 1:30 p.m., about two hours ahead of Train 15. According to Taylor's report, Ensign Floyd James was actually on Train 17, while his wife, Martha, had secured a berth on Train 15 (contrary to newspaper accounts that reported he was either on the same train or on an advance section of Train 15). Champlin and Taylor first informed James that his wife had been murdered. Regarding how the husband came to be on a different train than his wife, Taylor reported that "Ensign James . . . had left his wife at station at Seattle as he tried but was not permitted to ride Train #15." This information also contradicted news reports that the James couple was separated at Portland due to the overcrowded conditions and confusion of the winter snowstorm. Taylor reported that James also stated that the only person his wife knew on Train 15 was "a Mrs. Keaton," but that "she and his wife were not traveling together, that his wife and Ensign Keaton's wife had only met about 4 days before."[18] After securing these brief statements, with additional details about the James family connections in Norfolk, Virginia, detectives released him from further questioning and permitted him to board Train 20 to Eugene, where James claimed his wife's body.

Taylor and his ad hoc investigative team next turned their attention from Ensign James to the crew and passengers of Train 15, which they met when it arrived in Klamath Falls at 3:12 p.m. They assembled there an interagency investigative team that included at least thirteen people: Taylor and Banich of the SPRR police division; Sergeant E. W. Tichenor and officers Mark Sullivan and Clyde Lowery of the OSP; Sergeant Paul Robinson, Officer Archie Huff, and Oroville Hamilton of the Klamath Falls city police; deputies Dale Matoon and Jack Franey of the Klamath County sheriff's office; FBI Agent W. Wood; Klamath County coroner G. Adler; and Klamath County DA Sisemore.[19]

While the train was sidelined at Klamath Falls, the investigation took a more racialized turn, but Taylor, Champlin, and Sisemore also became more aggressive in their treatment of Banks and Anders—both White trainmen. Under the de facto leadership of Champlin, Taylor, and Sisemore, the disjointed, multiagency, public-private investigative team held the train with passengers and crew at the depot for over four hours. During that period, Sisemore set up shop in one of the deadhead diners, converting it into an interrogation room complete with a stenographer assistant. With the assistance of Champlin and Taylor, Sisemore took depositions from select witnesses and crewmen. They directed some of their sharpest questioning at Banks and Anders, treating them with less apparent respect than they had accorded Richard James. Taylor's notes from their depositions zeroed in on different components of their testimony than Banks stressed in his own subsequent report. Taylor acknowledged the conductor's estimate that Train 15 arrived at Tangent at 4:36 a.m. and departed at 4:41 a.m., and he noted Banks' estimate that the murder must have taken place "just prior to or while at Tangent." These two observations meant that the timeline for the murder would be somewhere between 4:25 and 4:35 a.m. Apart from that brief acknowledgment of one key element in the conductor's testimony, however, Taylor's account veers dramatically away from the primary points Banks emphasized in his own official report. Completely ignoring Banks' concerns about Wilson, Taylor mostly focused on detailing the number of "colored" passengers aboard the train, noting Banks informed the railway detectives of "two colored coach passengers and one colored soldier on train." Banks, however, did not even mention the number of Black passengers or soldiers on the train in his own written report, and that omission demonstrates a significant difference between how the two men thought about race as a factor in the investigation. Banks, who suspected Wilson's account, obviously did not think racial categories were relevant to the task of finding the murderer. Taylor, however, clearly accepted the marine's account at face value and ignored the trainman's more measured observations. The SPRR detective, a company man, questioned the judgment of two of the railroad's most experienced employees and accepted without question the inexperienced military man as a reliable, trustworthy source.

INVENTING A CLOSED-ROOM MURDER MYSTERY

Taylor's official report was a curious exercise in constructing an imaginary murder scene—a closed-room scenario—and then populating that room with imaginary characters and actors. The report simply ignored facts or details that didn't fit the trope of a closed-room murder scene—a staple of true-crime detective novels since the era of Edgar Allan Poe.[20] Taylor, for example, first emphasized the security of the crime scene, and then he asserted that the murderer remained on the train through Klamath Falls. With this assertion, he ignored two major disruptions to the crime scene: the removal of the body, bedding, and other materials in Eugene and the uncounted number of passengers who simply left the train without record in Eugene and Klamath Falls. It was absolutely not a closed-room scenario. Taylor, however, *pretended* it was. He suggested that if no one left the train while it was stopped at Tangent, and if the dining car stewards confirmed all of their crews were still aboard the train when it arrived in Klamath Falls, the only remaining possibility was that the murderer must still be on the train. Even more remarkably, Taylor pretended that no evidence could have escaped the train after the murder. His report emphasized, for example, the arcane detail from Anders' statement that the brakeman checked all vestibule doors while the train was stopped in Harrisburg, and that although one trap door was partially sprung in the vestibule to Car SP-2311 (five cars ahead of the murder car, toward the head of the train), snow on the steps to that vestibule "indicated no one had left through that door, that no other doors were found open."[21] While stressing this one small component of the trainman's statement, Taylor completely ignored Enell's testimony that directly discredited Wilson's claim that he searched to the rear of the train.

Taylor's report made no mention of Banks' suspicions of the marine, or the conductor's detailed account of how Wilson adjusted his narrative when confronted with discrepancies in his original statement. Instead, Taylor apparently accepted Wilson's claims about a dark-complexioned man in a pin-striped suit and focused on locating that man. His report racialized Wilson's account and conflated the marine's statement with Brakeman Anders' claims that "he observed a negro on train, who he does not believe is an employe [sic], that he was unable to locate this negro on train after murder, that this negro conversed with two colored passengers in head coach evening of murder." Taylor also provided the description of that Black passenger, as provided by Anders: about five feet nine inches in height, about thirty years old, wearing a light brown pin-striped coat, weighing about 160 pounds. Taylor then claimed, "This negro was later identified as John Funches, employee [the waiter] from dead head diner,"[22] disregarding the brakeman's statement that the man he saw was not an SPRR employee.

Taylor was clearly determined to connect the murder with a railway employee and avoid blaming the military man. He mixed and matched details he took out of context to link his suspicion of railway employees with Wilson's claim that he saw a dark-skinned man running from the scene. Taylor focused on minor points the two White trainmen mentioned only in passing, while he completely ignored major portions of their statements that were more directly pertinent. He wove together any detail they offered that remotely supported the military man's story, while he rejected anything that tended to undermine Wilson's alibi. He ignored the portion of Anders' statement that emphasized the Black man he saw at the Albany station was not a railroad employee, but he used Anders' description of that man's pin-striped suit to link him with the Black railroad employee, Funches, of the SPRR dining car division. In this way, Taylor made the Black waiter his first official suspect.

POPULATING THE CLOSED ROOM WITH EVIDENCE AND DETAIL

Taylor's team constructed a façade of police work that substituted a blizzard of detail for logical inquiry, populating the case with witnesses who testified to elements irrelevant to the question of who actually killed James. The militarized, racialized, and corporate bias of the Klamath Falls interrogations was apparent in the record of statements that investigators generated while holding the train at Klamath Falls. Sisemore's interrogations in Train 15's dining car produced twelve official depositions in four hours—each lasting about twenty minutes, on average. He deposed four trainmen, four passengers from the murder car, and four passengers from elsewhere in the train. Of the four passengers, three were White military servicemen (Wilson, William Van Dyke, and R. M. Kelso), and one was a White man from Daley City, California, whom investigators mistakenly identified as a serviceman (Eugene Norton). Sisemore did not depose any of the other thirty-two passengers in Car D (most of them women). The four passengers from elsewhere on the train included a Black couple (Soloman Studyway and Jessie Hall) from Seattle, reportedly seen talking with the waiter (John Funches) who initially came under suspicion because a White woman (Bernice Ball) complained that a "colored man" had spoken with her. The other two passengers Sisemore deposed included Ball and Mrs. G. A. Keaton. Keaton was a White woman who travelled from Seattle to Portland with Martha James and whose husband was a navy ensign in the same unit as the victim's husband. The four trainmen Sisemore deposed in Klamath Falls included two Black men and two White men: Second Cook Folkes; Pullman Porter Hughes; Head Brakeman Anders; and Pullman Conductor Bryant.[23] In all, Sisemore's crew deposed five Black and seven White witnesses. In a train with some three hundred passengers and crew, this was neither a random sample nor a logically selected range of witnesses. None of the women in berths nearest Lower 13, for example, were deposed in Klamath Falls.

The questions interrogators asked witnesses varied by race and employment status, according to the resulting written statements, and the nature
of their questions and avenues of inquiry suggest Sisemore's team accepted
Wilson's claims at face value. They focused only on identifying *which Black
employee* on the train committed the murder. It was an exceptionally narrow
inquiry, especially considering that the investigating team held the entire
train, passengers and crew, while they questioned these twelve people over
four hours. Taylor forwarded to O'Connell copies of the twelve depositions
from Sisemore's inquiry, plus a narrative explaining how they related to the
emerging storyline that framed his investigation. During the depositions,
Coroner Adler collected blood evidence from Lower 13 in Car D and from
along the corridors leading from Car D to the rear of the train. Adler also
reportedly "stripped and examined bodies of Harold Wilson, John Funches,
Robert Folkes, Jessie Hall, and Soloman Studyway," while police officers
inspected their personal effects, but Taylor reported that these efforts
"located no evidence."[24]

The importance attributed to Ball's complaint that a Black man in the
chair car spoke to her, and the otherwise narrow range of witnesses Sisemore
formally deposed, demonstrates how Wilson's story framed Taylor's investigation. On the basis of these few statements, Sisemore detained Funches and
Wilson, sending them back to Albany as "material witnesses." He also arranged
with the chief dispatcher to cut the murder car out of the train so that OSP
pathologist Beeman could examine it later, in Albany. Taylor reported Ball's
testimony that in the early morning hours of 23 January, while she was a passenger in coach Car 2311 of Train 15, "a colored man stopped at her seat and
sat down on the arm rest and said, 'where are you going.'" Ball stated that
when she did not reply, "this negro walked towards head end of train [in the
opposite direction from where Martha James was later murdered]." Another
White witness, Ivan Bond, corroborated Ball's account in an informal statement. Both Ball and Bond later identified Funches as the "colored man" in
question, and they both claimed he was wearing a brown pin-striped suit
when he "stopped and talked with Mrs. Bond." Other witnesses and a search
of his belongings, however, indicated the only suit he had on the train was of
brown-checkered cloth.[25]

Ball's deposition illustrates how Taylor's team compromised whatever
fragments remained of the closed-room case he pretended was at issue: even
the small group of witnesses that Sisemore deposed were not segregated

from other passengers and witnesses. Ball reported her exchange with Funches only after she spoke with Wilson on the train ride from Eugene to Klamath Falls (a conversation Banks noted in his own report). Sisemore apparently detained Funches even though the murder happened near the back of the train, more than seven cars behind the chair car where Ball was seated. Funches, for his part, as Taylor reported, "readily admitted he was the person who conversed with Mrs. Ball." Speaking to a White woman was not a crime, and he was a waiter travelling in diner Car 913, which was "deadhead-ing" ahead of (not behind) the chair coaches in Train 15, more than eight cars ahead of the murder scene.[26] Funches confirmed he did not go any far-ther back than the first chair coach (where Ball was seated) at any time that night, and no other witnesses contradicted that claim. Sisemore nonetheless ordered the waiter detained as his chief suspect, despite having no evidence whatsoever to hold him.

COVERING THEIR TRACKS:
RAILROAD INVESTIGATORS AND THE THIRD DEGREE

The investigation in Klamath Falls was clearly bungled and amateurish, and it left the investigative team looking foolish and incompetent. They had lost control over what Taylor and Sisemore tried to pretend was a classic, closed-room murder mystery. Evidence was scattered around Oregon, carried off the train in Eugene by the Lane County coroner and investigators and by the county coroner in Klamath Falls. Passengers disembarked in Eugene and Klamath Falls without leaving names, statements, or contact information, and numerous people compromised the crime scene. At Klamath Falls, trainmen shifted Car D onto a siding and left it unguarded for days, awaiting a north-bound train to Albany. Trainmen reassigned passengers from Car D berths to seats in other cars on Train 15 without recording original seat assignments or even the names of passengers formerly travelling in berths near the murder victim. Meanwhile, in Klamath Falls, Car D languished on the siding near the bars and taverns adjacent to the National Guard Armory, which was one of the busiest USOs in Oregon during the war. The Armory district teemed with servicemen and other revelers seeking entertainment and diversion. The nearby "murder car" was an irresistible lure to curiosity seekers or vandals—its location and appearance well known and pictured in local papers.

After less than one day, the case was already a public relations disaster for the SPRR and lawmen, even before Train 15 reached Dunsmuir the next morning. Nearly a full day after the murder, the only two people in custody were unacceptable suspects. Sisemore and other officials had publicly praised Wilson as a heroic marine who leapt to the defense of helpless women. Funches, who never should have been a suspect, had an airtight alibi that stretched across eight railcars separating him from the scene of the murder. Train 15 left Klamath Falls at 7:40 p.m. on 23 January, after a delay of about four and a half hours, and while en route to Dunsmuir, Taylor and his SPRR colleagues, Banich, Champlin, and Huber, scrambled to cover their tracks, belatedly collecting another thirty-eight statements from other passengers and crew. This was still a small subset of potential witnesses—most of those interviewed gave two or more statements. Nearly a full day after the murder, and after three major stops where uncounted, unnamed passengers disembarked, the investigative team finally began compiling a list of passengers still on the train. At Dunsmuir, two more SPRR investigators, officers Cottar and Murphy, joined the effort. Taylor reported that he put them to work securing names and addresses of "all coach passengers [still] on train, [and] . . . names and addresses of as many Pullman and Tourist passengers as possible." Taylor enclosed the resulting list in his report to O'Connell.

Investigators apparently considered passengers in the Pullman and tourist cars privileged citizens of a different class than those in coach seats, and they were reluctant to impose on them, or even deprive them of the services of their Pullman porters. This perception, that sleeping-car passengers were a better class, shielded them from scrutiny as potential suspects, or even from close questioning as material witnesses. Initially, their association with this privileged class also shielded Pullman porters from close scrutiny. By the time Train 15 reached Dunsmuir, late on the first night after the murder, however, Weinrick had reviewed the information Sisemore and Taylor's team provided and apparently concluded Funches could not be convicted. Weinrick, consequently, wired SPRR agents in Dunsmuir, urging them to find other suspects. Company detectives focused exclusively on railroad employees as potential suspects. As the train travelled between Dunsmuir and Redding, SPRR special agent F. E. Ramirez and Officer R. F. Banahan began taking statements from Pullman porters. Taylor reported that, apart from earlier interviews with Porter Hughes and Porter Charles Scurry (who was responsible for Car 60), immediately behind Dining Car 10110 (where Folkes worked), the interview team, until that morning, delayed interviewing porters out of deference to Pullman passengers.[27] In other words, in addition to their obviously militarized bias and their suspicion of railroad employees, company detectives also discriminated on the basis of class.

With porters virtually off-limits, not because of their own status but because of concerns about inconveniencing privileged sleeping-car passengers, investigators focused on the only other Black men with access to Pullman sleeping cars: dining car crews. Apparently, any Black railroad employee would do, if detectives could show he was in the vicinity of the murder car. Sisemore's inquiry prematurely and exclusively focused on Bernice Ball's false lead about a Black man in a pin-striped suit, because Taylor and the Klamath Falls district attorney had jointly constructed a racialized theory of the crime based on Wilson's story. Their theory shadowed Train 15 southward toward Los Angeles, and it settled darkly around the slim shoulders of Robert Folkes.[28] Wilson had indicated that the man he supposedly saw was dark-complexioned, about five feet ten inches tall, at least thirty years old, and "very heavy, about 175 or 185."[29] Folkes, according to notes one investigator scrawled in the margins of one of the cook's 23 January signed statements, was twenty years old, about five feet six inches tall, a slim 145 pounds, and a "yellow negro [with] small mustache, thick lips, blue serge coat, brown eyes, [and] kinkey black hair."[30]

Even if Wilson were telling the truth, Folkes did not even vaguely resemble the description the marine originally provided, but physical resemblance to the man in the pin-striped suit was apparently unimportant. In Klamath Falls, and en route from there to Sacramento, Taylor's team repeatedly interrogated Folkes in browbeating sessions that extracted several written statements. In all of those signed statements, the young cook consistently denied any knowledge of the murder. Detectives, however, compiled a list of supposed discrepancies, termed them "lies," and suggested they indicated guilt. Champlin and OSP officer Lowery also thoroughly searched Folkes' workplace—Dining Car 10110— "checking on knives and forks and examined all linen." Taylor's report of their findings asserted Folkes "lied about times he was in Car D in the rest room, ... lied about asking porter Hughes the time of day and he acted very preculiar [sic]."[31] Their search of the diner did not turn up any physical evidence connected in any way with the murder, but the "preculiar" behavior of a young dining car worker was apparently more important to SPRR detectives.

Taylor applied an obvious double standard, characterizing minor discrepancies in Folkes' statements as lies while ignoring blatant contradictions, logical inconsistencies, and abrupt, substantive changes in the statements other people made. Folkes' youth, race, diminutive size, and exuberant cooperation worked against him. Those same characteristics should have exonerated Folkes, if investigators really believed Wilson had seen the murderer, because the young cook obviously differed in age, size, physique, and demeanor from the description the marine provided. Taylor, however, seemed unconcerned about inconsistencies in testimony from any witnesses other than Folkes, whether Black or White. He and other investigators singled out *this particular Black man* for close scrutiny.

All facts aside, even before the district attorney instructed them to intensify their focus on Folkes, SPRR agents aboard Train 15 singled him out for special treatment. Folkes was their prearranged fallback suspect. With no obvious alternatives other than Funches or Wilson, investigators put the screws to Folkes. By the time the train reached Redding, railroad agents had reconstructed Folkes as the man they would blame for the murder. They took very minor statements Folkes made on innocuous points over nearly two days of repetitious, intimidating, and disorienting interrogations and labeled them major inconsistencies and evidence he was a habitual liar and exhibitionist. Folkes, according to Taylor, denied in his statement to Sisemore on the afternoon of 23 January, and again in his statement to Officer Huber later that evening, that he had ever been in the car "where lady was killed." Taylor claimed, however, that Folkes contradicted that statement later the next morning, when, at 5:30 a.m., he admitted "he had been in Car D just a few moments prior to time of murder."[32] Between 5:00 p.m. on 23 January, when he was interrogated in Klamath Falls, and 5:30 the next morning, Banich and Taylor put Folkes under physical stress and deprived him of sleep and then picked out supposed discrepancies in one-page statements representing a "conversation" that, in at least one case, likely lasted more than five hours.

The story of what a twenty-year-old slight Black youth endured at the hands of three burly middle-aged White railroad detectives through twelve hours of relentless questioning in darkened corridors and compartments on Train 15 can never be fully known. All that survives are terse reports with copies of "statements" (signed and unsigned) that detectives claimed Folkes made. One White passenger, R. M. Kelso, witnessed at least a portion of those interrogations, and he reluctantly testified to what he saw, stating he wanted no part in their "hanging of an innocent man."[33] Banich loaded his report with insinuations about the cook's demeanor and offhand comments en route to

Redding. The detective noted that he, together with Ramirez and Taylor, questioned Folkes in a Pullman car restroom aboard Train 15 as it moved from Dunsmuir to Gerber, California, and that they secured a written statement in that restroom. His official report claimed the three agents pushed Folkes into the men's room at five o'clock that evening (about two and a half hours before the train left Klamath Falls). They forced Folkes to strip naked, and Ramirez reportedly took the clothing out of the restroom "to examine it" while the other two agents interrogated the naked youth in the poorly ventilated, darkened, cramped space of a train lavatory reeking of smoke, urine, and an overtaxed toilet system. Twelve hours later, Kelso walked in on them while the train was under way. Kelso, a navy officer whose Lower 12 berth was immediately adjacent to Lower 13 the night of the murder, later testified that detectives were still interrogating Folkes when he entered the lavatory. Folkes, he recalled, was sitting, unclothed, in that small space, with windows closed and blackout shades drawn in the dark hour between 5:00 and 6:00 a.m.[34]

Banich apparently tried to influence Kelso to change his testimony. The detective visited the reserve navy officer at his home in El Cajon, California, four days later, reportedly suggesting Kelso testify he actually saw the three detectives strip Folkes naked at 5:00 a.m. on 24 January (which would have shortened the timeline of his interrogation by a full twelve hours). According to Kelso's official statement, however, he simply came upon an interrogation already in progress, and the agents continued questioning Folkes as if he were not there. For his part, Kelso made no effort to leave the room and merely went about his business, as if the sight of three burly detectives standing over one slight, naked Black youth in that claustrophobic space was neither unusual nor disturbing.[35] Considering the small size of the room, and the large size of the three agents (each well over six feet tall, towering over Folkes by at least half a foot), that pretense would have required a considerable act of willful ignorance by Kelso.

Nothing witnesses could say diverted investigators from their efforts to link Folkes with the murder. Detectives were as unfazed by Kelso's frank statement that he believed Folkes innocent as they were unconcerned about Banks' blunt warning that Wilson was likely guilty. Banich reported that, although Kelso admitted witnessing a portion of the interrogation, he "could not identify this man [Folkes] as being the same one he had seen in car 'D' prior to the murder," and, the detective admitted, "Kelso stated that he gave his statement [while still on the train] to the best of his knowledge so that he would not be involved in the probable hanging of an innocent man."[36] Curiously, Kelso did figure largely at the eventual trial because he testified he saw a man in the aisle near Lower 13 on his way to the washroom, just before other passengers sounded the alarm. As a military man, however, Kelso's own reasons for being up and about, adjacent to the murder scene, about the time of the murder, went unexamined. He, like Wilson and unlike Folkes, was not a suspect.

The young cook was well aware his life was in jeopardy, and from the scant evidence in stilted reports from Banich and Taylor, Folkes seemed to be in a negotiating frame of mind. Banich claimed he first wrote down Folkes' "statement" and only then took him out of the lavatory into an adjoining dining car, "due to the bad lighting conditions" where they had interrogated him. In the dining car, the detective instructed Folkes to read and sign what Banich had written—supposedly a summary of all that Folkes said over the long ordeal of the previous night. The entire statement was less than three-quarters of a page. According to Banich, Folkes first asked if Taylor and Ramirez had already decided to charge him with murder. Banich reported he told the cook he did not know the answer to that question, but "he was in trouble due to the fact that he gave so many conflicting stories." In response, Folkes reportedly said, "They'll pin the murder on me, but I'm innocent." Banich concluded, "During this conversation, Folkes was very nervous and seemed to be concentrating very deeply." There is no record that anyone else, Black or White, was first stripped and then interrogated in conditions anything like those Folkes endured in that railroad lavatory. Detectives apparently singled him out because he was younger, weaker, more isolated, and less experienced than other Black trainmen.[37]

Folkes endured extreme physical and mental distress aboard the train from Klamath Falls to Redding. By the time Folkes signed the "statement" Banich wrote and presented for his signature, he had not been allowed to sleep for more than twenty-four hours. Kelso stumbled upon the interrogation during one of the most tortuous, winding sections of the main line south of Dunsmuir. By that point, Folkes had worked one complete shift the day of the murder, then he was interrogated all night long. Immediately after signing the 24 January statement, he reported for his next shift, working from six o'clock in the morning until past ten o'clock that evening. It is not clear whether he was allowed to sleep the second night or not, but regardless, he was exhausted, sleep deprived, and seriously disoriented long before the train reached Los Angeles.

Given the intimidation, sleep deprivation, and other abusive treatment Folkes had endured, his story was remarkably consistent—he clearly and repeatedly denied any involvement or guilt in the murder. Even the written statements that Banich and Taylor wrote and then attributed to Folkes during the first two days of the investigation do not support the claims they made in their reports. In an unsigned statement of 23 January, Folkes reportedly replied to the question (from Sisemore) "What did you see last night" with the statement "I didn't see anything." He asserted he was in the diner when the murder took place, and that "the first person I saw was a military police [officer]." He stated he propped the door to the galley open for ventilation that morning "because the fans wouldn't run," and shortly after he opened the door, the military policeman went by without saying anything to him. Next, he reported, he saw a brakeman going by, flashing his light, and then he recalled, "I think another soldier asked me if I seen anybody go by and I told him no, not that I knew of." This last soldier, according to Folkes, asked, "Did I know there was a murder on the train and I asked him was he drunk." When asked, "Did you go up in the car where the woman was killed?" Folkes reportedly replied, "No." In context, Folkes was saying he did not visit the murder scene in Car D after he learned about the murder from the soldier (apparently Wilson). It was not a denial that he visited Car D before the murder, although that was the meaning Banich drew from this statement in his official report.[38]

Although Banich and Taylor may have suspected and persecuted Folkes just because he was a Black trainman, they apparently singled him out because he was relatively young, inexperienced, and cooperative. A major factor working against him was that his signed statements included specific timelines, unlike those from other Black trainmen who kept their responses vague and uncertain, claiming and/or feigning confusion. Those other trainmen also requested and retained copies of their signed statements. From their responses, SPRR detectives clearly did not consider Black trainmen capable of providing reliable details and did not press them for clarification. Folkes, however (at least in written statements), apparently tried to provide details, perhaps because interrogators insisted he do so, perhaps because he was trying to cooperate and had not honed the survival skill of playing dumb. His earnest cooperation may be why investigators considered him "preculiar." If he hoped truthful detail would help his cause, Folkes was sadly mistaken—investigators chose, from among many conflicting timelines other witnesses provided, those that best suited the storyline they wanted to construct.

A longer statement that Folkes purportedly signed in the presence of Huber during the interrogations aboard the train on the evening of 23 January demonstrates how he struggled to provide a time estimate that satisfied investigators. According to the document, Folkes claimed that after he retired to his berth, he remained there until about 4:35 a.m., at which time he walked forward one car to the men's smoking room (restroom) in Car D, asked Porter Hughes the time, stayed there about five or ten minutes, then walked back to the diner to prepare coffee and breakfast. Adjusting for the fact that Hughes later reported he ran his watch at least ten minutes fast, and following Banks' reconstructed timeline for the murder, this statement suggests Folkes made his way through Car D to the washroom perhaps five minutes before the murder, and then left Hughes about five minutes after the murder had already taken place. In the statement, Folkes noted, "When I walked through the Pullman car to the men's smoking room [where he encountered Hughes] I observed a man climbing down from an upper berth . . . about the fourth or fifth berth at the right side [approximately the location of Wilson's berth]." Folkes claimed that on his way back to the diner from the smoking room, "I saw this man again hanging around in the passage way near the drinking fountain, or at the rear end of Pullman coach [near the women's lounge in the corridor behind berths 15 and 16]. I then noticed that this man was wearing brownish pants, no hat."[39]

Once he committed himself to a time, however inaccurate, detectives expected Folkes to repeat that time, precisely, each time he was interrogated, but the circumstances of his interrogations would have confused even a more experienced witness with less reason to fear for his life at the hands of three angry White men. The statement Folkes later signed for Banich early on 24 January, after the overnight "interrogation" in the Pullman car restroom, indicates he awoke around 4:00 or 4:15 a.m., dressed, and went into Car D to use the restroom. He said he asked Porter Hughes the time, and, according to this statement, Hughes told him it was 4:30 (not 4:35, as noted in his earlier statement). Adjusting again for Hughes' watch, and for Banks' timeline, Folkes left Car D and entered the kitchen shortly before the murder. In this statement, Folkes said that on his way back to the diner, he "bumped into a man just leaving his berth, wearing dark pants and a white upper shirt." Folkes stated he excused himself and continued on back to the kitchen. He stated the man was "in the middle of and [*sic*] Pullman car on the right hand side, going towards Los Angeles, when I bumped into him."[40] If so, this man may likely have been the murderer.

The timelines that Folkes, Banks, and Wilson recounted posed a problem for investigators trying to build a case against Folkes, and the narratives they assembled from other passengers and crew in the first day after the murder further complicated their task. Depending on which statement from Folkes detectives chose, he was either in the washroom with Hughes when the murder happened, or in the kitchen working. If the murder took place before the train reached Tangent or while it was at Tangent, as Banks argued, then it must have happened between 4:25 and 4:35 a.m. At least one of Wilson's accounts put the murder closer to 4:30 a.m., which corresponded more closely to the estimate that Banks provided. Other witnesses, however, reported learning about the murder sometime between 4:30 and 4:50 a.m., and of course, the initial time cited in front-page newspaper reports across the country placed the murder nearer 4:00 a.m. In an effort to pinpoint the time of the murder, investigators turned to statements provided by the porter assigned to Car D that morning, Harry M. Hughes, and to those provided by a man who admitted being in the aisle at about the time Folkes claimed to have encountered a man there: H. M. Kelso. In doing so, they paired the narratives of a White naval officer and a Black railroad employee.

Kelso and Hughes, in their initial statements, seemed to agree on at least one key point: they both remembered Kelso was in the restroom with Hughes when other passengers first raised the alarm. In other particulars, their narratives conflicted with one or all of the stories that Banks, Wilson, and Folkes provided, and with each other's. Kelso, whose bunk was immediately adjacent to berth 13, next to both Wilson and the victim, initially stated that when he first emerged from his bunk (Upper 11) into the aisle sometime "after 4 o'clock . . . as far as I could see I was the only one there." Thinking he would shave early, he walked toward the washroom, encountering a man in the aisle of Car D who "had a porter's uniform on" and who directed Kelso toward the men's restroom. Given numerous opportunities, later, to identify that man as Folkes, Kelso refused to do so, but he did elaborate, stating it was a "man with a white coat and white hat, colored fellow." Pressed as to whether it might have been a cook's hat, he demurred: "I wouldn't say. I'd rather not make that a statement." When Kelso arrived in the smoking room of the men's restroom, he found Porter Hughes lying there on the bench. When Kelso entered the room, Hughes sat up and inquired, "What are you up so early for?" and Kelso answered, "I can't sleep, will get a shave before anyone else." According to this first statement, he then "sat on the toilet for a certain few minutes" and then came out and tried to open his shaving kit, but the zipper was stuck. Hughes helped open the zipper, and Kelso began shaving. Then, Hughes heard the call bell and rushed out to discover the murder. In this initial statement, Kelso made no estimate of time beyond the fact that he emerged from his bunk "after 4 o'clock."[41]

Hughes, in a statement detectives wrote out and presented for his signature the morning of the murder, provided a muddled time estimate that placed the alarm for the murder at somewhere between 4:30 and 4:37 a.m., adjusting for his watch and some vagueness in his chronology. He said that after "checking the car just before to see if anything was OK," he "fixed a zipper bag for one of the chief petty officers [Kelso] at the time scream was heard where he checked bag in zipper I untangled that as he heard the scream." When the interrogator asked, for clarification, "Was he with you at the time?" Hughes replied, "Yes, sir." He then volunteered a time frame for these events: "I asked why getting up so early he said used to getting up early and couldn't sleep, it was 4:35 exactly, about 10 or 12 minutes after that the scream was heard." Hughes clarified, in response to follow-up questions, that he didn't actually hear the victim scream, but rather, he heard Wilson "hollering" at the same time as the passenger in berth 12 rang his bell. Hughes confirmed Folkes had come into the lavatory and smoked a cigarette "previous to this," but Hughes emphasized he watched Folkes leave the car, enter the diner, and begin "making the fire in stove" before the porter returned to his "smoker."[42]

If investigators followed Hughes' statement, assuming his narrative and chronology were correct (and adjusting for his watch), the alarm bell and discovery of the marine standing over the body came somewhere between 4:35 and 4:37 a.m. Hughes' statement did corroborate the petty officer's claim that he was in the washroom when the body was discovered, but they differed on what Kelso was doing when Hughes heard the alarm—Kelso claimed he was already shaving, but Hughes claimed they were struggling with the zipper on Kelso's shaving kit. Kelso, in this first statement, did not say what time he entered the restroom, nor did he mention asking Hughes for the time, whereas Hughes volunteered a time consistent with when Folkes claimed to have been in the smoking room and confirmed Folkes was with him shortly before Kelso entered. He also confirmed Folkes left the Pullman car, as he had claimed, and was working in the galley of the diner, stoking the fires, when last seen. Hughes' claim that he asked a man why he was up so early, and that he verified the time he asked that question as 4:35 (or 4:25, correcting for his watch) also closely corresponds with Folkes' later account of his own conversation with the porter, although Hughes attributed that conversation to his interactions with Kelso. It is possible Hughes, not Folkes, misrepresented this detail, especially since Kelso did not corroborate it.

Investigators, confronted with the irreconcilable contradictions of early statements (further complicated by the porter's intentionally offset watch), selected elements of each narrative that reinforced the apparent veracity of military witnesses, no matter how incredible, while denigrating the reliability of railway employees, no matter how respectable. Even though Porter Hughes admitted walking through Car D shortly before Kelso entered the washroom, they pressed Kelso on whether the porter he claimed to have encountered in the aisle of Car D might instead have been the second cook, Folkes, and they insisted Kelso (not Wilson) was the man Folkes saw getting out of a berth midway through Car D. They were undeterred by Kelso's refusal to identify Folkes as the man he saw in a "porter's uniform," made no mention of asking if the man wore checkered pants, and ignored the discrepancies in time between Hughes' account and the estimates Banks provided. They cited Hughes' (unadjusted) timeline, however, in their assertions Folkes was lying about the time he entered the smoking room. They insisted Folkes provide precise times for when he awoke, dressed, entered the restroom, and returned to the diner, but they ignored Kelso's studied vagueness about when he left his bunk or when he entered the men's restroom. They also disregarded Kelso's differences from Hughes' statement regarding what they were each doing when the porter heard the alarm from berth 12.

As investigators assessed the statements of Wilson, Banks, Hughes, Kelso, and Folkes through the fog of a militarized bias, they also embraced racial stereotypes regarding the character and perceptiveness of witnesses. A White employee, Banks, questioned Wilson's honesty and supplied evidence and witnesses supporting the premise that whoever committed the murder had not left the train. Banks obviously meant that Wilson, who was still on the train, had committed the murder, and early police reports acknowledged that argument. Taylor and Sisemore, however, directed their suspicions at the Black waiter, Funches, who mostly matched the description Wilson provided of the man he supposedly saw fleeing the murder scene: Funches was about five feet ten inches tall, weighed about 180 pounds, wore a brown suit, had dark hair that he wore in a sort of short pompadour, and was a light-complexioned Black man who might be mistaken for a dark White man. Sisemore's interrogation team in Klamath Falls initially focused almost exclusively on Funches; however, Weinrick notified the investigating team that their case against Funches would not stand up in court. Sisemore was in a bad spot. He had already released statements implying Funches was a suspect, while praising Wilson's supposed heroics. Sisemore either needed another (surprise) suspect, or else he had to reverse his earlier characterization of Wilson's role. Sisemore consequently telegraphed Dunsmuir, directing SPRR detectives to more intensively interrogate Folkes, and they apparently applied brutal methods for the rest of his journey to Los Angeles.

The militarized bias, company outlook, and racial prejudice of the investigators clearly drove their efforts to tie Folkes to the murder as they assembled a revised timeline that would make that task easier. In doing so, they disregarded contradicting evidence from another prominently located White military man. Marine Corporal William W. Van Dyke's account included important evidence that Wilson might have had time to commit the murder, hide any evidence he had done so, and then sound the alarm as if he had just discovered the body. Van Dyke shared Lower 12 in Car D with his wife, Dorothy, the night of the murder, one berth back and just across the aisle from Lower 13. He stated he and Dorothy retired at about 11:20 p.m., while the train was still in Portland. They awoke to a "blood curdling scream" and the words, "'I can't stand it anymore, Oh, god, he's killing me." Van Dyke recalled he was "a little dumbfounded" but gathered his wits, "leaned over, and saw the streak, blood streak, shoved the curtain back. . . . Just as I rang the bell the Marine [Wilson] above hollered this is murder, stop the train." Van Dyke didn't know where he was when he first "hollered," but "the minute I looked out I asked if he was a Marine, he said yes, I shook hands with him, he had blood on his right hand, but not on his left."

Van Dyke's account established that there was a significant delay between when Martha James screamed and when witnesses looked out of their bunks and saw Wilson standing over her, and he also confirmed Wilson did not sound the alarm until after someone else rang the bell for the porter. Asked to estimate the time between when he heard the scream and when he heard Wilson "holler," Van Dyke noted he waited about sixty seconds after the scream, because he was "too damn nervous," then, when he looked out, he didn't ring the bell until he saw the feet of the murdered woman, and then, "it took a minute to ring the bell." He also emphasized, "the minute I ring the bell he hollers." By this estimate, Van Dyke indicates a delay of two or three minutes between the time he heard the scream and the time Wilson raised an alarm, and he notes he did not see the marine in the aisle when he first looked out and saw the woman lying there in a pool of blood.[43] Those two or three minutes directly contradicted Wilson's statement that he leaped from his bunk when he first heard the scream and helped the woman as she clawed her way out of her bunk. Van Dyke's observation of blood on Wilson's right hand also corresponded with later evidence from the autopsy report that the murderer cut the woman's throat using a right-handed motion.

Other nearby witnesses barely registered in the notes investigators made during the first two days, which reveals a gender bias in the investigation beyond the apparent militarization and racialization of the case by company detectives and Sisemore. Aside from Wilson, who occupied Upper 13, the berths nearest Lower 13 in the direction of the men's restroom (toward the front of the train) were Upper 11 (Kelso), and Lower 11 (occupied by Maxine Flieder). Across the aisle, in the same direction, the passengers nearest the murdered woman included an "unknown woman" who occupied Upper 12 (she never provided a statement or name, and only the porter's call slip and later recollection records her presence), and the Van Dyke couple in Lower 12. In the other direction, going toward the ladies' restroom at the back of the train were sections 15 and 16. A party of five, including a woman (Mrs. R. G. Donnelly) travelling with her mother-in-law (Mrs. W. H. Donnelly) and three children (two girls and a boy, ages four, three, and one, respectively), occupied Upper 16 and Lower 16, sharing a bulkhead with the vacant pair of berths in section 14 (the only vacant berths in the car). Mrs. Davis Chamberlin occupied berth Lower 15, sharing a bulkhead with Lower 13, and slept with her head near the bulkhead closest to the berth where Martha James was murdered. In that sense, Chamberlin was closer to the murder scene than any other passenger. Upper 15, the berth closest to Wilson's in the direction of the back of the car, was assigned to Mrs. Alton Bailey.

Various investigators collected cursory statements from some of these women, but most made no on-record statements at all prior to the date newspapers reported details of Folkes' alleged "confession," which included the police timeline for the murder.[44] Investigators did collect an early statement from Maxine Flieder (Lower 11), who claimed she awoke "about 4:50" (although she had no watch or clock), when she heard a woman gasp "O, Oh," then "about a minute or so after she spoke I heard her scream. She screamed once, very loudly and I then looked out of my berth and saw a woman lying in the aisle with blood on her feet."[45] Chamberlin's 23 January statement noted she heard "muffled screams" at "around 5 in the morning." Like Flieder, Chamberlin had no watch and admitted she was only guessing at the time. She "raised up and noticed that the lights in the coach were dim. The next thing I've heard was the buzzer ring very urgently. Then it sounded like someone's feet touching the floor hurriedly." Chamberlin said she then "parted the curtain and saw and recognized the young man as the Marine who was riding with us from Seattle in the same train [Wilson]. He said this is awful. Saw a lady laying on the floor and blood splattered all over the floor."[46]

There is no record Mrs. R. G. Donnelly (berth 16) was ever interviewed, but her mother-in-law, Mrs. W. H. Donnelly, was interviewed on 24 January, the day after the murder, producing only a very brief statement in paragraph form. She said she was "awakened by a noise [that] may have been scream." Then she heard "what sounded like a person jumping from berth." When she started to look out, she found a "man standing by my berth dressed in uniform who said 'Don't look out for your own sake, please.' So remained dozing but couldn't hear anything except un-understandable talking."[47] There is no evidence of follow-up questions, unlike many other statements inspectors collected from male passengers.

Virtually none of the passengers nearest the murder scene had any precise method for telling time—most were simply guessing. Many made those guesses several days, weeks, or even months after the night of the murder, well after police widely publicized their theoretical timeline. The only nearby female passenger who claimed she verified the time with a clock or watch was Mrs. Alton Bailey, the twenty-five-year-old spouse of a third class petty officer. Bailey, a nurse travelling alone from Spokane to California in Upper 15, stated on 25 March 1943 (two months after the event) that she first learned of the murder when she heard a man's voice in the aisle saying "something about murder" and advising that "women should not look out of their berths for their own good." Upon hearing that warning, which might also be interpreted as a threat, Bailey lay quietly in her berth. Only after several minutes did she look at her watch. Obviously quite some time after the actual murder, then, she noted it was 4:50 a.m. Bailey, sleeping immediately above Chamberlin with her head adjacent to the bulkhead between her berth and Wilson's, claimed she did not hear the murdered woman scream or say anything.[48]

Bailey's interview illustrates the priorities of those involved in the murder investigation and how their approaches to witnesses depended on the subject's military or employment status, as well as their race, gender, and class. She was just one example of a witness whom investigators approached for a follow-up interview during the three months between the time of the murder and the eventual trial. Each witness described their own personal experiences on Train 15 in stories that built on their own life experiences from before and after the events of that night. Men with a military affiliation, for example, projected a public identity that was familiar and reassuring to many other travelers—when Van Dyke realized Wilson was a fellow marine, he shook his bloody hand as a comrade in arms, not as a witness shaking hands with a likely murderer. Men who lacked a military affiliation, by comparison, were less reassuring. Banks wielded great authority aboard the train, but one witness described him as only a "man in a railroad uniform." White passengers commonly referred to porters as "colored boys" (or by the generalized nickname "George"). Women travelling alone identified themselves according to the status of their husbands and assumed identities as war brides, navy wives, or simply "Mrs. Davis Chamberlin." Investigators barely concerned themselves with this latter group, collecting mere fragments of their stories in statements of only a few typed lines, with no follow-up questions.

Early in the investigation, proximity to the murder scene, familiarity with the victim, and coherence and consistency of a person's story seemed less important to investigators than the gender, military status, race, and class of a witness or suspect. Investigators dissected the moving world of Train 15 after the murder by zeroing in on the Black workingmen who served the passengers, collected the tickets, prepared the meals, made up the berths, handled the luggage, announced stops, and handled other day-to-day operations. Detectives viewed these identifiable members of the company workforce with more suspicion than passengers who rode the train in relative anonymity, whether men or women.

There are no pictures in the record depicting Folkes or Funches smiling jauntily and standing next to Coroner Adler at Klamath Falls depot, but there are several of Wilson in that pose. There are, similarly, no pictures of women standing in groups on that siding, outside the murder car, curiously smiling at the camera. There are, however, many such pictures of White military men

Marine corporal Van Dyke outside Tourist Pullman Car D in Klamath Falls the morning of the murder, with a Pullman porter (unidentified) guarding the entry to the car, and with various unidentified passengers in the background. Original photo in OSP case file, SPR collection, CSRM Library and Archives.Courtesy California State Railroad Museum.

in uniform who congregated along the tracks waiting for the investigation to conclude. In the background of such photos, however, there are Black men in uniform—trainmen, not military men—doing the work of guarding the train's doorways, monitoring the comings and goings of passengers and investigators, looking serious and professional and protective of their charges. These trainmen, always in the background, served in job classifications few passengers recognized as military service. During the investigation and subsequent trial, however, these men and their understanding of the interior world of that moving train stepped out of the shadows and walked headlong into the limelight of public scrutiny and legal machinery in Oregon.

Chapter Four

The Trials of Home and Away Lives in Portland, Albany, and Los Angeles

The trial of Robert E. Lee Folkes forced race and labor conflicts to the forefront, challenging the façade of wartime solidarity and cultural homogeneity that most residents of Linn County, Oregon, preferred to present as their public face to the outside world. Leading up to the trial and continuing through the appeals process, corporate officials and labor leaders assumed prominent roles in a legal melodrama that made headlines around the country from mid-winter through early spring 1943. The trial trapped common workers from the railroad's dining car division in a landscape of racist exclusion and prejudice in the mostly rural mid-Willamette Valley. In a city where Black residents were not only unwelcome but excluded, the trial attracted crowds of local Albany residents who watched with growing fascination as a parade of witnesses—many of them Black trainmen—described events that had happened nearly two months earlier aboard a blacked-out train rolling through their county. Despite the centrality of Black trainmen as key witnesses, Albany-area hotels refused to rent them rooms, forcing the sheriff's office to arrange alternative accommodations. With reporters and onlookers queuing up in courthouse hallways, waiting for a seat in the overcrowded courtroom galleries, legal officials and officers of the court clearly played to public opinion, as well as to the all-White jury of local men and women. The trial and its aftermath, however, stripped away the veneer of rural seclusion and exposed the myriad connections linking the mid-Valley with the growing problems of labor unrest, racial discord, and militarized notions of justice in the rural and urban West during the war.

Black men who worked as dining car cooks and waiters during a time of wartime mobilization travelled through segregated landscapes of work and leisure while enduring the constant scrutiny and suspicions of White passengers and trainmen. Even the modest privacy of their personal quarters dissolved during the daylight hours into public spaces in which passengers relaxed while cooks and waiters served them. These service professionals worked with no hope of privacy before the last visitor left their diner each evening. The James murder trapped eleven such men in the public-private space of Dining Car 10110 for nearly two full days of interrogations while they also continued to cook and serve meals for a train full of stressed travelers. Those who worked in the pantry or kitchen may have escaped public scrutiny during duty hours, but their relative isolation in those unprivate spaces also marked them as different and apart from other crewmen. That characteristic dogged Folkes after the murder, and interrogators treated him differently than everyone else they interviewed.

When Robert Folkes finally walked out the doors of Dining Car 10110 onto the Union Station platform in Los Angeles, he was not a free man. Los Angeles Police Department detectives whisked him away to their interrogation rooms at downtown police headquarters in city hall and then sent him to the nearby Central Jail. Over the next three days in those LAPD facilities, he endured relentless pressure and insistent demands that he "confess" to the murder his antagonists insisted he must have committed.[1] Between 23 January and the end of April, LAPD and other authorities released various statements they attributed to Folkes, none of which bore his signature nor even those of interrogating officers. Prosecutors later read two of those statements aloud before jurors in the Albany courthouse, adding their own inflections and insinuating voices to the raw words on the page. Three of the supposed statements were in the form of a multipage transcript of a question-and-answer interrogation. All were the product of a transcription process similar to the one witnesses later testified had altered and falsified their own statements. Folkes, through his lawyer and in letters to his mother, steadfastly denied making the "confessions" police included in those "transcriptions." Regardless of the circumstances whereby police generated those statements, or the degree to which they accurately reflected anything Folkes actually said, the story prosecutors and reporters later told about them became more important than anything that might have occurred on board the train that night of 22–23 January 1943. Verbal dramatizations of those statements at trial, in fact, overwhelmed their actual content. In the end, they were all prosecutors needed to convince jurors to convict Folkes and recommend he be executed in Oregon's gas chamber.

TELLING STORIES ABOUT THE "AWAY" LIFE IN PORTLAND

Downtime in Portland figured large in the story prosecutors assembled for jurors during the Albany trial, and the stories trainmen told about that lay-over time opened a window on race relations, class, and status in the City of Roses during the war years. For a few short hours between the time they arrived on the northbound train and the time they reported back for the southbound leg of their journey, trainmen enjoyed a brief respite from the controlling oversight of railway officials. SPRR detectives viewed those unsu-pervised hours with great suspicion, and the murder investigation provided an opportunity for scrutinizing what trainmen did with their time beyond the reach of corporate managers.

When interrogating Black trainmen, investigators focused narrowly on their activities in Portland between the time they arrived on the northbound train and the time they reboarded the southbound train. This contrasts with the deeper life-history background investigators sought from White witnesses like Wilson. The first fully transcribed "statement" attributed to Folkes during his Los Angeles interrogations followed fairly closely the story he told SPRR detectives in various interrogations aboard the train between Eugene and Los Angeles. Those detectives assisted Tetrick and Rasmussen in grilling Folkes in LA. According to that statement, Folkes described his movements in Portland the night before the murder. Like others in the din-ing crew, when he left the train early that Friday afternoon, he walked "down on some street in Portland to the liquor store," where he purchased a pint of whiskey, then "walked on some other street to catch a bus." Several buses passed him by in the snowstorm without stopping, so he walked all the way from Union Station across the river and north on Interstate Avenue to the Medley Hotel, where he registered for a room on the second floor (room 229 or 226) that the railroad customarily reserved as sleeping quarters for the second, third, and fourth cooks on layover. When Folkes reached the room that night, the only person there was "Forty" (the fourth cook, Arthur Stein).[2] When Folkes offered a drink, Stein said he'd have one later if Folkes would wait for him downstairs in the lobby. Folkes went down to wait at the bar, and when Stein came down, they went into the dressing room to drink from the second cook's bottle. Then they went back in the bar, played a record, and Stein bought a bottle of beer. He sat at a card table to drink while Folkes sat at the bar and talked with a woman—apparently the front desk clerk.

The Los Angeles interrogators (specifically, McCreadie, at this point) pressed Folkes for details on the race of people in the bar and tried, without success, to introduce sexual innuendo into the cook's account. On the race of people at the Medley, Folkes casually observed, "They are all colored." He explained he sat in the lobby with Third Cook Sterling Bolton, until Elmer White (a waiter) came in with a friend. Folkes followed them into the bar, where White bought his friends rounds. Folkes stated another man came in with "two good looking girls"—one was the man's wife and the other his mother-in-law. His interrogators pressed for details, asking, "Did you feel like you would like to have a little piece of strange woman?" But Folkes replied, "No sir, I was feeling very fine and didn't feel like nothing."

If the police report is to be believed, Folkes was mostly interested in social drinking. He, White, and Bolton, according to this account, walked from the Medley to a nearby restaurant and ordered three glasses and one 7Up, apparently so they could mix their own drinks—a cheaper option than purchasing mixed drinks at a bar. The waitress warned them it was against the law to mix their own drinks in her restaurant, so they walked to a nearby laundry, where, with one glass and a bottle of Squirt, they mixed drinks with whiskey from bottles White carried in his grip. After sharing drinks, they went back to the bar. Folkes found the clerk he had been talking with had left, so he headed down the street to Forester's Pool Hall. On the way, he encountered Chef Baker. He offered to walk together, but Baker complained it was too cold, so Folkes walked alone across the street to catch a bus. While he waited, Pantryman Edward Smith walked up and said he was going to the commissary to stock up. Folkes offered Smith a nip from his bottle, and then they caught the bus to the commissary, two stops past the station. Smith told Folkes he was going to go "stock the wagon" (hand truck). Folkes went inside the station to get out of the cold and fell asleep on a bench. According to the statement, Folkes said another man waiting in the station woke him about 9:00 p.m. and warned the train was getting ready to go (it did not actually leave until after one o'clock the next morning, due to the snowstorm). Folkes boarded the train at a chair car to get out of the cold and walked through that car and Tourist Car E, adjoining Car D.

Finding the door to Car D locked, he got out on the platform, walked past Car D, and boarded his diner.

Once in the diner, according to this statement, Folkes changed into his work clothes and found Chef Baker, who was busy stocking the car. Baker had not yet put the fish away, so Folkes put them on ice and wiped down the workbench. Once finished, he walked forward, finding the steward's party under way at the front of the diner. He asked if the steward wanted sandwiches for the group, which included a man, his wife, and "some other fellows who I didn't know." The steward asked for about three sandwiches, which Folkes made with turkey from the chef's box. Then he made a fourth after "someone hollered into the kitchen from the pantry and told me to make four sandwiches." He also cut off a steak and set it on the stove to eat later. Folkes' statement indicates he set the sandwiches on a tray, added four pieces of pie, and then delivered the lot to the steward's party. In return, several partiers offered him a drink.

Folkes' interrogators tried to get him to admit he was drunk when he boarded the train, insinuating he later committed the murder in an alcohol-fueled stupor. Folkes, however, denied he was drunk, stating he took only small nips to ward off the bitter cold. Detectives nevertheless characterized those nips as "drinks" of a full shot or more. Whatever Folkes drank, apparently less than a half pint, was stretched across nearly six hours, from the time he visited the liquor store that afternoon until the time he delivered the sandwiches between 10:30 p.m. and midnight. After delivering the sandwiches, Folkes said, he went back to the kitchen, locked the door, and went to his berth, nearest the galley at the rear of the diner. He crawled under the covers and fell asleep somewhere between midnight and before the train got under way (about 1:15 a.m. or so). When he awoke the next morning, Folkes put on his (checkered) pants, shoes, and white jacket and headed up to the car where the steward's berth was located (Car 60—the first standard Pullman behind the dining car. Stewards were assigned berths in an adjacent Pullman car, when available). From there, he walked back to the lavatory in Car D, where Folkes found Porter Hughes "sitting on his bench." He spoke to Hughes, then went through the second door into the toilet chamber. When he came back out, he had a smoke on the bench next to Hughes, asked the porter what time it was, and then, learning it was about 4:30 a.m., he headed back to the kitchen.

CORROBORATING STORIES TELLING OF THE "AWAY" LIFE IN PORTLAND

Like Folkes, many other railroad men who worked aboard Train 15 the night of the murder later told interrogators stories about the world they inhabited at the far reaches of their "away" lives, reachable by walking or taking a streetcar from Union Station in Portland. These layovers of typically less than six hours were unsupervised time when dining car and Pullman car workers (mostly Black men) temporarily escaped the regimented, claustrophobic world of life on board the train under the ever-watchful eyes of their (White and male) supervisors (conductors, chefs, and stewards). The crew assigned to Dining Car 10110 on the evening of 22 January 1943 left an unusually detailed record of their activities from the time they arrived in Portland, around 2:00 p.m., until the time they awoke to a murder investigation around 5:30 the next morning. Details of their away-life routine survive on the record only because of an unusual circumstance that attracted the attention of SPRR detectives: their proximity to the murder in Tourist Pullman Car D that night. Over the next several months, investigators scrutinized the activities of each member of the crew, expecting them to account for every minute of their private and working lives in that fifteen-hour time window. The resulting record outlines their activities and establishes boundaries beyond which they refused to allow the official gaze of their inquisitors.

These corroborating stories of the "away" life of trainmen on layover in Portland document, in their mundane and evasive detail, a power struggle pitting relatively powerless, but unionized, employees against the marshalled authority and intimidating power of company agents. At a point of contentious labor relations, in early 1943, SPRR detectives tried to leverage these workingmen for information, but they encountered stubborn resistance. Eleven men worked on the dining crew assigned to Dining Car 10110 on the evening of 22 January, and they, with their interrogators, produced a set of negotiated narratives that describe only fragments of their experiences. The written records of those narratives were, in most cases, statements that each man signed. In several cases, they retained signed copies, demonstrating they lacked trust that railway agents would accurately report their statements. Each man spoke from a different position of power, by comparison with their inquisitors, who were uniformly small groups of White men in positions of power. Company detectives conducted interviews in official spaces that enhanced their authority. In those offices, mostly at Union Station in

SPR dining car workers (above, left) load supplies from handcart into a dining car. At right, SPR dining car workers load supplies from commissary onto handtruck for delivery to a dining car. Original photos from the SPR collection at the CSRM Library and Archives. Images courtesy the California State Railroad Museum.

Portland, SPRR agents posed questions to isolated men of color—employees who lacked personal or professional security, and who answered questions while confined in spaces from which they were normally excluded.

Speaking to men they did not know, in unfamiliar rooms, and from positions of deference and discomfort, the men investigators interviewed said as little as possible, and explained even less. Their interrogators disassembled each man's story, isolated small details from surrounding context, and reconstructed them into new and imagined narratives. Then the interrogators confronted each person they interviewed with statements they asserted were "facts" and insisted each witness explain why his story differed from those supposed facts. In this way, company investigators shaped the story each person told. The subjects of their inquiry mostly responded by rejecting the stories their interrogators presented without fully providing alternative explanations. They deployed silence and vagueness as tools of resistance. Assembled below is one interpretation of the combined written record of these various interrogation sessions. It is important to consider, while reading this account, that the written statements represented here are mere traces of the physical and verbal confrontations by which authority figures attempted to intimidate relatively powerless working people.

Each member of the eleven-man crew offered a slightly different timeline for when they arrived in Portland the afternoon of 22 January, but they generally agreed it was somewhere after 2:00 p.m. when supervisors released them with instructions to report back by 7:30 p.m. Train 15 was scheduled to leave Portland at 10:00 p.m., and the company required a loading crew at the commissary two and a half hours before departure time to pick up supplies and load them into the diner. Other members of the crew not assigned that duty were supposed to report back half an hour before departure time. Most of them met that schedule, even though the train was delayed for more than three hours. Number 2 Waiter Benjamin Russell Johnson, a twenty-three-year veteran of the railroad, was the only man who stayed aboard the diner after everyone else left, riding it up to the yards and staying with it until it was retrieved and brought up to the depot around 7:00 p.m. He later explained he and Pantryman Edward Smith began stocking the car on schedule—at about 7:30 p.m.—with some help from Chef Baker. Second Cook Robert Folkes, according to Johnson, later joined them and helped stock the car, working mostly in the kitchen out of sight of others in the car.[3] Johnson's experience, however, was unique.

Everyone else in the eleven-man dining crew left the train yard shortly after 2:00 p.m. and delayed their return to the dining car as late as possible, stretching as much unsupervised time into their layover as possible. At liberty in a city at the far reaches of their "away" life, each man sought a temporary refuge where he could rest safely in relative ease. With two exceptions, none of them had any long-term ties in Portland. Most headed over to the neighborhood near Interstate and Albina, across the Willamette River northeast from Union Station. In that area, the Medley Hotel catered to railroad men on short-term layover, and a community of casual acquaintance congregated in its lobby.[4] John C. Logan, a forty-five-year-old native of Portland with fourteen years as an SPRR waiter, was one exception. His mother lived in the 2300 block of NE Rodney Avenue, so Logan spruced up at a barbershop on 6th Street, near the station, and then went to his mother's house, where he enjoyed a nap, dinner, and conversation before heading back to the depot around 8:50 p.m.[5] Another exception was Steward Charles Greenman—a White man for whom railroad life was relatively new. Greenman, who had served as steward only since September 1942, was a resident of Shasta, California, who briefly served as division timekeeper for SPRR's Shasta Division from 1909 to 1911. In a demonstration of the racialized boundaries that divided even congenial coworkers during their downtime, Greenman generally avoided the Medley, preferring to room in hotels that White passengers frequented. On 22 January, he took a room at the Hoyt Hotel for his five-hour planned layover. He spent the evening there with five air cadets and a married couple he described as "Mr. and Mrs. Zinni," first visiting in their room, then inviting them over to his room, and then heading downstairs with them for a dinner with the cadets, some of whom later accompanied them to the diner for an after-hours "party" that lasted until anywhere from 10:00 p.m. to nearly midnight, depending on who told the story.[6] Greenman and his "guests" arrived at the diner at about the same time as Logan, by most accounts, but what time the party ended was in considerably more dispute.[7]

The other seven crewmen all wound up at the Medley by meandering routes, most commonly via a stop at the Oyster House—a popular eatery near Burnside—then a nearby liquor store catering to people of color, and finally the hotel lobby. Once at the Medley, crewmembers had several options. Some, like Third Cook Sterling Bolton, found a comfortable seat in the lobby and chatted with friends. Others, like Elmer White—a married man with two children in Los Angeles—accompanied Bolton on his circuitous route to the Medley and then spent the next five hours in the lobby, chatting with Bolton and Folkes, and finally the "colored girl" at the front desk who sat with them in the lobby when things were quiet. Around 9:30 that evening, White headed back to the dining car, alone. When he arrived there (around 10:00 p.m.), he found the steward's party clustered around a table at the head of the diner. Asked later whether the couple that Greenman referred to as "Mr. and Mrs. Zinni" might have been Mr. and Mrs. Keaton, from Tourist Car D, White replied, "It might have been."[8]

The Medley Hotel was clearly the center of their "away" life in Portland for Southern Pacific dining crews. Even Chef Clermont Baker, a White man, headed down to the Medley, where he briefly mingled, somewhat awkwardly, with his Black crew. He recalled that Folkes approached him in the lobby that evening to remind him they had to head back to stock the car at 7:30, but Baker told his second cook the car was delayed several hours. At that news, according to Baker, Folkes responded he would head down early to load the hand truck and wait for the dining car. Baker remained at the Medley until shortly before 9:00 p.m., when he headed back to the station, arriving to find Folkes asleep in the annex. The chef claimed he tried, futilely, to waken Folkes, then stepped over him and went on to stock the car alone, not mentioning any assistance from other crewmembers (this conflicts with every other account). Baker claimed he finished at 10:30 p.m. and went to bed.[9] The chef made no mention of the steward or his party, of Johnson's presence in the car, or of his assistance in stocking the diner, and his story varied wildly from other accounts on many other details.

Unlike Baker's account, which is largely uncorroborated, the stories of Bolton and White meshed closely with Johnson's account, and with the stories of Edward "Sarge" Smith, Ralph Hickman, and Elmer Devereaux, all Black waiters who had worked together for a number of years before that night. Smith, a forty-five-year-old waiter with twenty-two years of experience with the SPRR, served as "pantryman," and he was responsible for helping stock the diner. He, Devereaux, and Hickman headed down to a nearby fish market when the train first pulled in that afternoon, and they each purchased two quarts of oysters plus a couple bottles of whiskey, taking the oysters back to the car, then heading over to the Medley with the whiskey. They took a room together, lounged on the bed and chairs, drank whiskey, and napped until 6:30 p.m., when Smith headed downstairs to the lobby, planning to head over to the commissary. After chatting briefly with Folkes at the corner of Albina and Interstate, Smith recalled, they both caught the bus to Union Station and walked together from there to the commissary. Smith reported to the commissary at 7:00 p.m., three hours before the train was scheduled to leave, and about half an hour before he was required to be there, but he discovered the diner not yet returned from the yards and the train likely delayed up to three additional hours. He recalled that when the dining car did come up, about a half hour later, he went back to the commissary, "pulled the [hand] truck back up," and met Russell Johnson and Chef Baker. Together, they went back to the diner and stocked the car, finishing their work by about 10:00 p.m. Smith recalled that although they were initially the only ones there, Folkes worked in the kitchen while they stocked the car.[10]

Devereaux, a thirty-five-year-old waiter with five years of experience on SPRR dining cars, challenged the steward's claim that the party ended early that evening, and other waiters seemed to support his recollection. They mostly agreed that Devereaux got back to the car about the time the steward arrived with "a lady and two men." Devereaux added that after he and Hickman got back to the diner at 9:30 p.m., the steward's "party" came in "about 10:00," when he was already in bed.[11] Smith claimed he went to bed around 11:00 p.m. in a berth immediately adjacent to the steward's party. He later recalled that Elmer White woke him about 2:00 a.m., looking for keys to the diner.[12] White, the forty-two-year-old lead waiter and a nine-year veteran with the SPRR, later admitted that when he arrived at 10:00 p.m. he was the last of the crew to report back, which he could tell because "all of the curtains were up, and each fellow makes up his own bed and puts up his curtains," and he noticed the steward's party already there, noting they left after about another hour, and, he said, "I was the last man he [the steward] talked to before he went to bed."[13]

Hickman's story generally confirmed, despite some differences in chronology, Smith's narrative of the oysters, whiskey, and crash party at the Medley with the three of them, including Devereaux. He recalled going out with Devereaux for Chinese food after Smith woke up and headed down to the station at 7:30 p.m. He claimed, however, that after dinner, the two waiters reported back to the dining car around 8:55 p.m., finding Smith and "the old man, Russell Johnson," stocking the car. He and Devereaux loaded oranges and grapefruit on the car for Johnson, then "put the tables in place and I got our beds out of the hole." Hickman claimed he went to bed about 9:55 p.m. He heard the steward walking down the aisle talking to some people sometime after 10:00 p.m. but didn't see them. Later, he heard the steward call, "Robert, I'm hungry," and "Robert [Folkes] said he could fix him some sandwiches." Hickman recalled that "Old man Russell [Johnson] told the Steward to keep quiet so we could sleep too." He said (1 February statement) that he also heard someone in the car (apparently one of the other waiters) say, "White, shut up." Using the plural, Hickman recalled, "We said we wanted to sleep. They [the steward and his party] were talking loud and we were very sleepy, and it sounded like they said, 'White, shut up.'" Later he said (1 February statement) that after the party left, he was awakened when he heard Elmer White and the steward talking: "They said, 'The train will be going pretty soon' and I said, 'I will be glad when it does.'"[14]

Booker T. Johnson, the thirty-three-year-old waiter number 5, who had worked for the SPRR since 1930, confirmed the late hour of the party and added details that suggested the Jameses and Keatons possibly participated. Taking a somewhat different route to the dining car through the segregated nightlife of Portland, Johnson first went from the station up the street to "Fosters," "a colored restaurant on 6th street." Then he walked to the liquor store, bought a pint of whiskey, and then walked to "a lady friend's house" on the east side, on the corner of 49th Avenue and Powell, stopping to shop along the way (a turkey, some fish, and some bacon), arriving at her house around 6:00 p.m. He stayed there for dinner but left "kind of early" because he was concerned buses would be delayed by the snowstorm. He arrived back at the diner around 9:30 p.m., boarded the car, and put his groceries in the icebox in the kitchen, where he had "a few words" with Folkes, whom he found working there. Then he helped stock the car and went to bed about 10:45 p.m., but he lay awake for a while, smoking cigarettes. He noticed there were two "fliers . . . officers and two ladies with them." In his earlier statement (1 February), Johnson noted these were "very nice people. They tipped very well and were very very nice people and naturally when tips are your business you like that kind of people."[15]

John C. Logan, waiter number 4 and a fourteen-year veteran with the Southern Pacific, also contradicted the claims of both the chef and the steward, further complicating the chronology of events. Logan was a long-term, experienced employee who had worked with Chef Aaron and Russell Johnson for the previous three years. When he headed back to the diner from his mother's place in northeast Portland, arriving at the depot at 8:50 p.m., he passed Johnson on the platform, headed toward the station from the commissary. On the car, around 9:00 p.m., he found Smith, Devereaux, and "two or three of the cooks . . . in the kitchen," including Folkes. Logan noticed, by 9:10 p.m., that the steward was already up in front with a party of three or four guests. His (1 February) statement noted they were seated around a "big table," and he stressed that, with the other beds all made up, the party could only be seen by walking up there, past all the berth curtains. He saw Robert Folkes walk by "about 9:30" with a tray of sandwiches. Logan got up "about 10:00" and went into the pantry, where he worked "alone all the time" preparing and squeezing the oranges and grapefruit and preparing salad bowls. At about 1:00 a.m. he headed up to the first car ahead of the diner (Tourist Car D) to use the restroom. By that time, he said, the diner was dark, all the berth curtains set up, with no one else awake except the porter, who told him to wait until the train pulled out. He waited until 1:45 a.m. and then went forward to use the lavatory in Car D, where he met a White middle-aged man, about thirty-five or forty, near the corner of the smoking room. In the lavatory, he found Porter Shaw with "a Marine." Logan returned to the diner by 1:50 a.m. and fell asleep by 2:30.[16]

All these accounts, collectively, raised problems for the chef and steward, who were obviously evasive and misleading in their statements. Given all the witnesses involved, even the steward had to admit he violated company rules by allowing a private party in the diner and providing them with drinks and sandwiches from company resources. The chef, if he was on board during the party, was accountable for this misuse of company resources, and all accounts except his own placed him in the kitchen with Folkes when the second cook prepared sandwiches. Investigators especially focused on whether the steward's party consumed whiskey, who supplied it, and whether they were reimbursed for doing so.

Company investigators clearly used the murder investigation as a pretext for pursuing their primary mission: surveillance of dining car workers whom they suspected of selling company resources on the sly. SPRR detectives reminded Steward Greenman that he had been instructed not to serve any complimentary meals, but Greenman admitted Folkes served six turkey sandwiches to his party, even though the steward *claimed* he told the second cook not to do so. The steward also adamantly denied serving any drinks, claiming Folkes and one of the waiters simply donated their own whiskey to the party. Greenman was questioned closely about whether he actually had drinks in mixed company with two White couples, other military personnel, and "colored members of [his] crew? That is, they actually mixed at this so-called 'steward's party'?" But Greenman avoided the racial "mingling question," emphasizing that detectives overstated the number of drinks Folkes had taken, noting, "I would not allow that familiarity," and later stressing, "He [Folkes] seemed to me as innocent as a newborn babe."[17]

Greenman's account of his "party" emphasized the notion that his crew volunteered their time, services, and supplies to his guests, suggesting that his lapse was only in allowing the servicemen and their wives to come in out of the bitter cold and in not being more assertive in insisting his waiters and cooks refuse them hospitality. He admitted taking the party to two small tables near the front of the diner, next to Johnson's berth, where he had Folkes serve turkey sandwiches, and he claimed "Mr. Kirkland," one of the "flier cadets," shared a half pint of whiskey. Greenman claimed White also gave Kirkland his own bottle. The steward claimed his guests left by 10:00 p.m., after staying only about fifteen minutes, and that Greenman then talked with White for about fifteen minutes,[18] until around 10:30 or 11:00 p.m. Sometime after 11:00, Greenman said he headed back to Porter Scurry's Pullman Car 60 to use the lavatory and sat and talked with him for fifteen minutes, going to bed around 11:15 p.m. and sleeping until he awoke around 5:45 a.m.[19]

The eleventh man on the diner that night was Robert Folkes, the second cook whose activities and demeanor on the morning of 23 January, from all accounts of his coworkers, seemed perfectly normal for a man responsible for making watch on a train bulging at the seams with civilian passengers, military personnel, and crew. Most crewmen woke between 4:30 and 5:30 a.m.

to find they had travelled only seventy miles in the seven hours since their train was supposed to have left Portland. They found Folkes exactly where they expected to find the second cook on a bitterly cold, snow-filled morning—in the diner kitchen, serving hot coffee, muffins, and hot cereal. In the blacked-out darkness of predawn on that January day in the second winter of the war, the kitchen was an island of wood-fired warmth, with smells of coffee, baked goods, and sizzling pans as Folkes fried up eggs, bacon, and other short-order breakfast items. Pullman porters, brakemen, conductors, and dining car workers stopped by the kitchen for their first cup of morning coffee, a muffin, or a hot bowl of cereal to start the day. They all recalled, later, the familiar smiling face of Robert Folkes, perfectly calm, efficiently working, busily preparing meat and stock pots for the noonday meal as they chatted with each other in the doorway to the diner.

Without exception, when investigators asked each of the ten men working with Folkes on that diner whether they suspected him of murder, they expressed complete disbelief, often stoutly defending him. Those who knew him best and longest were most supportive in their comments, but even the two White men—Chef Baker and Steward Greenman—the two relative newcomers jointly responsible for managing the diner on the run from Portland to Los Angeles, refused numerous invitations to implicate Folkes. Detectives pressed the issue, misrepresenting earlier statements, claiming knowledge they did not have, pretending to hold evidence that did not exist, and threatening witnesses of color with imprisonment and the loss of their jobs for making allegedly false statements. In some cases, investigators implied other Black trainmen might be charged in place of Folkes unless they implicated him. Despite all that, those who worked most closely with Folkes, who knew him as a reliable, hardworking man, refused to turn against him. Some Black trainmen, however, did implicate the White steward and the White chef in violations of company policy and government regulations regulating alcohol sales, or at least they made statements dramatically contradicting the claims of those two White managers.

BRINGING BLACK WORKERS AND THEIR STORIES TO ALBANY

Black trainmen who moved relatively freely through the familiar landscapes of their "away" life in Portland lost that freedom during the legal proceedings at Albany in early spring 1943. Company officials and the Linn County district attorney's office colluded in controlling and restricting their movements throughout the trial. Trainmen, however, resisted those efforts and asserted, by direct action, their rights to freedom of association and mobility. They demanded fair treatment, housing, and compensation similar to what Weinrick provided White witnesses. As reporters focused on the courtroom melodrama targeting Folkes, Black trainmen with bit parts in those proceedings struggled to free themselves from the controlling authority of company handlers in Albany. They turned for support first to union representatives and then to the Portland civil rights community. They also appealed directly to the Linn County sheriff's office and the Oregon State Police. Their efforts helped link the Folkes case to broader civil rights efforts that outlived the trial and the man it targeted.

Before and during the trial, African Americans who travelled to Albany as witnesses or observers entered a landscape of prejudice that extended far beyond the trial venue. Investigators, who were all White men, treated Black trainmen with suspicion, claiming their testimony was tainted by "race solidarity," and they treated them differently from White trainmen. The privilege of a subpoena was one of the most important points of discrimination in the period leading up to the trial. Prosecutors issued official subpoenas for White witnesses, but they worked informally through the railroad to compel the presence and testimony of Black trainmen. Subpoenaed witnesses qualified for county-funded compensation for their meals and lodging, plus a daily stipend for their time. In most cases, the prosecutor's office required only very informal statements of expenditures before authorizing a check drawn on county funds. The informal process prosecutors adopted for securing testimony from Black trainmen, however, offered no such compensation, and it functionally imprisoned those witnesses, limited their mobility, and deprived them of wage-earning work while forcing them to pay the costs of food and shelter in Albany out of their own pockets. Given these conditions, Black trainmen only reluctantly left the familiar landscapes of Portland's central train district for the uninviting environment in Albany. Prosecutors viewed them as hostile but necessary witnesses in their case against Folkes, and local residents treated them as reviled curiosities in a town with segregationist policies and practices.

Linn County district attorney Harlow Weinrick collaborated with SPRR company officials and Pullman Palace Car (PPC) company agents in controlling and interrogating Black trainmen whom they considered pertinent to the case against Folkes. In February 1943, as Weinrick built his case for seeking the death penalty, SPRR and PPC agents collaborated with police investigators, bringing to Albany certain trainmen who worked on Train 15 the night of the murder. The PPC assigned District Claim Agent M. K. Sheehan to Albany for the duration of the investigation and trial, and Sheehan arranged accommodations for porters held there as witnesses for the trial. SPRR representatives were technically responsible for making similar arrangements for the dining car waiters and cooks Weinrick called as witnesses, but since those were also African American men, Sheehan's reports regarding the Pullman porters also described the situation for other Black trainmen in Albany.[20] Weinrick and company agents, in other words, classified witnesses by race and only secondarily by company or significance to the case.

In the weeks preceding the trial, Black trainmen whom prosecutors and defense attorneys planned to call as witnesses—first before the grand jury and later during the criminal trial—clearly wanted to stay in Portland with day-trip commutes to Albany on the days they actually served as witnesses. In Portland, they could freely circulate in centers of African American community, where they would more likely find welcoming refuge, such as the Medley. Union Station, in Portland, was the central hub of the away-life community for Black trainmen, and they clearly preferred to stay there during the trial.

Contrary to the interests and preferences of Black trainmen, prosecutors and railway agents preferred to isolate them in the hostile, racially exclusive environs of Albany, where company managers could more easily monitor and control them. Sheehan brought three Pullman Company employees to Albany for grand jury proceedings beginning 18 February, including Pullman Conductor J. A. Bryant (a White man) and Porters Hughes and N. L. Shaw (both Black men). He collaborated with Weinrick and special agents from the SPRR.[21] Early in the investigation, Sheehan reported difficulty securing housing in Albany for the company's porters, noting that "even some of the S.P. men who are well known here could not get accommodations at the hotels." As one possible solution, he suggested the company park a Pullman sleeping car in the Albany train yard, claiming it was too difficult to arrange daily transportation to and from Portland.[22] He did not explain why regular train service would not suffice for that purpose.

The same positions of employment that secured Black trainmen status and prestige within the African American community of South Central before the war became virtual prisons of forced labor during the period of wartime mobilization.[23] Sentiments toward these railroad men turned especially ugly in Albany after January 1943,[24] when Weinrick threatened to arrest and jail the entire dining crew unless SPRR officials agreed to "retain" them "in service" through the trial. SPRR authorities agreed to those terms, without consulting the men involved, and coordinated a similar agreement with PPC company officials regarding Hughes and Shaw. For the duration of the trial, the status of these Black trainmen dramatically declined. Previously, they were company employees with significant autonomy and authority managing affairs on railcars where they were assigned. During the trial, they became company dependents trapped in a perverse version of their "away" lives for the duration of those legal proceedings. Deprived of the personal freedoms and unfettered mobility they enjoyed during layovers in Portland, they found themselves under Sheehan's constant supervision. They entered a state of limbo from early February through late April 1943.[25]

Under conditions of threatened imprisonment and de facto forced employment, railroad men who had worked closely with Folkes on Train 15 returned, under escort, to Albany. By the time they arrived in Albany, local newspapers were filled with stories that Folkes had been charged with murder and had supposedly "confessed" to authorities in Los Angeles and in Linn County.[26] Sheehan and Bryant, both White men, officially "escorted" Hughes and Shaw, both Black porters, to Albany for grand jury hearings on 18 February 1943. Sheehan secured reserved berths for himself and Bryant for the round-trip commute that day, while Hughes and Shaw travelled "in regular line," meaning they were required to report for duty, serving as porters on Pullman cars travelling between Portland and Albany.[27]

The grand jury indicted Folkes, on 18 February, for first degree murder, after hearing testimony from the Eugene City coroner (Poole), the bereaved husband (James), passengers Connor and Wilson ("the Marine"), porters Shaw and Hughes, Pullman Conductor Bryant, Train Conductor Banks, OSP pathologist Beeman, and Sisemore. In addition to these witnesses, Weinrick informed Pullman officials he would also require Pullman Tourist Car 4001 (Car D—the so-called murder car), along with porters Scurry and Sibley, in Albany for the trial, and that he expected the company would arrange their presence. When Bryant, Shaw, and Hughes returned with Sheehan to Portland on the 9:45 p.m. train the day of the grand jury hearing, [28] they demonstrated that, contrary to Sheehan's claims, it was entirely possible for Black trainmen to participate in the Albany trial as day commuters from Portland.

Sheehan later explained he travelled with Bryant, Hughes, and Shaw as day commuters to the grand jury proceedings only because he was unable to find overnight accommodations in Albany for "our colored porters." He requested help from SPRR officials, asking whether they had any ideas about how to house "the colored dining car men" whom Weinrick also planned to call as witnesses. By early March, however, more than a full month after the murder, neither Pullman company officials nor representatives of the SPRR had any ideas about how to procure housing for Black trainmen in a town where hotels refused them overnight accommodations.[29]

The problem, Sheehan claimed, was that hotel proprietors in Albany "felt it would be rather dangerous to attempt to accept negroes" into their hotels. Sheehan reported that the Albany Hotel and the St. James Hotel both "declined to accept them" and that the only other hotel in town, the Vanderan, advised they would "probably not have room for them at the time of the trial," even though they usually "catered to railroad people." Sheehan noted that the proprietor of the St. James was especially concerned about the fact that, due to the proximity of Camp Adair, a major military cantonment between Albany and Monmouth, many White servicemen from Texas, and their wives, would frequent his hotel during the trial. Sheehan suggested the PPC should "spot" a sleeper car in Albany for use by the SPRR dining car crew and the Pullman porters. By contrast, he casually noted that with regard to the company's White employees whom Weinrick also required in Albany as witnesses, "We can obtain rooms for them."[30]

A number of the Black trainmen were apparently radicalized by their treatment in Albany. Porter Hughes led several coworkers in a campaign of resistance, challenging the company's assertions it could control and restrict the off-duty activities of its employees. Hughes, who had first consulted with the home office of the Brotherhood of Sleeping Car Porters, of which he was a member, informed company handlers that only the sheriff's office could wield that authority, and then only with a properly served subpoena. Beyond that legal argument, Hughes also criticized the PPC for treating its Black porters differently than its White conductor (Bryant). This approach apparently surprised Sheehan, who reported "considerable discontent on the part of the employees," noting that Hughes was especially concerned that the company required him and Shaw to work their way to Portland, whereas the company forwarded Bryant to and from Albany on a free pass. Hughes argued, to Sheehan, that the state of Oregon, rather than the Pullman Company, should have paid his mileage and housing expenses, and he pointed out that, due to the murder, he and his fellow porters were "losing money by having to appear as witnesses and not being paid for what they would have earned had it not occurred."[31]

Hughes and other Black trainmen also resisted company efforts to control and manage the content of their testimony before the grand jury and at trial. Beyond discriminating in their treatment of employees called as witnesses, depending on whether they were White or Black, and limiting the free mobility of their African American employees in Albany, PPC officials used their influence to prevent porters from talking about the case with attorneys representing Folkes. This became an issue when official court records revealed Hughes' presence in Albany, showing he had testified before the grand jury. That news attracted the attention of Leroy Lomax, the Portland-area trial lawyer representing Folkes in Oregon, and he attempted to contact Hughes, seeking to depose him on what he witnessed as porter in the murder car. Hughes, as required by company policy, notified PPC officials on 10 March that Lomax had contacted him, asking to meet in Portland. Sheehan and PPC representative C. M. Fitzgerald, upon learning of that request, instructed Hughes not to acknowledge it, "and to disregard it completely."[32]

Hughes and the other Black trainmen initially abided by company policy and effectively stonewalled Folkes' lawyer, but their growing discontent with unfair treatment broke into the open in March 1943. The tipping point came when Weinrick proposed, as a cost-cutting solution, that Tourist Car 4001 (Car D) be returned to a siding near the Albany depot, where it could be used for housing the porters and also be available for showing jurors the murder scene. The idea actually originated with Sheehan, who previously mentioned this possible "solution" to the "problem" of housing Black trainmen in a city where local hotels refused to rent rooms to customers who were not White. PPC managers had already run Car 4001 through company shops for cleaning, refitting and redesignating it Tourist Car 4294, shortly after Beeman's official inspection in late January. Weinrick now insisted the company not only send the car back to Albany but also reassign it the "4001" designation that it carried the night of the murder, because (according to Sheehan), "he [Weinrick] felt that it would be of greater psychological value [in terms of influencing jurors to convict Folkes] if the car was numbered as it was at the time of the murder." Sheehan's subsequent efforts to track down Tourist Car 4294, however, revealed it had been shunted around the country, from Seattle to Middleton, Tennessee, and from there to Yuma, Arizona, and thence to

San Luis Obispo, California. SPRR officials observed that, although they initially had operated PPC Car 4294 in "local service, . . . anticipating just such
a request as this," the company had later withdrawn the car from regular line
operations for "emergency" military service.[33]

In the melodrama that Weinrick intended to stage for the circuit court
when Folkes came to trial, the DA planned to reassemble in the Albany yards
a mini-train consisting of only Car D and Dining Car 10110 and then lead
jurors through that pretended "reconstruction" of the scene of the crime.
Jurors would tour only those two cars, presented as if they were simply unbiased physical evidence. Without the other nine cars that originally made up
Train 15, however, leading jurors through just the diner and Car D would
indelibly link Folkes' workplace with the crime, while encouraging jurors to
forget that some three hundred people aboard that train had access to Car
D on the night of 22–23 January. Pullman Cars E and 60, for example, were
each filled with nearly forty people the night of the murder, all in close proximity to Car D. Passengers in those Pullman cars, like those in Car D, could
easily move around without attracting the attention a uniformed dining car
worker would attract in the aisle of a sleeper car. In staging Car D and Dining
Car 10110 together, Weinrick was not simply presenting jurors with "physical
evidence" of "the crime scene." Instead, he edited the crime scene to suggest
that Dining Car 10110, but not Car 60, Car E, or any other except Car D, was
connected to the murder. That edit decided Folkes' fate.

In a public-private conspiracy to discriminate against and control Black
trainmen, SPRR and PPC agents collaborated with prosecutors to withhold
evidence and imaginatively restage Car D and Dining Car 10110 as if they
were "the crime scene" and (in Sheehan's words) to maximize their "psychological effect" on jurors. This corporate-government collusion encouraged
jurors to look past facts and act, instead, on prejudice. SPRR agent O'Connell
and Weinrick urged PPC officials to present Car 4001 for this purpose, and
they also proposed using it as sleeping quarters for all Black trainmen the DA
called to testify at the trial—porters and dining car workers. In response to
PPC inquiries regarding compensation for their Black employees, Weinrick
replied that "all he could pay these witnesses was $2.00 a day" and he hoped
the PPC and SPRR companies would cover any additional expenses beyond
that amount.[34]

All parties involved in the investigation stonewalled requests from defense
lawyers for access to trainmen involved in the inquiry. In response to repeated

requests from Lomax to meet with Porter Hughes, Sheehan falsely stated he "did not know whether Mr. Hughes was in town and that he [Hughes] . . . did not report at the office when in town as he knew his regular assignment and reported direct to the car." Sheehan also learned from attorneys for the SPRR that Lomax had requested a passenger list, but that "District Attorney Weinrick did not look with favor upon furnishing this information."[35] In this exchange of letters (copied to colleagues with the PPC and SPRR), corporate officials documented Weinrick's active campaign to prevent defense attorneys from acquiring names or statements from passengers or crew who might have challenged the case he was weaving against Folkes.

Asserting physical control over the trainmen was part of a larger scheme to manage the flow of information and to support company efforts to control its workforce. As part of his efforts to suppress evidence and misrepresent the murder scene, Weinrick also urged company officials to strictly limit the individual liberty of Black trainmen in Albany. Sheehan reported that he "gathered the impression, when Mr. Weinrick was here, that he would like both Pullman employees and S.P. employees to stay as near to the station as possible and to go up town only when necessary." By that point, SPRR officials had already agreed to Weinrick's terms for housing dining car workers in railcars.[36]

Porters Hughes and Scurry understood the public-private collusion to restrict their mobility without a subpoena as an unfair labor practice and infringement of their civil rights. They refused to surrender their personal time to either PPC agents or Weinrick, and they asserted their rights to fair accommodations and per diem pay for the time they spent in Albany. They began with deferential excuses but escalated their resistance to direct confrontation and then preemptive action. Hughes met with Sheehan in Portland during the first week of April, asking whether the PPC agent had "rented a house for us." When Sheehan told Hughes he had arranged to house the porters in the restaged Car D, the porter's initial response was simply that "it must be filthy and probably stinks." When Sheehan countered that Car 4001 had "been shopped and had been in service and it was clean," Hughes informed Sheehan that he and Porter Shaw had spoken with "a colored man" in Albany who indicated he might be able to arrange local housing for them.[37] Both porters refused to spend even a single night in the murder car, insisting the company either house them in a hotel or return them to Portland. Sheehan eventually reported to superiors that he had located accommodations for the porters at an "auto court" (motel) near the outskirts of Albany, but he insisted the porters would have to assume a portion of the cost.[38] This report misrepresented Sheehan's negotiations with the porters, who, in fact, made those arrangements independently and then insisted Sheehan compensate them with PPC funds.

Negotiating a solution to the housing "problem" involved a two-pronged approach, in which Black trainmen deployed deferential strategies of passive resistance alongside more confrontational, activist responses. The porters mostly avoided directly confronting Sheehan, instead focusing criticism on Weinrick. They allowed Sheehan the pretense that he was not responsible. Instead, they questioned Weinrick's motives. Hughes asked Sheehan, for example, why Weinrick had not directly subpoenaed the porters. He noted that, while in Los Angeles, he had personally contacted the DA to ask when he would be needed as a witness in Albany, but Weinrick had not responded. Hughes questioned why Weinrick only communicated with Black trainmen through company officials (e.g., Sheehan), while he communicated directly with White witnesses. Shaw asked Sheehan why Weinrick managed to secure rooms for all the other (White) witnesses, but not for the (Black) porters or dining crew, noting prosecutors had more than six weeks to prepare for their arrival. Sheehan claimed, in his report to company superiors, "I tried to reason with Shaw but he was convinced that they were being discriminated against even by the District Attorney." Worker discontent spread quickly to include Porters Sibley and Scurry. Scurry, for example, announced he would return to Portland if there were no Albany accommodations other than a Pullman car.[39]

Sheehan clearly sympathized with the company line and attempted to assert authority over the porters, but he also wanted to avoid bad publicity and, for that reason, tried to work out a compromise with Weinrick. In his correspondence with superiors, Sheehan expressed frustration and surprise that the porters adamantly refused to sleep in the murder car. In his negotiations with porters, Sheehan attempted to deflect criticism from the responsible person (Weinrick) to the more abstract and unchangeable "conditions in the town [Albany]"—by which he clearly meant presumably racist local residents. Finally, he tried to divert porters with a promise of a "fee" of two dollars per day, plus a "bonus" at trial's end.[40]

The four porters (Sibley, Hughes, Shaw, and Scurry), at some point in their negotiations with Sheehan, sought support from the Brotherhood of Sleeping Car Porters (BSCP), including legal advice on procedures, under

Oregon law, for subpoenaing out-of-state witnesses. Scurry telegrammed the BSCP, seeking guidance. Sibley, meanwhile, pressured Sheehan, first indicating he was willing to sleep in the murder car, but when Sheehan expressed his appreciation for the porter's "cooperative" attitude, Sibley dropped the other shoe: "as soon as they were served with subpoenas he would go on out to the car." The sticking point, Sheehan reported, was Weinrick's failure to issue subpoenas directly to the Black trainmen. Although the porters, according to Sheehan, interpreted that failing as calling into question whether they would in fact be paid, they were also challenging the discriminatory treatment of Black trainmen. Sheehan, consequently, promised to have Weinrick individually subpoena the porters.[41]

Sheehan's efforts to follow up on that pledge revealed that Weinrick's refusal to issue subpoenas to Black trainmen was part of a larger plan to hide witnesses from defense counsel. Weinrick used the PPC agent's authority over the porters to manipulate and control their movements, to isolate them from the venue of the trial, and to sidestep legal requirements under Oregon law that he comply with discovery requests from the defense. In response to Sheehan's request, the DA first made a show of drafting subpoenas in Sheehan's presence, promising to have them signed by the court. Sheehan reported to the porters that subpoenas were "on the way," but they refused to budge until subpoenas were actually served. Later that day, Sheehan again approached Weinrick, warning that the porters were threatening to leave Albany and return to Portland, and he asked why the papers had not been delivered. In response, Weinrick revealed his purpose in working through the company rather than issuing individual subpoenas: implying that he had never intended to ask the court for the signatures, "he explained they did not wish to reveal to the defense the witnesses they intended to call, but the men [meaning Black trainmen] could be assured they would be paid. Mr. Sisemore then accompanied me to the men and explained it to them and they seemed satisfied *on that one point* [emphasis added]."[42] By this account, Sisemore, the Klamath County DA, apparently colluded with Weinrick to avoid standard requirements of discovery and fair disclosure.

The porters had not been subpoenaed and so might easily have returned to Portland without testifying, since there was no court order requiring them to appear, but Weinrick and Sisemore banked on the coercive authority the PPC management wielded over its porters. They worked with SPRR and PPC officials to arrange a virtual imprisonment of African American witnesses in two railcars hidden from view in a small roundhouse behind the rail yard: the renamed Car 4001 and Dining Car 10110, hitched together as sleeping, cooking, and living quarters—a self-contained holding-cell-on-wheels. Both cars were inside the Albany roundhouse, with steam lines and electricity hookups for warmth and light. After Sisemore assured the porters they would be paid, Sheehan was under the mistaken impression that the only remaining hitch was the matter of bathing facilities (there were no showers or bathtubs in either car). He tried to arrange for the men to bathe in the gym showers at the nearby Moose Temple but reported that members of the Moose Lodge refused to allow Black trainmen access. Hughes, meanwhile, independently contacted OSP lieutenant Howard, asking him "to see if he could not locate an Auto Court."[43]

In thwarting the designs of the district attorney, the PPC, and the SPRR, Hughes demonstrated the independent problem-solving skills, self-assuredness, and proud professionalism for which Pullman porters were known. He bypassed company handlers and county officials, engaging directly with state authorities to secure housing for himself and his fellow porters. Acting with the assistance of Howard, Porter Hughes (not Sheehan) located two cabins at the Albany Motel, about one mile beyond the roundhouse and even farther from downtown. The proprietor of the semirural motel was willing to house the four African American men for the duration of the trial at the rate of four dollars each per day—roughly what Weinrick authorized for White witnesses at hotels nearer downtown. Howard also informed the porters that the DA would pick up the tab for the motel. Sheehan found himself outmaneuvered and he felt obliged to apologize to Weinrick and Howard "for the trouble our employees had given them." He discovered, however, that Weinrick had other priorities: "Mr. Weinrick and Mr. Howard . . . both said that it was alright as the main thing was to keep them happy in as much as the defendant is of their race."[44] The new arrangements, of course, also conveniently removed the witnesses farther from downtown.

RACE SOLIDARITY AND THE ALBANY EXPERIENCE

Concerns about race solidarity extended beyond the context of the trial and permeated "away" life for Pullman porters and dining crews. As they passed through towns and cities en route from their home terminal to their destination and back again, Black trainmen met and nurtured relations with friendly faces, seeking sources of refuge and assistance for those inopportune times when later circumstances might strand them in an unfamiliar community.

Albany, Oregon, according to the census of 1940, had only one Negro man, R. H. Hale, who, with his wife, operated a shoe-shine parlor near the courthouse. Hale's shop offered both refuge and interim employment for Pullman porters and other Black trainmen stranded in Albany during the trial. The congregation of African Americans in Hale's shop also brought them into contact with other principals in the trial and aroused the suspicions of prosecutors and company agents. Secure in the knowledge that they were a dominant majority, White men who wielded unquestioned power in Albany closed ranks against the despised, miniscule minority of Black trainmen, while castigating those virtually powerless workers for their presumptuous "race solidarity."

The small-town setting of the trial in Albany brought prosecutors, witnesses, and the families of victims and the accused into uncomfortably close quarters, increasing the potential for friction and conflict. During a noon recess in the first week of the trial, for example, Sheehan encountered Clara and Jessie Folkes while he was "walking down the street" ahead of a party of railroad men, including himself, Bryant, and Hodges (all White men), along with Hughes (a Black man). Hughes, he noted, "made a great show of joining them [the two women] and proceeding along the street with them. It was obviously an act of defiance on his part and I have not given him the satisfaction of commenting on it." On Saturday evening, later that week, Sheehan encountered Weinrick, Sisemore, and their wives walking downtown with an SPRR agent, William Stone. In this chance meeting, Sheehan learned that Stone and Hodges (another SPRR colleague) went into Hale's shop for a shoe-shine and found Hughes and Scurry working there. Hughes explained he was "the kind of fellow that had to keep busy . . . especially when they had to pay $4.00 for their rooms at the Motel" (although the sheriff had agreed to pick up the tab, he indicated he would reimburse them only after the trial—just as he did with the White witnesses). Sheehan, who paid Hughes for his shoe-shine, protested that neither porter needed to work to get money, offering to supply funds "if they were short." Such funds, however, were an "advance" on their future wages,[45] subject to repayment, whereas Hughes and Shaw clearly hoped to earn money on days when the company required their presence for the trial but did not assign them a paying position.

Concerned that Hughes might be swayed in his testimony by "race solidarity," as evidenced by his openly consorting with Clara and Jessie Folkes, Weinrick and Sheehan took elaborate measures to ensure that only the porter's oral testimony, not his more detailed deposition, would enter the trial record. Sheehan claimed during the trial that Hughes "goes out of his way to be annoying," but he assured Weinrick that Hughes "would not let him down when he finally appears as a witness."[46]

Despite those assurances, Sheehan took extraordinary measures to conceal from the court any evidence that Black trainmen had previously provided written statements to private investigators or police. Throughout the early proceedings, defense attorney Lomax frequently claimed the DA was withholding evidence, including witness names and statements, but Weinrick steadfastly denied the existence of such evidence. At that point, Sheehan noted, "I took all the statements I had with me and mailed them to myself at Los Angeles, in order to say, if asked, that I did not have any statements." When Porter Hughes testified on 11 April, however, he confirmed that he made three prior signed statements: two en route to Los Angeles and one to the Pullman Company. In one of the most theatrical moments of the trial for the defense, Lomax asked Hughes if he had brought copies of any of those statements, to which the porter replied he had, and extracted them from the left pocket of his shirt.[47]

This incident galvanized Sheehan into action, and he complained to PPC superiors that Hughes obviously conspired with the defense attorney to undermine the prosecution, out of "race solidarity." Hughes testified that both stenographers who recorded his lengthy statements to the Pullman Company and to Weinrick had altered or otherwise failed to include significant parts of his testimony, including the fact that Wilson initially told him the assailant was a White man. Hughes claimed that when he asked for copies of his signed statements from police on the train, and from Sisemore, they refused to provide them, and for that reason he could only produce the copy of his statement to the Pullman Company. Most damagingly, Hughes testified that Sheehan told him, in Los Angeles, that he (Sheehan) would not provide to the defense attorney copies of any statements that Pullman Company employees had made because "the Pullman Company believes Folkes guilty."[48] In response to Weinrick's immediate objection, the trial judge ruled that comment "hearsay" and ordered it stricken from the record, but it survived in Sheehan's daily digest of trial proceedings.

The trial broke down the pretense of paternalistic concern behind which Sheehan had previously hidden his controlling impulses. Evident tension between Sheehan and his charges escalated during Hughes' testimony, and the PPC agent discussed with Weinrick the propriety of charging the porter with perjury. Pullman Conductor Bryant, a White trainman, however, reminded the DA and Sheehan that he supported Hughes' comments on many points that other White witnesses (Van Dyke, Conner, and Brakeman Anders) claimed to be false.[49] Faced with this multiracial criticism, which directly challenged the apparent race solidarity of those other White witnesses, Sheehan and Weinrick exhibited growing anger in their communications from this period of the trial. Tensions peaked when Hughes came dangerously close to exposing the shell game Weinrick and Sheehan had waged to conceal key pieces of evidence from Lomax. After Hughes revealed the copy of his statement, the DA and the PPC agent scrambled to reacquire complete copies of the other statements Sheehan had intentionally shipped to himself in Los Angeles earlier in the trial. SPRR agents assisted by providing their own copies to the prosecutor. The case, however, suddenly took a positive turn for the prosecution when Porter Shaw's courtroom testimony omitted his own recollection, as documented in an earlier signed statement, that Wilson initially claimed the assailant was a White man. Reassured by this omission, Weinrick asked Sheehan to again dispose of the copies they had just recovered from SPRR officials.[50] Two days later, however, under cross-examination by Lomax, Shaw dramatically produced a copy of his own written statement, just as Hughes had done, and he then reiterated his earlier statement that Wilson initially claimed he saw a White man fleeing the murder scene.[51] This embarrassing sequence, before the jury, should have discredited Weinrick's denial that his office was stonewalling discovery requests from the defense.

The trial highlighted the tense labor relations that divided PPC management and porters in the aftermath of the March on Washington Movement. At the end of each day of testimony, Sheehan checked on his charges, and Hughes apparently reveled in needling the company agent, taunting his handler with the apparently facetious claim that he was thinking of "taking a pass" to go up and work at a logging camp farther up the Santiam River. Sheehan reported that Hughes worked another side job as a taxi driver in Albany, reportedly earning nearly twenty-four dollars in tips on a single Sunday afternoon, largely from shuttling servicemen from Camp Adair around town in their search for drinks and other adult entertainment.[52]

The collusion of officials in both companies with local prosecutors in managing PPC porters and SPRR dining crews demonstrates how they controlled and manipulated their workforce during the war. Labor organizations like

Pollard's Dining Car Cooks and Waiters Union Local 582 struggled against those conditions in the militarized climate of the Second World War, initially adopting a "support the troops" stance and assuming high-visibility roles in war bond drives during 1942.[53] Labor tensions in Albany, as evident in Sheehan's strained and disbelieving relationship with Hughes, echoed ongoing problems in Los Angeles, where union officials closely monitored the trial. Los Angeles was a refuge of sorts from the discriminatory policies that Hughes and other African American men reported from Albany, and, for union members from South Central, the attitudes of people in Oregon were difficult to comprehend. After the trial, the Linn County sheriff only partially delivered on his promise to reimburse Black trainmen for their room and board. Each received only three dollars per day for fourteen days plus a mileage allowance of two cents per day when they were released from service. White witnesses received four dollars per day plus mileage.[54]

NEGOTIATING TERMS OF SURRENDER:
THE CONFESSION NARRATIVE(S)

The courtroom melodrama that Weinrick staged in Albany required the presence of Robert Folkes, who returned to that city only after a brutalizing experience in Los Angeles that involved manipulative mind games and a surreal tour through the streets and haunts of the South Central neighborhoods where he grew up. The LAPD detectives who led him through that twisted experience of his hometown told the press he confessed to the murder within three days of his arrival in their custody. Whatever other witnesses, Black or White, testified to during the trial, the only voice that ultimately mattered was the one represented in the written document that police, prosecutors, and the judge referred to as a "confession." They claimed that the voice in that document belonged to Folkes, and they presented it as if it were a single, continuous story he had told them. What little evidence survives regarding the circumstances under which that statement was authored, however, suggests that, at best, it was a negotiated document crafted in an unmonitored process during which Folkes had no resort to counsel while police operated with impunity. The integrity of the process was compromised to the extent that it is likely police either fabricated or creatively embellished some or all of the document. Folkes never signed it, and he repeatedly renounced it, through his lawyers, unlike several previous statements he signed on the train from Klamath Falls (all of which included clear denials of any involvement in the murder).

LAPD detectives interrogated Folkes in Los Angeles over a period of three days, eventually producing, in multiple copies, a transcript of a disjointed "confession" that they claimed he made voluntarily and without coercion. Their interrogation of Folkes immediately followed the brutal treatment he endured on board the train from the morning of 23 January until he stepped out on the platform in Los Angeles two days later. Those who witnessed or participated in those interrogations differed dramatically in their accounts of what, exactly, he said, in what circumstances, and in which interview. They disagreed on his physical condition, the settings of the interviews, the duration of the interrogations, and the degree to which his interrogators accommodated his physical needs for rest, nourishment, personal safety, and fluids. The police "transcript" provided virtually no details of the physical setting or psychological context of the interrogation. Alternate versions that also appeared in written form described in more detail the surrounding context of the words attributed to Folkes, but those versions lacked the imprimatur of the official police version. In each case, however, the process that converted spoken conversations into written statements reproduced only a small fraction of the human interaction involved. The actual sounds, smells, and experience of the interrogation disappeared in a document of mere words and punctuation. In a prolonged and emotionally charged pattern of intimidation, LAPD interrogators applied physical stress and psychological tactics intended to coerce a confession from Folkes over those three days. In the end, they could only produce a written statement he never saw, never signed, and denied making.

The official police transcript and other accounts that appeared in area newspapers all began with individuals who wrote down what they or someone else thought they heard, or what they wanted other people to think they heard. Police assigned a stenographer the task of producing a written transcript of their meetings with Folkes. That person (always a woman, in this case) later typed up a version of what she thought she heard or had been told—in some cases more than a month after the interrogation. The transcriptionist relied on her own shorthand record plus sketchy notes that interrogating officers compiled over several days of questioning their captive. Newspaper reporters likewise relied on the memory of key participants, asking them to recall events and then recasting their fragmentary recollections as seamless "eyewitness" accounts. Whether transcript or news story, the written records were presented as if they were verbatim accounts of things people actually said in a single, continuous conversation. That, however, was not the case. In this sense, each transcript was a detailed record of an imagined story.

Residents of South Central learned through a variety of formal and informal networks the story of how police extracted a confession from Folkes. Most accounts of that process do not survive in the historical record. One important version that made its way into the collective memory of the South Central community, however, came via the intermediaries of his wife, Jessie Louise Folkes, and the local reporters and members of that community to whom she told her story. Jessie, whose last name was variously listed in the case file as Folkes, Taylor, and Wilson, granted several different interviews in which she discussed what Folkes supposedly told police officers, and under what circumstances. Reporters from the *Los Angeles Sentinel* and the *California Eagle*, the two most prominent locally owned newspapers in South Central that particularly appealed to African American readers, converted their interviews with Jessie Folkes into a detailed written account, and Jessie later repeated portions of that narrative in court testimony.[55] The full context of her remarks, however, was mostly denied jurors and onlookers in the Albany courtroom where Folkes stood trial for his life. Beyond South Central, other newspapers largely ignored her account, and the jury and trial judge ignored it during their deliberations.

The *Los Angeles Sentinel* printed the "full story" Jessie Folkes provided reporters, in which she described the circumstances of her husband's detention and challenged the LAPD version of his interrogation and supposed "confession." According to that lengthy article, she first learned of his arrest at 3:00 p.m. on Monday, 25 January, when she discovered a calling card that police detectives left at her front door. By that time, Robert had been in LAPD custody for more than seven hours. Jessie rushed down to city hall, where Officer Richard B. McCreadie showed her a Western Union telegram from Weinrick asking the LAPD to detain Folkes "for questioning." McCreadie told her it would go easier for Robert if she convinced him to confess. When she asked, "How do you mean, by making it easy?" McCreadie explained that the LAPD "held no malice against him [Folkes]... We know he did it, because he's told two or three different stories and each one has changed each time." McCreadie admitted to Jessie that Folkes said he did not commit the murder, but the officer suggested, she later recalled, that perhaps Robert was "trying to protect the person who did the murder, and me." After that conversation, McCreadie and "other detectives," including SPRR detective A. J. Kelley, took her into an interrogation room to visit with her husband.

Detectives clearly tried to manipulate Folkes through his wife, urging her to tell him to "confess" and then pretending to leave them alone in a room that was obviously under observation. Jessie found Folkes seated at a long table, facing the door in a small room at LAPD headquarters. She recalled, "Robert appeared to be very sad and said 'Hello Baby, How are you?'" When she replied, "How are you feeling?" He said, "Pretty tough." He tried to stand up, but an officer told him to sit down and had her sit down to his right. McCreadie gave them each a cigarette, then left her alone with Folkes, instructing them both to remain seated, not move, and not give each other anything. Once they were alone, Robert told her, "I'm in a pretty tough jam, ain't I?" She asked, "Did you do it?" and he replied, "No, I didn't do it." At that point, a detective came back in the room, gave Folkes a second cigarette, and warned them to "make it snappy, I can't let you stay in here all night." After he left, Jessie asked her husband, "Why would they hold you and no one else?" He said he thought it was because he was the only one awake at the time of the murder. He told Jessie he wanted to sign over to her his last paycheck and that he wanted her to return Eddie Dooley's colorful blue-green overcoat. Then, Folkes gave his wife five dollars from his wallet, and as she left the room, he told her, "Be a good girl and keep your chin up." She asked the detectives if it was okay if she kissed him good-bye, and when they agreed, she kissed him, and the detectives said, "That was a good one, give us a movie one this time," to which Robert replied, "They're funny guys."

The next day was a grueling and terrifying ordeal for Folkes and his wife. After leaving the interrogation room at city hall, Jessie Folkes did not see her husband again for nearly twenty-four hours, from 3:30 p.m. on Monday, 25 January, through 3:00 p.m. on Tuesday, 26 January, and then only through the bars of a holding cell at Central Jail, under the watchful eyes of his keepers and cellmates. In between those two meetings, she rushed back to their home on 25th Street, more than thirty blocks away, and then rushed back to city hall—covering a total of over sixty city blocks in only two and a half hours. She arrived at city hall by 6:05 p.m. with cigarettes and papers for her husband, but officers at police headquarters told her she was too late to visit and would have to come back during visiting hours the next day. She returned at 10:30 the next morning, as instructed, after a second round trip of over sixty city blocks, and asked to see Officer

McCreadie. The desk sergeant told her McCreadie was out, but she could wait. She waited three full hours until several detectives came out to talk with her (around 1:45 p.m.), but they would not let her visit Folkes before 3:00 that afternoon. Around 3:00 p.m., she later recalled, they finally took her to see her husband, but he was not at police headquarters: "He was at Central Jail in one of the cages. . . . The right side of his face appeared to be puffed." She said he was moving stiffly, complaining of a sore back, and unable to stand. She asked, under the watchful eye of his jailers, if they had beaten him: "He said, 'No.'" Then he told her, gesturing at others in the cage, "They say we're guilty until we're proven innocent."

Robert's jailers forced Jessie Folkes to leave him there in the Central Jail "cage," where he was obviously in pain, apparently from severe beatings. Horrified by what she had seen and heard, she headed home. Four hours later, around 7:30 p.m. on Tuesday, 26 January, Rasmussen and Tetrick arrived at her front door with Folkes in tow. Jessie was distraught and mentally and physically exhausted from rushing from her home to city hall to Central Jail and back again, several times over the previous twenty-four hours, and she was recovering in bed. Seven other family members had gathered to keep her company in her small one-bedroom house: her mother, Marry Tuggle; her aunt, Gracie Lee; her daughter, Johnny Mae Wilson; her sister and brother, Pearline Abnacker and Arnold Abnacker; and her sister and brother-in-law, whom she identified only as Mr. and Mrs. Leon Washington (Leon Washington worked as a reporter for the *Los Angeles Sentinel* and appeared in photos accompanying coverage of this story). Jessie noted her husband was wearing, that night, the same clothes he had worn when he left home six days earlier, minus Dooley's overcoat (which the police confiscated as "evidence" and never returned—it was never introduced at trial and simply disappeared in police custody). Folkes and the two detectives crowded around her bed in the small room. She noted that Robert seemed to be intoxicated, even before he reached into his pocket and pulled out a half-pint bottle of whiskey, offering her a drink. Then he asked the detectives to leave them alone for about ten minutes. When they refused, he asked them to step outside with him for a moment. When they returned, Folkes asked Tetrick and Rasmussen each to take a drink with him from the bottle, stating, "Will you guys keep your word if I keep mine?" to which Rasmussen said, "I always keep my word, I never tell a lie." Jessie Folkes explained that her husband then sat down next to her and said, "Baby, I'm going to tell them I did it, but I didn't do it."

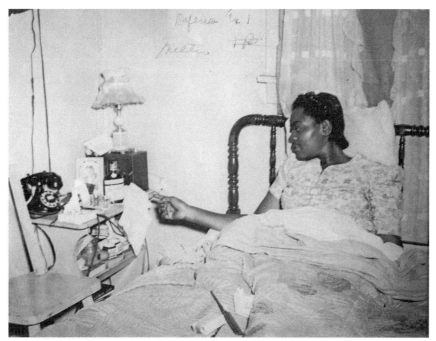

Jessie Taylor Wilson Folkes in the bedroom where police alleged Robert Folkes "confessed" to them. From OSSC case file, Oregon State Archives (original print used as Defense Exhibit 1 at trial). Image courtesy the Oregon State Archives.

The story Folkes next told the detectives, according to the version his wife related to reporters later that evening, outlined a series of events that veered in and out of the stories his coworkers told investigators in statements detectives filed with the SPRR investigative team and the OSP. Jessie Folkes later recalled, "He told me that he wanted to come home and the lawyer up there [at Central Jail] told him if he'd confess they'd bring him home." According to other court records and witness accounts, Folkes was denied access to any lawyers throughout this three-day period, but Jessie's story suggests one of his interrogators at Central Jail posed as a lawyer to trick him into confessing. Folkes told his wife, "Even though they're going to burn me or hang me, remember in your heart that I didn't do it." Only after that disclaimer did he begin his tale of how he supposedly murdered Martha James.

The story Folkes told police in his wife's crowded bedroom was circuitous and disjointed, suggesting he was seriously confused, disoriented, or dissembling. According to both Jessie and his mother, Clara Folkes, he seemed intoxicated. Folkes began, according to his wife, with a statement about the steward's party: He admitted he was drunk when he made sandwiches for the steward's guests, including a navy pilot and his wife, plus three or four guests—all White. Then he described a brief conversation with "the lady by the vestibule [apparently the pilot's wife]," after which "a man in a uniform [whom he later described as "the marine"—not the navy pilot] approached me. . . . [He] said to me, you know the woman you were talking to by the vestibule, I want to get rid of her, because she is my wife and then [he] hesitantly said, she is my girl friend." This "marine" further explained, according to Folkes, "he wanted to get rid of her, because she had been messing up." According to Jessie, the marine asked Folkes what it was worth to him to murder the woman for him, and when the second cook jokingly said, "Anything from a nickel up," he replied, "If you can do it and fix it so she can't talk any more, I'll give you $1000."[56]

After relating this series of events to detectives in the presence of his wife, Folkes explained that "the lady" about whom he'd been talking with "the marine" later came over and "asked him to get her husband, who was in another part of the train." After pretending to look for her husband, Folkes told the detectives, he reported back to her that the man was in a conversation and did not want to be disturbed. He asked the woman what time she was going to bed and promised to bring her husband to her berth about half an hour after she retired. According to Jessie, Folkes next focused on the time he woke up the morning of 23 January. He said he set his clock for 3:15 a.m., and when it went off, "he remembered what he had to do about this woman." He retrieved his boning knife from the kitchen, sharpened it on his sharpening stone, walked back to the kitchen, stripped down to his workpants (checkered trousers) and undershirt, pulled on his overcoat (the blue-green one he borrowed from Dooley), put the knife in his coat pocket, and went back to the Pullman car. As he passed by the men's lavatory, according to this account, he heard the sound of someone shaving, and he assumed it was the chief petty officer (Kelso).

As he spoke, Jessie recalled, Folkes seemed to wander and get confused about the story he was telling, the order in which events happened, and even which events he was describing. Detectives kept reminding him to get back on track—it seemed clear to her that Folkes was not only being coerced, but also coached, to tell a story someone else worked out for him ahead of time. After first telling his wife to remember that, no matter what he said, "I didn't do it," Folkes floundered around, repeating the most innocuous parts several times while avoiding any mention of the murder. Especially when he got to the part about Kelso, each time, she noted, "he wandered off and told the whole thing again." After each narrative circle, he explained how he opened the buttons on the curtain to berth 13, looked in, "and found her coat there." Then, Jessie said, "in a rambling matter [he] went over the whole situation [yet again]." Finally, he told a story about the murder. The woman in the berth, according to his repetitious, rambling narrative, "was sound asleep. He . . . went forward into the berth and attempted to button the curtains behind him. Then he climbed out of the berth, pretended the train was going so fast that he stumbled into the berth. She awoke, and asked who it was out there. He said 'never mind.'" When she threatened to scream, "He told her if she screamed it would be her last scream. He climbed into the berth, and put his knees on both sides of her." When she attempted to push him off her and out of the berth, Folkes said, "he had no intentions of killing her. He wanted to scare her. He then said he might as well kill her, if he didn't she would scream. He said he cut her throat on the right side." One detective asked how many times, and he replied, "Once."

After very briefly, vaguely, and inaccurately describing, just once, how the murderer cut Martha's throat, the rest of the statement Folkes made in Jessie's presence focused exclusively on later events. After he finished talking, one detective asked, "What side did you say you cut her on?" When Folkes reconfirmed "the right side," the detective asked, "Are you sure it was the right side?" He said, "Yes," and the detective asked again, "Are you absolutely sure?" With that prompting he changed his story: "Oh yes, it was the left side, I read it in the paper"—then he hesitated and said, "I mean that's the way I did it."[57] As a matter of fact, the autopsy report specified the murderer cut Martha's throat on the left side, but Folkes had trouble getting that part of the story right without coaching.

In South Central, Jessie's account of Robert's supposed "confession" carried more weight than anything police later claimed, and her version clearly implied Folkes only told that story because he feared his jailers would otherwise kill him. Moreover, even LAPD captain Rasmussen afterward denounced the supposed confession and, according to the *Sentinel*, stated that "he had no belief in Folke's [*sic*] confession and that he [Folkes] appeared to be screwy." The article, which included a front-page banner headline reading "L.A. Dining Car Cook Admits Train Murder" above a four-column-wide photo of Folkes on the platform in LA surrounded by detectives E. A. Tetrick, J. J. Kelly, J. J. Finneran, and R. B. McCreadie, also included the subheading "'It's a Frame-up'—Mrs. Folkes" and a second superscript headline, above the banner, reading, "'He Didn't Do It,' Says Wife."[58] The article noted that Mrs. Tuddle (sometimes spelled Tuggle), the young cook's mother-in-law (Jessie's mother), told reporters that "a detective at Central station" told her that "doctors had requested that Folkes be placed under the influence of liquor to see how he reacted."[59]

TELLING STORIES DOESN'T MAKE THEM TRUE: STATEMENTS, TRANSCRIPTS, AND REPORTS

Folkes' performance in front of his wife and other witnesses was unconvincing, even to police detectives in the room, but they characterized it as a confession and, later that evening, after returning Folkes to an interrogation room at LAPD headquarters, they worked to craft a more concise written version, which they later released to the press and forwarded to prosecutors in Oregon. That version of the story, and not the version in the *Sentinel*, made its way into the Associated Press newswire, where newspapers across the country, including Portland-area dailies, picked it up as front-page news.

The circumstances of the "confession" that Jessie Folkes described for *Sentinel* reporters raised serious questions about coercion and intimidation methods in city hall and at Central Jail, and the story Folkes told in front of his wife contrasted sharply with earlier statements he made, both on the train and after arriving in LA. The idea that LAPD officers might coerce, threaten, or even kill a Black man held prisoner at Central Jail was nothing new to residents of South Central. In fact, between the time Martha James was murdered and the eventual trial of Robert Folkes, the LAPD was the focus of an ongoing investigation into methods of torture and interrogation that included killing witnesses and suspects while in custody at Central Jail.[60] LAPD detectives Rasmussen and Tetrick later admitted Folkes told a different story earlier in the interrogation process, but they considered that statement unworthy of transcription. Instead, they delivered to Weinrick two conflicting transcripts of lengthy interrogations that they staged with Folkes in LA—one that preceded the statement at his wife's bedside, and one that they claimed he made at ten o'clock the following morning. They also verbally repeated, at trial, a heavily edited version of the story he told in the presence of Jessie Folkes.

The two transcripts Rasmussen and Tetrick forwarded to Weinrick as alleged "confessions" were each formatted as if they were verbatim accounts of everything anyone said during a single interrogation, but that was a false impression of the actual process. The two interrogations that these separate documents allegedly represented supposedly began no later than 5:15 p.m.

on 26 January and 10:00 a.m. on 27 January, respectively—a span of at least fifteen hours. Neither transcript indicated when the interrogation ended; however, the transcript of the first "confession" covered eight legal pages in single-spaced type, while the second one covered only four legal pages in single-spaced type. Folkes did not sign either one. Apart from conflicting oral accounts by his wife and interrogators, no written record of his bedside "confession" survives.[61] Other witnesses, however, provided additional evidence of the relentless grilling he endured at Central Jail and at LAPD headquarters before he allegedly confessed.

STORYLINES NOT PURSUED

In the context of wartime censorship, prosecutors and police controlled which stories made their way into the press and which did not. OSP files from early in the investigation include an extensive interrogation of Wilson that raised suspicions about his role in the murder, but it was never released in public or introduced at trial. Doris Price, a singer-dancer of some regional repute, told authorities on the day of the murder an incriminating story about Wilson that they buried for the duration of the trial. Price reported that she boarded the train in Seattle in the early afternoon on 22 January, after working a series of nightclub acts in that city. While waiting for the train, she encountered a young man dressed in civilian clothes whom she had previously met in a club, and they struck up a conversation. Wilson, standing nearby, joined in uninvited. When she turned to respond to Wilson, the first man walked away, leaving Price alone with the marine. According to Price, Wilson was "quite a talker and talked continuously." He boarded the train with Price, loaded her luggage, and sat with her in the coach car from Seattle to Portland.

En route to Portland, Wilson told Price obviously bogus stories about himself and his (imaginary) twin brother "Bob." The twenty-two-year-old recruit with less than a year's service in the marines told Price he was in Pearl Harbor during the 7 December 1941 attack, that he had been in the marines for three years, and that he was on a mosquito boat that was blown up in the Pacific, leaving him stranded on a desert island. Then he pressured her to join him in the vestibule of the car. Price, clearly creeped out by his obvious advances, refused. She did, however, autograph a picture of herself that Wilson cut out of the Seattle paper. When they got to Portland, he followed her onto the platform. In order to discourage him, she told him her father, a federal marshal, was meeting her inside the station. At that point, he left her there on the platform, at about 11:30 p.m. Price noticed another woman on the platform whom she later recognized as Martha James, wearing a leopard-skin coat and brown beanie with matching fur bow. She recalled that Martha was accompanied by a navy ensign and a navy flight officer with one other woman.[62] This was around the time of the steward's party, by some accounts.

Price's statement suggests Wilson crossed paths with Martha James, her husband, and the Keatons on the Portland platform, five hours before James was murdered in the Pullman berth immediately below Wilson's. Price's signed statement survives in the investigation files, and it corroborates another signed statement Wilson provided while in Albany, before the LAPD produced Folkes' supposed confession. Neither the account Price provided, early in the investigation, nor the lengthier account Wilson provided in Albany, however, ever appeared in newspaper reports or trial records. Instead, investigators released Wilson's other statements that shifted the focus from himself to first Funches and then Folkes.

TAKING UP THE FIGHT: DEFENDING ROBERT E. LEE FOLKES

More than a full year after the Folkes trial, the *California Eagle* reported that the NAACP's Los Angeles branch voted in its regular meeting to give "moral and financial support to the fight to free Folkes, after hearing his mother [Clara Folkes], and listening to a report of the case from William Pollard, of the Dining Car Cooks and Waiters Association, who as chairman of the Robert Folkes Defense Committee [RFDC], has waged almost singlehand-edly, a campaign to get justice for the youth. A letter written by Folkes to his mother was read by her at the meeting." This letter, reprinted in the *Eagle*, is the only verifiable statement on record that Folkes drafted and signed in his own hand. In the letter, Folkes observes, "I was convicted of this heinous crime. I was not convicted with evidence, I was convicted through prejudice. I truly believe that I could take any one of those jurymen that convicted me, or even the judge who heard the case, and on the same grounds, either one of those people could be placed in front of a Negro jury and convicted. Of course, this incident will never happen, but I assure you it is amazing what prejudice can do." The grammar, syntax, and style of this signed letter from Folkes are completely at odds with the supposed "statement" police attrib-uted to him and introduced at trial. After hearing the presentations from Pollard and Clara Folkes, the Los Angeles branch of the NAACP announced that its goal was to enlist one dollar from each of America's fifteen million Negroes for an appeal fund.[63]

Central to the effort to free Folkes was the issue of how to deal with the document prosecutors represented as a "confession." Throughout the trial and appeals process, his defenders tried to introduce evidence that LAPD detectives who interrogated Folkes were guilty of manipulating evidence and extorting false confessions. Most compelling was the fact that, unlike virtually all other statements collected from Folkes and other witnesses before he reached LA, all the supposed "confession" statements were unsigned. Nowhere in the voluminous case files does Folkes admit, by his own hand or under his own signature, that he had any role in the murder. At trial, Tetrick claimed under cross-examination that, in all his time as a police officer, "I have never asked a man to sign a confession . . . [because] I don't think a signed confession is of any value." When defense attorney Lomax alertly challenged that statement with the question "In your estimation, a man's signature on a piece of paper doesn't mean anything?" Tetrick responded, "Yes, it does." Then he claimed under oath that when detectives brought in stenographer Jean Bechtel to take down a verbatim statement from Folkes, she never actually transcribed it, because Folkes "ran on about" events that did not involve the murder.[64]

In what must have seemed a triumphant exchange for the defense, Lomax adroitly turned Tetrick's claim against the prosecution, discrediting both Tetrick and Sisemore in the process. First, he cornered Sisemore into denying that there was any record Folkes made a statement at police headquarters on the afternoon of 26 January (in which he *denied* guilt), and then he forced Weinrick to produce the statement Sisemore denied ever existed. Asked directly if the LAPD secured any statements from Folkes other than the one introduced as State's Exhibit K (a statement police claimed Folkes made on 27 January, the morning after he visited his wife's bedside), in which he supposedly admitted guilt, Sisemore stated at trial, "So far as I know, this [the 27 January transcript] is the only statement we have."[65]

Lomax then posed the same question directly to Weinrick: "Will you state in open court and before his Honor that this [the 27 January transcript] is the only statement and that you have no conflicting statements with this statement?" Weinrick was lead prosecutor—he could hardly claim partial knowledge of the case if charged with perjury. He finally admitted, "I can hardly say that. I think there is another statement in the file, but it doesn't conflict with this statement and doesn't cover the things this statement covers and it wasn't taken by Miss Lyman [whom prosecutors previously called to the stand to establish a foundation for introducing Exhibit K]." Under follow-up questioning, Weinrick haltingly admitted there was at least one other statement Folkes made in LA, with Jean Bechtel as stenographer, but, he argued, that statement was interrupted when Jessie Taylor (aka Jessie Folkes) arrived at city hall and asked to see her husband. Lomax, following this exchange in the April 1943 trial, then asked for a recess so Weinrick could retrieve the "Bechtel statement." After the recess, Weinrick returned with an eight-page document that Lomax triumphantly introduced as "Defense Exhibit 2."[66]

The statement of 26 January (Defense Exhibit 2) was a crucial link in the strategy by which Lomax portrayed Folkes as the victim of police coercion in Central Jail. Between the 5:15 p.m. time noted on the 26 January statement that Bechtel drafted and the 10:00 a.m. time noted on the 27 January statement that Lyman crafted, Folkes' physical and mental condition markedly deteriorated, as his mother and wife both explained before the jury. Clara Folkes testified she called Jessie's house while her son was there with Rasmussen and Tetrick, and when she learned Folkes was there, she walked the several blocks from her house, arriving at 1163½ 25th Street around 8:30 p.m. By then, she testified, her son was acting peculiar, "like he was highly intoxicated; he acted very funny. He was highly intoxicated, or something was wrong with him." She explained, "He didn't look natural. . . . His face looked like it were bloated or something wrong with it." Although Clara said she spoke to her son and he spoke to her, she contradicted detectives' claims that they allowed her to have a "conversation" with him, noting that they were present the whole time she was there. When she entered Jessie's bedroom that evening, Clara noted, she didn't think her son recognized her, "because he didn't seem natural—he didn't act normal."[67]

Jessie Folkes, whom Clara identified to the court as "Miss Jessie Wilson," testified more bluntly that her husband had been beaten before he arrived at her home that evening around 6:30. She said investigators manipulated and intimidated Folkes before, during, and after the oral statement he made in her bedroom. She testified that no one in the room took any notes while he was speaking, and that Tetrick was on the phone most of the time he was in her house, discussing the progress of the interrogation with someone "up north." Earlier that day, Marine Corps major James B. Hardle arrived in Albany, where he conferred with Weinrick and offered his assistance "toward progress of the investigation."[68] While Hardle conferred with Weinrick, Tetrick called to tell them Folkes was in the process of confessing.[69]

After they left Jessie's home with Folkes and his mother, somewhere around 8:45 on the evening of 26 January, and after they dropped Clara off in front of her house, Tetrick and Rasmussen apparently returned Folkes to Central Jail, leaving him there overnight. The next morning, twelve hours after they dropped him off, they retrieved him to police headquarters and, at 10:00 a.m. on 27 January, the transcript later known as "State's Exhibit K" supposedly began. Lyman, the stenographer for this four-page statement, later testified that she had previously taken "quite a number of statements from intoxicated persons" in her position as stenographer with the LAPD homicide division. Her testimony seemed to indicate it was common practice to first ply suspects with whiskey and then coerce a confession. Prosecutors hastily requested a recess, after which Lyman changed her testimony to claim she "sometimes" took such statements. Then she admitted, under cross-examination, that prosecutors Weinrick and Sisemore coached her during the recess to make that change in her testimony.[70] The LAPD stenographer claimed she took the statement in shorthand notes but, she admitted, "I didn't type it up right away," and she would only say she brought the finished transcript to Rasmussen "later on." Neither Folkes nor anyone else ever signed the transcript or otherwise verified its content, nor did Lyman, Tetrick, or Rasmussen ever claim they reviewed it with Folkes, and they never asked him to sign it. Folkes denied the statement, in its entirety, through his attorneys.[71]

The 27 January statement that the LAPD attributed to Folkes came shortly after Joseph Beeman submitted his autopsy report to the summit of investigators that Weinrick convened in Albany and within an hour after Governor Snell telegrammed his fellow Mason, Governor Colgate Darden of Virginia, assuring him, as reported in the *Virginian-Pilot*, that "authorities in Oregon were doing 'everything possible' to bring about the apprehension of the slayer of Mrs. James."[72] At Albany, representatives of the US Navy and US Marines met with prosecutors about the time Rasmussen and Tetrick were on the phone with Weinrick during the Folkes interrogations of 27 January. At key moments during the statement, the document notes Rasmussen and Tetrick left the room to take calls from Albany. Lyman testified that although the heading on the statement indicates the presence of six men and herself in the room with Folkes during the interrogation, everyone else except

Tetrick and Rasmussen left the room before Folkes even began his statement. The transcript she prepared, however, shows that Rasmussen entered the room only after the statement began, and that he then left the room with Kelley, Ramirez, and Banich, leaving Folkes alone with Tetrick, Lyman, and Finneran.[73] In other words, the statement is internally contradictory.

The statement prosecutors introduced at the April trial as Exhibit K was very brief and, apart from a few preliminaries, consisted largely of a monologue of one and a half legal-size pages of closely spaced small type, allegedly representing Folkes' response to Tetrick's invitation to describe his actions "from the time you got up [on the morning of 23 January]." The resulting narrative, however, reads as if it were spliced together from various passenger statements and observations that police gleaned over the previous four days, and it lacks internal consistency, even beyond obvious conflicts with other accounts. At the outset, when Tetrick asks, "You want to tell anything?" the transcript indicates Folkes replied, "I made my statement last night. That is okay, it stands like it is." In response to a second prompt, he says only, "I stuck to my word." Prompted a third time to "tell us the same story you told last night," he demurs: "If I told the same story it would be a mistake," and he observes, "I went over this so many times and every time I did it was wrong." Finally, after a fourth and fifth prompt, in the portion of the conversation included in the transcript, the "confession" narrative begins: He arose that morning (23 January) at four o'clock. The night before (22 January), he went back to the Pullman car to use the restroom. He found a woman sitting on her bunk, "about number 13." The woman asked him to help her get into the next car to see her husband. He told her he would look for her husband, but he "went back in the dining car, sat down and joined the crowd." After some time, he "went back and said, seen her husband, he was in a conference with a gang of fellows." He directed her to wait in the vestibule until he gave her the signal, then walk quickly through the dining car to the next Pullman behind the diner, "keeping her head high, and no one would notice her." He said she did so, and then went back to her own car and went to bed. Shortly after, he also went to bed, sleeping until his alarm went off at 3:15 a.m. He lay there for fifteen minutes "half awake and half drunk." After about fifteen minutes, "it came to me about this lower berth 13. I went to the restroom there in this same car 'D' and sat on the bench and talked to Mr. Hughes and smoked a cigarette. I then went back to my dining car."[74]

The portion of Exhibit K describing the murder begins halfway through the monologue, and the last two pages are a series of questions and answers about that scene. The transcript details how he returned to the kitchen to build a fire, but did not build a fire. He started thinking about berth 13. He "staggered over to the bench" where he kept his knives. He took a knife and tested its edge on his thumb. He walked through Car D to make sure it was clear. He went back to the kitchen and realized he should disguise his identity. He took off his white coat and put on a coat from the closet. He made, from one end of the tourist car to the other, about three trips, although he didn't know for sure how many trips he made. On his second trip through the car, he encountered the petty officer (Kelso). He directed Kelso to the restroom, followed him partway, and then "sunk back and went to the end of the tourist car again." Then he "walked back to the tourist car." He unbuttoned one button from the inside of the curtain. He kept going to the end of the tourist car, where he knew Hughes was with the petty officer. He walked back toward the dining car and unbuttoned another button from berth 13. He walked back through the tourist car again and heard the petty officer's razor "zizzing." He went back to berth 13, entering the berth with his left knee. "Somebody," he recalled, "raised up from that berth and asked who was I . . . it was all in a fog to me." He told her it made no difference and instructed her, "Button those curtains. . . . It was a lady, true enough. She buttoned the curtain. She acted as if she was going to button them . . . but I was loaded and I felt she had more power than I. . . . Evidently in my mind I figured she was not going to do that and there is where I killed her."[75]

The remainder of the narrative was a series of questions from Tetrick, followed by mostly "yes" or "no" answers from Folkes. Tetrick asked if he thought she was trying to throw him off ("Yes"), did he kiss her ("No"), did he touch her body with his hands ("No"), did he remember where he cut her ("Yes, sir"), did he stab her more than once ("I think it was only once"), did he run after the killing ("Did I run? I run"). In several digressions, the statement seems like an effort to clarify points of confusion and contradiction among various stories witnesses had provided police. He said she did not make any sound at all: "Not a loud sound for anybody to hear. All of it was false pretenses. It was somebody going to be implicated in the case. At the time this happened the only thing that was said was just her gasping for breath." He was unsure where he cut her but said, "I think it was her head." Asked, "You think you cut her with your right hand?" He said, "Yes, with my right hand, if I killed her. I know I killed her." He said he went back to Car D a "second time" after he left the berth and went back to the dining car, "after I knew she was cut. When I came back, I knew there was going to be alarm. . . . I removed my coat and put my work coat back on." Asked, "What coat were you wearing?" he replied, "My black overcoat."[76] There is no mention of the bright blue-green overcoat Folkes borrowed from Dooley instead of the dark overcoat he left at home, and there is no indication he removed or otherwise covered up the unmistakable checkered cook's pants that all witnesses agreed he was wearing that morning, just minutes after the murder.

The remainder of the "confession" focuses on what Folkes did after the murder. Tetrick closed the interview with a statement: "No threats or violence has been used against you, nobody beat you." The (unsigned) transcript indicated he replied, "No." Asked, "Nobody could force the story out of you?" the last answer indicated on the transcript reads, "If I was not guilty I would not make this confession. I have kept my word. As long as she [the stenographer] has it down and I read thoroughly and understand I will be willing to take the medicine which the killer should take."[77] This confused, internally contradictory, obviously incomplete account was the statement defenders of Folkes somehow had to refute—or at least convince learned jurists, on appeal, that it should not have been admitted as evidence. That should not have been difficult if jurors began with the presumption of innocence.

Chapter Five
Men and Women of Conviction

Prosecutors in the case against Robert Folkes enlisted forces of prejudice in their efforts to convict the young Black man they accused of murdering Martha James. Those who supported that effort wielded far more power, influence, and status than either the defendant or his attorneys could muster. Once prosecutors told Wilbur Brinson that Folkes was the man who murdered his daughter, that well-connected, bereaved father drew on all his considerable resources—fiscal and otherwise—to ensure the Oregon criminal justice system first convicted and then executed Folkes. Virginia governor Colgate Darden—a near neighbor and friend of the Brinsons—directly pressured fellow Mason and Oregon governor Earl Snell, who took a personal interest in the case and, in so doing, encouraged DA Harlow Weinrick and his multiagency investigative team to secure a conviction and a death sentence. First, however, there was the matter of a trial.

Snell, and other voices of authority in Oregon, approached the trial as an opportunity to demonstrate that the state's criminal justice system could work in wartime. In that sense, they understood the trial as part of the war effort. Long before the trial began, it was clear that conviction and execution, not acquittal and release, was the only outcome that would adequately demonstrate, in the eyes of skeptical guardians of militarized order, that the state's criminal justice system was up to the task. Executives with Southern Pacific and the Pullman Company added their voices to those of representatives from the US Navy and the Marines in a growing chorus of influence and power, all aimed at ending the life of the twenty-year-old Folkes. With no substantive evidence supporting their charges, prosecutors relied almost entirely on two statements they claimed Folkes made: one in Los Angeles and the other while awaiting trial at the Linn County jail on the top floor of the Albany courthouse. Without those two unsigned documents, both of which Folkes denied having made, they had no case. There was no physical evidence linking Folkes to the murder, there was no evident motive, and there were no eyewitnesses who claimed to have seen him committing the murder. There simply was no substantive case without those statements, which leading legal experts at the time argued should not be admissible in court.[1]

As it turned out, prosecutors did not need a substantive case. The trial was never about seeking truth—it was about demonstrating control and authority in wartime. Snell and his subordinates in the state justice system approached the case as a test of their political will to legally convict and execute a young Black trainman, and that outcome depended more on telling a familiar story than on producing evidence or eyewitnesses. All prosecutors needed to do was assemble and cast the parts a credulous judge and jury would accept as fitting their preconceived notions of how a melodramatic murder case should unfold.

AN "OREGON DIFFERENCE": PREJUDICIAL LANDSCAPES AND MILITARIZATION IN THE MID-VALLEY

In preparing for trial, prosecutors could rely on deep-seated forces of prejudice in western Oregon that dominated state government during the 1920s and shaded public policy well through the election and first term of Governor Earl Snell. Potential jurors and courtroom observers in the case all lived through an era of extreme racial prejudice that was a phenomenon not merely locally but statewide. Historian Lawrence Saalfeld, in a study of Klan influence during the early 1920s, found numerous examples of Klan strongholds in mid-Valley cities, including initiation rallies and public demonstrations in Corvallis, Albany, and Salem, as well as in larger urban centers like Medford, Eugene, and Portland. Near Albany, midway to Corvallis on State Highway 20, Saalfeld observes, the Klan sponsored construction of the Children's Farm Home—an alternative to Catholic-sponsored orphanages. Widespread support for the Klan's agenda led to a Klan-endorsed Republican-majority Oregon legislature in 1923, which came to power in the same election cycle in which a Klan-backed Democratic Party nominee, Walter Pierce, won Oregon's gubernatorial race. During that period, Klan-backed initiatives targeted Catholics and Asians in Oregon, with widespread support from the same electorate. The Klan moved more furtively after the US Supreme Court struck down Oregon's Klan-sponsored mandatory public schools measure in *Pierce v. Society of Sisters* (1925), but evidence of the secret organization's continuing influence survived in western Oregon's towns and cities, and the mid-Valley was notoriously unfriendly to African Americans through the 1940s. Even after Oregon's constitutional provision excluding Black people from the state was finally revoked in 1926, and even though the prohibition on "Negro, Chinaman, and Mulatto Suffrage" was lifted in 1927, evidence of continuing prejudice remained. Nearly two-fifths of voters, for example, opposed the 1926 measure repealing the exclusion clause. Nearly the same fraction challenged the 1927 measure on suffrage. The relatively large numbers of voters who opposed these efforts to end segregationist clauses in Oregon's constitution demonstrated continuing animosity against people of color, even as the state moved to align its laws with the US Constitution.[2]

Barely sixteen years separated the Folkes trial from the constitutional reforms of 1926 and 1927, and the militarization and paranoia of the early war years quickly reversed those gains for civil rights in Oregon. Prosecutors exploited the wartime circumstances of 1943 and those earlier racist tendencies in framing their case against Folkes. In the prevailing climate of fear and prejudice in early 1943, legal authorities in Oregon were under pressure to produce a conviction, but Weinrick, Sisemore, and Beeman had all obviously bungled the initial investigation and had no real case, unless they decided to target Wilson. Even with Wilson, they faced a problem: eyewitnesses saw the marine standing with bloody hands above the still-breathing victim as she bled out on the floor in the aisle next to Wilson's berth, but no one came forward to say they saw him commit the murder, and investigators could not find a murder weapon. Apart from his proximity to the crime, there was ample room for reasonable doubt, especially since Wilson managed to distract investigators and redirect their attention toward Black trainmen. Wilson had escaped their direct oversight for several hours of unsupervised time as the train travelled from Tangent—where the murderer killed Martha James—to Klamath Falls, where Sisemore conducted his farcical inquiry targeting Black trainmen to the exclusion of anyone else. During that time, Wilson had plenty of opportunity to cover his tracks, if he actually was the murderer, and there was certainly enough room for a good lawyer to raise questions about the integrity of the crime scene, regardless of who was charged. Prosecutors, consequently, scrambled to find a more vulnerable defendant.

In the racist militarism of the early war years, Weinrick's team apparently embraced the premise that it would be easier to convince a jury to convict a Black civilian than a White military man, given the lack of any substantive evidence. As the War Relocation Authority (WRA) manipulated wartime propaganda, targeted Japanese Americans for removal from western Oregon, and further inflamed racial prejudices, prosecutors prepared the ground for a trial that played to the prejudicial assumptions and biases of judge and jury, without regard for truth. Emotions, not facts, would govern the outcome. Weinrick's investigative team leaked to the press details of statements they attributed to Folkes, characterizing them as "confessions," but they denied the defense access to those statements. Anyone reading newspapers in the months leading up to the trial could not have missed front-page stories divulging details about those statements because the news made front-page headlines all across the country, including in local and regional newspapers in Albany and Portland. Prosecutors cultivated and nurtured a prejudicial atmosphere, laying the groundwork for jury selection and the trial, all the while refusing to cooperate with requests from the defense team for information about witnesses, evidence, or other details about the case. By stonewalling standard discovery requests, Weinrick's prosecution team forced the defense attorney, Leroy Lomax, to depend largely on sensationalized news stories for information about who might have information and where potential witnesses might be located.

ACT ONE: WOMEN (AND MEN) OF THE JURY

The first act in Weinrick's staging of the Folkes trial melodrama was the process of jury selection, during which observers gained their first glimpse of how prosecutors and defense attorneys would approach the case. The courtroom audience was overwhelmingly White, local, and by most accounts, disproportionately women from Albany, but it also included daily observers from the Portland area, and a smaller, more diverse mix of people who travelled there from distant corners of the country. It included family members and friends of the accused from South Central, representatives of the NAACP and the Urban League from Portland, labor officials from the Dining Car Workers Union who travelled from Southern California, family members of the victim who travelled from Virginia, and a parade of witnesses that included mostly Black and White trainmen, other passengers, and policemen from many jurisdictions through which Train 15 passed on its way from Portland to LA. Also in the audience were representatives of SPRR and PPC corporate interests and from the various branches of the US armed services, including the Marines and the US Navy. It was possibly the most cosmopolitan of any wartime gathering in that small county seat of mostly rural Linn County, Oregon. This means that, to the degree jurors felt pressured by the prejudices of their audience, a cosmopolitan outlook—and not just local or rural biases—influenced the resulting verdict against Folkes.

The jury that Lewelling's court empanelled was both historic and biased in favor of White middle-class women. In a case where a young Black man from South Central stood accused of murdering an upper-middle-class White woman, that bias complicated the task of preparing a defense. The jury was among the first in Oregon to include women, and in that gendered sense, they were less peers of the accused than of the victim. Less than two months before the trial, on 19 February 1943, a newly amended law took effect in Oregon removing the provision that exempted women from jury duty solely on the basis of their gender.[3] That exemption had previously prevented women from serving on juries, but on 1 March 1943, barely a month before the Folkes trial, the Linn County clerk drew a new list of potential jurors that was updated to include women. The list included five hundred residents of Linn County whose names were drawn from county voter rolls to establish a pool of potential jurors for cases that would come before the court over the next two years. Each name was listed by voting precinct.[4] Jurors in the Folkes case were drawn from that pool in early April, and on 8 April 1943, the trial of Robert E. Lee Folkes commenced presenting evidence to an empanelled jury that included eight women and only four men. In addition, one alternate, also a woman, sat through the trial with other jurors and heard all the evidence that the court presented before that jury.[5]

During juror selection, prosecutors pointedly screened out candidates hostile to the approach that eventually led to conviction and execution, but Lomax faced the more difficult task of discerning racial prejudice during that formal in-court process. On the first day of the trial, 7 April, Lomax, according to one gender-bound report in the *Oregon Journal*, "questioned almost every juryman on his racial feelings, asking several if they had any 'racial prejudices.' He rejected several who were Southerners or said they had family connections in the South." The offhand comments of reporters, however, suggest racist assumptions were deeply ingrained in the popular culture of Oregon, not just the South. The *Oregon Journal*, for example, casually noted that next to Folkes sat his "Negro friend," W. E. Pollard,[6] identifying the labor leader only in reference to his race. Reporters focused more on the appearance of the defendant and his lawyers than on the substance of their argument.[7]

In a state that had pioneered opposition to the death penalty only one generation earlier, one irony of the Folkes trial was that, in one of the first capital murder trials in Oregon to include women on the jury, the prosecution carefully filtered out all jurors who honestly expressed moral reservations about the death penalty. Although women shifted the balance against capital punishment in one of the first statewide referendums after gaining suffrage, prosecutors gambled that women would support capital punishment in this particular case. In working to place as many women on the jury as possible, Weinrick was especially vigorous in challenging jurors without explanation, exhausting all but one of his allowed peremptory challenges, whereas defense attorney Lomax repeatedly waived his twelve peremptory challenges and accepted each panel of potential jurors, regardless of gender, except for those who openly admitted racial prejudice.[8] The *Oregonian* confirmed that the most common reasons potential jurors were dismissed from the pool were, in order, vocal opposition to the death penalty, openly admitting racial prejudice, or flatly stating they "had already formed an unalterable opinion."[9] The prosecutor, however, also rejected jurors who "previously expressed doubt over the validity of circumstantial evidence."[10] What remained, by the end of the second day of the trial, were eight women and four men who largely agreed on three points: they (1) favored the death penalty without moral reservation, (2) saw no problem with a case made entirely of circumstantial evidence, and (3) were morally comfortable denying they harbored racially prejudiced opinions, even though they lived in small, close-knit, mostly rural communities that actively excluded Black people.

The final list of jurors represented well the geographic diversity of Linn County, but they were ethnically, culturally, and intellectually much more homogeneous than the courtroom audience or the assortment of witnesses either side called to the stand during the trial. Nine different towns or precincts were represented on the jury, and only three jurors listed as their hometown a place that met the census bureau's standard for "urban" in 1940. In addition to being mostly composed of women, the jury was also overwhelmingly rural. Most jurors were farm-dependent, married residents of a county that was virtually all White. Court documents and news reports listed all nine women on the jury (including the alternate juror) as married, and none of the women listed an occupation other than "farm wife" (two jurors) or "housewife" (six jurors and one alternate). The same sources identified all four men on the jury by their occupations, without mentioning their marital status, including two listed in "worker" positions at wood or paper mills, one as an "operator" at a grain mill, and one as a "farmer."[11] In this agricultural community, a majority of the jury members were employed in agriculture-dependent industries or directly engaged in farming, either as a farmer or as a farm wife or housewife in a farm household. Only a third of the jury members were engaged in an occupation not directly related to agriculture, and those were all people who worked in wood products industries or maintained a household dependent on those industries.

Even before prosecutors called their first witnesses, the defense team came up short during jury selection—typically one of the most important phases of any criminal trial. The all-White jurors were mostly either conservatively dressed, matronly housewives of relatively comfortable status and wealth, or else relatively prosperous businessmen or skilled workers, at least by the standards of Linn County.[12] It did not require a great leap of imagination for them to identify with Martha James and her husband: she was a White housewife married to a man who fit the Willamette Valley model of rural masculinity. Her husband was a taciturn farmer who volunteered for military service and bore his grief with stoic dignity, appearing in public only in his navy uniform. The accused, by contrast, was a Black man from Los Angeles who clashed with rural and agrarian ideals of manly virtue: he had avoided military service by finding employment in a draft-exempt position, he took a wage-earning job with a railroad corporation, he lived in a metropolitan area of California, he wore fashionable formal wear during leisure time, and his assigned duties included mostly cooking and cleaning. Moreover, he lived most of the time away from his family, and he was not formally married to the woman he called his wife.

Further complicating matters for Folkes, his lawyer overreached during opening arguments, promising a story that was difficult, if not impossible, to deliver: Lomax, a renowned Portland defense attorney, claimed he would prove "somebody else" committed the crime. With that theatrical assertion, he unnecessarily accepted the burden of proof for solving a crime that from all appearances defied certain solution. His concern, of course, was that "reasonable doubt" was equally unobtainable before an all-White jury sitting in judgment on a Black man, unless he could unequivocally show jurors another person was clearly guilty. Before the trial even began, consequently, Lomax gifted to Weinrick's prosecution team a sympathetic and inexperienced jury that was unlikely to consider reasonable doubt sufficient reason for acquittal.

Rather than assuming the innocence of the accused, they were instead primed to expect that Folkes' defense team would prove he was not guilty. Outside the world of true-crime detective novels, that expectation was an unreasonable standard for a capital murder case.

PRELUDE TO ACT TWO:
ORCHESTRATING THE PARADE OF WITNESSES

Weinrick's team orchestrated a moralizing melodrama of ten component parts as prosecutors immersed jurors in a confusing blur of detail, shuffling witnesses through the witness box in a shell game of legal misdirection: (1) they crafted a theatrical set with two railcars arranged in a fanciful "murder scene" in the Albany roundhouse and then guided jurors through that setting in a tour that framed the case as a classic "closed-room" murder mystery; (2) they neutralized the most credible White voice that threatened to complicate their simplistic script, limiting his testimony to mundane details about the train and its scheduled passage through the Willamette Valley; (3) they alternated other, pretentiously authoritative White voices with the testimony of Black trainmen in a rhythm that suggested White jurors should trust and identify more closely with the former than the latter; (4) they questioned Black trainmen on very narrow and controlled topics while using other witnesses to enthusiastically narrate a dramatic story that juxtaposed virtuous defenders of White innocence against sinister forces of darkness; (5) they withheld important clues and evidence until after all Black trainmen testified, building tension for a surprise twist in the story; (6) they introduced "surprise" (military) witnesses who dramatically reversed the flow of the story at a critical point to reinforce the credibility and appeal of their star witness (Wilson); (7) they presented a "surprise" witness in the person of an innocuous female ingénue whose dramatic testimony seemed to (but did not actually) place Folkes at the murder scene; (8) they equated the physical presence of Folkes in Car D with the implication he committed the murder; (9) they ended with a parade of authoritative White voices (police and railroad detectives and prosecutors) who read a narrative version of the murder story into evidence in dramatic voices while claiming to be speaking the words of the defendant confessing to the crime; and (10) they stressed the brutality and senselessness of the crime, implying that the very lack of a clear motive was, in itself, proof the crime was committed by a Black man whom they falsely claimed had a record of sexual violence and exhibitionism.

In all these strategic turns, Weinrick relied on Lewelling to limit the range of defense questioning while permitting unsubstantiated attacks on Folkes' character and reputation. Virtually none of the facts prosecutors presented in the case bore directly on the guilt or innocence of Folkes. Rather, they were part of calculated efforts to craft a moral framework within which jurors might weigh the depravity of the accused villain against the innocence of the virtuous victim. In that context, a guilty verdict was the obvious, emotional outcome of a trial that was more a staged morality play than a search for truth.

ACT II, SCENE 1: STAGING THE "MURDER SCENE"

Prosecutors, with the collusion of the trial judge and the acquiescence of the defense team, successfully created the illusion, right from the outset, that the case was a classic "closed-room" murder mystery typical of the genre popularized by Edgar Allan Poe and Arthur Conan Doyle.[13] As one of their first official acts, jurors toured the "murder car" and the dining car that prosecutors staged in the Albany roundhouse for their benefit. Even before prosecutors presented any sworn testimony, or even opening arguments, this tour planted in jurors' minds the idea that the dining car and its crew were related to the murder of the passenger in Lower 13 in Car D. It also created a false familiarity with the real landscape of the murder: the actual setting for the crime was a much larger train with many more cars beyond those the jury toured, but only these two cars had real substance and presence in the experience of jurors. The court bailiff led the empanelled jurors and alternate through the murder car and the dining car, pointing out the Lower 13 berth, the smoking room, the ladies' dressing room, the kitchen section of the diner, and various berths where leading witnesses (not yet sworn in or even introduced to jurors) supposedly slept the night of the murder.[14] In this way, an official representative of the court impressed on novice jurors which evidence and witnesses were important and how they connected to the murder scene.

When jurors returned to the courtroom from their tour of the restaged "murder scene," Weinrick explained his theory of how they should think about those railcars in relation to the case against Folkes. In an opening statement lasting some fifteen minutes, he reviewed Martha James' movements before and after boarding the train, then he described his version of Folkes' movements that night, and finally, he claimed prosecutors would present physical evidence and eyewitness testimony that would prove Folkes was guilty.[15] The story Weinrick told the jury was a streamlined version of the one that appeared in the written statement LAPD detectives claimed they took from Folkes while they detained him at Central Jail in LA. The subsequent trial, however, failed to produce either eyewitness testimony or physical evidence linking Folkes with the murder. In fact, it yielded evidence that actually seemed to exonerate him.

In an energetic effort to discredit the prosecution's opening statements, defense attorney Leroy Lomax actually misread the rural sensibilities of jurors, eroded his own credibility, and put Folkes at a disadvantage. Lomax responded to Weinrick's opening statement with apparent outrage, observing this was the first time he had heard the prosecution's theory of the case. This claim was technically true, but it rang false to observers who lived in a county where lurid reports of the investigation had choked formal and informal news networks over the previous three months. Lomax, moreover, seriously misjudged his audience by challenging the integrity of uniformed authorities and court officials in the supercharged atmosphere of patriotic sacrifice and militarization in those first years of the war. In a fiery and combative opening statement, Lomax accused the OSP, SPRR, the Pullman Company, and Weinrick of colluding to prevent him from contacting passengers who were on the train the night of the murder. He stated those public and private authorities refused to disclose reports, statements, evidence, or even theories of their case to the defense. Although this was evidently true, it seemed shrill and overdramatic in that quiet county courthouse during a challenging phase of a difficult war. The SPRR representative at trial, W. H. Stone, privately focused, with some concern, on the conspiracy claims Lomax raised, but the *Oregonian* mostly dismissed and ridiculed Lomax's claims as legal histrionics. Lomax, in a similarly misguided effort to garner sympathy for his client, also informed the press Folkes had just received his draft notice the morning of the trial.[16] Coming as it did in the second full year of the war, this appeal rang hollow in a rural community where many young men of military age had already voluntarily enlisted. In the pervasive atmosphere of wartime crisis, it gave the impression Folkes was complaining, through his lawyer, about a personal sacrifice most local residents viewed as a badge of virtuous masculinity.

The line of defense Lomax invoked on behalf of his client was unintentionally patronizing and insulting to his rural audience and what they valued in terms of masculine virtues in wartime. Rather than focusing on the remarkable employment record and reputation for reliability that Folkes had earned as a responsible, hardworking laborer who contributed to the economic

Defense Attorney Leroy Lomax, Robert Folkes, and William Pollard at the defense table in the Albany courtroom at the start of the trial. A cropped version of this image appeared in the *Oregon Journal* on 8 April 1943. Image courtesy the Associated Press.

support of his family for nearly half his young life, Lomax referred to his twenty-one-year-old client, during opening statements, as "a boy charged with murder."[17] It was a defense strategy that seriously misrepresented the respectable identity this young workingman had carved out for himself over nearly a decade of gainful employment.

Lomax had badly misjudged his mid-Valley audience. Everyone on the all-White jury lived in towns or hamlets with populations under ten thousand and mostly fewer than two thousand.[18] They presented the collective appearance of taciturn farm folk skeptical of lawyers and city slickers. The urbane and theatrical defense attorney's task was complicated by the fact that his client was a stylishly dressed Black man wearing what local reporters misidentified as a "zoot suit," and his assistant in the case, William Pollard, was a studious-looking Black man in a well-tailored business suit. None of these three members of the defense team blended well with small-town culture or rural traditions in Linn County, where the median educational level was only eight years of schooling.[19] Even if jurors remained unaware of Pollard's radical credentials, the labor advocate's studious, well-dressed, intellectual presence visibly jarred with the common appearance and demeanor of others in the courtroom.

In his most successful effort to reframe the case for jurors, Lomax questioned why the prosecutor was so willing to accept Wilson's story. He told jurors a plausible alternative version, offering a plotline that more fairly represented the many statements Folkes gave investigators aboard the train. The most important corroborating witness to this alternative storyline was Porter Hughes, whose timeline, if jurors accepted it, would have virtually eliminated Folkes as a possible suspect. Lomax also emphasized that certain key witnesses individually refused to cooperate with defense investigators, notably including Chief Petty Officer Kelso.[20] In an opening thirty-minute statement that skeptical observers described as "quite theatrical,"[21] Lomax devoted the bulk of his opening remarks to a story that placed Wilson at the scene of the murder, behaving inexplicably, redirecting investigators in the opposite direction from where he claimed the murderer fled, and rummaging through used towels to carry away those with blood on them. Sometime later, Lomax said, Wilson went back through the train and wiped blood on a towel in the second car behind the death car.[22] Nothing Lomax offered, however, was as substantial as the "murder scene" prosecutors framed as if it were unbiased evidence. The staged scene of two railcars in Albany's roundhouse told a story more powerful than the theatrical voice of one histrionic lawyer. Pragmatic farm folk trusted their eyes and local authorities more than a sharp urban lawyer from Portland.

ACT II, SCENE 2:

STAGE-MANAGING WITNESSES AND THE ORDER OF EVIDENCE

Weinrick's prosecution team presented the case in a manner designed to distract and misdirect jurors rather than clarify inconsistencies or gaps in the evidence. They called more than thirty witnesses to the stand and questioned them in ways that differed depending on their race, gender, occupational background, and class. They segregated Black witnesses from portions of the trial that explored details of the crime scene or other problematic testimony. They called White witnesses with potentially damaging testimony to appear early in the trial, before their significance to the case was apparent and before prosecutors broached issues that would have allowed the defense to productively cross-examine those witnesses. They asked early, potentially problematic witnesses only narrowly defined questions and then abruptly cut them off whenever they tried to explain their answers. They sandwiched the testimony of Black trainmen between reliably authoritative voices of White witnesses, and they strictly limited the number of female voices (only two adult passengers, one child, plus two police stenographers). They concluded with a parade of investigating officers who repetitiously retold the story prosecutors had introduced in opening arguments.

All through the early days of the trial, prosecutors refused to admit they had any written statements in their possession, and then, near the end of the trial, they read into the record precisely those statements they had previously pretended not to have. In doing so, they pretended they were quoting the full text of what Folkes actually said to them, and they adopted affected voices and other dramatic flairs to make the oral reading of those statements more interesting and compelling. The entire production went off with only a few minor glitches, notably involving the testimony of Wilson, Hughes, and Shaw, each of whom took the stand as witnesses for the prosecution and then, in various ways, challenged the simplistic, moralizing storyline prosecutors wanted jurors to remember.

By the time jurors began deliberations in the third week of the trial, few observers seemed confident which way the verdict might go, not least because, from a dispassionate distance and to a small but significant minority of observers, the contradictions in the story prosecutors had presented seemed obvious and fatal to their case against Folkes. That case, however, was neither dispassionate nor distant from jurors, who lived through a theatrical experience that warped their perception of events on Train 15.

The authoritative voice of the White train conductor, William Banks, posed the most serious threat to the story prosecutors wanted the jury to believe, but they cleverly maneuvered him into supporting their claim that the case was a "closed-room" murder mystery. The conductor was among the first on the scene of the murder, and he managed the initial investigation, but after Weinrick introduced him to jurors early in the trial, the prosecutor narrowly limited his questioning of Banks, asking only for details of the train's scheduled stops, the makeup of the train, and procedures for managing passengers. Prosecutors put the conductor on the defensive with sharp questioning that forced him to explain his management of the train after he first discovered the murder, and Banks was most emphatic in asserting no one had left the train when he held it on the siding at Harrisburg.[23] The clear implication was that the murderer was someone on the train, and jurors were primed to think of "the train" as including just the "murder car" and "the diner." This narrowed the range of possible murderers to people in those two cars.

In broad outline, prosecutors effectively concealed contradictory testimony by excluding it altogether or by surrounding it with marginally relevant or wholly irrelevant details. Jurors who sat through all the testimony for nearly three weeks in Lewelling's courtroom seldom heard contradictory testimony in context with opposing views. Instead, prosecutors overwhelmed them with a repetitive string of witnesses who told stories that seemed broadly familiar, but only because the details of earlier, conflicting testimony had mostly faded into distant memories. When they finally presented Wilson's story, for example, well-informed trainmen like Banks, Shaw, and Bryant had all previously testified, but they were not allowed to testify on matters relating directly to their perceptions of Wilson or his story. Lomax was handicapped by the refusal of prosecutors to release any statements they had acquired from those witnesses. When he cross-examined Shaw, for example, Lomax had no idea what Wilson or Hughes would later testify, nor did he know all that Shaw had told investigators about what he observed the night of the murder. By the time he learned Shaw had supplied investigators with written statements, the defense attorney had already completed his cross-examination of the witness. When he learned of the existence of Shaw's written statement, Lomax asked Lewelling to direct prosecutors to produce it, but the judge ruled, "The time to have done that was when he [Shaw] was on the witness stand."[24] Rulings like this supported Weinrick's efforts to conceal from jurors obvious contradictions in the prosecution's version of the case.

Shaw's testimony was damaging to the prosecution's case, but he was a Black porter, and without corroboration from a White witness, prosecutors clearly believed the White women and men on the jury were unlikely to accept his story over Wilson's. In a pattern apparent throughout the trial, they followed the Black trainman with a White witness: Pullman Conductor Bryant, who tended to support both Shaw and Folkes. Bryant was a seventeen-year veteran of PPC, and a resident of the prosperous and overwhelmingly White suburban community of Arcadia, California, northeast of LA near Pasadena. His testimony described Martha James as agitated, assertive, and independent—not at all a passive, timid young woman.[25] This characterization challenged the prosecution's efforts to establish the victim as a vulnerable and exploited damsel in distress and threatened the emotional underpinnings of their case.

Under cross-examination, Bryant directly challenged the credibility of prosecutors, and in doing so, he offered the biggest opening in the case to the defense. Bryant disclosed that he personally secured statements from each passenger in the murder car, immediately after discovering the murder, and he testified that he estimated the number of passengers in Car D at twenty-nine or thirty people, most of them women who were never called as witnesses. Bryant also confirmed that SPRR officials independently secured separate written statements from each passenger in the car. These admissions substantiated the claim Lomax made in his opening remarks that company officials concealed evidence from the defense. More directly, he denied that Folkes made repeated trips through Car D prior to the murder. Bryant testified that on his own many trips through Car D between 12:30 a.m. and 3:00 a.m., he never encountered Folkes.[26] Curiously, in an effort to discount Bryant's admission that trainmen took statements that were not provided to the defense, Weinrick pressed the point that the Pullman conductor had not secured signatures from passengers on those handwritten statements,[27] implying that they were, for that reason, not legal "statements." He later made the opposite argument, claiming that unsigned statements prosecutors attributed to Folkes constituted his legal "confession."

Bryant's admissions on the stand threatened to undo Weinrick's case against Folkes. The experienced district attorney, however, abruptly refocused jurors away from the issue of who did the crime and focused, instead, on the heartrending story of how wartime circumstances left the innocent young White war bride stranded, alone, and without her luggage in a world of Black trainmen on a lonely station platform. He called to the stand Portland passenger agent Harold Hoffert—a White man—followed by the supervisor of janitors and redcaps at Portland—a Black man named Phil Reynolds. Together, these two witnesses explained how they located Martha James' two missing bags in the unclaimed baggage from Seattle.[28] The testimony of Reynolds and Hoffert actually undercut Weinrick's case against Folkes by tracking the movements of Martha James from the platform through the time she retired for the night. By their combined testimony, she was never alone at or near her berth with any Black trainman other than the redcap or the porter, neither of whom wore a uniform remotely resembling a cook's.[29] Their combined testimony, however, distracted jurors from Bryant's, which more directly challenged the case against Folkes, and the seasoned DA quickly redirected their attention with a White matronly witness who told a story more likely to resonate with women on the jury.

ACT II, SCENE 3: THE MARINE, THE MAN IN THE DARK OVERCOAT,
AND THE FAST RUNNER

Prosecutors relied almost entirely on male voices to build their case against
Folkes, but they used female voices to encourage jurors to disregard inconsistent timelines and to accept the premise that, apart from Folkes, no one
should be expected to account precisely for their whereabouts at particular
times. They called on Mrs. Davis Chamberlin to introduce the first details
of the circumstances surrounding the murder and as a lead-in to their star
witness, Wilson. Chamberlin's female voice introduced events without concern for precise timing, acclimating the jury to a case that held together only
if they ignored how more specific timelines tended to exonerate Folkes.
Prosecutors encouraged Chamberlin, and then Wilson, to speculate on precise times, even though both witnesses admitted they had no way of telling
time. Wilson's rambling account, which followed directly after Chamberlin's,
was riddled with internal contradictions, confusing asides, and uncertainties.
Most importantly, nothing in his official courtroom testimony implicated
Folkes, and when given the opportunity to do so, he explicitly refused to
identify the defendant as the man he claimed to have seen running from the
victim's berth. Wilson's courtroom testimony left Stone and other members
of the prosecution shaken about prospects for conviction, but they shored
up gaping holes in his story by producing "surprise" testimony from three
White male passengers: Ralph Conner, Eugene W. Norton, and William W.
Van Dyke, followed by Marjorie Wasserman, a teenager from Los Angeles.
Conner, Norton, and Wasserman all testified in ways that helped jurors accept
Wilson's otherwise implausible and constantly changing story, and all three of
them dramatically altered their courtroom testimony from their own earlier
statements. After Wasserman, prosecutors called the brakeman (Anders), the
petty officer (Kelso), and then, finally, Porter Hughes.

Weinrick clearly expected women on the jury would empathize with
Chamberlin—a White middle-aged woman much like themselves—and that
her description of the brutally murdered James, a vulnerable innocent, would
outrage and blind them to factual gaps in the case against Folkes. Chamberlin
described how she comforted the much smaller, distraught Martha James in
the women's dressing room sometime around midnight. Her timeline contradicted previous testimony, but neither prosecution nor defense challenged
her inconsistencies regarding when, exactly, their encounter took place.
Chamberlin testified James was "concerned" because she had lost her bags,

and the younger woman left the dressing room "just a few minutes" after their chat. Some fifteen minutes later, Chamberlin returned to her berth (Lower 15), finding James sitting on Lower 13, fully clothed, still without luggage. About an hour later, as the train left Portland (1:30 a.m., from other testimony), Chamberlin returned to the dressing room, finding James "preparing to retire," relieved to finally have her luggage.[30]

With Chamberlin's testimony, Weinrick encouraged the jury of mostly rural farm women to consider how they or one of their daughters might have experienced travel in the difficult conditions in that overcrowded Pullman car. She told the court it was her first train trip in over twenty years, and unlike Shaw or other experienced trainmen, she found her passage that night confusing, unfamiliar, and disorienting.[31] Her testimony gave jurors their first description of the murder scene, filtered through an older woman's perceptions while she was suspended in a dreamlike state between sleep and wakefulness.[32] Banks, who might have offered more details, was prevented from testifying on that issue.

Chamberlin's testimony broke with the opening story prosecutors told jurors about the positions of the assailant, the victim, and Wilson around the time witnesses heard James scream. Lomax asked whether Chamberlin saw anyone in the aisle when she first looked out after hearing the scream, and Chamberlin replied with certainty, "I didn't see anyone. There was no one in the aisle." Asked repeatedly if the light was sufficient to see if someone were there, she confidently replied, "Yes, you could have seen them." Asked specifically if she would have noticed a man standing with one leg protruding from Lower 13, she agreed that there was nothing in the aisle that attracted her attention at all.[33] Her testimony directly conflicted with Wilson's earlier statements, which claimed he heard the scream, looked out, and saw the man in the pin-striped suit backing out of the berth and running from the scene as Martha lurched into the aisle. Wilson also claimed he jumped down to ease James to the ground. Chamberlin saw none of this, but she described how, sometime after the murder, she heard Wilson's voice announcing the murder and warning women not to look out from their berths.[34]

By introducing Marine private Harold Wilson through the matronly eyes of Chamberlin, Weinrick positioned him as a chivalrous protector of feminine frailties before jurors had a chance to hear other witnesses offer less forgiving descriptions. In a memo describing his strategy before the trial, Weinrick laid out two primary hurdles for success: first, prosecutors had to show that Folkes committed the crime; second, they had to show Wilson had not. Wilson was Weinrick's star witness but also the greatest risk to the prosecution, not least because he was the most obvious suspect. His testimony conflicted, on crucial points, with most other witnesses', and it was riddled with internal contradictions and obvious evasions. His story also changed dramatically from early in the investigation, but jurors were supposed to consider only evidence presented at trial. Many courtroom observers noticed how his story changed, but those differences were unimportant to prosecutors—unless, of course, they were interested in solving the crime rather than simply convicting Folkes. Wilson was the only witness who, in written statements prior to trial, positively claimed he saw a man fleeing Lower 13. If he claimed in court that man was the defendant, it would seal the case against Folkes. Weinrick needed Wilson's testimony to counter the problems Shaw and Bryant had introduced.

Wilson testified longer than any other witness, allowing prosecutors more time to camouflage his inconsistencies and shape how jurors thought about the case. His time on the stand stretched across six consecutive news days, from Friday, 9 April, through Wednesday, 14 April, including three days when court was in recess (Saturday, Sunday, and Tuesday). During those six days, prosecutors and investigators frequently conferred with him. Wilson openly admitted, under cross-examination, that prosecutors coached him during recesses, and Lomax successfully detailed for the jury many ways in which the marine's story changed as a result. Lewelling, however, offered jurors no advice regarding whether, in coaching their witness, prosecutors had crossed an ethical or legal line.[35]

The key to Wilson's continuing "credibility" as a witness for the prosecution, despite his obviously shifting, contradictory story, was the degree to which jurors accepted him as a symbol of military correctness and responsibility. That military identity distinguished him from both Shaw, who was Black, and Bryant, who was White. Weinrick cautiously wrapped Wilson's testimony in the marine's serviceman persona. He first established Wilson's military credentials without mentioning rank—"You are employed with the United States forces?"—and then stressed his connection with Oregon, not his earlier background in Minnesota. Wilson testified only that he was "employed" with the US Marines, not that he was a recently recruited private or that he was released from the brig at Bremerton Naval Base the same day he boarded Train 15. In fact, there was no mention, in court, that police discovered his criminal past or record of sexual assault. Wilson only stated he was with the Naval Air Station at Tongue Point, and that he was travelling from Seattle to Portland "under Government orders" to report at "San Diego, California, Fleet Marine Force." Weinrick stressed repetitiously that Wilson was travelling by "government transportation" and "under military orders," implying he was on a secret or critical mission of some sort. Unlike the details prosecutors extracted from Richard James specifying how he and Martha travelled from Seattle to Portland, Weinrick asked Wilson to start with when he arrived in Portland,[36] sidestepping why the Marines shipped him from the Bremerton brig to San Diego without his unit.

Militarization infused the tone and substance of Wilson's testimony, and prosecutors papered over his inconsistencies with implications that the marine's military judgment was more reliable than civilian timelines or expertise. He answered each question with military terseness, frequently responding only "Yes, sir" or "No, sir." As a hedge against Wilson's inconsistent chronology, Weinrick encouraged him to admit he did not have a watch, noting his malleable time estimates were "merely guesses or your best judgment," thus preempting concerns he might be an unreliable or untruthful witness. Wilson claimed he first secured a berth in Car D at about 2:00 a.m., when Porter Shaw directed him to Upper 13. He took off his uniform coat and dress shirt, walked back to the men's lounge to clean up, stayed there until about 2:20 a.m., and then went back to his berth and went to sleep. This timeline conflicted with Porter Shaw's by at least twenty minutes.[37]

Wilson's testimony provided a timeline that differed from other witnesses', but it was much more consistent and less problematic for the prosecution than ones he offered in earlier statements, either to police or to reporters. Wilson testified he fell asleep within half an hour after returning to his berth, which, by his own timeline, would have been 3:00 a.m. He claimed he slept until 4:30 or 4:45 a.m. When Weinrick asked, "How did you establish that time?" Wilson replied, "By the lady's scream."[38] Since he had already testified he had no watch, that statement illustrates how he adjusted his time estimates to fit his understanding of the prosecutor's proposed timeline for the murder, but Weinrick encouraged the jury to consider Wilson's adjusted timeline as authoritative, eyewitness evidence that the murder, in fact, took place during a window of time that was after 4:35 a.m. and before 4:50 a.m.—a fifteen-minute window when no one could verify Folkes' whereabouts except that he had breakfast cooking and ready by 4:50 a.m.

Weinrick next led Wilson through a detailed summary of his actions after hearing the scream, telling a story familiar to anyone who followed early news reports, but with significantly revised details tailored to the jury audience and the case against Folkes. There was no more mention of a pin-striped suit. Wilson, instead, testified that when he looked down over the curtain rod, he saw a man in "dark clothing" who was "just departing from berth 13" and wearing "a dark overcoat." He had no recollection what the man's hair looked like and claimed he couldn't tell if it was long or short. He hedged on the direction the man went, first testifying he went "to the left," but when the prosecutor asked him whether that meant he went forward in the train or toward the rear, Wilson testified the man "pivoted" forward (away from the diner, which would have been to the rear of Car D). This testimony contradicted the story prosecutors wanted the jury to understand. Weinrick, consequently, led the witness to support the case against Folkes: "As I understand it, he proceeded to the rear of the train?" Wilson then reversed himself, saying, "He did." Weinrick then quickly changed the subject.[39]

Wilson also adjusted his testimony about the position of the body, correcting the contradiction in his previous story that Banks had brought to his attention early in the investigation. The marine testified that after the man ran around the corner toward the rear of Car D, Wilson saw Martha James emerge from her berth "frontwards," then slump to the floor "with her left arm and her head resting on the arm of lower 14 berth and her right arm was on the mattress."[40] This addressed the concern Banks previously raised, in his written statement, that Wilson's original explanation to the conductor of how he found Martha's body lying prone in the aisle did not match the way the victim's blood had completely soaked the mattress in Lower 14.

Other parts of Wilson's testimony were laughably impossible. When Weinrick asked Wilson to describe the distance the murderer ran after he left berth 13, the marine responded, "About nine steps." The total distance between Lower 13 and the corner of the hallway at the rear of the car (one berth away), however, was only slightly over six feet two inches. Wilson, a former high school athlete, claimed the man ran very quickly in that direction but required, at a full run, at least nine steps to cover only six feet. Later, under cross-examination, he repeatedly claimed, in response to incredulous questioning from Lomax, that it took the man ten or twelve seconds to run, not walk, that distance. As the man passed the light at the end of the corridor, Wilson claimed he glimpsed the man's hair and part of his face, just before he rounded the corner.[41] He estimated it took the man another four running steps to disappear from sight, around a corner less than three feet wide, or a total of thirteen running steps to cover only nine feet. These statements should have thoroughly discredited the witness in the eyes of the jury, and prosecutors were clearly shaken by this testimony. Rather than rethink their approach, however, they moved to shore up his credibility.

In an effort to rebuild juror trust in Wilson's story, Weinrick encouraged him to speak with authority about mundane details he noticed in the kitchen, where he first encountered Folkes shortly after the murder: the door was open; the cook was preparing to fry, not just some eggs, or one egg, but precisely two eggs. With this uncorroborated example of Wilson's ability to pay close attention to and remember detail (as compared with his obvious inability to do so at the more remarkable scene of the actual crime), Weinrick then encouraged Wilson to repeat, verbatim, a conversation he had with a "young negro cook" in the kitchen of the dining car at 5:00 a.m. nearly three full months before the trial. Folkes, according to Wilson, "kind of smiled" and told him, "I have been here a little later than usual." In response to news a murder had been committed, Folkes asked whether Wilson had been drinking. The marine testified that he replied, "No, this is military information; I have to have it." With Wilson's military authority thus established, the marine claimed that Folkes instantly adopted a more deferential demeanor, and when asked how long he'd been there, the cook "looked at the clock which is up on the shelf, and he said about twenty minutes to half an hour."[42]

None of the witnesses, including Wilson, could link Folkes directly to the crime, but Weinrick managed to stage an opportunity where his star witness pointed directly at Folkes, before the jury, and positively identified him—even though it had nothing to do with placing him at the murder scene. After leading Wilson through a detailed recap of his interactions with the man in the kitchen, who was exactly where his job required at 5:00 a.m., Weinrick theatrically asked Wilson if he could identify the cook, and if he could point him out in the courtroom. In this way, the prosecutor arranged to have the marine, who previously claimed to have seen the murderer fleeing the scene, point to the defendant in the courtroom, as if the fact he saw him at his duty station in the kitchen, at a time when he was supposed to be precisely there, had anything at all to do with the murder. Weinrick then asked Wilson to detail each subsequent time he saw Folkes, from the time they spoke in the kitchen through the time the marine left the train in Klamath Falls. Wilson claimed he saw Folkes walking along the tracks in Eugene, carrying a pail, and then he testified that while Folkes was held in Linn County jail awaiting trial, and while Wilson was also held there as a material witness from 23 January through 22 February, sheriff's deputies assigned him (Wilson) the responsibility of taking Folkes his meals each day.[43] This testimony positioned Wilson as Folkes' jailer, rather than a possible alternative suspect or even merely a witness.[44]

Weinrick desperately needed Wilson to counter earlier testimony that Folkes was hard at work in the kitchen when the murder took place. He asked Wilson if he observed "anything unusual about Robert Folkes when you saw him there?" The marine obligingly testified that Folkes was stammering and nervous and "seemed to be perspiring quite heavily. . . . Beads of perspiration were coming out on his forehead and starting to run down his face." Asked whether there was a fire in the stove at the time, Wilson claimed the stove was cold and the kitchen was cool.[45] This sequence of questions left the impression, first, that Wilson was a keen observer and, second, that Folkes was acting strangely and pretending to cook on a cold stove, shortly after the murder. By the time Weinrick reached this point in the interrogation, it was nearing 5:00 p.m. on a Friday afternoon, and the judge called a recess until 9:30 the next morning (Saturday). In stretching Wilson's testimony across several days, Weinrick isolated this claim that the marine saw Folkes pretending to cook on a cold stove from Wilson's earlier testimony that he had seen not one but precisely two eggs frying on that same, supposedly cold, stove.

The court did not reconvene until Monday morning because Lomax fell ill over the weekend, and when Wilson finally resumed the stand he admitted, under cross-examination, that he had discussed his testimony with Weinrick and OSP lieutenant Howard over the weekend.[46] Despite that admission, Lomax seemed at a loss how to proceed. Wilson's testimony contradicted even itself, never mind that of previous witnesses. The points of contradiction were so varied and numerous that the defense attorney could choose many possible starting points for constructing a story that would expose the marine's inconsistent narrative. With so many mundane points of difference, however, Lomax also risked confusing jurors about which facts were unimportant and which were crucial. After several false starts, he finally asked Wilson whether Folkes was the man he saw running from Lower 13. Wilson replied, "I don't know."[47]

Wilson implausibly argued that his ability to recollect details of events he witnessed actually increased rather than decreased over time. He claimed

greater detachment from emotions of the moment encouraged clearer thinking. He indicated that whereas his statements immediately after the murder
included many details about what he saw, he later came to believe those
details were incorrect, and that his subsequent reconstruction of events, in his
own mind, provided more reliable details than what he claimed to remember
in the first half hour after the murder was discovered.[48] Lomax asked whether
Wilson discussed his recollection of a brown pin-striped suit with Weinrick,
and the marine admitted he had, but he denied Weinrick had suggested it
may have been a dark overcoat, and he claimed he came up with that idea
on his own, even though it contradicted his own earlier statements. Lomax
adroitly asked questions that demonstrated to the jury how Wilson's narrative changed over time, emphasizing his interactions with prosecutors, thus
demonstrating he had been coached to change his story to make it more consistent with the prosecutors' theory of the crime.

While Wilson emphasized his military credentials and experience, Lomax
resorted to thinly veiled ridicule to break through the marine's veneer of militarized authority. He asked Wilson, regarding the victim, "Did you say she
jumped, skipped, or stepped and ran out of the berth?" The witness replied,
"No, I said she came lunging out of her berth." Lomax, suggesting Wilson had
altered his testimony on that point after conversations with Weinrick over the
weekend, asked why he changed that detail from his description the previous
Friday, when he said Martha James "came running out of the berth" and that
she had come out "frontwards." In the midst of this promising and aggressive
cross-examination, however, Lomax suddenly felt ill and abruptly asked for a
recess, interrupting a series of questions that seemed to be shaking Wilson's
confidence and effectively highlighting his unreliability.[49]

Whenever Lomax managed to make headway against the prosecution's
case, the judge intervened in ways that eroded the defense attorney's credibility with the jury. At one point, Lomax exposed the prosecution's failure to
provide copies of witness statements that the defense sought during discovery, and then he tried to secure an order from the judge directing Weinrick
to surrender those documents. Lewelling, however, denied that request,
and when Lomax challenged that ruling, the judge rebuked him before the
jury, undermining the defense attorney's standing. As prosecutors gained
confidence in similarly favorable rulings, they more aggressively challenged
defense motions. When Lomax insisted prosecutors produce Porter Shaw's
written statement, for example, Sisemore demanded that the judge order

stricken from the record the insinuation that the state withheld evidence from the defense. Lewelling rejected Sisemore's motion, but he ruled Lomax had missed his chance to request the statement while Shaw was on the stand. He then denied a defense request to recall Shaw to the stand. Lomax protested that those rulings effectively denied defense access to state records. Lewelling snapped back, "I said nothing of the kind, and you know I did not. . . . There is no showing it is a state record, and I resent those kind of statements." Lomax apologized and asked the court to inquire into the matter, but Lewelling responded, "I don't know anything about it. . . . Proceed with the cross examination of this witness [Wilson]."[50]

The testy exchange with Lewelling distracted jurors from the substance of Wilson's testimony, and it eroded Lomax's standing in the court as a professional voice of reasoned authority. Lewelling forced Lomax into a string of apologies, all in front of the jury. Rather than simply accepting each apology, the judge repeatedly and aggressively restated his dissatisfaction with Lomax, forcing a total of three separate apologies, all in open court. Only then was Lomax allowed to return to cross-examining Wilson. This confrontation empowered the beleaguered witness. After the exchange, Wilson was suddenly more evasive and answered most questions from Lomax with terse phrases bereft of his habitual use of the honorific "sir." He mostly replied, thereafter, in curt monosyllables: "Yes," "No," "It was," or "I don't remember." Finally, he denied ever telling anybody the man he saw leaving Lower 13 was a White man.[51] At that crucial point in the cross-examination, Lomax again took ill and requested a recess until later that afternoon (Monday). When court reconvened at 2:00 p.m., however, Lewelling informed the jury that on advice of a doctor (DeRiver, who later testified in court for the prosecution regarding his examination of Folkes at LAPD headquarters), Lomax would not be able to continue until at least two days hence. With that, Lewelling called a recess until Wednesday morning at ten o'clock, admonishing the jury to avoid discussing the case with each other or with anyone else.

The courtroom transcript, despite Stone's positive assessment of Wilson's testimony, actually documents the marine's increasing confusion and testiness in response to questions from Lomax. The defense attorney, for example, cornered Wilson into admitting he gave three prior signed statements, including one to PPC agents, one to SPRR detectives, and one to OSP investigators. Lomax also extracted from Wilson a timeline that differed from what he testified in response to Weinrick. Under cross-examination, Wilson claimed he was with a previously undisclosed friend, "Al," in a chair car until about 2:00 a.m.,[52] and that he stayed in the men's smoking room in Car D for some time before retiring in Upper 13. Perhaps most importantly, Wilson revised his story about how the man he claimed to have seen pivoted after leaving the victim's berth. In a testy exchange, Wilson corrected Lomax, who had accurately quoted the marine's prior testimony (apparently reading from courtroom notes) in which the witness claimed the man pivoted first left, and then right, before running to the rear of the train. Wilson interrupted, insisting the man "pivoted to his left and ran to the elbow of the car and then pivoted to the right."[53] This conflicted not only with Wilson's prior testimony but also with the layout of Car D.

Near the end of Wilson's time on the stand, Lomax made telling inroads on the marine's credibility as a military figure, in a series of questions that probed the recruit's knowledge of his own unit and chain of command. With no access to any statements Wilson had previously supplied prosecutors, Lomax probed blindly until he stumbled across an astonishing gap in the marine's story. Referring to courtroom transcripts from Wilson's earlier testimony, Lomax asked Wilson to reconfirm where he was headed, on orders from Bremerton, and Wilson replied, "Fleet Marine Corps, San Diego." Lomax followed up with, "What Battalion and Regiment did you belong to?" Wilson replied he was with Guard Company One in the Sixth Battalion. Asked, "What regiment?" he replied, "I don't know." Lomax then asked which unit he was ordered to join in San Diego, and Wilson replied, "Just Guard Company 1." In the apparent belief the witness misunderstood his question, Lomax clarified, "No, I mean when you left Bremerton, what regiment were you assigned to?" Wilson repeated, "Guard Company 1." Lomax followed up with a series of questions seeking to clarify whether Wilson's entire company was relocating to San Diego, but the witness initially replied, "I don't know." Finally, Wilson admitted he was travelling alone. Asked his commander's name, Wilson could only identify him as "Captain Woody." [54] At that point, Lomax abruptly ended his cross-examination, leaving jurors with the memory of a marine who not only did not know the details of his unit designation in Bremerton, but could not even recall his commanding officer's full name and did not even know whether his own unit was relocating with him to San Diego.

ACT II, SCENE 4:
THE "SURPRISE WITNESSES" AND DRAMATIC DISCLOSURES

With Wilson's credibility as a military expert shaken, prosecutors revived their case with a dramatic flourish they borrowed from true-crime novels of the interwar period: a series of "surprise witnesses"—all of them White—who told remarkably different stories in court than they had previously offered in sworn statements. Marjorie Wasserman, Ralph Conner, and Eugene Norton each offered testimony that diverted attention from areas of obvious confusion in Wilson's narrative. Previously, only Wilson claimed to have seen a man fleeing the scene of the crime, and only Hughes positively stated he saw Folkes in Car D at any time prior to the murder. Hughes' various statements and eventual testimony, to the chagrin of prosecutors, actually solidified Folkes' alibi, establishing details about his movements and the timing of the murder that made it virtually impossible for him to have committed the crime. At trial, however, both Norton and Conner testified that they saw a man in a dark overcoat—possibly blue or green—fleeing down the aisle after the murder, and Marjorie Wasserman, a fifteen-year-old girl, testified in court she saw a man who "looked like" Folkes talking with James near her berth sometime after midnight that night. The courtroom testimony by each of these three witnesses directly contradicted their earlier sworn statements, but neither jurors nor Lomax were ever told those statements existed. With these surprise witnesses, the case suddenly shifted dramatically against Folkes, even though no one—not even Wilson—ever confirmed he was the man they supposedly saw in that coat or talking to Martha.

The three surprise witnesses testified in ways that further complicated the story with new contradictions that served the purpose of distracting jurors from Wilson's miscues. Unlike Conner, who testified the lights were bright in Car D, Eugene Norton testified just a few minutes later that lighting was "very poor." Norton said he saw James "lunging on to the floor near [not into] what I would say was berth 14." This contradicted both Wilson and Conner, who both claimed she lunged part way into berth 14 while clutching the curtains. Norton claimed he was distracted for a moment when he saw "a man's head up over the top of [berth 9]," who he later learned was Conner. When he looked back into the aisle, he saw Wilson standing above the woman, placing "something white" under her head. Norton was emphatic that he "could never imagine where this man come from. . . . There was nobody there for a short interval prior to that other than the lady lying in the aisle."[55] This statement contradicted Wilson's testimony that he helped lower the woman to the aisle by gripping her beneath her armpits from behind. Norton also noted Wilson was "one berth and a half" behind the woman's body, "in this little place, just before you make the turn [at the back of the car in the angled aisle leading to the dining car]" when he hollered, "This is murder, stop the train," throwing his hands up in the air.[56] In other words, Norton first saw Wilson suddenly appear from the rear of Car D, from precisely the direction where Norton and Conner both claimed they saw a dark shape fleeing, only moments earlier. No one saw Wilson emerge from Upper 13, and no one saw him peering over the top of the curtains, as he testified he had done, although Norton did notice the passenger in Upper 9 doing that.

Lomax responded to the melodramatic disclosures of the surprise witnesses by grilling the least sympathetic witness of the three—the man mistakenly identified in some early reports as a serviceman—on whether he previously provided investigators signed statements that might corroborate his suddenly detailed memory of events that happened more than three months earlier. Norton, who was employed as an SPRR machinist at the time of the murder and was not a serviceman, admitted that he gave four prior signed statements—one to Sisemore, one to Weinrick, one to SPRR detectives, and one to OSP investigators. He also confirmed he refused Lomax's request to question him prior to the trial.[57]

An alert juror, given enough time with access to a printed transcript of courtroom testimony, may have noticed how Norton's testimony conflicted with previous witnesses', but jurors had only their own memories of what each witness said, swaddled in a suffocating blanket of insignificant detail. Closely questioning Norton about details of his sworn testimony, Lomax demonstrated the witness was seriously confused about the sequence of events from the time he first noticed Wilson to when Porter Hughes arrived on the scene. Norton's testimony conflicted with Wilson's narrative and with Marine sergeant Van Dyke's recollections on where and when Wilson first appeared in the aisle and began shouting. He testified Van Dyke "put his head out" from Lower 12, then pulled it back in, just before Wilson began shouting, and that "just as he [Wilson] was hollering . . . the bell rang."[58] Most damaging for the prosecution's case, Norton testified, under cross-examination, that Wilson had blood on the back of his left arm, up midway to his elbow, and not only on his palm.[59]

Norton also contradicted his own sworn testimony. He admitted under oath that Weinrick visited him at the SPRR offices in the San Francisco Bay

Area, coached him on how he should testify, and supplied him with transportation from Daly City to Albany for the trial. Earlier, under direct questioning from prosecutors, Norton had testified he had not previously discussed the case or his testimony with them.[60] Clearly, he had perjured himself, either in his initial testimony or under cross-examination, and Weinrick swiftly moved to counter that impression with the next "surprise" witness.

The third of the "surprise witnesses" Weinrick melodramatically sprang on the jury was a young girl who had travelled with her father on Train 15, and the prosecutor prepared the jury to listen to her quiet, hesitant, childlike voice by positioning her after two other particularly sympathetic witnesses. First, he called the injured marine, Sergeant Van Dyke, who testified just before a female caregiver—army nurse Alice Reard. Then, finally, the youngest of all the witnesses, Marjorie Wasserman, came to the stand. This progression of witnesses gradually moved the prosecution's narrative in diminishing degrees of masculinity from assertively male voices to passive and feminine voices—from the self-confident railroad machinist, Norton, to the hesitant and uncertain voice of the injured marine, Van Dyke, and then Reard, the soft-spoken yet self-confident and pragmatic nurse whose quietly female voice prepared jurors for the hesitant, uncertain, teenaged voice of Wasserman. When she finally took the stand, Wasserman was the only person whose testimony vaguely placed Folkes anywhere near the scene of the crime. Unbeknownst to the jury, she presented evidence that LAPD lieutenant Tetrick had helped her remember or reconstruct during their pretrial interview at the Wasserman home in LA over a month after the murder.

Wasserman's testimony demonstrates the racialized context of the trial. Hers was perhaps the most hesitant and vulnerable voice on the stand in that courtroom, and it was impossible for Lomax to challenge her testimony without playing into Weinrick's strategy of appealing to the emotions rather than the logic of the jurors. The fifteen-year-old high school student from Fairfax High School in LA spoke so softly from the stand that Weinrick repeatedly admonished her to "speak a little louder" and "keep your voice up."[61] Wasserman described the man she saw talking to Martha as "rather short, rather medium build; he was a colored man, and I guess that is about all I can say." When pressed for more details, the young woman replied, "I don't know exactly how he was dressed. . . . It seemed like some sort of uniform." Asked if the so-called uniform was "not white?" she replied, "Yes, sir." Her answer left some ambiguity as to whether she meant it was white or "not white." Most tellingly, she had not noticed any checkered pants. She noted the man was not wearing a cap or a hat, and that "he had rather large lips and kind of a square body."[62] Asked if she could point him out in the courtroom, she stated, "That man looks like him." Asked to clarify if he was or was not the man she had seen, she replied, "I can only say he looks like the one."[63] The trial transcript did not clarify at whom she pointed. Stone, in his synopsis of her testimony, stated she "pointed to Folkes seated at the counsel table."[64]

Lomax tried to expose contradictions in the prosecution's case, countering vague insinuations with detailed, specific questions on cross-examination, but his appeal to logic fell flat. Weinrick more successfully appealed to juror emotions, introducing dramatic turns and surprise testimony that lacked substance but played to their prejudices and assumptions. Jurors remembered Wasserman saw "someone who looked like" Folkes, which outweighed her later admission, under cross-examination, that she remembered that detail only after Tetrick coached her to do so, over a month after the incident. Wasserman admitted to Lomax that the statement she made on the train shortly after the murder "was a little different" than her courtroom testimony. Asked in what respect her testimony differed from that initial statement, she replied, "Well, the one on the train I didn't recall seeing any man talking to Mrs. James, and I didn't remember anything about that at the time until I saw a picture [of Folkes] the next day in the papers."[65]

More importantly, of course, all Wasserman had actually seen was an apparently unremarkable conversation between a Black man "in some sort of uniform" and a White woman whom she did not know, and all of this took place in a public space about five hours before the murder. The closest either Lomax or Weinrick came to getting Wasserman to deny or confirm that Folkes was the person she had seen talking to James came late during cross-examination. Lomax, stressing the significance of the moment for the defendant, asked her to confirm whether Folkes was really the man she saw talking to Martha. Wasserman backed off: "I didn't say that was the man; I said that looks like the man." The lingering image, for jurors, however, was the earlier one: a fifteen-year-old girl pointing at Robert Folkes and saying, "He looks like the man." The unspoken part was "who I saw talking to a White woman."

With Wasserman's testimony, Weinrick successfully staged the second, melodramatic opportunity for a witness to point accusingly at Folkes before the jury. In this case, it was a young woman who personified the vulnerable sister that, in the wartime propaganda posters, needed protection from the menacing, racialized foe. The prosecutor's melodramatic staging impressed upon sympathetic jurors the supposed significance of Wasserman's accusing finger. Weinrick quickly rushed to the next witness before jurors could fully process her testimony, and before they might realize she remembered almost nothing about the man other than his skin color. After stumbling over the color of the man's uniform or even the style of his clothes, she had, in fact, pointed at the only Black man inside the courtroom bar, and then said only, "He looks like him" before admitting reasonable doubts that it was the same man.

Weinrick moved quickly to change the mood by bringing in several authoritative, assertively confident White male voices. He first called Brakeman Anders, and then he called Chief Petty Officer Kelso. The petty officer was remarkably vague in his testimony before the jury, and he "disremembered" virtually everything that happened the morning of the murder, except for his chance encounter with a man in the aisle as he made his way to the washroom. Apart from recounting his own toilet activities, Kelso offered nothing of substance to support prosecutors' claims or defense questioning that the man he encountered was Folkes. He denied hearing an alarm buzzer, screams, or shouting, finally claiming he was "a little deaf."[66] Stone, in his summary report, noted with evident disappointment, "Kelso seemed to be a reluctant witness, and his only desire apparently was to return to his home in El Cajon, California, as soon as possible."[67] Given his studied vagueness, Kelso's testimony served the sole function, for the prosecution, of placing a uniformed White man before the jury between the testimony of the White brakeman, Anders, and the Black porter, Hughes.

Hughes had the potential, more than anyone else, to directly challenge Wilson's narrative and the prosecution's entire case. His assertive stance during pretrial conflicts over housing in Albany led railway officials and the prosecutor's office to suspect he would defend Folkes on the basis of what they called "race solidarity." Apparently unconcerned about their own race solidarity with the victim's father, prosecutors sandwiched Hughes' testimony between that of two imposing White authority figures: the tall, gaunt Chief Petty Officer Kelso, and the cigar-chomping, hulking SPRR detective Clarence W. Champlin. Inspector Champlin was the lead investigator for SPRR, and his testimony, delivered in a gruff, authoritative voice, reestablished for jurors the narrative he previously constructed as the foundation of the initial investigation. On key points of difference, the all-White jurors weighed Champlin's calm, direct, hard-bitten investigators' demeanor against the South Central inflections of Hughes, whose Pullman porter's uniform exuded authority aboard the train but nowhere else.

Pullman Porter Harry McKinley Hughes was a challenging witness for both defense and prosecution because he refused to stay within the deferential boundaries White officials expected a Black trainman to respect, in or out of the courtroom. Hughes apparently relished antagonizing his corporate handlers who forced him to cool his heels in Albany before and during the trial, and when he eventually testified, he blew holes in the prosecutors' case. His physical presence, however, as a large, challenging Black man, apparently made more of an impression on jurors than his words from the witness stand. His testimony obviously worried prosecutors and PPC observers, but Lomax struggled to take advantage of the openings the porter provided. In the courtroom melodrama Weinrick orchestrated before jurors, it was unclear what role Hughes was supposed to assume, and as a result, jurors apparently disregarded his testimony and responded emotionally to his racialized presence. This did not bode well for Folkes.

Most of Hughes' testimony focused on the timeline for when he encountered Folkes and Kelso in the men's smoking lounge in relation to the time Van Dyke rang the porter, sounding the first alarm about the murder. Hughes was forceful and assertive, standing by his earlier statements that placed the murder sometime earlier than 4:35 a.m., and his firsthand account of when and where he saw Folkes during and immediately after the probable time of the murder virtually eliminated the second cook as a possible perpetrator. Moreover, his account contradicted Wilson's testimony on many critical points.[68] Most notably, Hughes testified that Wilson had tried to redirect him forward in the train while he (Wilson) searched toward the rear of the train. He also testified Wilson told the porter the man he had seen fleeing the murder scene was a White man.[69]

Prosecutors tried to represent Hughes as a fat, lazy, inattentive Black man, in a racialized attack intended to discredit the most important challenge to their case against Folkes. Since Hughes was the first trainman at the scene of the crime, Weinrick couldn't ignore him, but he called him as a prosecution witness in a strategy designed to compartmentalize and neutralize the man's testimony. Hughes fought back against racialized slurs on his character, detailing his official activities as the Pullman porter responsible for monitoring Pullman Tourist Cars D and E and Standard Pullman Car 60 during the critical hour between 3:30 and 4:30 a.m. Pullman Car 60 was the first-class car immediately behind the diner. Hughes helped a woman board the train with two other passengers at Salem between 3:20 and 3:30 a.m. and showed her to Lower 8 in Car 60, leading her through Car D and the diner on the way there. From there, he returned through the dining car, passed through Car D to Car E, checked the status of Car E from midway along the aisle, then returned to Car D, finally settling into the smoking room, emerging to check each of the cars every fifteen minutes thereafter.[70]

Hughes' testimony refocused jurors on Wilson's initial claims he saw a man with a chunky build, weighing around 180 pounds, in a dark, pin-stripe suit, and he testified that when Wilson, whom he knew only as "a passenger in my car," told him to search forward in the train, Hughes looked closely at the marine, "to memorize his features so that I could identify him [clearly implying he did not trust Wilson]. Then I went forward and got the conductor Banks." Hughes clarified he was not taking orders from Wilson but doing his duty as a trainman, which was to closely monitor the people in his car and notify the conductor of the crime as soon as possible.[71]

Jurors could believe either a White marine who claimed he took charge of the situation or a Black trainman who claimed that he, not Wilson, was the authoritative voice. Hughes, unlike Wilson, testified that just minutes after the murder he found Folkes in his kitchen, working over a stove in which "the fires were especially hot," heating water for coffee and cereal, and with muffins in the oven. His testimony contradicted Wilson's claim that Folkes was perspiring while pretending to work over a cold stove. In cross-examination, Lomax reconfirmed with Hughes that Folkes was in his smoking room until approximately 4:30 a.m. and that the porter personally saw Folkes walk into the dining car kitchen to resume his duties sometime before 4:35 a.m.[72] This left virtually no time at all for Folkes to have committed a murder within the timeline Banks and Hughes established by their testimony. Prosecutors, consequently, argued that the murder actually took place somewhere between 4:35 and 4:50 a.m., which conflicted with the recollection of every witness in a position to accurately mark the time they learned of the murder.

Hughes also managed to shatter the credibility of the prosecution in front of the jury, although that panel of jurists apparently looked past flagrant misrepresentations by Weinrick's team. Under cross-examination, Hughes dramatically produced from his coat pocket his written, signed statement, shortly after prosecutors claimed it never existed. Weinrick, at that point, attempted to cross-examine Hughes, even though he had originally called the porter as a witness for the prosecution. Lomax incredulously challenged Weinrick's efforts to impugn his own witness, and then he objected to the prosecutor's effort to discredit the porter's sworn testimony by quoting from Hughes' written statement, after previously having told the court and jury that statement did not exist. Weinrick appealed to Lewelling, but the judge agreed with Lomax and disallowed Weinrick's line of questioning.[73] In doing so, Lewelling actually assisted the prosecution in two ways: On the one hand, he established a veneer of fairness by appearing to side with the defense on a vehemently argued point. On the other hand, he protected prosecutors from an authoritative witness whose written statement contradicted their lead witness on every significant point.

On another question that directly challenged the integrity of the entire legal proceeding, Hughes questioned the accuracy of the stenographer's transcript of his statement. Weinrick opened the door for Hughes to make those comments in front of the jury when the prosecutor began to quote from his previous statements. In response, Hughes suggested the stenographer left out a significant detail: "I told you about it here . . . two months ago when I was up here the first time. Whether the lady [transcriptionist] got it or not, I don't know. That in front of witnesses he [Wilson] did state it was a white man. N. L. Shaw was present and I was present—the only two of our kind [Black trainmen] there."[74]

ACT III: REVEALING THE PLOT USING THE DETECTIVE'S NARRATIVE VOICE

With the prosecution reeling from the effects of Hughes' challenging testimony, Weinrick resorted to a time-worn literary device borrowed directly from the true-crime detective novel: hard-bitten detectives narrated the "reveal," connecting the dots for a credulous audience, telling jurors who committed the crime, what they were thinking, and why they acted as they had. The story detectives told from the stand, despite many inconsistencies with established facts and other testimony, and no matter how internally inconsistent, offered jurors a compelling narrative that guided them through the maze of detail from the three-week trial. Lewelling aided their effort by allowing the detectives enormous latitude to repeat entire conversations that they had heard from other people months before the trial.

Lewelling's hearsay ruling, during Hughes' testimony, set a standard that he did not apply to the parade of authority figures—railroad investigators, police, and sheriff's deputies—that Weinrick summoned to the stand. For more than a third of the trial record, Lewelling allowed those voices of authority to speak with impunity about what they claimed they heard witnesses say. Most damaging to the defense was Lewelling's decision to allow into evidence—verbally and in written form—unsigned transcripts of "statements" those same authority figures claimed Folkes made while they interrogated him in the Los Angeles and Albany jails. Railroad detective Champlin, who followed Hughes to the stand, for example, asserted that when he asked Kelso during an interrogation in Klamath Falls to identify the man he saw in the aisle on the way to the smoking room, Kelso supposedly pointed at Folkes and said, "That looks like the man."[75] Kelso, testifying before the same jury, had already denied making that statement, but Lewelling allowed into evidence Champlin's claim he heard Kelso say it.

With Champlin, prosecutors Weinrick and Sisemore shifted the focus from victim and witnesses to investigators and their theories. After Champlin, they paraded a series of detectives and police officers through the witness stand, including OSP officers and the Linn County sheriff and his deputies, setting the stage for lengthy testimony from LAPD detectives Tetrick and Rasmussen and LAPD stenographer Nancy Lyman. These last three witnesses, finally, introduced the confession Folkes allegedly made in LA.

Lewelling barred only the jury and other subpoenaed witnesses from the room during hearings to determine the admissibility of the so-called statements, which allowed everyone but the jurors the opportunity to see how key witnesses contradicted each other on the critical question of whether those statements were coerced or fabricated. Lewelling stated from the outset he was only interested in whether officials applied so-called third-degree methods, by which he strictly meant physical torture. The judge clearly accepted the premise that the unsigned statements accurately rendered what Folkes had said, and Lewelling did not allow defense attorneys to challenge that assumption. Despite these restrictive boundaries, Lomax showed, through close questioning, that the officers were either concealing or misrepresenting how they produced those statements, and he demonstrated they were otherwise lying about the circumstances and the statements themselves. Despite that showing, Lewelling allowed them into evidence, and he also allowed verbal recollections of police and other detectives who claimed they remembered, word for word, extended soliloquies by the defendant. The result was a repetitious parade of authority figures who layered embellishments and assertions over previous allegations, constructing an elaborate edifice of a story that overwhelmed courtroom observers and the jury with its artifice and detail, condemning Folkes in the process. This portion of the trial outweighed and distracted from everything that preceded and Lomax could not overcome its momentum and authority.

Throughout the hearing, Tetrick and Rasmussen told Lewelling conflicting accounts of the night they took Robert Folkes to his wife's house to extract what they described as his "confession." Each detective told his story separately, in response to questioning from Weinrick and Lomax, without knowing how the other might have responded. Tetrick spoke at length about the detention and interrogation of Folkes at LAPD headquarters and at Central Jail. His story differed from Rasmussen's on both large and small matters, including the route they took to the house, when and where they stopped to buy the bottle of whiskey Folkes had when they reached the house, and where he was detained while at headquarters. Tetrick sometimes changed his story in the middle of a sentence. He claimed, for example, that on the way to the house, "We stopped at 12th Street and Central liquor store and bought a half pint of H&H whiskey—no, I retract that. The defendant gave me the money and I bought it for him."[76]

Unlike Tetrick, who claimed Rasmussen stood at the foot of the bed while Folkes gave his statement, the captain claimed he was "sitting upon a corner of the dresser." Where Tetrick had claimed he was seated on a trunk in the room, Rasmussen testified the lieutenant was "sitting on a chair . . . near the foot of the bed."[77] Unlike Tetrick, Rasmussen claimed Clara Folkes asked him for a ride back to her house after Folkes gave his statement. Tetrick claimed he asked Clara if she wanted a ride. Clara Folkes later testified she did not ask for a ride, but that one of the officers offered her one. Back at headquarters, Rasmussen claimed he, not Tetrick, called the night watchman to return Folkes to Central Jail. Unlike Tetrick, who claimed he retrieved Folkes from Central Jail at ten o'clock the next morning, Rasmussen claimed he saw Folkes in his office, room 43 at city hall, before 9:30 that morning. Lomax seemed unaware of these inconsistencies, or at least made no mention of them in his questions, and in fact, he protested the amount of detail the prosecutor was presenting.[78]

If the point of the hearing was to establish the credibility of the two police detectives, Rasmussen and Tetrick, Lomax successfully demonstrated to the judge and courtroom observers that they were completely untrustworthy.

Their stories conflicted on both major and minor details, and Tetrick's characterization of Folkes' response to how he'd been treated appeared snide and
disingenuous. On cross-examination, Lomax extracted details from Tetrick
on the route he followed from city hall to Jessie Folkes' house on 25th Street,
and then, when questioning Rasmussen, he drew out similar details that contradicted Tetrick's account, indicating they took a completely different route,
not least because the route Tetrick laid out involved going the wrong way on a
one-way street.[79]

Lomax tried to convince Lewelling that Tetrick and Rasmussen violated his client's constitutional rights, and he pointed to recent Supreme
Court decisions that rejected a similarly tainted confession for reasons that
closely paralleled the circumstances of Folkes' interrogation. Lomax cited
the US Supreme Court case *McNabb v. United States* (October 1942)—a
case originating in the Tennessee courts. Lomax apparently struggled to
hold Lewelling's attention with a review of the US Supreme Court ruling
that made McNabb's confession inadmissible, based on the length of time he
was detained and interrogated without benefit of counsel. Lomax also linked
the treatment of Folkes with the ongoing investigation of LAPD abuses at
Central Jail. He noted that fourteen LAPD officers had recently been indicted
by a grand jury for assault and another three for manslaughter in relation to
the Beebe case that he had previously mentioned. He particularly stressed
that Rasmussen and Tetrick were closely associated with the same investigative unit of the LAPD implicated in Beebe's death.[80]

Immediately after Lomax concluded his argument, Lewelling abruptly
ruled in favor of allowing prosecutors to present the Lyman statement, obviously without taking the time to read the McNabb case. Instead, Lewelling
asserted that, "so far as the evidence here shows, he [Folkes] was in possession
of all his faculties, was not under duress or some belief or hope that he would
be better treated by reason of his statement, or was not in fear of anything."[81]

The jury heard none of the contradictions between Tetrick's and Rasmussen's
accounts that might have alerted them to their untrustworthy nature. By the
time Weinrick called the two LAPD officers to the stand in the jury's presence,
he had delayed long enough for them to meet and compare notes, and they
managed to smooth out areas of obvious contradiction. The story the jurors
heard, consequently, was relatively seamless, and the two officers substantiated
each other's claims on most significant points. During the hearing, the two officers seemed to be covering up the truth with a story that they made up as they

went along, but in front of the jury, they gave more consistent answers or else claimed they did not remember. Courtroom observers, however, had seen them give a completely different, less convincing performance just a day earlier, and a number of those observers were prominently involved in later appeals and public criticisms of how the judge handled the case the jury heard.

Once Lewelling ruled on the admissibility of the Los Angeles statement, the prosecution presented the jury with multiple versions of what they claimed Folkes had confessed. First Tetrick and then Rasmussen testified at length, recounting what Folkes verbally told them at his wife's house. Each officer pretended to be quoting Folkes word for word, even though neither had taken notes and no stenographer had been present. They each phrased things differently and included factual claims that differed from what the other claimed to recall. Both officers then testified on the substance of the written statement Nancy Lyman supposedly witnessed the next morning. In their oral testimony, they repeated much of the story they claimed they had heard from Folkes the previous night. Tetrick claimed, in his account of this second statement, that at one point, while Folkes was talking, "the girl" [stenographer Lyman] stepped out of the room, leaving Folkes alone with him and Finneran. At that point, Tetrick claimed, Folkes stated he killed Martha James because "she looked like my type of woman, and I just couldn't get her off my mind." In this instance, even the police stenographer could not corroborate the detective's claims because, according to Tetrick's story, she was not in the room. Lyman's transcript does not include any reference to the statement, nor does it state that she had left the interrogation room.[82] Finally, after these repetitive restatements of the unsigned, obviously incomplete, and possibly falsified statements that police attributed to Folkes, Sisemore read the Lyman document out loud, into the record, in the presence of the jury. In this way, the jury heard five different versions of Folkes' supposed LA "confession," which he denied, through his lawyers, ever having made.

After losing the prolonged fight to exclude the Lyman statement (introduced as Exhibit K), Lomax shifted tactics and pressed Weinrick to admit that police detectives in Los Angeles had extracted an earlier statement Folkes made on the first day of his interrogations in which he denied guilt. After debating the issue before the jury, Lomax won the embarrassing admission from Weinrick that prosecutors did, in fact, have that earlier statement, which he and Lomax subsequently referred to as the "Bechtel statement"—named for the stenographer who sat in on the interrogation on which it was based.

Lomax demanded defense attorneys be provided copies of both the Lyman document and the earlier Bechtel statement. Lewelling ordered Weinrick to comply with that request and then adjourned the court to give Lomax time to review the materials. That recess was the first time either Folkes or his attorney was allowed to see either statement, both of which police attributed to him.

Reading the supposed statements into the record helped prosecutors regain the authoritative voice they needed to convince jurors to look past the evidence and to trust the narrative Weinrick's team wanted them to believe. The district attorney needed to recover his credibility with the jury, which should have been shattered after his debate with Lomax over the existence of the Bechtel statement. After Weinrick first denied, before the jury, that it existed, he was trapped into admitting, again before the jury, that he had it in his possession. At that point, however, Weinrick abruptly changed the subject by introducing a surprise third statement he had not previously mentioned, which he claimed Folkes voluntarily gave while awaiting trial in Albany. The prosecutor called Linn County sheriff Herbert Shelton to the stand to lay the groundwork for introducing the Albany statement after the recess Lewelling granted Lomax for the purpose of reading the two LAPD statements.[83]

The Albany statement added a new layer of contradictions to those already apparent in the two LAPD statements, and those differences helped Weinrick's team insinuate that Folkes, and not the investigators, was responsible for those inconsistencies. Increasingly, prosecutors began to suggest that Folkes was slightly deranged, but not so much as to render him legally insane. Shelton described a fourteen-hour interaction with Folkes that began when he and Deputy Kirk spirited Folkes off the train in Eugene on the pretense they wanted to avoid a lynch mob supposedly waiting at the Albany station. While Folkes was still disoriented from the twenty-four-hour train ride from Los Angeles, they forced him into the back seat of a police car and took him on a circuitous, bewildering, and intimidating two-and-a-half-hour ride into the early morning mists on winding backroads through the foothills of the Cascade Range and finally back down to Albany. The trip from Eugene to Albany normally required about half that time via the mostly flat roads in the Willamette Valley. They arrived at Linn County courthouse sometime after 8:30 a.m. on 31 January, where Shelton, Kirk, OSP officers Howard and Tichenor, OSP pathologist Beeman, and at least one SPRR agent interrogated Folkes until nearly 10:30 p.m. in an empty courtroom. During that span of fourteen hours, between six and eight burly detectives grilled Folkes without respite, holding him without sleep or food.[84] Shelton claimed they took Folkes to the lavatory around 3:30 p.m., but apart from that one break, they allowed him no meals or other toilet breaks, although they did ply him with a steady diet of nicotine and caffeine in the form of cigarettes and coffee. Somewhere around 6:30 that evening, Folkes suddenly found himself alone in the smoke-filled courtroom with Beeman and Howard, and those two OSP officials extracted a statement nearly fifty pages long, following a marathon four-hour session that lasted until 10:30 p.m.[85]

Weinrick paraded a string of authoritative White witnesses before the jury, including OSP officer Howard, OSP pathologist Beeman, and OSP stenographer Kathleen K. Miller. After these witnesses established a foundation for offering the transcripts as evidence, Weinrick and Sisemore read into the record the Albany statement they attributed to Folkes, and they made copies of all three supposed statements available for jurors to consult, as trial exhibits, during their deliberations. Those statements were the only written narratives of the case allowed in the jury room during deliberations. Jurors had no access to trial transcripts or any other records of witness testimony after they retired to deliberate. Once he accomplished the objective of placing those incriminating statements before the jury in oral and written form, Weinrick rested the state's case against Robert E. Lee Folkes.

CRITICAL REVIEWS: BLACK TRAINMEN, WHITE ALBANY, AND THE CASE FOR THE DEFENSE

The trial ended with an anticlimactic critique, by the defense, of the prosecution's case. That critique, however, never came close to the standard Lomax had set for himself during opening arguments. Lomax could not solve the case for the jury, and he could not prove to them who, besides his client, was the real killer. He could catalog a long list of contradictions in the case prosecutors had presented, and he could challenge their claim that Folkes confessed, but he had not managed to give jurors a dramatic alternative to Folkes. If they expected him to extract a confession from a witness on the stand, nothing so melodramatic happened. In the end, he left jurors with a bunch of loose ends, unexplained contradictions, and a storyline prosecutors presented as if it were authoritative.

The prosecution's case boiled down to nothing more than a string of White authority figures who claimed Folkes told them he was guilty. Their word held, even against protestations from the defense that Folkes denied admitting guilt. Their word held, even against eyewitness accounts that placed Folkes in the dining car at times and under circumstances that made it virtually impossible for him to have committed the murder. Other eyewitnesses confirmed that physical evidence in the diner supported Folkes' claim that he was working hard, in the kitchen, at the time prosecutors claimed the murder happened. Hughes and others confirmed the timeline that Folkes provided in numerous statements aboard the train en route to LA, accounting for his whereabouts far more precisely than anyone else on record. Finally, the autopsy report asserted an angle and direction of the killing wound inconsistent with the way Folkes held a knife, with his dominant hand, and close inspection of the kitchen and his clothes revealed no traces of blood from the victim, even though the murder scene was completely soaked in her blood after the assailant severed a major artery in her neck.

Weinrick's dual strategy of overloading the case with irrelevant detail while appealing to jurors' emotions and prejudices left Lomax few options. He followed the 738 transcript pages of the prosecution's case with a defense that consumed only 70 pages, calling only thirteen witnesses, most of whom had previously testified as state's witnesses. The list of trial exhibits was lengthy but inconsequential. Apart from the Lyman and Miller statements that Lomax alleged were fabricated and/or coerced and therefore inadmissible, the state had literally no evidence implicating Folkes. Prosecutors piled on exhibit after exhibit of physical evidence, none of which they linked to Folkes. After nearly three weeks at trial, they only managed to prove he was on the train, working in the kitchen, and occasionally using the men's room in Car D. Neither Wilson, nor Wasserman, nor Kelso ever positively identified Folkes as the Black man they each claimed they encountered at various times prior to or after the murder. No one, not even Wilson, positively claimed they saw a Black man, let alone Folkes, either committing the murder or even leaving the scene of the murder. When Wilson pointed at Folkes in the courtroom, it was only to confirm he was the man working in the kitchen when Wilson looked in the kitchen door. There was no physical evidence directly or even indirectly linking the murder with Folkes, or even with the dining car. Forced to mount a defense against a virtually nonexistent case, Lomax offered only two exhibits: the Bechtel statement and a photo of Jessie Folkes sitting in her bed and pointing at the bottle of whiskey that she and Clara confirmed Robert Folkes and the police brought to her house.

Lacking any real alternatives, Lomax requested the attorneys retire to the judge's chambers with Lewelling, and in chambers, he asked for a directed verdict of acquittal on the grounds the state had not provided sufficient evidence of guilt for the case to go to the jury, and on further grounds the so-called statements did not constitute valid "confessions" before the law. He argued that in the event Lewelling decided those statements did meet the standard of a confession, then the defense would be forced to argue they were inadmissible due to intoxication and mistreatment of the defendant. Lomax also argued the Albany statement was extracted under suspicious circumstances and only after Folkes had stated he did not wish to talk about the case, on advice of his lawyer. Finally, Lomax argued the transcripts were demonstrably incomplete records of the defendant's alleged statements, by the admission of the officers involved in extracting them. At that point, the verbatim transcript of the hearing abruptly ends with the curt notation, "Argument by Mr. Lomax followed." The next entry in the trial transcript read, "The Court: Motion overruled."[86] In shorthand, the stenographer simply refused to complete the transcript of the defense attorney's argument. Weinrick later certified that transcript was a "full and complete" copy.

Lomax clearly recognized that his client's fate rested more on how jurors perceived Folkes and less on how they evaluated the evidence and testimony. Most of the witnesses Lomax called for the defense, consequently, testified to the good character and virtues of Folkes. Lomax attempted to show the jury that the accused was himself a victim of circumstance and collusion. Defense witnesses included five trainmen—Folkes' direct supervisor (the chef), a waiter, two porters, and the steward—as well as the young cook's mother, his wife, and several arresting officers. Whereas prosecutors viewed trainmen as untrustworthy witnesses influenced by race solidarity, the defense treated trainmen as indispensable witnesses, regardless of race. Most notably, these included Chef Baker and Waiter Johnson.

Lomax had nothing to offer the jury that could counter the authority of the detectives and district attorney who melodramatically read or recalled for that captive audience the supposed confessions they attributed to Folkes. Lomax tried to get their attention by reading into the trial record Defense Exhibit 2—the so-called Bechtel statement that LAPD investigators generated after they interrogated Folkes the first day he was detained in LA (26 January).[87] Although it included a direct denial of guilt, it was just one brief statement coming late in the trial, after the jury had already heard two other far more dramatic and damning statements in which the suspect purportedly confessed.

Lomax had his greatest success with three Black porters, near the end of the trial, but their testimony came late in the process, and as Black working-class trainmen, they lacked status or authority before the all-White jury comprising mostly middle-class housewives and farm wives. Porters Shaw, Sibley, and Scurry clarified, as a defense witnesses, details about Wilson's actions that should have called into question the marine's reliability as a witness, his influence on the early phases of the investigation, and his suspicious tampering with evidence at the crime scene. Scurry affirmed he heard Wilson describe the man he saw leaving James' berth as a "white man," and he also produced in court copies of statements he previously gave to the PPC and to the OSP, thus demonstrating yet again that prosecutors willfully misled the court when they claimed they had no such statements.[88] Shaw also revealed that the first section of the train, on which Martha's husband travelled, remained on the tracks at Portland's Union Station for quite some time adjacent to the second section to which she was assigned, and that the two trains left Portland on the morning of 23 January somewhere between 12:40 and 1:20 a.m. Earlier narratives that prosecutors provided implied the James couple was separated before arriving in Portland, and that there would not have been time for them to reconnect at Union Station.[89] Shaw's timeline suggests they had considerably more time to attend the steward's party and participate in other activities while waiting for the call to board. Shaw's testimony also revealed he observed blood on Wilson's left palm, right thumb, and right shoe, and on the right sleeve of his full-length-sleeved shirt just above the wrist. The detail of blood on his right hand and sleeve was important because the autopsy indicated the killer likely wielded the murder weapon in his right hand while holding down the victim with his left hand, cutting the left side of the victim's throat. Shaw also corroborated Hughes' timeline.[90]

Porters Sibley and Scurry directly contradicted Wilson's claim he searched all the way to the rear, where Sibley's Standard Pullman was the last car on the back end of the train.[91] Scurry, who was responsible for Standard Pullman Car 60, immediately behind the diner the night of the murder, offered testimony that reveals the double standard Lewelling applied on the question of hearsay in this trial. In response to questions from Lomax, Scurry testified he first learned of the murder from Hughes, who rushed into the car with a cane in his hand. Scurry recalled, "He looked at me and he said, 'Have you saw anybody?'" At that point in the testimony, Weinrick immediately objected and Lewelling advised Scurry, "You are not permitted to say what he said; tell what he did." Scurry, a twenty-year-veteran Pullman porter, attempted to continue, "He looked at me and said did I see anybody go through the—." At that point, the transcript indicates, Lewelling interrupted with a sharp warning: "I just cautioned you not to repeat that conversation. It constitutes hearsay evidence."[92] Lomax then apologized to the court on behalf of the witness, claiming, "I don't think the witness understood."[93]

By the standard Lewelling applied to Scurry, everything the state presented in the way of police testimony regarding what Folkes told them would have been hearsay evidence, and most of the remainder of the state's case leaned heavily on statements various witnesses claimed they heard from Folkes or other principals in the case. In this court, however, White men who were detectives, police, or military men were allowed to repeat at length comments they claimed they heard other people say, but Black men were barred from doing so, on the claim that it was hearsay evidence. Lewelling also allowed prosecutors to directly upbraid witnesses for veering into testimony they considered unnecessarily detailed.[94] Trainmen—White or Black—were accorded less respect than military men or investigating officers.

At the end of the trial, shortly before issuing instructions to the jury, Lewelling heard arguments, in chambers, from Lomax, Sisemore, and Weinrick, regarding defense concerns that prosecutors had failed to cooperate (and had actually colluded to conceal evidence) during the pretrial discovery phase. Lomax noted prosecutors refused to supply lists of passengers or crewmen, despite repeated requests they do so.[95] Lewelling responded with a circular argument: "There is no evidence in this case indicating that there are any other persons who have any knowledge of this case whatsoever. . . . The court must presume that all the witnesses who had any knowledge of it have been before the court. Counsel for defendant has not indicated that there are any other witnesses who have any information that would assist the court and the jury."[96]

In response to Lewelling's argument, Lomax pointed out that prosecutors stipulated there were at least thirty people on board Car D the night of the murder, and Weinrick admitted, before the judge, in chambers, that in all probability there were more than thirty passengers aboard Car D the night of the murder. Only a fraction of those potential witnesses, however, testified at the trial. Lewelling, responding to that admission, agreed that two different witnesses had corroborated that estimate, which on the face of things, seemed to contradict his earlier response to Lomax. The transcript of discussion in Lewelling's chambers abruptly ends at that point, but there is no indication the judge reversed his ruling, and when the court record resumes, it records Lomax busily swearing in OSP sergeant Earl B. Houston before the jury, with no further mention of the state's failure to disclose evidence.[97]

TRIAL'S END: INSTRUCTING THE JURY

As it turned out, prosecutors did not need a substantive case. The trial was never about seeking the truth—it was about demonstrating control and authority during wartime. Snell and his subordinates in the state justice system approached the case as a test of their political will to legally convict and execute a young Black trainman, and that outcome depended more on telling a thrilling and gripping story than on producing evidence or eyewitnesses. All prosecutors needed to do was assemble and cast the parts that a credulous judge and jury would accept as fitting their preconceived notions of how a melodramatic murder case should unfold.

The sheer volume of testimony overwhelmed the ugly little fact that prosecutors had no tangible evidence or direct eyewitnesses linking Folkes to the crime, but Lewelling's summary instructions to the jury focused more on how to convict than how to acquit. Rather than warning them about relying on the questionable "statements," Lewelling encouraged them to base their decision largely on those documents. He urged the inexperienced jurors to "consider the manner in which the witnesses have testified, their motives, and it is for you to determine whom you will or will not believe, taking into consideration your experience as men and women of affairs."[98]

In the relative weight of his instructions, Lewelling also implicitly encouraged the jury to apply the death penalty. He cautioned jurors to begin their consideration of testimony with a presumption of innocence, but after that pro forma nod to due process, the most important details in his instructions and the bulk of his directions offered jurors advice on the meaning of "premeditation and deliberation." Lewelling explained that if the jury found the defendant guilty of acting with premeditation and deliberation that would constitute a finding of murder in the first degree, which carried a mandatory death penalty. Premeditation and deliberation, he argued, need only precede the act of killing by "an appreciable length of time sufficient for reflection and consideration of a definite purpose to kill, however short that time may be." To ensure jurors did not misunderstand his meaning, Lewelling restated the concept no less than six times within a single page of the trial transcript. He argued, "The human mind acts with a celerity which it is impossible to measure, and whether the premeditated design to kill was formed must be determined by the jury. . . . It is sufficient if there was such a design or intent in the slayer's mind at any moment before or at the time of the commission of the acts resulting in death." He further instructed, "There may be no perceptible space of time between the forming of the design and the acts resulting in death," and he instructed that the standard would be be met, even if "the design to kill was formed by him at the instant of the act."[99]

Before the jury had even decided on the guilt or innocence of Folkes, Lewelling urged them to consider whether to impose the death penalty. He advised jurors, "You are instructed that direct proof of deliberation and premeditation is not necessary, but it may be inferred from the facts proven." Among those "facts," Lewelling specified, "statements made by defendant after he is under arrest" could be considered, if they were "freely and voluntarily made." Just in case jurors missed his meaning, as it applied to the statements police attributed to Folkes, Lewelling clarified that it was their responsibility, as jurors, to pick and choose, from the statements he allowed into evidence, those portions of the statements they believed to be voluntary, excluding other parts they judged to be involuntary or coerced. He stressed that, even if jurors found the defendant to have been intoxicated at the time he gave those statements, they would still be admissible, unless he was intoxicated to the point of mental incapacity.[100]

Jurors struggled with the verdict for nearly thirty hours, coping with difficult conditions and unfamiliar surroundings, under guard and without liberty to leave, imprisoned in the same courthouse as the defendant whose fate they were deciding. Lewelling issued his instructions on the morning of 22 April, and the jury retired to the jury room at 10:15 a.m. Nearly six hours later, at 4:00 p.m., the jury foreman, Doerfler, asked Lewelling to clarify how many of them must agree in order to find the defendant guilty of murder in the first degree without recommendation for life imprisonment (meaning a mandatory death penalty). The other alternatives they apparently considered at that point included murder in the first degree with recommendation for life imprisonment, or, possibly, murder in the second degree (also without applying the death penalty). Lewelling clarified they needed a unanimous verdict for a first degree finding, regardless of recommendation, but a finding of murder in the second degree required a vote of only ten of twelve jurors. With that, jurors returned to deliberations until midnight, when they informed Lewelling they could not reach a verdict. The judge, however, ordered them locked in the courthouse overnight, sending in bailiffs with food and bedding. Jurors slept, under guard, in makeshift beds on hardwood floors in two different courtrooms, divided by gender—four men in one room and eight women in another. After a restless night, they resumed deliberations at 9:00 a.m. on 23 January, and at 3:00 p.m., after nearly another full day of deliberations, they notified bailiffs they had a verdict.

The verdict came as a surprise to many courtroom observers who expected, if not an acquittal, at least an inconclusive outcome. The jury, however, ultimately agreed with prosecutors who had argued for either death or acquittal. The hastily reassembled court heard the jury's verdict of guilty of murder in the first degree without recommendation, which compelled the judge to issue a sentence of death in the state's gas chamber in Salem, Oregon. News of the verdict visibly upset defense attorney Leroy Lomax. After a stunned pause, he insisted the judge poll the jury, and each juror somberly affirmed they agreed with the decision. In a summary statement that abruptly concluded proceedings, Lewelling set a sentencing date of 26 April 1943. On that date, at 1:30 p.m., he sentenced Robert E. Lee Folkes to be executed in the state prison gas chamber on 28 May 1943. Shelton, Kirk, Howard, and Chambers promptly transported the defendant to that facility, and Folkes sat on death row for the next twenty months.[101]

In all the strategic turns in the case, Lewelling limited the range of defense questioning while allowing prosecutors unfettered leeway for introducing unsubstantiated claims smearing Folkes' character and reputation. Virtually none of the evidence prosecutors presented bore directly on the guilt or innocence of the accused. Rather, it was calculated to craft a moral framework within which jurors might weigh the depravity of an accused villain against the innocence of a virtuous victim. In that context, a guilty verdict was the obvious, emotional outcome of a trial that was more a staged morality play than a search for truth.

Chapter Six
Trials of War and Hopes for Postwar Progress

Clara Folkes, upon hearing the jury's decision, reportedly sat as if stunned into immobility, remaining in her seat long after everyone else filed out. As she finally left the empty courtroom, she told one reporter, "This is the worst shock I ever had." Other accounts reported Lomax broke down in tears at the verdict, while the courtroom erupted into celebratory and surprised pandemonium. Folkes, by various accounts, stared impassively ahead as the judge read the verdict, but newsmen observed his demeanor was sober and subdued when he later told reporters, "I'm sorry the jury thought I did it, as I didn't, and I'm sorry my mother and Jessie had to go through this."[1] When Deputy Sheriff Kirk moved to shackle Folkes and remove him from the courtroom, William Pollard reportedly reached out a hand, sympathetically touching the young defendant on the arm, but the surrounding law enforcement officers roughly threw Pollard back and threatened to arrest him.[2]

That interaction illustrates the prejudicial attitude public officials brought to the case of Robert E. Lee Folkes in Oregon during those early stages of the war. Pollard, a well-dressed, well-educated, studious-looking Black man, was not remotely a physically intimidating or threatening figure. The burly White officers, who outnumbered and physically towered over both Black men, responded to Pollard's simple human gesture with brute force, and they threatened to arrest him. In a setting where an all-White jury had just convicted and condemned Folkes—also a slight, well-dressed, fairly well-educated Black man—those were intimidating threats. Brute force and White privilege, not humane justice, prevailed that day in Lewelling's courtroom. Over the next twenty months, Pollard joined Clara Folkes in a long battle to reverse those priorities. The focus of their struggle shifted, after April 1943, from the county courthouse in Albany to the state capitol in Salem, about thirty miles farther north in the Willamette Valley.

Between April 1943 and December 1944, the struggle to free Folkes followed a circuitous process of appeals, while the context for understanding his case shifted from prewar racialized hysteria to the struggle for shaping the postwar readjustment. The James murder of January 1943, and the trial and sentencing of Folkes in April that year, came at a critical turning point in the war, amid news of desperate battles for Guadalcanal, Leyte Gulf, and Tripoli.[3] Those struggles marked the beginnings of a long-term strategy that eventually turned the tide in favor of America and its allies, but at great cost in human lives and resources. Over the next year, lawyers for Folkes appealed his verdict, while American strategists unleashed an island-hopping campaign against Japanese forces in the Pacific. In landing after landing, marines launched amphibious assaults against Japanese positions, while American naval forces engaged the Japanese fleet and pressed relentlessly northward toward the Philippines and the Japanese home islands. On the European front, the struggle for North Africa and the Soviet Union's desperate stand against Nazi invaders at Stalingrad preoccupied Americans around the time of the trial. America and its allies made relatively little progress against German forces elsewhere until about a year later, when Allied forces stormed the beaches at Normandy, gaining a foothold in northern Europe. By the end of 1944, Americans were more confident of victory in both Europe and Asia. The racialized Japanese enemy was mostly contained, and as victory seemed more likely, Americans increasingly turned to planning for the postwar period of demobilization and demilitarization.

The appeals process for Folkes, consequently, played out against a very different political context than his initial arrest, interrogation, and trial. At the time of the murder, fear and hysteria shaded newspaper coverage of the war. Before and during the trial, newspapers and prosecutors told the story of the murder as a melodrama in Black and White. Their story resonated with the nighttime fears of a populace gripped in the darkest winter of the war. Only a year later, the murder story was old news that seemed less compelling than more substantial triumphalist narratives of military progress and planning for a postwar world. Newspapers profiled Black men in uniform in front-page stories that trumpeted the successes of the Allied war effort, and SPRR newsletters featured articles about Black trainmen who served with bravery and accomplishment, either in the military or in defense-related jobs.

After the trial, optimistic appellants for Folkes told a story about color that they staged against the brightening horizon of an impending victory over the forces of darkness. They appealed to popular hopes for a more just and diverse, more virtuous, future. Their story, however, competed with alternative visions of a return to prewar conditions of racial exclusion, segregated employment, and White supremacy in Oregon. Before the war ended, the case of Robert Folkes gained prominence in metropolitan Portland and in South Central Los Angeles as a test case in the struggle for securing more permanent civil rights for Black Americans. In that sense, it was a Pacific Northwest variant of a larger nationwide struggle for civil rights that emerged during the Second World War. As part of that struggle, in the Pacific Northwest and elsewhere, African American labor organizers joined forces with advocates for progressive reform, and in the particular case of Robert Folkes, William Pollard led the effort to link the case of his condemned union brother to that larger regional and nationwide movement.

POLITICAL REPOSITIONING FOR POSTWAR DEMILITARIZATION

The Second World War opened doors for Black workers seeking higher-paying jobs, particularly in war-related industries in Portland and other port cities on the West Coast, and those advances prompted concerns about what might happen in the postwar period of demobilization. Higher employment and better wages energized civil rights activists who hoped to extend those advances into the postwar world, but even before the war ended, a reactionary backlash threatened to reverse those gains. These trends were regional manifestations of a broader nationwide struggle. A. Philip Randolph and other Black leaders lobbied union authorities in the United Auto Workers (UAW), the American Federation of Labor (AFL), and the Congress of Industrial Organizations (CIO) to end union racism, gaining some ground with the UAW and the CIO but encountering stiff resistance in the AFL, where most locals supported the national office in opposing equal employment opportunities for Black workers.[4] Civil rights advocates had more success appealing for government action rather than for private concessions. Randolph's March on Washington Movement (MOWM), during summer and fall 1941, pressured Franklin D. Roosevelt to issue Executive Order 8802, which established the Fair Employment Practices Committee (FEPC)—a relatively toothless organization Black activists struggled to convert into a more functional federal agency that might aid the struggle against discriminatory hiring practices and working conditions. Their efforts were partly responsible for Roosevelt's Executive Order 9346, issued in May 1943 (one month after the Folkes trial), which established a new Committee on Fair Employment Practices with a larger budget and more direct support from the executive branch. Unlike the order that established the FEPC, EO 9346 specifically included labor unions among institutions forbidden to discriminate by race, sex, or creed.[5]

Executive Order 9346 and the Robert Folkes Defense Committee (RFDC) entered the consciousness of the Portland-area civil rights community about the same time,[6] and the local campaign to overturn the Folkes conviction, consequently, was entwined with the struggle over unionization of Black workers in Portland-area shipyards. After initially conspiring to exclude Black workers from shipyard jobs, the AFL-affiliated Portland local of the Boilermakers and Shipbuilders Union responded to federal pressure by organizing separate Black auxiliary unions and negotiating agreements with Kaiser shipyard employers allowing them to hire Black workers, who were required to pay union dues but were not allowed to join the actual union.[7] William H. McClendon, who restarted the *People's Observer* in Portland that summer, specifically linked the Folkes verdict with the struggle against racist exclusion in Portland's shipyards in the inaugural issue of his newspaper in June 1943, and he became one of Portland's leading voices for civil rights during the two-year campaign to overturn the conviction.[8]

At this critical stage in the transition from wartime to postwar planning, the RFDC marshalled an impressive multiracial coalition of labor activists, church leaders, legal authorities, and conscientious objectors who joined forces in the two-year effort to save Robert Folkes. In doing so, they provided a focus for progressive reformers in the state. Their sustained campaign, which reached across local, state, and regional boundaries, linked the civil rights community in Oregon to a broader national movement committed to advancing civil rights in the postwar era. The RFDC helped link the regional response of shipyard unions with the struggle against the death penalty and with other civil rights organizations and labor unions in Portland, in the mid-Willamette Valley, down the West Coast, and nationally. Most notably, it provided a common cause for labor activists in the railway industry and for shipyard workers and community organizers in Portland and in South Central Los Angeles. In addition to McClendon, other prominent voices in the effort included Reverend J. J. Clow—pastor of the Mt. Olivet Baptist Church and a leading figure in Portland's Council of Churches. Clow took over as local president of the Portland-area NAACP during Folkes' trial and appeals, while he was also pressing federal housing authorities to provide adequate housing for Black workers in that city. Clow claimed that "police hysteria" and "damaging newspaper publicity," as in the Folkes case, sparked a virulent wave of anti-Black activism in Portland. He was a visible presence at the trial, and he pointedly argued that police were inflaming public prejudice by arresting innocent people.[9]

The Folkes case also exposed long-treasured myths of rural refuge that blinded many Oregonians to long-term issues of racial prejudice and labor unrest. The uniquely virtuous rural communities that long-term Oregonians imagined as their joint heritage conflicted with the disorderly realities of wartime urbanization and industrial transformation that confronted rural residents of the mid-Willamette Valley. Rural communities in Oregon were distant but not isolated from the urban landscapes and issues that absorbed residents of Portland and other West Coast cities, and the story of why the state executed Folkes shows how the war drew those rural and urban worlds closer together. The war made it more difficult for rural residents of the mid-Valley to ignore the changing, more urban, structure of race and labor relations in the early to mid-twentieth century. On the surface, Linn County, Oregon, was relatively remote from wartime dislocations that transformed urban centers like Portland, Los Angeles, and Seattle during the first years of American involvement in the Second World War, and prosecutors relied on the comparatively homogeneous characteristics of that rural populace as they framed their case against Folkes. The apparent sameness of that population, however, belied an undercurrent of anxiety afflicting the farm folk of the mid-Valley.

The Folkes trial, in these circumstances, might be understood as a public ritual that focused attention on a simplified version of race relations at a time when wartime mobilization and militarization otherwise redefined, reshaded, or complicated previously drawn color lines. The melodramatic trial assigned each character with an exaggerated, stereotypical role that substituted for subtler shades of a multiracial society with more nuanced interests and values. That melodrama exaggerated rural-urban differences at a time when the war was actually blurring many such distinctions. The man prosecutors accused of murdering Martha James was a defendant whose differences from most local young men of the mid-Valley were obvious and visible: he was a young Black man who favored ostentatious styles of dress, speech, and physical demeanor that were distinctly urban. He was also a member of a relatively radical labor union in a period when A. Philip Randolph's Brotherhood of Sleeping Car Porters and the March on Washington Movement transformed the way White Americans thought about African American trainmen: earlier images of innocuous service attendants were set aside, and in their place, White passengers perceived Black trainmen as threatening and challenging symbols of racial difference.

THE ROBERT FOLKES DEFENSE COMMITTEE

Whereas militarization framed the initial investigation, arrest, trial, and sentencing, the appeals process wound its way through a political landscape that increasingly challenged prewar notions of gender- and race-skewed justice. Those who defended the conviction and sentencing of Folkes resorted, somewhat desperately, to racist arguments for punishing him, while those who appealed his conviction more commonly focused on the racist motives of his interrogators and the trial principals: prosecutors, jurors, and judge. Defense attorney Leroy Lomax raised similar concerns during the trial. Lewelling and newspaper reporters, however, claimed the court's approach to the case was race-blind, even as they exploited racialized stereotypes. In the post-trial phase, however, African American leaders organized a more race-conscious response, exploiting that community's more broadly visible role in the military effort. That response provided a more assertive, self-confident backdrop for the narrative that the RFDC presented to the Oregon State Supreme Court (OSSC), and later to the governor of Oregon.

Clara Leach Folkes and William E. Pollard, who jointly organized the RFDC and attended each day of the trial, continued working together after the verdict, seeking financial support for the appeals process. That process ultimately included a review from the OSSC and an appeal to the Supreme Court of the United States (SCOTUS). It culminated with a clemency petition to the Oregon governor. President James J. Clow of the Portland chapter of the NAACP and chapter secretary Ruth Haefner (who also chaired the Race Relations Council of Church Women of Oregon) also attended the trial and worked closely with Clara Folkes and Pollard on the appeal from 1943 to 1945.

The RFDC, with the supportive involvement of Clow and Haefner, helped transform the defeat in Lewelling's courtroom into a call for progressive action in Oregon. Their effort galvanized a resurgent Black press that was virtually silenced as a voice of dissent during earlier stages of wartime reaction. Little more than a month after the scheduled sentencing, a publication oriented toward African American issues hit the streets in Portland, targeting businesses owned or operated by or for the benefit of Black residents. One prominent sales outlet was the Medley Hotel, where Black trainmen typically gathered during their downtime between trains. The first issue of the new publication, the *People's Observer*, featured the Folkes case on page one, next to a statement of purpose by the Portland-area African American business-man identified on the masthead as its publisher: William H. McClendon.

The newly revived *People's Observer* included a race-conscious call on 29 June 1943 for a community commitment to secure justice for Folkes. McClendon restarted the newspaper after suspending publication earlier in the war, using the Folkes case as a vehicle for jump-starting community interest. Alongside his "declaration of policy" he printed a synopsis of irreg-ularities in the case against Folkes. McClendon announced, "The People's Observer is convinced that during these turbulent times the Negro people have been afforded ample opportunity to learn and understand the curse of faint-heartedness and submissiveness. We have, as all minority groups must, come to honor and appreciate courage, militancy, and aggressiveness." He pledged support to all those "who are unwavering and unrelenting in their opposition and attacks upon restrictions, legislation and statutes that threaten to curtail the progress of labor and the Negro People." Finally, he pledged that the paper would be "a valiant defender against segregation and its related evils; a vigilant champion for freedom, liberty, equality, and jus-tice; an alert guard against all social atrocities; a [vitriolic] analyst and severe critic of discriminatory practices; a sentinel to warn of all impending retro-gressive social trends and tendencies."[10]

Meanwhile, Robert Folkes disappeared into the bowels of the Oregon State Penitentiary immediately after the trial, and the story of the Lower 13 murder largely disappeared from mainstream newspapers,[11] but the story that NAACP activists and the *Observer* told (with the help of Pollard and Clara Folkes)—of a young man unjustly accused and convicted in a rigged trial—energized civil rights activists within and beyond the African American com-munity that summer. Responses to the verdict were largely racialized: most White commentators expressed relief the killer had been caught, convicted, and sentenced to death. Most African American reports, however, articulated outrage at the prospect that a likely killer—Wilson—got away scot-free, while an innocent young man was going to the gas chamber in his place. White Oregonians, it seems, mostly wanted to forget about the case, but a resurgent civil rights community in Oregon transformed the courtroom defeat into a rallying cry for resistance and community action.

McClendon's analysis of the Folkes case in the *Observer* emphasized the questionable use of transcripts from the second cook's alleged oral "statement," and he focused on the coercive methods of the LAPD and its interrogation of the young Black suspect. He reported that the "Pacific Coast branches of the NAACP and the [Dining Car Workers Union] PODCW Local No. 563 of Oakland, California" were working with Reverend J. J. Clow, president of the Portland branch of the NAACP, to organize the "Robert Fowlkes [sic] Defense Committee," in a fundraising effort aimed at covering the cost of appealing the case to the OSSC.[12] After listing a series of other, lesser, irregularities and the omission of physical evidence from the trial (such as the results, suppressed at trial, of Beeman's analysis of fingernail scrapings taken from Folkes or other witnesses—all of which revealed no presence of human blood, except in the case of Wilson), McClendon concluded, "We are convinced that Folkes did not have a fair and impartial trial and that there was a gross distortion of justice in this case." The editor also argued that mainstream newspapers distorted and misrepresented the case: "Relative to the statement published by the metropolitan newspapers quoting Fowlkes [sic] as having said 'he was ready to pay for his crime' upon hearing the decision of the jury; this is untrue and without a doubt a falsification of this youth's attitude."[13] White reporters emphasized the fatalistic resignation of Folkes after sentencing, claiming he was happy and joking with his captors, but McClendon portrayed Folkes as determined and consistent in denying guilt and renouncing the supposed statements as fabrications and distortions.

RFDC organizers clearly hoped that, as demonstrated with the wartime advances on the employment and housing fronts, and with the involvement of the FEPC, the public mood in Oregon was shifting on matters of race. In hopes that Oregonians of this new era would reject the verdict as overtly racist, they scrambled to position the case as an exposé of lingering, retrograde racism in the state's legal system. McClendon's first editorial in June 1943 opined, "Court procedures are notoriously unfair to Negroes. Investigations show that Negroes are convicted with less hesitation than any other racial group; most times they are repeatedly convicted on evidence which for whites would be inadequate." The editorial then directly linked the Folkes case to ongoing race-related labor strife in Portland shipyards, accusing Tom Ray, leader of Portland Local No. 72 of the Boilermakers and Shipbuilders

Union of fomenting an artificial claim of "labor shortages" despite a surplus of available Negro workers. He also linked the African American struggle for justice in Oregon with the nation's fight against the Axis powers: "There are at present a multitude of fascist whites who would rather risk defeat than grant freedom to the Negro People. These people . . . believe that a victory for Hitler would create a situation whereby they will be in a position to force the Negro back into shackles and chains." He concluded, "The Negro people are gradually realizing some advancements in industry and in government. . . . The Negro People are now awakening to the clarion call of Frederick Douglas . . . who taught his people eighty three years ago that men 'Who would be free, themselves must strike the blow.'"[14]

During Folkes' appeal, the NAACP in Portland was enveloped in a major fight with racist unions. In response to criticism from a 10 November 1942 summit meeting of government and union officials that focused on the need to end the union's discriminatory practices, Tom Ray reportedly proposed organizing an "auxiliary union for Negroes." Referring to opponents of this move, McClendon observed that the Portland NAACP and the Negro Shipyard Organization for Victory were resisting the "white supremacists" and the "poll-taxers, Jim Crowers, pro-lynchers and race baiters."[15] In pairing this story with the Folkes case, McClendon reframed the RFDC as a progressive response to larger patterns of racist reaction, labor unrest, and unequal working conditions in Oregon.

THE FOLKES CASE IN RELATION TO LATE-WAR LABOR RELATIONS IN PORTLAND

McClendon constructed the story of Folkes' experience as a parable of union activism and collective action. He emphasized Folkes' working-class identity as a unionized dining car worker who was tried for murder in racially exclusionist Linn County, and he used the trial as a metaphor and an entry point for discussing the experience of Black union activists in Kaiser shipyards. Black shipyard workers suffered mass layoffs and blacklisting during the same period Linn County prosecutors constructed the narrative that convicted Folkes. McClendon reported that layoffs at Kaiser targeted men who were "part of the staunch negro rank and file movement which is demanding acceptance into the local No. 72 Boilermakers Union." He reported that company spokesperson "Mr. Ashley, personnel manager of Kaiser Company, informed them that they would not receive clearances to work anywhere in this area."[16]

On the same day the LAPD had somewhat miraculously produced transcripts of Folkes' alleged confession, the Oregon Shipbuilding Corporation, headquartered in Delaware, terminated the employment, in Portland, of a Black shipyard worker named Lee Anderson.[17] The next month, Clow and Haefner met with the FEPC, which was holding hearings at Hudson House, in Vancouver, Washington. Those hearings included a mass meeting of the Negro Shipyard Organization for Victory.[18]

Somewhat belatedly, in California, Charlotta Bass and the *Eagle* followed McClendon's lead, exploiting widespread outrage over the farcical conviction of Folkes to rally support for, and interest in, the wartime movement to secure equal and fairer treatment for Black workers and, particularly, to secure relief for Black trainmen overwhelmed by wartime militarization of SPRR trains. Bass and the *Eagle* collaborated with Dining Car Workers Union leadership, notably Pollard, calling for FEPC hearings "to probe discrimination against railroad workers," to "declare a special legal status for undermanned railroad trains," and to "secure full utilization of existing manpower by upgrading Negro porters and dining car waiters [ironically excluding mention of dining car cooks and chefs]."[19] The committee's counsel, Bartley C. Crum, observed, "Negroes in the United States have suffered continuous, wholesale and increasing discrimination in employment by most of America's largest railroad systems. . . . It is imperative that Negroes be allowed full and equal participation in all phases of the war program."[20]

Against this backdrop of racialized labor strife in Portland and Los Angeles, Robert Folkes and his lawyers appealed his conviction, first petitioning the OSSC, then the SCOTUS, and finally, Republican governor Earl Snell. Snell was embroiled in the racialized labor unrest in Portland during the post-trial phase of the Folkes case, which forces of reaction commonly (and defensively) equated with late-war challenges to White racial privilege. Portland's Black community similarly adopted a more race-conscious approach to confronting those reactionaries. McClendon's paper, in late October 1943, reported a shakeup in the Portland chapter of the NAACP, which had expelled chapter president Wyatt Williams for his role in helping the Boilermakers and Shipbuilders Union organize a segregated auxiliary the outraged editor labeled "detrimental to the local Negro population." McClendon reported that Williams, during the 1942 gubernatorial election, wrote a letter to Governor-elect Snell, claiming the Portland-area NAACP had supported Snell's campaign. Terming Williams a "Trojan Horse: Negro

Apostate," McClendon railed against Snell, asserting he "was not the logical choice of the Negro people for governor." Describing Williams as "the local boy who never does any good," the editor noted Clow subsequently defeated Williams with the support of "the progressive element."[21] In the battle to save Folkes, Clow and McClendon rallied that progressive element in Portland's Black community against local and regional forces of reaction. Their efforts transformed the RFDC into a symbolic focus of a progressive insurgency in Oregon during the latter years of the war.

TRANSCRIPT IMPRISONMENTS AND THE SECOND RAILROADING OF FOLKES

While the NAACP and the Black press in Portland and Los Angeles focused on labor issues, Folkes, his mother, Clara, Lomax, and Pollard prepared his case for review by the Oregon State Supreme Court. Their appeal flew beneath the radar of most news coverage, except for periodic notices of requests for an extension of the deadline for filing. The defense team was handcuffed by delays in the Linn County district attorney's office, which was responsible for producing and certifying a true copy of the courtroom transcript from the original shorthand notes that court reporter Kathleen K. Miller compiled during the trial and then transcribed between April and November 1943. Miller, who testified for the prosecution at trial, deposited with Lewelling's circuit court, on 27 September, a sworn statement certifying the completed transcript was a full and complete record of court proceedings, but it was another two months before the prosecutor's office forwarded the massive document to the OSSC.[22] The higher court relied primarily on that transcript, isolated from the surrounding social context of news stories, police interrogations, or other materials that were common knowledge to anyone following the case since January. In shaping and controlling what Miller included in the transcript, Weinrick and Lewelling, during and after the trial, defined the range of argument that defense lawyers could present on appeal and OSSC justices would consider during deliberations. The final court opinion, consequently, largely confirmed and certified the conclusions of Lewelling's court and the Albany jurors.

The RFDC struggled to keep the case before the public during the long hiatus between the sentencing hearing and the public disclosure of the OSSC ruling, which came more than a year after the original verdict. Most of the delay originated in Albany (Lewelling's court), not Salem (seat of the OSSC). Weinrick's office was remarkably slow in producing the lengthy trial transcript, which included, yet again, multiple versions of the supposed statements Folkes allegedly made, first to the LAPD and then to OSP detectives in Albany. Each statement appeared twice in the trial record: once as an exhibit for the prosecution and once as part of the trial transcript at the point where prosecuting attorneys read the document into the court record. Just as prosecutors overwhelmed jurors with their oral presentations, this repetitious retelling of the supposed confessions in the trial transcript overwhelmed the record. Defense attorneys first had to argue on appeal that the statements should not have been allowed into evidence, and second, in case the higher court disagreed, they had to argue why the statements should be discounted in relation to other evidence. Supreme court protocols allowed very little leeway for introducing new information into the appeals process, meaning the OSSC decision was largely framed within the parameters Lewelling established in his courtroom.

The trial transcript, when it was finally completed more than five months after the trial, was riddled with inconsistencies that suggested prosecutors tampered with the court record. Most glaringly, the transcript included sudden breaks in the numbering of pages, unexplained insertions, and conspicuous omissions. Court reporter Miller, in certifying the document, admitted "the figures [pages numbered] 375 consecutively through 387 and figures 390 consecutively through 399 were not used in numbering the pages of this transcript." These pages were simply missing from the record, but she asserted the document, nonetheless, was "a full, true, and correct transcript of my shorthand notes and the whole thereof." This admission aside, Miller noted the transcript was paginated "from one to 656 and 662 through 831, including 618-a and 715a," but she neither noted nor explained the obvious omission of pages 657 through 661, nor did she explain why pages 618-a and 715-a were inserted into the transcript.

The trial transcript was an obviously compromised record of actual courtroom proceedings, and Miller's certification was transparently incomplete and inaccurate—all issues that should have raised questions about other transcriptions she prepared, including the supposed Albany statement that prosecutors attributed to Folkes. Even the irregularities that Miller itemized in the certification document were inaccurate and incomplete. The actual copy of the transcript filed with the OSSC moves directly from "Hickman-D-377" to "Hickman-388-D" and from "Hickman-389-D" to "Hickman-400-D." Miller did not address, in the certification documents, why those twenty-two pages were omitted. Then, although Miller specifically certified otherwise, the transcript *did* make use of figures 375, 376, and 377, as well as figures 388 and 389, before skipping to figure 400, omitting figures 390 to 399 (as Miller noted in the certification documents but did not explain). Moreover, the notation system in the pages that contradicted the certification document differed from the rest of the transcript, reversing the order of the page number and the "D" or "X" that Miller used to denote "direct" or "cross-examination." The quality and composition of the typescript also change at that point from heavy white paper to onionskin.

One OSSC justice argued, in his eventual dissenting opinion, that the sudden, unexplained changes in material composition of the transcript drew attention to certain parts of the manuscript, quietly altering how readers focused on key points in deliberations. This use of materials to punctuate and highlight certain portions of the transcript effectively altered the meaning readers took away from the document. Expense and time constraints may partly explain these differences; however, preparation and delivery of the trial transcript spanned over half a year. Weinrick's office clearly had plenty of time to correct these errors, suggesting they were more than accidental. The only indication, finally, that the transcript was officially "accepted into the court" appears as a scrawled notation by Weinrick near the bottom of the cover of the transcript copy.[23] Despite its internal inconsistency, lack of contextual integrity, and missing imprimatur from the trial judge, this deeply flawed, obviously compromised document was the foundation for all subsequent reviews and appeals.

DISAPPEARING THE STORY OF ROBERT FOLKES: THE APPEALS PROCESS

As the Folkes case assumed symbolic importance for the resurgent civil rights movement in Portland and Los Angeles during the later stages of the war, forces of reaction in Oregon tried to bury the case in the bureaucratic vacuum of the appeals process. Between April 1943 and December 1944, nonetheless, the RFDC successfully repositioned the case near the center of public concern in Portland and, less successfully, into public awareness at the national level. As Clara Folkes and Pollard battled for the life of her son, they attracted the attention of more established and long-running newspapers oriented toward the African American community and even some other, more mainstream, outlets aimed mostly at White readers. The trial's outcome surprised many observers. Even the *Norfolk Journal and Guide*, in James' hometown, reported in early May that "prominent white leaders in Norfolk's civic, social and professional life have openly expressed surprise at the verdict of the Albany, Ore., jury." The article noted, "Several Norfolkians, including veteran lawyers who would not let their names be used, have openly stated that they seriously doubt Folkes' guilt, based upon the evidence presented at the trial." It emphasized Wilson's changing description of the man he claimed to have seen fleeing the scene, and it highlighted the claim Lomax made, in his closing remarks (none of which the court reporter included in the official transcript), of what the victim—a product of a privileged White upbringing in a racist, southern community—would more likely have said if she could have seen her attacker was Black: "This nigger is killing me"—not "This man is killing me."[24] Even in the racially charged atmosphere of wartime Norfolk, local White authorities believed a White man (meaning Wilson) and not a Black man (meaning Folkes) had murdered Martha James.

Despite widespread suspicions that the verdict was flawed, the RFDC began with few public supporters and struggled for more than a year to attract reliable support, even from the Black press. Apart from fragmentary accounts like the one in the Norfolk paper, the case largely faded from public view for most of 1943 and 1944, even in Oregon. After the excitement of the trial, the appeals process was bureaucratic and wrapped in stultifying, technical legal-ese with few of the dramatic hooks or lurid storylines that made the murder and subsequent trial a front-page story.[25] Folkes remained in the state peni-tentiary through summer and fall 1943 while his lawyers prepared briefs for the OSSC. Working with allies in Portland as well as in South Central, the RFDC recruited prominent clergymen and printed appeals in the Black press, desperately seeking funds, information, and political support.

Interstate networks connecting the Black clergy and the Black press on the West Coast were critical factors that helped the RFDC transform their lonely fight into a civil rights struggle with broader significance. McClendon and Clow, in particular, worked to connect the labor struggles and Black activism in Portland with the locus of the Black cultural renaissance in South Central, and Pollard's previous involvement with Charlotta Bass and other progressives in South Central helped link their effort to the wider reader-ship of the *California Eagle*. Clara Folkes was particularly active in recruiting support from the Black clergy in South Central after the verdict. Reverend J. Raymond Henderson, who presided over the Baptist Union in Los Angeles, visited with Clow and Lomax in Portland shortly after the verdict, apparently at the urging of Clara Folkes and Pollard, and he came away from that visit "convinced that Folkes is innocent of the 'Lower 13 Slaying.' I believe him to be the victim of circumstances and the trickery of someone who committed the crime and was smart enough to cover up and incriminate an innocent Negro with insufficient intelligence to protect himself." Henderson urged residents of Los Angeles to "go to your respective churches this Sunday prepared to give an offering." Henderson concluded, "Let us all become aroused, lest justice be once again miscarried."[26]

Growing concerns over other abusive police actions in South Central during spring and summer 1943 intensified local interest in the LAPD role in the Folkes case, and that connection helped link civil rights leaders in Los Angeles more closely with Clow, McClendon, and other Portland-area progressives. Near the time originally scheduled for Folkes to be executed, in May 1943, LAPD officers in South Central fired four shots into Lenza Smith, a thirty-six-year-old Black defense worker whose killing sparked a "near riot" on East 52nd Street. In the aftermath of the shooting, Black community leaders organized a unity rally at the People's Independent Church of Christ on 18th Street and Paloma in South Central, during which Henderson also appealed for funds to support Folkes. The unity rally and Henderson's appeal refocused long-running concerns about LAPD mistreatment of Black men, and in the aftermath of the riot, South Central's progressive organizations found a focus for their outrage in the Folkes case. The Negro Victory Committee, the NAACP, and the CIO Anti-Discrimination Committee all became more intently involved in supporting the RFDC in the aftermath of the Lenza Smith shooting.[27]

The RFDC recognized that the success of the appeals process rested as much on a successful public-sphere campaign as on formal legal channels, and they used their South Central connections to reframe public understandings of the case and to challenge how mainstream reporters misrepresented evidence and Folkes. Henderson's role in the RFDC attracted the support of the influential editor of the *California Eagle*, who printed an open letter from Henderson to the editor of the *Los Angeles Examiner* (a Hearst newspaper) on behalf of the Interdenominational Ministers' Alliance and the Baptist Ministers' Union representing the Combined Negro Churches of Los Angeles. Henderson protested the 23 May 1943 issue of *American Weekly* (an insert in the Hearst chain's weekend editions) in portraying "murder in Lower 13" with "dastardly

drawings and subtle implications." Henderson and the Baptist Union emphasized Folkes' guilt "has never been proven. The little prejudiced town of Albany,
Oregon, had condemned him before the trial. The unsigned confession means
nothing. It is even inadmissable [*sic*] evidence under Oregon law. The jury had
handed [to] them [the] typed copy [of] the testimony of the marine in the
case, which is prohibited by law in any court of real justice."[28]

The Black press succumbed to the melodramatic tone of the Folkes trial,
embracing the language and distortions but inverting the message. After
Folkes won a temporary stay of his execution in May 1943, the *Eagle* connected his case with a progressive challenge to the nationalist myth of wartime unity and race-blind militarization. With headlines screaming, "Folkes
was framed!" Bass belatedly linked the Folkes trial with the "zoot suit riots,"
promising more complete coverage in the *Eagle*'s "Youth Section," due out
17 June. In a teaser subheading that read like the cover of a true-crime news
rag before the war, the *Eagle* promised "the whole shocking story, revealing
the intimidation and corruption which worked full blast in this trumped-up
murder case." In one breathless appeal, Bass promised to reveal lurid details
previously withheld: "How Folkes was made drunk by Los Angeles Police—
how he was threatened with lynching to secure a phony confession—will be
unveiled in this gripping and tragic story. Do not miss it, young people! It
might have been your story."[29] Despite the advance buildup, however, nothing
about the Folkes case appears in the *Eagle*'s surviving copies of that week's
youth section, and Bass offered no explanation for why the paper did not
deliver on that promise.

Without the melodramatic elements Bass promised her readers that
summer, the appeals process attracted much less attention than the trial.
Conspiracy was easy to assume but hard to prove in the context of a militarized security state where reporters could seldom access records they needed
to support claims like those Bass published in the *Eagle* that June. Instead, the
official appeals process buried the drama of false conviction behind a façade
of fairness to officers of Lewelling's court, operating on the presumption the
judge, district attorney, and police investigators all acted in good faith. With
less concern about fairness to Folkes, the process bogged down in a legal pretense of confidence in the jury's decision.

The RFDC had to break through twin assumptions that the court acted
fairly and that the jury's decision was sound, and to do that they relied on a
list of exceptions Lomax noted during the trial. The formal bill of exceptions

he prepared and filed with the circuit court, which the county clerk included in the file forwarded to the OSSC on 24 November 1943, laid the foundations for appealing Folkes' conviction to higher courts, first at the state level and then to the federal Supreme Court. The nine-page document listed seven exceptions the defense reserved against Lewelling's rulings at the trial: (1) the introduction as evidence and delivery to the jury room transcripts of Folkes' LA "confession" (State's Exhibit K); (2) the introduction as evidence and delivery to the jury room transcripts of Folkes' Albany "confession" (State's Exhibit L); (3) admission of the LA transcripts despite evidence the defendant was intoxicated at the time of the alleged oral statements; (4) the trial court's failure to provide statutory instructions to the jury regarding their responsibility to view with caution oral claims and admissions; (5) the trial court's ruling that allowed the prosecution to impeach its own witness (Kelso) after the judge overruled defense objections and allowed hearsay testimony from SPRR detective Champlin to the effect that he heard Kelso describe the man he encountered in the aisle of Car D shortly before the murder differently than Kelso himself described the man in his direct courtroom testimony; (6) the court's ruling that allowed prejudicial testimony from Rasmussen implying (without corroborating evidence) that the defendant's house contained illegal weapons; and (7) the court's denial of defense motions for a directed verdict of acquittal on the grounds there was no evidence connecting the defendant with the crime except for purported oral admissions of the defendant listed in exceptions (1) and (2) and to which prosecutors offered no corroborating evidence from other witnesses. Exception (7) also noted that the officers responsible for taking the Albany statement both admitted they pressed the defendant to confess even after he protested he did not wish to discuss the case without his attorney present. Lomax also argued that court testimony confirmed the alleged transcripts were incomplete or altered.

Beyond these seven specific exceptions, Lomax argued in the state-level appeal that a complete understanding of exceptions and rulings from the trial court would not be possible without a full and careful review of the entire trial transcript.[30] Lomax reminded OSSC justices that the DA's unusually long delay in completing and providing copies of the transcript had prevented defense attorneys from compiling a comprehensive bill of exceptions, but he also implied they should consider the full context of the trial when reviewing the specific exceptions he included in the defense brief.

The Black press paid more attention to the appeal than did mainstream news outlets targeting mostly White audiences; consequently, readers more attuned to wartime civil rights struggles were better prepared for the post-appeal process of petitioning Governor Snell for clemency. Few of the details of the Folkes appeal made their way into newspaper accounts before or after the OSSC scheduled oral arguments, and the ultimate decision arrived with virtually no context or explanation for how Lomax framed each trial exception. Nearly nine months after the trial, readers of the *Eagle*, for example, finally learned, in late January 1944, that the OSSC had received the appeal, including "lawyers' briefs." The newspaper credited Pollard and James H. Anderson, cochairs of the RFDC Citizens Committee, with pressing the appeal and raising the necessary funds, with support from the Los Angeles and Portland branches of the NAACP, the Dining Car Cooks and Waiters Union Local 568, and various other organizations and churches in LA.[31] That report was somewhat premature, however. The OSSC received the Appellant's Brief (from Lomax) on 18 January, followed by the Respondent's Brief (from Weinrick and Sisemore) on 7 February, and the Reply Brief of Appellant (from Lomax) on 18 February. Two weeks later, on 1 March, the court finally heard oral arguments from Lomax and Weinrick. All these developments proceeded with virtually no notice from the local or national press.

Mainstream audiences divided along racial lines during and after the appeals process as a result of their differing exposure to the trial aftermath. Defense attorneys and RFDC supporters operated mostly in obscurity, and most popular outlets virtually ignored their efforts to change the storyline that prosecutors laid out in the trial transcript. At least five simultaneous stories vied for attention before the OSSC and in the press: (1) defense attorneys asserted OSSC justices should focus on how authorities trampled the rights of Folkes during the investigation; (2) defense lawyers claimed the trial was unfair and Lewelling's rulings violated state and federal laws and constitutions; (3) prosecutors asserted the people had already spoken in the person(s) of the jury and the resulting sentence was fair and just; (4) RFDC supporters contended the trial was a racist expression of Jim Crowism and the equivalent of a legal lynching; and (5) White journalists mostly argued the case was closed—with the defendant already convicted and sentenced, only the execution remained to conclude justice. None of these arguments directly addressed the question of who killed Martha James, although those who followed the Black press expected otherwise.

Mainstream newspapers represented the case as solved and the execution as a foregone conclusion, while publications oriented toward African American readers expressed skepticism but also hope that state or federal courts would ultimately overturn the conviction. Neither mainstream newsmen nor Black publishers outlined the legal appeal with any attention to detail. Readers were not informed of any specific arguments and news articles offered virtually no reference to specific timelines or court processes. As a result, news of the OSSC ruling, when it finally arrived in June 1944, came virtually without context long after most people had forgotten about the case and were preoccupied with preparations for postwar transitions. The meaning of the OSSC decision, therefore, was largely constructed after the event and in other contexts apart from the original arguments of the lawyers' briefs.

RECONSTRUCTING MEANING FOR THE FOLKES CASE IN THE OREGON STATE SUPREME COURT

By the time the OSSC issued its decision on the Folkes appeal, the case no longer resonated with the national mood, and coverage of the opinion was almost an afterthought in most mainstream news reports. Editors buried most updates about the case in perfunctory news-filler stories surrounded by large entertainment ads deep in the back pages. Defense attorneys deliberately downplayed sensational aspects of the murder, focusing narrowly on how authorities coerced statements from Folkes. Prosecutors relied mostly on the sheer weight of trial transcripts and the storyline the supposed confessions told in repetitious detail and rambling incoherence. They wrapped obvious contradictions in endlessly mundane verbiage, grinding down even the most determined readers, and then they delivered familiar, summary versions that referenced those statements, pretending they were internally consistent and conclusive evidence confirming Folkes' guilt. Prosecutors clearly signaled, in stultifying, unoriginal arguments, that they assumed the OSSC would routinely uphold the conviction.

Justices on the court varied widely in their degree of engagement with the trial transcript, and the majority opinion focused on symbolic issues of states' rights, positioning the OSSC in conservative opposition to a supposedly extremist, liberal court at the federal level. The majority justices on the OSSC, in other words, used the Folkes case to express solidarity with constitutional arguments underpinning the Jim Crow system of racial segregation and White supremacy. The OSSC majority demonstrated remarkable disinterest in the details the transcript revealed about how the trial court mismanaged the Folkes case, and prosecutors encouraged the court's inattentiveness with repetitious assertions that clearly aimed to obscure rather than clarify areas of contradiction.

The eventual OSSC ruling was anticlimactic, given widespread assumptions the trial had settled issues of guilt and punishment, and the decision was otherwise overshadowed by a surge of war-related news. Reports of the Battle of the Mariana Straits, in what one account termed "the opening round of a great showdown battle between the contesting navies of the Pacific,"[32] shouldered aside the OSSC ruling when it was finally announced on 20 June, and initial reports included virtually none of the court's majority arguments. The dissenting opinion of Justices Rossman and Kelley, ironically, was more widely available to curious readers than the argument Justice Brand authored for the five-to-two majority. Brand's opinion was tailored to an audience concerned more about transitions to the postwar era than the paranoid fears that had overwhelmed reason earlier in the war.

Brand's opinion retold, for audiences in the late-war period, a story that closely followed the journalistic account that first broke into headlines on that snowy January morning eighteen months earlier. It began with a tragic account of how wartime circumstances separated the young James couple in Portland, and it asserted a timeline for the murder that contradicted most of the testimony the prosecution privileged at trial. Brand ignored obviously conflicting testimony and brashly asserted a drastically simplified version of events. By his account, three passengers—Wilson, Conner, and Norton—actually saw the perpetrator, and two of those three actually saw the man backing out of Lower 13 dressed in a "long dark overcoat." This false certitude grossly misrepresented witness testimony. Brand admitted no witnesses identified Folkes as the man they saw, although they did see the man run toward the dining car to the rear of Car D, where the second cook worked.[33] Brand's opinion relied mostly on Weinrick's oral retelling of the case, streamlined with evasions and vague generalizations that papered over conflicting accounts.

The most important obfuscation involved Weinrick's refusal to admit the racial context of his case against Folkes. If Oregon's supreme court justices previously saw any local newspaper coverage about the murder and subsequent trial, they could not have missed the racial identities of the victim, the defendant, and the various witnesses. Those identities were ever-present, if unspoken, realities during courtroom deliberations and in newspaper coverage, including photographs. The pretense of a color-blind trial court that prosecutors and judge carefully cultivated, however, effectively removed most overt racial references from the official transcript. This left Lomax in the position of having to reinsert race into the appeal during oral and written arguments. In so doing, he challenged the court's decorum and its pretense of racelessness, and he opened the way for racist apologists to argue the defense had injected race into a case that was really about color-blind justice. Prosecutors calmly pretended they had not even noticed race, adopting an air of sympathy with justices and jurors who patiently endured an emotional onslaught of irrational accusations from defense counsel. Lomax, by contrast, emphasized in oral arguments "three assignments of error" in Lewelling's administration of the trial: (1) admission of transcripts as if they were oral confessions, (2) methods of interrogation that violated the constitutional rights of the accused, and (3) inadequate instructions from the judge to the jury regarding the use of oral admissions in a courtroom.[34] Beyond these arguments, Lomax questioned the pretense of police officers who claimed they remembered exactly what Folkes had said during interrogations. He noted that LAPD officers Rasmussen and Tetrick and OSP agents Beeman and Howard "testified at great length" concerning every word spoken by the defendant "without once asking to be allowed to refresh their memories."[35]

Lomax wanted OSSC justices to focus on his client's claim that he never saw transcripts of the statements police attributed to him, that his interrogators never read those statements back to Folkes, and that the defendant never signed nor otherwise acknowledged or reviewed the documents. Lomax noted that the defense never saw those transcripts before prosecutors introduced them as evidence in Lewelling's courtroom, and he argued that the repetitious manner in which they were introduced, first as oral testimony from various police officers, then as written narratives that prosecutors read into the record with dramatic voice before the jury, and finally as written transcripts that jurors took with them into the jury room where they consulted them during deliberations, transformed those unauthenticated and uncorroborated documents into juggernauts that overwhelmed all other evidence presented at trial. Lomax accurately stressed that, apart from those transcripts, prosecutors produced nothing linking Folkes to the crime.[36]

Although the OSSC majority seemed more interested in redefining the case as a precedent for asserting states' rights over federal authority, both prosecutors and defense attorneys apparently prepared oral arguments expecting the case would turn on the issue of whether Folkes was coerced into confessing. Weinrick devoted much of his oral argument not to emphasizing the legalities of whether the statements should have been admitted, but rather, emphasizing what they contained. He recapitulated, yet again, details of the Lyman statement, and then concluded, "That statement was a confession, under the definitions of this court which go all the way back." Under questioning from Justices Belt and Lusk, Weinrick explained interrogators never asked Folkes to sign the statement, arguing lamely, "They were rather length[y] and it took some time for the reporters [transcriptionists] to transcribe them and by that time it was felt to be unnecessary." Bailey skeptically questioned that excuse, noting that transcribing the forty-page Albany statement "would take about a day."[37] The justices showed discomfort with Weinrick's arguments, and their opinions mostly questioned the validity of those coerced and unsigned "confessions."

Weinrick argued that the only tests required for accepting as evidence an unsigned confession were, first, whether the statement was voluntary, and second, whether it was made by the defendant. Justice Hay challenged that premise: "You think a transcribed statement of what the defendant said is itself the confession? Isn't the confession what he said and the other a memorandum of it?" In answer, Weinrick argued that if Folkes sat down and wrote out the confession in his own hand, that would have been admissible, and then he asked a rhetorical question: "All right, what is the difference between that defendant using his hands to make his statement or using his mouth and teeth and lips to make the statement to a person taking it. . . . I cannot see any distinction. It is his confession; he says I am guilty."[38] On this point, Weinrick essentially argued there was no fundamental distinction between a primary source (the actual voice of a subject) and a secondary source (another person's report of what he or she thought the subject actually said), but none of the justices called him on that point. In all these exchanges, neither the justices nor Weinrick directly questioned the initial assumption: Had Folkes actually "confessed"? In other words, did the unsigned statements actually reflect what Folkes said in those interrogations, under duress? Trial testimony clearly showed no one ever read the statement to Folkes nor gave him the opportunity to read or correct it, and he had no attorney present in any of the interrogations.

Brand's majority opinion sidestepped the issue of the improper statements by first inventing a new narrative of the case that was inconsistent with actual testimony and then arguing that other testimony was so compelling the statements were not even needed to convict Folkes. Brand's version of the story noted that Folkes wore a "white coat" while speaking with Porter Hughes in the smoking room of Car D before the murder, that Wasserman saw "a colored man dressed in a white uniform" speaking with Martha James while the train was in Portland, and that she testified, "He [Folkes] looks like the one." Ignoring testimony to the contrary, Brand reinserted military authenticity into the story, emphasizing that "Witness Wilson, a United States Marine," had "searched all cars to the rear of car D." Without addressing defense claims that Lewelling allowed hearsay testimony, Brand noted Champlin testified that during interrogations in Klamath Falls "the defendant admitted that he was the person who had shown Kelso the way to the men's room."[39] Folkes, of course, never testified to this point or any other at his trial, and none of his signed statements from interrogations aboard the train were ever introduced at trial.

Brand argued that the story he narrated at the opening of his opinion, which he apparently pieced together from an arbitrarily selective sampling of widely divergent and mostly contradictory testimony, was important context, in that it "corroborates various portions of the admissions and confessions of the defendant." The remaining testimony, he (inaccurately) claimed, largely dealt with supposed admissions and confessions of the defendant (Exhibits K and L) and the circumstances in which they were made. Brand characterized Exhibits K and L as "transcribed stenographic notes of conversations with the defendant wherein the defendant confessed his guilt in great detail." In apparent reference to the oral arguments, and ignoring the written brief Lomax submitted, Brand inaccurately claimed the defendant presented only "three assignments of error and no more." He characterized the second assignment of error as relating to "oral admissions of the defendant," suggesting this was a second issue, apart from the first matter. Brand's majority opinion then approached each of the three assignments of error he was willing to recognize, separately and in sequence. He argued a confession need not always be signed by the defendant before it can be "deemed admissible as the written confession of the defendant," but he held "he must in some manner have acquiesced in the correctness of the writing itself."[40]

Folkes had specifically denounced the supposed "statement," through his lawyers, as a fabrication, and for that reason even Brand could not claim he "acquiesced" in its "correctness." By Brand's own standard, this meant the document was inadmissible. Somehow, Brand had to accommodate the fact in his argument that the conviction could stand, despite the fact that verdict was tainted by the jury's exposure to inadmissible evidence. Brand, consequently, argued that Lewelling erred in (a) allowing the Lyman statement (Exhibit K) in evidence, and (b) sending it to the jury room with other exhibits. Admitting that "the defendant never saw, heard, wrote or signed the instrument," Brand essentially agreed with Lomax that Lyman should only have been allowed to consult the statement while offering her verbal account of the confession she purportedly witnessed. In this way, he argued, the jury would have heard the statement but would not have seen it, and the oral rendering of the document would have been from the witness (a stenographer) on the stand, not from the district attorney (an officer of the court). The statement, in those circumstances, would have been no more than a "memorial of lost recollection, instead of being proven as a written confession in and of itself."[41]

Having convincingly discredited the decision to admit the written statements in court, Brand astoundingly asserted the error "was not prejudicial." He referenced a notation in the transcript, near the end, which claimed, without corroboration, that Folkes had said "as long as she has it down and I read thoroughly and understand, I will be willing to take the medicine which the killer should take." With no evidence whatsoever that the notation was in Folkes' writing or that it accurately reported something he said, Brand admitted it was not precisely as if Folkes approved the transcript, "for it had not yet been written." Nonetheless, he asserted, as a key feature of the majority opinion on the matter, "it was a manifestation that he would adopt it if it was properly taken down and if he should read and understand it."[42]

Leaving aside the question of whether Folkes actually made the statement or not, Brand implied that a willingness, beforehand, to approve an as-yet-unwritten statement if it were correctly taken down was legally the same thing as actually reviewing and approving that statement once it was written. Brand noted Rasmussen testified that Folkes offered to sign the statement (neglecting the fact it was not even written down in his presence), but that the LAPD officer refused to allow it. No evidence of this claim appears in Exhibit K, but Brand's majority opinion argued that this spurious claim by the interrogating officer was legally equivalent to the defendant's having reviewed and signed the statement. Rasmussen's claim, however, was actually impossible because the transcript, by his own admission, was not even written when Rasmussen disingenuously claimed Folkes asked to sign the phantom document.[43]

By twisted reasoning and selective reading of evidence, Brand officially recognized the indisputable truth that Lewelling erred in admitting as evidence a statement that Folkes neither reviewed nor signed, but at the same time, he also managed to pretend the error was a virtually irrelevant technicality. He argued along similar lines in ruling Lewelling erred in admitting as evidence the Miller statement (Exhibit L). He also claimed, however, without explanation, that "the accuracy of the court reporter's shorthand notes and of her transcription thereof was proven and is unquestioned." This claim ignored testimony from Hughes and other witnesses that alleged the same transcriptionist (Miller) fundamentally altered their statements and deleted or misrepresented important details, clearly indicating a pattern of error and possible deceit. It also ignored efforts by defense counsel during the trial to exclude Exhibits K and L on the basis of direct testimony from arresting officers that proved the transcriptionist left out important details from Exhibit L. Brand's opinion also ignored the ways in which Exhibit K conflicted with Exhibit L and other evidence and testimony. Instead, the majority opinion emphasized the "direct, detailed confession by the defendant that he murdered Mrs. James."[44]

Throughout the majority opinion, Brand simplified and misrepresented evidence and facts to give the false impression the trial transcript detailed an uncontested story rather than a complex mosaic of conflicting accounts. He selectively cited various "facts" from the trial transcript that fit the narrative he presented in the majority opinion, while ignoring other facts and testimony that directly contradicted the ones he selected. In areas where the accounts of Rasmussen and Tetrick directly contradicted each other, Brand resorted to simple vagueness, ignoring clear evidence that the two LAPD investigators were either lying or otherwise falsifying the record. In discussing the Albany statement (Exhibit L), by contrast, Brand cited the "uncontradicted" testimony of officers Howard and Beeman as evidence of the veracity of their accounts. Ultimately, Brand concluded, "We hold that none of the confessions of the defendant were rendered involuntary or inadmissible by reason of the length of the periods of questioning or the manner in which it was done."[45] As legal rationale, Brand specifically referenced the Layton case (State v. Layton, 174 Or. 148 P. (2d) 522), which the OSSC had decided in a ruling just two months earlier (on 25 April), noting lawyers in that case, as in the Folkes case, cited Ashcraft v. State of Tennessee as precedent. In considering a petition for rehearing the Layton case, Brand observed, "The questioning of the defendant [Layton] covered a much longer, continuous period than in the case at bar [Folkes]," and regardless, the OSSC (Brand's court) had ruled the Ashcraft precedent inapplicable in that case. Brand noted the jury in the Folkes case was admonished to consider whether statements were or were not voluntary, and he argued, therefore, that the jury "must have found that defendant had voluntarily confessed the crime."[46] In other words, the jury had already spoken, and Brand argued the OSSC should not second-guess their decision—even if that decision were based on tainted evidence placed before them in error.

Finally, Brand's majority opinion offered a politically inflammatory states' rights argument on the matter of whether the court was bound by *McNabb v. United States.* White supremacists, in years following the Civil War, built the postwar system of Jim Crow segregation on the foundation of states' rights, partly as a reaction to the period of military occupation and coercive federal authority known as Reconstruction. In *McNabb*, a reconstituted liberal court ruled inadmissible a confession a White peace officer coerced from an arrested person while failing to take the accused before a magistrate within the time required by federal statute. Brand denied the applicability of *McNabb* on the grounds that, as a federal case, it was not binding on state courts. He argued *McNabb* was "out of harmony with the law of this jurisdiction," and in an overtly politicized aside, he argued, "Notwithstanding the recent extension of the boundaries of procedural due process by the United States Supreme Court *as at present constituted* [emphasis added—a reference to nine justices on the SCOTUS appointed by Democratic president Franklin Roosevelt between 1937 and 1943[47]], we cannot believe that it will go to the extreme length of holding that one is deprived of due process of law whenever illegally obtained evidence is received against a defendant in a criminal trial."[48]

On the question of tainted evidence and coerced confession, and on the question of whether Folkes was denied adequate counsel, Brand's opinion categorically rejected *McNabb* as a federal intrusion on states' rights, and the bulk of his majority opinion relied, almost exclusively, on Exhibits K and L (the tainted statements) and the oral testimony of police officers. Where it considered other, contradictory testimony from Clara Folkes and Jessie Taylor,[49] the opinion acknowledged that the *literal* meaning of their testimony contradicted the officers and the transcripts, but Brand argued for a more *symbolic* interpretation of their testimony so that it might better fit within the broad outlines of the officers' claims. In this way, Brand stretched and pulled the evidence as presented in the trial transcripts until it matched the story he claimed "proved" Folkes guilty of the murder.

Ultimately, Brand argued, Folkes missed his chance to deny the validity of Exhibits K and L when he failed to take the stand. Brand asserted "the evidence that defendant's confessions were, in fact, voluntarily made is so clear, conclusive and uncontradicted that we will not encumber the record by quoting the testimony," and he then concluded, "Under these circumstances, the confessions constitute the highest sort of evidence." Brand's opinion included an obligatory nod to a defendant's constitutional right not to testify, but he argued, "The fact remains that by reason of his failure to testify or to produce any other evidence in contradiction of the confession, the testimony of the witnesses for the State is in every substantial particular unimpeached and uncontradicted, except as stated."[50]

Brand's majority opinion demonstrated a preference for assuming the integrity of police over the innocence of the Black defendant. Nothing in the majority opinion considered the testimony of the Black trainmen. The opinion argued that any differences between what Folkes supposedly said and transcriptions of those accounts most likely resulted from the defendant's inconsistency, and "it seems to us improper to assume that minor discrepancies are those of the officers who reported his statements."[51] Brand's majority opinion reads as if it were responding to concerns about discrepancies within the transcript itself, or concerns about discrepancies between the transcript and the testimony of the officers who appeared at witnesses. The brief Lomax filed with Brand's court, however, actually argued, as documented in the transcript of trial testimony from Hughes and Shaw, that what stenographers transcribed differed substantially from oral statements witnesses had made, and he argued that statements attributed to Folkes did not accurately or completely represent what Folkes actually said. Rather than discrepancies *within* the document, in other words, Lomax argued there were discrepancies *between* what Folkes said and what the document *reported* he said. Brand's opinion first misrepresented the concern and then waived it off as unsubstantiated, either in the transcript or in the testimony of the police.

Brand's opinion extensively quoted testimony Tetrick and Rasmussen offered in court, citing details of that testimony as if they proved Exhibit K was substantially a confession. He argued that because those portions of the transcript to which Lomax objected were substantially the same as other evidence that the defendant had not challenged and that Tetrick related as his oral recollection, the defendant's interests were not substantively harmed by the court's error.[52] Likewise, Brand argued, the oral testimony of Lieutenant Howard substantively corroborated Exhibit L, meaning the defendant also was not harmed by the court's error in allowing that exhibit as evidence.[53]

In a transparently political nod to the states' rights position of Jim Crow segregationists, Brand's majority opinion argued that precedents from other states, and not from the federal courts, guided his court's decision. The function of state supreme courts such as the OSSC, according to Brand (quoting a judgment of the Illinois Supreme Court), "is not to determine whether the record is free from error, but is to ascertain whether a just conclusion has been reached, founded upon competent and sufficient evidence, after a trial in which no error has occurred which might be prejudicial to the defendant's rights."[54] Ultimately, Brand concluded, the OSSC was bound by the provisions of O.C.L.A.§26-1325, which "requires the court to 'give judgment without regard to the decision of questions which were in the discretion of the court below or to technical errors, defects or exceptions which do not affect the substantial rights of the parties.'" Applying that test, Brand argued, "the verdict would have been the same had no error been committed in the case at bar [Folkes' conviction]."[55] The majority of Brand's court, with these words, agreed the trial was substantively fair, regardless of procedural errors.

REASSERTING POSTWAR RACIAL ORDER: THE CONCURRING OPINIONS

Brand's majority opinion sidestepped race by focusing on states' rights in a remarkably selective and misleading reading of the trial transcript, but his argument did not adequately address the concerns of concurring justices who went further in their arguments to define the limits of racial tolerance in Oregon. Justice Belt, for example, supported Brand's majority opinion with a "specially concurring opinion" that questioned why Folkes failed to testify. Then he added inflammatory accusations that, despite direct testimony that Martha James was not raped, Folkes actually had attempted to rape her (there is no evidence supporting this claim in case files). He injected racialized code words into the argument, stressing the "unquestioned integrity" of White interrogating officers and the "fiendish and brutal" nature of the crime committed by the young Black defendant. Regarding the defendant's Fifth Amendment rights, Belt opined, "It is true that he was not, under the Constitution, obliged to take the stand and tell what he knew about the case—as any innocent man would be glad to do—but he should not be permitted to remain mute and then . . . escape the consequences of a just verdict."[56]

Justice Lusk drafted an even longer concurring opinion emphasizing the standing of the White police officers involved and directly condemning his colleague, Justice Rossman, for impugning their character and reliability. Implying Rossman's dissenting opinion sided with the Black defendant against the White officers, Lusk questioned why Rossman disparaged the testimony of three of the four police officials who claimed they heard Folkes orally confess. Lusk, whose concurring opinion largely recapitulated, ad nauseam, the testimony of Rasmussen and Tetrick, directly addressed Rossman's standard for reversing a lower court's decision "unless the evidence produced by the state is so strong that it possesses an unusually high degree of cogency."[57] Lusk lauded, at great length, the nineteen-year tenure of Rasmussen with the LAPD, citing his academic credentials as a degreed professional with a "Bachelor of Law" from USC and his ongoing status as "instructor in criminal law." He also cited Tetrick's sixteen-year tenure with the LAPD, Howard's twelve-year record with the OSP, and Beeman's academic credentials as a licensed physician, surgeon, and pathologist and his standing on the faculty at the University of Oregon Medical School, where he taught, among other courses, medical jurisprudence. By contrast, Lusk denigrated the character and reliability of the two Black women, Jessie and Clara Folkes, whose testimony directly contradicted Rasmussen and Tetrick on certain key points, most notably on whether Folkes was intoxicated and whether he demonstrated murder strokes on his wife in her bed. He also attempted to explain and excuse why Defense Exhibit 2, the Bechtel statement Folkes gave in LA the day before his alleged confession, contained no reference to his supposedly repeated requests (according to Tetrick's testimony), during that interrogation, to be taken to his wife's house. In evaluating the testimony of the two LAPD officers, the justice dismissed any discrepancies in their accounts, while he questioned the believability of Black witnesses, suggesting they were tainted by race solidarity.[58]

In a shrill defense of White authority over Black suspects, Lusk's concurring opinion aggressively condemned any reasonable criticism of the obviously compromised testimony of the two LAPD officers, while he studiously ignored defense efforts to introduce the well-documented pattern of racist intimidation and LAPD brutality at Central Jail. Lusk, and other concurring justices in the majority, argued (falsely) that the defense made no effort to impugn the testimony of Tetrick and Rasmussen, and these justices also refused to acknowledge the numerous times Lomax attempted to raise in Lewelling's court the issue of ongoing grand jury investigations into the LAPD homicide division's abusive and murderous interrogation tactics. Lewelling warned Lomax, under penalty of contempt of court, not to veer into that territory, and he ruled out of bounds any questions regarding interrogation tactics of LAPD officers under investigation for torturing and murdering prisoners whom they incarcerated at Central Jail.

Lusk applied an obvious double standard in his assessment of the LAPD officers that went further down that road than the majority opinion. Unlike Brand, whose opinion simply ignored discrepancies between what Rasmussen and Tetrick testified and what Lyman detailed in Exhibit K, Lusk argued for two mutually contradictory interpretations regarding the testimony of these two officers. First, he argued, any discrepancies in their testimony actually exonerated them of any suspicion that they may have colluded to fabricate a story: "The officers are not in exact agreement as to everything the defendant told them. Had they been, it might have afforded reason for suspecting that they had gotten together and agreed on a story, in which case their credibility would have been affected."[59] In other words, the very fact the officers' stories contradicted each other "with respect to incidental and unimportant details," Lusk argued, was proof they were telling the truth. Second, however, Lusk cited as proof of the veracity of their testimony their "substantial agreement" with regard to "the defendant's unforgettable account of the murder itself, and his preparation for it."[60] In other words, in this second portion of his argument, Lusk argued that the fact their stories were the same proved, not collusion, but the veracity of their narrative.

ROSSMAN AND THE RECONSTRUCTION OF RESISTANCE IN POSTWAR OREGON

Faced with the arguments of five colleagues who concurred in the majority opinion, including the pointed and personal criticisms Justice Lusk lobbed directly at him, Rossman constructed a thirty-two-page argument more comprehensive and exhaustive than the ones either Brand or Lusk authored. Justice Kelly concurred in that dissent in the five-to-two decision. Rossman's summary paragraph argued that Folkes "ought not to have been handicapped through placing in the scales of justice prejudicial matter which weighed heavily against him and which consisted of (1) several accusations of crime (rape, assault, threat to kill, etc.) of which he was not guilty; and (2) stenographers' memoranda which the defendant never saw, signed or approved, but which were submitted to the jury as his written confessions." Rossman also argued that the court "should have directly instructed [the jury] to view his oral admissions with caution. A judgment of death which is infirm through grave error," he concluded, "ought not to be affirmed."[61]

Rossman's dissent, although ineffectual in shifting the court's ruling in favor of Folkes, was the keystone of a last-gasp effort to secure a governor's pardon for the second cook, and the pamphlet version of his opinion elevated the case into a symbol of determined resistance in the civil rights struggles in the latter stages of the war and into the postwar era. The struggle to save Folkes from the state's gas chamber played out against the backdrop of a "Negro rights" theme that framed the election campaign season during summer and fall of 1944. Amid expectations that Franklin Delano Roosevelt would select the incumbent vice president, Henry A. Wallace, as his running mate in the 1944 elections, the local Albany newspaper, which typically favored Democratic Party candidates, reported "serious rifts within the democratic party" that included demands from "Negro Spokesmen" that the national convention should "promise equal economic and political rights to Negroes," including specific concerns about poll taxes, lynching, "Jim Crowism" in the armed forces, and demands for a "permanent fair employment practices committee" to carry on the work of the wartime FEPC. Noting that the Republican Party's national convention had made "specific pledges on those issues" (but without detailing what, exactly, that convention pledged), an article in the Albany newspaper around the time the court published its ruling on the Folkes case lamented the racialization of the upcoming election: "The racial issue in the democratic south has loaded such demands with political dynamite for the democratic platform committee."[62]

State residents learned of the OSSC decision in the Folkes case in the racialized context of the fall 1944 elections and in the lethal climate of renewed interest in enforcing the state's death penalty. Oregon voters, who had elected Republican governor Earl Snell just two years earlier, had voted into office a man whose most important campaign themes sounded a tough-on-crime agenda that all but disavowed the governor's authority to issue pardons. Although Oregon's overwhelmingly White demographics enabled Snell and his opponent to avoid even talking about race during the 1942 gubernatorial campaign, the Folkes case forced Snell's hand and revealed the prevalence of race in Oregon's political culture.

Beyond Oregon, the OSSC ruling prompted calls for taking the campaign to free Folkes to the next level. News of the state supreme court's five-to-two finding against Folkes made a big splash in the *Eagle* and other news outlets oriented toward African American readers, who learned from that coverage that even the five justices who supported Brand's majority opinion agreed the "purported confession . . . should not have been submitted to the jury as if it were a signed confession."[63] The *Eagle* relied largely on communications from Dining Car Workers Union representatives, who referred to the case as "a second Scottsboro" and appealed for donations to the RFDC. Amid promises from Lomax to appeal the case immediately to the US Supreme Court, Pollard and the defense committee redoubled their efforts to mobilize community support for the next phase of the appeals process.

In the aftermath of the OSSC ruling, the political climate shifted in ways that favored the RFDC's agenda to save Folkes. Not only did Rossman's dissent attract the support of one concurring justice, his principled argument forced Brand's majority to admit that the written transcripts should not have been introduced as exhibits for the jury to consider. In that sense, Rossman's voice officially validated the narrative the editors of the *Eagle* and the *Observer* had constructed as a way to lend meaning and positive significance to the otherwise discouraging trial verdict, and it emboldened those working on the appeal to put a more public face on that effort. Clara Folkes, in the immediate aftermath of the OSSC ruling, asked the question mainstream newspapers simply ignored: "There was no evidence given by the 42 witnesses of the State that implicated my boy. His body and clothing were free of blood stains, yet one of the State's witnesses had blood stains on him in several places and human skin under his fingernails. I wonder why the Supreme Court overlooked that?"[64]

The Folkes case was just one of several civil rights cases that emerged, or reemerged, into the public sphere during the summer of 1944. Later that year, the California State Supreme Court ruled that Preston S. Jones, "a 17-year-old Negro Youth," was "beaten unmercifully by L.A. Police," who arrested him just a few months before they arrested Folkes. The California court's ruling, coming in the wake of a year-long grand jury investigation, affirmed the LAPD homicide squad routinely administered "daily beatings" in Central Jail during the period Folkes was interrogated there, and in the case of Jones, the court noted, LAPD officers beat the defendant at least twice a day for four days "to compel him to confess to murder." In a scathing critique of standard intimidation tactics that police officers in Los Angeles and San Diego commonly deployed in obtaining confessions, the California court asserted law enforcement officers must understand that the rights of persons suspected of a crime must be respected.[65]

News of the favorable ruling in the Jones case, together with widespread publicity touting the Rossman dissent in the Folkes case and successful efforts to convince the Republican Party to insert racial justice planks in its national platform, all seemed to suggest a direct appeal for clemency from Republican governor Snell might succeed. NAACP activists across the West Coast subsequently appealed for national support in the cause of the second cook unjustly convicted of murder. They emphasized the significance of standing up for principle in a case where no evidence linked the defendant to the crime, apart from unsigned transcripts of supposed "confessions" that Los Angeles police reportedly extracted in between brutal "interrogation" sessions at Central Jail.

Racialized labor strife in Portland shipyards that August, however, prompted a racist White backlash in Oregon at a critical point in the appeals process. In a wildcat strike at Swan Island, 80 percent of White electricians walked off the job after shipbuilders hired Black electricians in order to comply with an FEPC order. During the strike, which the *People's Observer* reported was in violation of the Smith-Connally antistrike law, the *Observer* documented a proliferation of "insulting signs" White electricians at Swan Island had "scrawled upon walls of restrooms" and reported that White girls were "advising each other not to converse with Negro Americans." During the FEPC hearing preceding the ruling, a White supervisor of the company argued that "no negro should be upgraded higher than a journeyman."[66]

Even with the racialized labor unrest in Portland that summer, the public campaign to secure justice for Folkes gained traction until late September, when the tragic death of Martha's husband, Richard James, on 29 September recaptured the mantle of victimhood for his dead wife. James, a navy ensign at the time of the murder, was a navy lieutenant by the time his training plane caught fire at fifteen thousand feet and crashed with no survivors about twenty miles northwest of Pasco, Washington. Most news reports framed the narrative of his fiery death against the backstory of his young bride's murder eighteen months earlier, and they noted the man convicted of Martha's slaying outlived them both, due to his pending appeal.[67] Just one month before the November elections, news that James' plane had crashed and burned indelibly linked the Folkes appeal with the deaths of two attractive, young, and pristinely White symbols of wartime sacrifice: the beautiful young "war bride," murdered in her sleep, and the handsome, bereaved naval officer, tragically killed while serving in defense of his country. The campaign to secure justice for Robert E. Lee Folkes played out against that symbolic backdrop and amid the racialized concerns of late 1944.

Symbolism weighed heavily against Folkes in the 1944 election cycle. Early in the investigation, local newspapers conflated his case with the racially motivated removal policies targeting Japanese Americans in Oregon. Just a week after Weinrick extradited Folkes from California to Linn County, former Oregon governor Walter Pierce came to Albany to speak on the issue of "removal," linking that issue with his own racialized notions of labor control. Pierce was first elected governor with an endorsement from the Ku Klux Klan in the 1922 campaign, when Klan-backed legislators gained a working majority in Oregon's lower house. He attracted large crowds on his return to the mid-Valley lecture circuit early in the war, just in time for the murder investigation. As OSP detectives interrogated Folkes without legal representation on the third floor of Linn County's courthouse, Pierce came to town to give a speech in which he reportedly compared the racial character and habits of Japanese Americans and African Americans, suggesting both races posed a threat to public safety: "Statisticians figure that, at their normal rate of rabbit-like breeding, they might have Japanese senators from California in fifty years. We cannot jeopardize our national life by introducing another race problem. The Negro is docile under normal control and when not given liquor. The Japanese is always aggressive and plotting for racial supremacy. They have a nation and a country and now they have added possessions rich in raw materials. . . . We cannot appease, but we must conquer and then we must rid our country of all the Japanese." The next day, headlines in the Albany paper announced the end of the battle for Guadalcanal, with "50,000 Japs Killed" in the "First Big All-American Victory in Pacific War."[68]

Many White Oregonians in the mid-Valley, like many in Portland, shared a generalized sentiment supporting racial exclusion. Just two months after Albany audiences applauded Pierce's racist remarks, and at about the same time Folkes stood trial there, Morton Tompkins, master of the Oregon State Grange, reconfirmed the racialized sentiments of mid-Valley residents. He claimed farmers of the region were adamantly opposed to the return of "so-called 'loyal' Japanese to the Western Defense Zone for the purpose of alleviating critical farm labor shortages of the area." In a virulent diatribe in the midst of a widely reported scarcity of qualified farmworkers, Tompkins opined, "I don't know who is behind this movement to permit Japanese farm workers to return to this area, but I can assure you that the farmers are not asking to have them back." Tompkins added, "The farmers don't want them, and what little they might be able to increase food production here will be far outweighted [sic] by the menace to our security which their presence would occasion.... When and if those enemy planes come [to bomb the Northwest], we want to be sure that we don't have any of Hirohito's friends in our midst."[69]

More than eighteen months after Tompkins' statement, the battleground for racial exclusion shifted, and the focus was less on the war and more on local divides and tensions. As defense lawyers scrambled to push back the date scheduled for Folkes' execution, Oregonians again confronted the aftermath of wartime "removal policies," and mid-Valley newspapers reported a racialized mood among farmers no less virulent than the reported musings of Pierce or Tompkins the previous year. The lead story on 18 December 1944 in the *Democrat-Herald* focused on two federal Supreme Court rulings that (a) removal of Japanese Americans was constitutional "at the time it was carried out," but that (b) "citizens must be permitted to return to their homes when their loyalty to this country is established." A companion article focused on reactions of Oregon officials in Portland and Hood River to the prospect of returning Japanese Americans—mostly expressing alarm and opposition—and a follow-up article, a week later, argued Japanese Americans should relocate to the Midwest.[70] Clearly, rural residents of the mid-Valley were not alone in supporting White racial privilege and repressing people of color in postwar Oregon.

In this climate of racialized labor unrest and overtly exclusionist, racist sentiments, Clara Folkes travelled to Portland in November 1944 to meet with welfare organizations and other groups mobilizing "to bring pressure upon Governor Earl Snell to show clemency in the case." Obviously no longer "stunned into silence," and no longer willing to leave her son's life in the hands of lawyers and judges, Clara travelled extensively and spoke frequently and with passion before public audiences of church and community organizations, seeking broad-based popular support for a clemency campaign petitioning Oregon governor Snell. Contrary to Brand's majority opinion, Clara Folkes and Pollard pressed the argument that, substantively and procedurally,

Lewelling's court had violated her son's civil rights. NAACP activist and legal consultant Julia Richardson travelled with Clara Folkes from Los Angeles. While in Portland, Richardson conferenced via telephone with NAACP representatives Walter White and Judge William Hastie, both of whom urged her to proceed with plans for the clemency campaign. White, representing the NAACP's national office, assured Richardson the organization would take full responsibility for funding and pressing appeals on Folkes' behalf, noting that it had already distributed in Portland reprints of the Rossman opinion in booklet form under the imprint "Facts of the Folkes Case."[71] Over the next month, the NAACP led a public and private campaign encouraging concerned citizens all around the country to send letters and telegrams to Snell urging clemency for Folkes. Rossman's dissenting opinion, widely circulated in pamphlet form as *The FACTS in the Robert Folkes Case,* provided the intellectual foundation for that effort and for last-ditch appeals to the US Supreme Court.

Nearly two full years after the murder of Martha James, the RFDC successfully repositioned Folkes, the card-carrying member of a radical labor union, as a regional symbol of civil rights activism, and in doing so, they linked local activists with broader national movements. Their efforts promoted a new counter-narrative: the story of the Folkes appeal was no longer about his guilt or innocence but rather the reliability and integrity of the criminal justice system in Oregon. This argument previewed the stance of others who attempted to thwart the dream for more substantial civil rights in the postwar era. Those who criticized the campaign to free Folkes asked rhetorical questions that appealed to Oregonians and their belief in their own unique virtues. Their version of an "Oregon difference" promoted a racially cleansed vision of the state's past and a curious paranoia about its standing and respect around the country: What right did people outside the state have to push their "race agenda" on Oregonians? Who was behind the "well-funded" campaign to "overthrow" the system the people of Oregon had established?

Chapter Seven
Executing Judgment Oregon Style

The notion of an "Oregon difference" gained credence during and after the Folkes trial, as mainstream news writers in Portland, Albany, and Klamath Falls praised the actions of the Oregon State Police, court officials in Linn County, and the Oregon State Supreme Court. The system, they argued, had worked. In the six months following the OSSC ruling upholding the Folkes conviction, they continued that positive spin. News writers praised the professionalism, commitment to process, and absence of "mob spirit" in Oregon's system of law enforcement. Over the same period, however, critics crafted a counter-narrative that also embraced the notion of an "Oregon difference." Their version emphasized the need to overturn the Folkes death sentence, which they argued was out of step with what they considered the shared values of most Oregonians. They argued Lewelling's court had failed Oregon, and they asked the governor to extend clemency to Folkes not merely to save the life of one man but for the good of the state. By setting aside the verdict, they argued, Snell would open the way for a new trial more in keeping with Oregon's true character. This argument included an important critique of the death penalty itself: critics of the verdict argued that executing Folkes would be an irreversible step that would tarnish the reputation of all Oregonians, and they argued for commutation to a life sentence, often adding the qualification "until the real killer can be identified." Clearly, they were concerned the state might execute an innocent man. Supporters of the original verdict, as well as critics of that result, both began with the rhetorical position that there was something special about Oregon setting it apart from other, presumably more racist, parts of the country, but they called for two radically different outcomes. In the first case, supporters argued it was necessary to execute Folkes to preserve the unique virtues of Oregon's system. In the second case, critics argued it was necessary to save Folkes to allow that system the chance to demonstrate its unique virtues.

Neither of these two arguments was grounded in reality: Oregon's history of White privilege was well established before the war, and the treatment of Japanese Americans and Hispanic farmworkers in Bracero camps during the war, along with racialized labor conflict in Portland-area shipyards, demonstrated deep and continuing problems with race and class in the state, despite public voices that proudly proclaimed Oregon somehow different, more virtuous than other states and regions of the country.[1] In this sense, the debate over whether Snell should extend clemency to Folkes was trapped within the rhetorical boundaries of the melodrama that Weinrick presented at trial.

Those who argued a state-sanctioned execution would violate their faith in Oregon's unique commitment to fair and equitable legal processes gained a powerful ally in the arguments of OSSC justice George Rossman, whose careful deconstruction of the case against Folkes reframed the meaning of the state court's majority opinion. Whereas other OSSC jurists mostly retold the same story LAPD officers introduced with the Lyman statement (even though the majority agreed it should not have been allowed), Rossman questioned the integrity and reliability of those investigators and their stories. Whereas other jurists hid their racial prejudice behind an exaggerated pretense of respect for the jury's verdict and the integrity of officers of the trial court, Rossman questioned the integrity and reliability of evidence Lewelling allowed prosecutors to place before that jury. Rossman, in short, asked his colleagues on the court to substantively honor the rights of the accused and to reject the Jim Crow style of pretended equality papering over racist inequality before the law. Oregon, he argued, expected more of its public officials than a legal lynching of a convenient suspect. Rossman's articulation of an "Oregon difference" resonated with civil rights activists who challenged the verdict late in the war, and it set the stage for broadening the fight for civil rights after the war. Local activists, beginning in the fall and winter of 1944 and 1945, used Rossman's dissent to broaden the discussion of "civil rights" from a racial context to include a challenge to the death penalty and other related issues of class and difference.

Written arguments from McClendon and Pollard, in addition to Rossman, reconstructed the moral framework for understanding the Folkes case as a challenge to civil rights in Oregon. Widespread circulation of those arguments on the West Coast energized public debate on how matters of race and class fit into postwar planning in the Pacific Northwest. Although lawyers for Folkes appealed the case to the Supreme Court of the United States, RFDC leaders and supporters recognized a gubernatorial reprieve was their best chance for overturning the verdict. They also understood that securing a pardon from Snell required both public pressure and private appeals. McClendon broadened the base for potential public support when he linked the case with broader issues of economic and social justice in the Portland area. As editor of the *Observer*, he framed the Folkes case within a broader campaign for extending wartime opportunities into more permanent gains advancing civil rights and economic access in the postwar era. He warned, however, of a coming storm: war production needs had prompted economic and demographic transformations that caused "prejudiced and provincial" leaders in the state great "mental anguish" in their efforts to ensure "the influx of Negroes" and also "migrant whites" who moved to Portland during the war "would find only a temporary economic existence."[2]

Pollard helped McClendon reframe the Folkes case as an opportunity for progressives to present a united front in the struggle to advance civil rights. Early in the petitioning drive and shortly after learning of the OSSC decision, Pollard drafted a twelve-page brief that questioned the moral framework prosecutors crafted during the investigation and trial phase. Moving beyond simply legalistic arguments, Pollard's letter challenged their implicit assumption that military voices were more virtuous, arguing the investigation was tainted with "war hysteria." That mind-set, he argued, "upset many fair-minded Americans." As an alternative, Pollard offered a more nuanced reading of militarized virtue that emphasized actual wartime service over merely uniformed authority. Wilson, he argued, was far from a military hero. Instead, the marine was actually a questionable figure who somehow avoided transport to the South Pacific when many trainmen were leaving draft-exempt positions and volunteering for overseas service. Generous contributors to the RFDC, he noted, included many "members of our armed forces" already stationed in the South Pacific. Wilson, in Pollard's formulation, was a poser who falsely claimed the mantle of militarized virtue that more properly belonged to those actually fighting against injustice and inequality at home and overseas. Pollard's letter, which circulated widely via the RFDC, informed the arguments of many public and private petitioners.

ACTIVISM AND REGION: AN ORGANIZATIONAL RESPONSE TO THE FOLKES CASE

By the time national officers of the NAACP finally offered to help the RFDC publish and distribute reprints of Rossman's opinion, the case had already grown well beyond rural Linn County to symbolize resistance to social and economic injustices throughout Oregon and the West Coast. In the person of OSSC justice Rossman, civil rights advocates—including the Civil Rights Committee of the Oregon Bar Association—found a hometown symbol of regional difference who was already well known and widely respected for previously standing up to the state's legacy of Klan-tainted influence. The RFDC successfully linked the case with an emerging self-consciousness about race prejudice and social injustice in the Pacific Northwest by war's end. They mobilized a progressive core of people who found common cause protesting Folkes' sentence. Petitions from fourteen Oregon-based clergymen plus additional group petitions from labor unions and benevolent organizations in Oregon and other states flooded Snell's mailbox before and after Christmas 1944. Other petitioners found each other independently, without any organizational framework, forming groups of people motivated by the case to act in concert with each other.[3] People of like minds found others like themselves and formed new groups for action.

Rossman's opinion mattered at several levels—his dissenting argument circulated widely within the state in reprint form at a critical point in the transition from wartime to postwar planning, and it enunciated fundamental principles of fairness and due process in language that captured the attention of civil rights activists. Equally important, Rossman's voice carried weight in the state's legal community, and it connected that community with regional and national networks of legal professionals. He was one of the most distinguished and respected legal scholars in the history of the Oregon State Supreme Court. He served as an OSSC justice for over thirty-eight years, from 1927 through 1965 (longer than any other justice) and as chief justice in the vital postwar period from 1947 to 1949. Rossman was a Pacific Northwesterner who earned national distinction and professional accolades. He grew up in Seattle and Tacoma from the age of two, attended local schools, and then, in 1907, graduated from Whitworth College. Three years later, in 1910, he graduated from the University of Chicago's School of Law and moved to Portland, where he passed the Oregon bar exam and set up a successful practice.

Long before the Folkes case made national headlines, Rossman earned a reputation for challenging the long tradition and legal underpinnings of racist exclusion in Oregon. He was already a seasoned lawyer and municipal judge in Portland by the time Republican governor Ben W. Olcott appointed him to a vacant position as circuit judge for Multnomah County in the 1922 election year—the same year Olcott's principled stand against the Ku Klux Klan nearly cost the incumbent governor his own party's nomination and ultimately cost him the election against the Klan-endorsed Democratic Party nominee, Walter Pierce. In that sense, Rossman's appointment to the circuit court was Olcott's parting shot at the KKK before he left office. Five years later, Republican governor I. L. Patterson appointed Rossman to fill an open position as justice of the OSSC, and he was reelected to that position every six years, beginning in 1928. He retired from the court in 1965, having also served as chief justice during the administrations of Republican governors Earl Snell and John H. Hall.[4]

Rossman's position and reputation reinforced the legal foundations for an emerging nonpartisan coalition of progressive voices who advocated for and defended civil rights in Oregon before and after the war. He earned the confidence of Republican, Democratic, and Independent governors alike. As an appointee of an anti-Klan Republican, Rossman was nonetheless an independent voice widely respected across party lines and at the national level. He was an established authority on evidence, administrative law, and judicial procedure. He served on the Board of Editors of the American Bar Association Journal and chaired the judicial administration section and the administrative law section of the American Bar Association. During the mid-1930s, Oregon's Independent governor, Julius L. Meier, appointed Rossman to chair committees charged with drafting proposed legislation to improve the administration of justice in Oregon courts. Democratic governor Charles H. Martin later reappointed him to those assignments. Beyond his official duties on the OSSC, Rossman was an active volunteer public servant and academic professional. He chaired the Marion County chapter of the American Red Cross for nineteen years; directed the Freedoms Foundation of Valley Forge, Pennsylvania; and served as a long-standing member of the Congregational Church and the Masonic and Elks Lodges. Prior to his service on the OSSC, he taught courses on evidence, corporate law, and pleadings at Northwestern Law School in Portland, and he later presided over the Board of Directors of Pacific University.[5]

THE FACTS IN THE ROBERT FOLKES CASE: FROM LEGAL ARGUMENT TO PAMPHLET

Given Rossman's credentials as, arguably, the most distinguished and nationally prominent justice on the OSSC during the 1940s, it is not surprising that civil rights advocates enthusiastically distributed his dissenting opinion. The pamphlet called *The FACTS in the Robert Folkes Case*, published by the NAACP, was circulated widely throughout Portland and the Willamette Valley by Oregon progressives in late November and early December 1944.[6] It was also widely referenced in Black newspapers beyond the state. In this format, Rossman's otherwise obscure legal opinion directly inspired many who petitioned Snell seeking clemency for Folkes. His published dissent pointedly and systematically dismantled the credibility of Brand's majority opinion, and Folkes' lawyers relied heavily on Rossman's opinion in formulating their appeal to the Supreme Court of the United States. RFDC leaders understood, however, that their best chance was to directly petition the governor for clemency.

In the mid-twentieth century, Oregon was one of only fourteen states that granted its governor sole power to commute, reprieve, or pardon convicted criminals. Other states placed that decision in the hands of a state parole board (in some cases including the governor), or they required the governor consult with a state parole board. In Oregon, however, the Deady Code of 1864, revised by century's end as ORS 144.640.670, placed this power solely in the hands of the governor. Through the 1940s, fewer than 3 percent of death penalty defendants from Oregon pursued a habeas corpus remedy in federal courts. In virtually all death penalty cases during the 1940s and 1950s, judicial appeals beyond the OSSC were futile: "If one was sentenced to death," a leading authority on the state's death penalty observes, "one's most promising remedy would be commutation of the death sentence by the governor."[7]

Prominent efforts to link the Folkes case with broader civil rights issues and labor struggles in the Portland area apparently biased the governor against petitioners for clemency. Portland's NAACP leadership, in the wake of the gubernatorial election of 1942, publicly and vocally denounced its previous president for cozying up to Snell during that campaign, and the *People's Observer* published a harsh critique of the new governor in its recapitulation of that controversy in summer 1943, shortly after the Folkes verdict was announced. The *Observer* account (as detailed in previous chapters) linked differences between the local chapter of the NAACP and Snell to the previous summer's dispute involving Lee Anderson's racial discrimination complaint against the Oregon Shipbuilding Corporation in Portland shipyards. If members of the RFDC hoped to sway Snell's opinion regarding Folkes, the *Observer* made their task more difficult by linking the case to a broader campaign for extending wartime opportunities into more permanent gains for civil rights and economic access in the postwar era. Moreover, McClendon's paper positioned Snell as an opponent of that campaign, arraying White privilege against Black workers in the shipyards case.

The NAACP national office also complicated matters for the RFDC in Oregon by introducing the pamphlet with an essay that framed the case as a simplistic, moralizing melodrama. Written in the style of advocacy journalism, that introductory essay distracted readers from Rossman's more scholarly and judicious arguments. It presented a luridly speculative version of the case that veered away from evidence presented at court with little regard for the distinction between rumor and evidence. The essay introducing the NAACP pamphlet was a transparent effort to recast the heroes and villains in the melodramatic case. Rossman's legal opinion narrowly considered only the actual evidence and testimony included in the trial transcript, but the NAACP introduction focused on the drama surrounding the investigation, interrogations, and pretrial publicity involving Folkes. Beginning with his arrest, the essay argued, "newspapers in Oregon and all over the country began a campaign of agitation and appeals to latent race prejudices." Due to all the publicity, the pamphlet concluded, "it was impossible to get an unprejudiced jury" in Albany.[8] This argument implicated jurors in the prejudicial decision. The eight women and four men on the jury, by this account, should have known better. Emphasizing the complete lack of evidence against Folkes, the preface concluded, "Unfortunately, however, Folkes is a Negro. The victim was a young white woman. . . . This is the equivalent of a legal lynching." As a remedy, the introduction urged "every fair minded man and woman to write or wire Gov. Snell, Salem, Ore., and request the commutation of Folkes' sentence from death to life imprisonment!"[9]

Rather than embracing NAACP rhetoric that asserted Oregon courts and citizens were fundamentally tainted by racist motivations, most Oregonians who petitioned the governor took the more measured approach that the verdict was an error and not a fundamental flaw in the system or an indictment of their fellow citizens. They deluged Snell with cards, letters, telegrams, and petitions from late fall 1944 through early January 1945, sometimes alleging race prejudice and demanding justice, but more often urging the governor to proceed cautiously and fairly where Lewelling's court and the jury had acted rashly and unwisely. Despite NAACP assertions the Folkes conviction was simply a "legal lynching," most petitioners avoided allegations of race prejudice, demonstrating judicious restraint in respectfully addressing a White governor in a mostly White state. They were obviously motivated, however, by one of the most overtly racialized appeals that had thus far appeared in print favoring acquittal of Folkes. The first four pages of the pamphlet, which outlined the NAACP narrative of the case, introduced twenty-five densely packed pages of Rossman's legalistic prose. Some readers may have examined the entire pamphlet, but most of the notes and letters that survive in Snell's correspondence file on this case reference details and examples borrowed from the NAACP preface, and not Rossman's more dispassionate, academic deconstruction of the case.

GOVERNOR SNELL AND THE PUBLIC RELATIONS CONTEXT OF THE FOLKES CASE

National events disrupted regional and local efforts to transform the Folkes appeal into a general campaign that would refocus public attention on civil rights abuses in Oregon and prepare the way for more equitable postwar race relations in the Pacific Northwest. Federal agents, in November 1944, closed the net on a multiyear sting operation that targeted Union Pacific dining car workers implicated in a "conspiracy to steal from dining cars moving in interstate commerce." Their efforts, begun about the time of the Lower 13 murder, essentially reversed the multiyear corporate campaign to rehabilitate Black trainmen in the perceptions of White passengers during the latter stages of the war. The timing of the FBI sting operation, together with a second high-profile murder case in the mid-Valley, mobilized reactionary advocates for continuing White privilege in postwar Oregon and opened a path of retreat for Governor Snell from the growing flurry of demands for executive clemency. Folkes, the Black trainman and the specter of Black labor radicalism, resumed center stage in the state's racial melodrama, distracting from the NAACP effort to recast him in the role of Folkes, the victim of racist prejudice and legal lynching.

In a seemingly unlikely convergence of events, the FBI sting operation broke into the open just as the petition campaign to save Folkes got under way. Although none of the trainmen in the Folkes case were involved (because they were employees either of the rival SPRR or of the PPC), the mass arrests, mostly of Black trainmen on the Union Pacific Railroad (which also connected through Portland's Union Station), made headlines that undercut the public image of other dining car workers around the country. The *Eagle* reported, shortly after Thanksgiving 1944, that a federal grand jury had indicted 136 dining car employees (including seventeen chefs) as "co-conspirators."[10] As the most prominent criminal case involving a dining car worker convicted of a violent crime wound its way toward execution in Oregon, the FBI sting operation recast the (mostly Black) dining car workforce as not only shirkers, but also corrupt wartime profiteers.

Even as the FBI sting challenged the standing of Black trainmen as virtuous defense workers, the execution of a White former police officer provided Snell with a powerful answer to those who alleged Oregon's criminal justice system was racially biased. Oregonians learned in early December that Lewelling had resentenced Robert Folkes to die in the state's gas chamber on 5 January 1945 and also that Snell had denied citizen petitions to commute the death sentence of Richard Layton, a former police officer from Monmouth, Oregon. Layton, whom most observers described as mentally slow, was a White man convicted of murdering Ruth Hildebrand, of Dallas, Oregon, by drowning her in the Willamette River at Wells Landing near Independence late one June evening in 1943. The two cases were similar, in that Layton protested his innocence, even though prosecutors introduced, and characterized as confessions, written statements he allegedly made to OSP pathologist Beeman and OSP lieutenant Howard (both of whom also led the interrogation producing the Albany statement they attributed to Folkes). As in the Folkes case, Layton's lawyers argued police extracted those statements from their client only after a prolonged and unsupervised interrogation that involved abusive treatment over an extended period of time. Like Folkes, Layton protested his innocence to the end, denying he made the statements police attributed to him in a typewritten, unsigned transcript that prosecutors in Polk County portrayed as his "confession." The widely publicized Layton trial took place in overwhelmingly rural Polk County, just north of Albany, two months after the Folkes trial, but the OSSC ruling in the Layton case, in April 1944, preceded their decision in the Folkes case by about two months.[11] After Layton's execution, Snell frequently referenced the case as evidence that justice in Oregon was race-blind: the two cases, he argued, were substantially the same, suggesting Folkes (who was Black) was treated no differently than Layton (who was White). Oregon, he implied, practiced even-handed (race-blind) justice.

Unlike the Folkes case, however, the majority opinion in Layton's case rested its findings on the testimony of the defendant, noting "the repulsive fact" that the thirty-six-year-old former police officer, who weighed 225 pounds, admitted before jurors he was "intensively amorous toward" the five-foot-four-inch, 125-pound, seventeen-year-old Ruth Hildebrand.[12] On another important point of difference, the transcript of Layton's trial, unlike the Folkes case, includes ten pages of direct testimony by the defendant himself, in which Richard Henry Layton describes his grueling experience through thirty-six hours of nonstop interrogation. Layton's defense, that the drowning was an accidental outcome in the playful aftermath of consensual sex, failed to sway jurors, who noted the former police officer was a married man who, nonetheless, "permitted his lechery to mark the course of his conduct" in seeking sex with a minor. In a unanimous seven-to-zero opinion they ruled that Hildebrand's death, accidental or not, was his responsibility.[13] In that case, allegations of immoral behavior clearly weighed against the defendant.

Layton's execution, on 8 December 1944, armed opponents of the Folkes clemency drive—and Governor Snell—with a formidable argument: the OSSC had denied Layton's appeal, even though his lawyers cited many of the same precedents and constitutional arguments Folkes' lawyers cited in his appeal. Despite a concerted campaign seeking gubernatorial clemency, the state followed the jury's recommendation, executing Layton, a White man, on 8 December 1944. Prosecutors in Layton's case, as in the Folkes case, built their arguments for the death penalty around a purported confession Beeman and Howard extracted using questionable methods. Housewives from Monmouth, Independence, and Dallas spearheaded an energetic petition drive on Layton's behalf that depicted the defendant as a feeble-minded simpleton. Psychiatrists testified Layton had the mental maturity of a nine-year-old,[14] and his lawyer provided the governor with a copy of Layton's statement at sentencing, pointing out how dramatically it differed, in its simplistic vocabulary, syntax, and pacing, from the more complex statements Beeman and Howard attributed to him but that Layton claimed he never made.[15]

None of these arguments convinced Snell to show clemency toward Layton, and many petitioners and the governor himself cited that decision as an argument for denying clemency for Folkes. Among all the petitions and letters that Snell fielded regarding Layton, one particular letter from the man's lawyer, in November 1944, indicated Layton's eagerness to submit to a lie-detector test and included his request that the interrogating OSP officers (Beeman and Howard) also be required to take a similar test. Layton clearly believed, despite his admittedly limited intelligence, that those officers lied when they claimed he confessed to the murder and also when they claimed a written, unsigned transcript actually reported his verbal statements. Layton attempted, in his last statement to the court during the sentencing hearing, to explain his suspicions. The judge informed Layton, however, that, even if his assertions were true, it was too late for him to make those claims, and the judge could not stay the execution.[16] Layton went to the gas chamber on 8 December 1944, just as the governor began answering clemency petitions for Folkes, whose case involved similar concerns about police perjury involving the same two OSP officials (Beeman and Howard), as well as the two LAPD detectives (Rasmussen and Tetrick).

ROSSMAN AND THE LEGAL CASE FOR CLEMENCY IN THE FOLKES CASE

Petitioners who disagreed with the governor's premise that consistency required the same decision in the Folkes appeal as the Layton appeal could point to Rossman's dissent. Rossman concurred in the OSSC's unanimous decision in the Layton case, but his vociferous dissent in the Folkes case clearly delineated how it differed. Unlike the somewhat melodramatic NAACP preface, Rossman's opinion directly addressed, in careful and precise legal terms, the illogic of "erroneous" court rulings, explaining how investigators first settled on Folkes and then set about convicting him. Unlike the Layton case, where the defendant admitted, in open court, that he was on the scene when Hildebrand drowned, no such admission emerged in the Folkes case, and prosecutors never placed the second cook at the scene of the murder. In the Layton case, jurors weighed the question of whether Hildebrand's death was in fact murder, whereas in the Folkes case, no one questioned whether James was murdered; rather, they considered the question of whether Folkes was the person who committed that murder.

Rossman's dissent dispensed with the majority's fixation on the youth, beauty, and innocent virtues of the victim, observing: "I deeply deplore the crime which took the life of Martha Virginia James. If it were possible to bring back to life that beautiful young woman . . . by disregarding the errors which were committed during the trial at the expense of this defendant, I would do so; but the restoration of her life is beyond our powers." Instead, Rossman argued, "We can do nothing but answer truthfully the question: Was the defendant found guilty and sentenced to the forfeiture of his life in a trial conducted free from prejudicial error?"[17]

In an argument that carefully avoided criticism of the Oregon system of justice or the assumed virtues of its citizen jurors, Rossman focused on the individual errors of the circuit court judge. Everyone on the OSSC bench, Rossman noted, agreed Lewelling committed errors, and the only remaining question dividing the majority from his dissent was "whether or not the defendant was prejudiced [harmed] by those errors." Rossman was not interested in second-guessing the jury on whether Folkes was guilty or innocent, or criticizing the ability of a jury comprising mostly women to rationally evaluate the evidence they were presented. He was only concerned with whether jurors were unduly influenced by court error in reaching the conclusion Folkes deserved the death penalty. He argued that Brand's majority opinion—that they were not influenced by court error—leaned heavily on Exhibits K and L, even though Brand and other concurring justices in the majority agreed those statements were, in fact, inadmissible.[18]

Rossman's argument sidestepped the melodramatic morality play prosecutors had staged and focused on the defendant's legal status of presumed innocence, rather than the assumed villainy Lomax burdened himself with disproving at the trial. Rossman observed there was no evidence in the trial record that Folkes ever previously committed a crime, and he stressed, moreover, the defendant was actually a minor. He noted prosecutors offered no motive or evidence for his involvement in the murder, and given these circumstances, Rossman concluded, the court's errors in admitting both Exhibits L and K actually introduced jurors to unauthenticated police claims that Folkes had had prior run-ins with the law, including allegations he raped, threatened to kill, and committed assault and battery, in addition to exhibiting public drunkenness. Weinrick's purpose in reading those statements to the jury, Rossman argued, was to incite an emotional response in order to secure (a) a conviction, and (b) the death penalty. The judge erred, first, in allowing those statements into the record and, then, in allowing the district attorney's office to physically alter the statements with tape and scissors in such a way as to literally bookmark for jurors a passage introducing even more egregious statements that Lewelling should have ruled inadmissible but did not.[19] The written record, in this way, was even more prejudicial than the oral representations of the statement. Rossman argued Lewelling's errors with both statements were sufficient to warrant a retrial.

The idea that different people might read the supposed "confessions" in different ways, depending on their educational level and attention span, also figured prominently in Rossman's deconstruction of the prosecution's case. Exhibit L, he thoughtfully observed, was effectively two narratives—at the level of first impressions, it seemed to show Folkes as a hardened killer with a bad criminal record, but with a closer reading, the document primarily consisted of accusatory questions that Folkes, according to the transcript, either denied or answered with non sequiturs. Even assuming the document was a fair "transcript" of the interrogation, as prosecutors claimed, Rossman established that if subjected to a critical reading, it might be seen as contradicting the claims Weinrick made against Folkes. By withholding that document from defense until late in the trial, however, prosecutors protected it from close scrutiny.

Beyond the written word, however, Rossman also stressed the third narrative resulting from "the effective use which the prosecutor's tongue made of these erroneously admitted pages." In that oral reading, Rossman observed, "the defendant was undoubtedly branded as a felon whose life was worthless."[20] With these observations, Rossman demonstrated how a single written document assumed different meanings depending on who read it, whether the reader considered it closely or only went through it quickly, and the context or assumptions or subtexts they applied to that reading. Each person who read these documents, in other words, might draw different meanings from the same written words. The defendant, moreover, not only neither reviewed nor otherwise indicated those words accurately reflected his spoken statement, but in fact Folkes strenuously denied, through his lawyers, that Exhibits K and L accurately represented what he told police. In the case of the jury, Rossman was particularly concerned their reading of that document during deliberations unfairly reinforced the prosecutor's oral rendition of those exhibits before the jury.

Most importantly for the direction of the civil rights movement in Oregon after 1945, Rossman's dissenting opinion focused especially on the morality of the death penalty itself. The errors of the trial judge, he argued, were particularly serious because the case involved the death penalty, and he rejected as irrelevant any precedents the prosecution offered that did not involve a defendant whose life hung in the balance. In all cases where the jury was responsible not only for determining guilt but also for recommending punishment, Rossman noted, the relevant precedents all called for reversing convictions and ordering a new trial where court errors influenced the finding of degree of guilt and turpitude of the crime. "No one," he argued, "can say that the jury would have imposed the death penalty if Exhibit L, with its accusations of extraneous crimes, had not been sent to the jury room."[21]

CIVIL RIGHTS, THE DEATH PENALTY, AND ROSSMAN'S DISSENT

Rossman's dissenting opinion spoke more eloquently to moral concerns about the death penalty in Oregon than to the question of whether the state applied the law without regard to race or creed. His argument, which stressed the moral gravity of applying the death penalty, established a precedent of legal reasoning that strengthened the position of those who opposed the death penalty, and it largely reinforced allegations of racialized bias that the NAACP stressed in its reprint of the Rossman dissent. The first half of Rossman's dissent focused almost exclusively on the jury's role in affixing the death penalty, and only after laying that foundation, which called into question the death sentence itself, did he address the issue of guilt or innocence. Rossman did not challenge the correctness or virtue of the jurors but stressed, instead, the errors Lewelling made in instructing jurors on their responsibilities under the law. The Oregon justice system, in Rossman's dissenting argument, was not fundamentally flawed, and Oregon's citizen jurors were not necessarily impaired by their own racial bias.

After framing the case before the OSSC as a precedent-setting one that dealt primarily with the problems of applying state law in death penalty cases, however, Rossman's opinion clearly and explicitly argued that the state utterly failed to prove its case against Folkes. According to his dissenting argument, the most compelling evidence the prosecution managed to muster boiled down to four facts: (1) Folkes was aware of Martha James' presence on the train, (2) he was in Car D shortly before the homicide, (3) the murderer fled in the direction of the diner, and (4) when seen working in the kitchen a few moments after the homicide, Folkes was perspiring. None of those facts, Rossman concluded, conflicted with the perfectly obvious normal duties for which Folkes was responsible: he was in Car D to use the lavatory, as all dining crew were instructed to do, and he was in the kitchen shortly after the murder because that's precisely where he was supposed to be at that time as second cook making watch. Given the state's lack of any facts or direct testimony linking Folkes to the murder, Weinrick's case wholly relied on the purported "confessions," which Rossman argued "were nothing but the memoranda of the two stenographers who wrote them." Those memoranda (Exhibits K and L), Rossman observed, each bore headings that "gave it a false official cast," and worse, "the headings were not removed when the papers were sent to the jury." Instead, the court erred in deeming Exhibits K and L the defendant's written confessions, and Lewelling's instructions "repeatedly referred to both documents as 'statements made by the defendant,'" thus reinforcing the "false official cast" that the headings conferred.[22]

On one of the most important aspects of the case relating to civil rights, Rossman challenged the apparent presumption, in Lewelling's court, that officers of the law and military personnel were more truthful than other witnesses. When interrogating officers differed in their testimony regarding what Folkes allegedly said in oral admissions, Rossman argued, those discrepancies demonstrated either that they failed to understand the defendant or they failed to repeat, correctly, what he said. He questioned Brand's willingness to rely on the written transcripts as if they were a more reliable, "verbatim report of questions and answers" than the contradictory testimony of the officers themselves, which, he argued, raised serious questions about their believability.[23] Referencing classical literature, Rossman quoted Puritan philosopher John Ray's aphorism "If it is in print it must be true,"[24] and then he questioned the judge's ruling that allowed jurors to take Exhibits K and L into the jury room, where they could read and reread them at their leisure, unlike other evidence. The majority's claim that they were no different than oral testimony was, in Rossman's view, simply untenable.

In affirming the admissibility of unsigned "confessions," the Brand majority, according to Rossman, had taken a dangerously flawed and activist stand that would undercut civil rights in Oregon for future generations, and he argued it raised serious concerns about the fairness of the death penalty. Rossman observed, with apparent alarm, that while Weinrick's written brief and oral arguments did not claim Lewelling's errors were harmless and non-prejudicial, Brand's majority opinion advanced that theory without reference to the state's arguments. Most remarkably, Rossman argued, Brand claimed that "where guilt is conclusively proved by competent evidence, and no other rational conclusion could be reached, conviction should not be set aside because of unsubstantial errors." In a scathing rebuttal, Rossman noted that none of the cases Brand cited as precedent for that proposition involved capital punishment. "Nothing is gained," Rossman admonished his colleagues, "by comparing the slip-ups in minor cases with the irregularities in a case where the life of a human being is at stake," and he reminded them it was equally as important to consider the precedent they were setting as to detail the precedents that they were following. He not only accused his colleagues of "not following the precedents," but he also warned, "I fear the effect of the one which they are creating."[25]

Most insidiously for future civil rights in the state, Brand's opinion asserted that the testimony of police officers should be considered incontrovertible in Oregon courts. Rossman saved his most scathing criticism for the majority's opinion that officers Tetrick, Rasmussen, Howard, and Beeman offered incontrovertible evidence independent of the exhibits that all of the justices agreed should not have been introduced at trial. The only evidence the state had presented that indicated Folkes committed the murder, Rossman argued, was the purported confession, as rendered in Exhibits K and L, neither of which were admissible. Aside from those four officers, the only other persons present during the making of the supposed statements were stenographers Lyman and Miller, and Weinrick. Rossman observed that Weinrick did not take the stand as a witness, neither Lyman nor Miller testified as to what Folkes said in their presence, and Beeman's testimony revealed virtually nothing of what he heard Folkes say. Of the remaining witnesses, Rossman noted, Rasmussen and Tetrick offered testimony that was directly contradicted by other witnesses. Quoting extensively from Clara Folkes' testimony, Rossman detailed the ways in which her sworn testimony directly contradicted the officers' claims that they had heard Folkes confess over the phone to her, and again in person after she arrived at Jessie Folkes' house.[26] He noted that Jessie Folkes directly contradicted Rasmussen and Tetrick on whether Folkes arrived at her house already drunk and carrying a whiskey bottle in the company of those officers. She also denied their claim that Folkes demonstrated on her body how he cut Martha James' throat.[27]

In a portion of the ruling with far-reaching implications for the authority of the state over its citizens, Rossman refused to accept the premise of Brand's opinion that the court could wink at inconsistencies in the testimony of public authorities while holding private citizens to a higher standard. His dissenting opinion explored this point by drawing on the document Lomax forced Weinrick to reveal in court: the Bechtel statement (Defense Exhibit

2). That nineteen-page defense exhibit, originally produced by an LAPD stenographer, supposedly recorded statements Folkes made from 5:15 p.m. Tuesday until at least seven o'clock the same evening. Rossman demonstrated how the Bechtel statement directly contradicted Tetrick's claim that Folkes "repeatedly" asked to be taken to see his wife. It made no mention at all of any such request, suggesting either Tetrick's testimony was false, or else the written statements were incomplete and inaccurate records of what Folkes said, contrary to police assertions.[28] Either way, Rossman concluded, police claims regarding what Folkes actually said during those interrogations were wholly unreliable, whether they appeared in writing or in oral testimony. Rossman declined to detail "other of the incidents which place in issue the credibility of the two officers," citing instead the standard instructions Oregon's code required judges issue to all jurors: "A witness false in one part of his testimony is to be distrusted in others."[29] Applying that standard, Rossman argued that neither the police-generated transcripts nor the police testimony itself could be trusted as incontrovertible.

PETITIONING FOR CIVIL RIGHTS: PUBLIC SPHERE AND PRIVATE INFLUENCE

The civil rights activists who coalesced around the RFDC in Oregon during 1944 could not directly influence the governor's decision and instead resorted to indirect action through the popular and advocacy press and, more privately, through direct petitions to the governor. In framing private petitions and public appeals, they relied mostly on the NAACP pamphlet and the arguments Pollard and McClendon disseminated through informal networks, including union locals and the readership and cooperating partners of the *Portland Observer*. Without those resources, those involved in the petitioning campaign otherwise would have learned of the OSSC ruling in the Folkes case only through regular news outlets. None of the newspaper accounts of the court's decision carried the full text of the decision, offering instead only a brief synopsis of the ruling in a narrative that privileged Brand's reasoning. Most news reports inaccurately claimed Rossman and one other justice had been motivated to dissent over the issue of whether the "confessions" should have been admitted to evidence. As a matter of fact, however, that was an issue on which the dissenting justices actually agreed with the majority opinion. They only differed on whether the error was so prejudicial that the lower court's ruling should be reversed. Of those who bothered to petition the governor, the overwhelming weight of argument was clearly opposed to the execution. In a state where many citizens claimed Oregon's criminal justice system was especially virtuous, of course, most Oregonians saw no need to intervene in a case they assumed was justly settled.

Oregonians were less motivated to write their governor on behalf of Folkes than people from outside the state, if the raw number of petitioners is any indication, but of those state residents who did so, the overwhelming majority were clearly concerned it was a miscarriage of justice. In doing so, petitioners demonstrated considerable engagement with the concerns about fairness and constitutional rights that Rossman raised in his dissenting opinion. The NAACP pamphlet and Pollard's firsthand account of the trial were the most common sources petitioners cited as the basis for their understanding of the case, except for those who asserted they personally attended the trial in Albany. Overwhelmingly, they were concerned the trial court unduly privileged the testimony of Wilson and the police, and in doing so, they argued, the court failed to protect the constitutional rights of the accused.

A significant contingent of Oregon's legal community joined the campaign seeking clemency for Folkes, and their arguments closely followed the legal framework of the Rossman opinion. At least nineteen lawyers and judges from Oregon responded to the NAACP pamphlet with carefully worded, neatly typed appeals on office letterhead that referenced legal cases and precedents while advising the governor for or against clemency. Of all petitioners who wrote or telegraphed the governor, those favoring clemency outnumbered those arguing for the death penalty by a margin of at least two to one regardless of whether the petitioner was a lawyer, judge, or layman. The legal community in Oregon, in particular, was strongly opposed to the execution and argued eloquently and with academic rigor for the governor to set aside the verdict. Clearly Oregon was not, as a state, committed to the discriminatory and prejudicial practices that critics described as a legal lynching of Robert Folkes.

Indirect approaches had little hope of success in a political climate where a governor who was elected on a platform of law and order was mostly concerned about seeming decisive and resolute during the transition to postwar authority. Rather than convincing Snell to change his mind, the deluge of petitions actually seemed to steel his resolve to follow through on his campaign pledge that he would not intervene in death penalty cases decided in the courts. As clemency petitions poured in, from mid-December through early January, the governor's response gelled into two distinct form letters, with only minor modifications for personalized comments. Those letters, which gradually hardened into perfunctory and unwavering responses, suggest the governor had made up his mind—long before the petitioning campaign began—not to intervene in the execution, even though he claimed in most letters that he had not. His rationale for that decision, however, did evolve over time, and those changes bear the imprint of reactionary letters from forces of White privilege who urged the governor to make an example of Folkes that would send a message to other Black trainmen and African American residents. The governor mailed each petitioner who favored clemency a brief three-line message advising the correspondent, "The matter to which you referred [insert date] has been and will continue to receive careful attention, study and consideration [insert salutation]."[30] He mailed a longer, three-paragraph letter to each petitioner who favored execution, beginning with the more gracious introductory sentiments, "I appreciate your kindness in writing to me concerning the Folkes case," then drawing parallels to the Layton case (in which he had refused to intervene) and observing that these sorts of decisions were very difficult, and finally ending with a brief closing paragraph offering "thanks for your thoughtful letter."[31]

The governor clearly tried to present himself to the African American community in Portland as a fair-minded man who might yet be swayed by a reasoned argument, despite clear evidence he was not, in fact, open to argument on this racialized issue. On the eve of the Layton execution, in his response to a petition from a Portland-based African American clergyman, Snell claimed he was struggling with the moral implications of his decision in that case. In answering Reverend Browning C. Allen of the Bethel African Methodist Episcopal Church, who authored one of the first petitions to the governor on Folkes' behalf, Snell drafted, on the third anniversary of the Pearl Harbor attack, a personalized letter to "Dear Dr. Allen" in which he compared his decision in the Layton case (Layton was scheduled for execution the next day) with his view of the Folkes case, arguing the two cases were essentially the same. At that early stage in the petition campaign, and in the immediate context of a voluminous petition campaign regarding the Layton case, Snell observed, "These are decisions that really tear at men's souls—decisions most difficult and weighty—decisions which sap the very life of any governor."[32] At the time he wrote, however, he had already decided not to intervene in Layton's execution, and less than twenty-four hours later, the state of Oregon killed Layton in the gas chamber at the state prison in Salem.

As word spread about the petitioning campaign for Folkes, forces of reaction organized a counter-petitioning campaign that operated mostly in the shadows using private and personalized appeals rather than appeals to a larger public. Between 7 December 1944 and 4 January 1945, the governor's tone obviously hardened during the holiday season in response to a deluge of petitions for and against clemency. The widely publicized petition drive, and the widespread distribution of the NAACP pamphlet to members of the Oregon Bar Association and through civil rights organizations in Oregon and California, prompted a backlash of petitions urging the governor to stand firm behind Lewelling's circuit court rulings and sentencing. This backlash notably included letters from seven Oregon attorneys, mostly drafted and mailed in the week between 14 December and 22 December 1944. During that same holiday season, Virginia governor Colgate V. Darden sent another personal appeal to Snell, noting he was writing on behalf of Wilbur Brinson's family and in response to news reports in Virginia of a petition campaign in Oregon seeking executive clemency for Folkes. Darden urged Snell not to give in to those demands.[33] Also, in a typewritten note detailing several conversations between an advisor to Snell and a number of socially prominent and wealthy White attendees at a "Sigma Chi banquet," the unsigned memo indicated that "Shipping Club President" Chuck Spear advised the governor, "Sentiment strong against commutation."[34] These private petitions indicate that certain interests among Oregon's economic elite pressured Governor Snell to shut down an increasingly popular challenge to the authority of White leadership. Executing Folkes had become an important symbol of political and class authority.

Snell responded to the urging of his reactionary constituents by hardening his line against petitioners for Folkes. Although the petitions from those who supported clemency included thirteen lawyers, a sitting judge, and several retired jurists, Snell's form-letter response to petitioners favoring clemency shrank during late December and early January into a terse, virtually immutable, three-line acknowledgment. Snell's unwavering line toward those pleading Folkes' case apparently built on arguments from racially charged letters that opponents of clemency mailed him earlier that month. Timber industrialist G. B. Nunn, of Wheeler County, Oregon, for example, wrote that "strong efforts" under way to induce Snell to commute the sentence were "well financed." Implying outside interests were pushing for clemency, he argued, "Financial gain . . . is more important than the object they seek." Nunn cited the military sacrifice of "American boys . . . in far places in the world." Clearly, he meant to suggest Snell should think about the sacrifices of White, not Black, servicemen in deciding whether to intervene in this case against a Black, not White, defendant, but he claimed, "The issue is not White vs. Black, but money and sob sisters against the dignity of our courts."[35] Attorney E. W. Sims, a few days later, also urged Snell not to interfere with a matter already decided in the court system, noting, "I have an abiding conviction in the ability of our courts," and arguing, with apparent sarcasm, "White men have been executed for similar crimes and if we are to have capital punishment, it certainly ought to apply to negro as well as white, even where the negro is convicted of assaulting and murdering a white woman."[36]

Snell retreated into a denial of racialized difference, invoking the example of Layton's execution to advance the argument that justice in Oregon was race-blind, even as he referenced Layton's racial identity to make that argument. Throughout December, the governor extended reassurances to those who opposed clemency in the Folkes case by comparing it with the 8 December execution of Layton, a White man. The governor argued the two cases were virtually identical, expressed his confidence in the courts, and confirmed his reluctance to interfere in a legal matter already settled in those courts. In some cases, he claimed to have additional information (never disclosed) convincing him of Folkes' guilt. Posturing as a governor who would never deny any citizen a hearing, Snell assumed a populist stance that echoed the themes Salem resident F. E. Swopes expressed in a handwritten five-page letter mailed on 21 December 1944. Swopes first questioned why there was no orchestrated lobby for "the common people" and then offered his own deconstruction of the Rossman dissent, presumably from the perspective of one of those common people.[37] Swopes expressed frustration with the publicity accorded the Folkes case, arguing it resembled the "Jordan case:—a negro now serving a commuted life sentence in the Oregon penitentiary" and claiming the supreme court, at the time of Jordan's case, "was closely packed by a band of 'communists' who journeyed there with the avowed purpose to intimidate the court." In this way, Swopes attempted to portray the case against Folkes, a member of a progressive union, as a test of the governor's resolve to stand up against a supposed communist conspiracy. Rather than looking backward at the situation in the war at the time of the murder, Swopes clearly was more concerned about the postwar period, which he envisioned as a confrontation between the United States and the forces of communism.

Many opponents of executive clemency, including Swopes, liberally laced their arguments with racist assumptions and diatribes that the governor's acknowledgment letters never renounced. Snell's response letters differed little, whether corresponding with those who casually referenced race or those who indulged in ranting diatribes. Mrs. Vera Jackson of Salem, for example, darkly warned: "Do you know that is what causes mob violence & lynchings in the South? When a Negro committs [sic] an unforgiveable murder, the people don't wait around for the courts to postpone & then give 'clemency' in the case any more." After claiming close parallels with the Layton case, Jackson asked, "Why should the Negro get more consideration that [sic] Layton?" At that point, she observed, "There are quite a number of Negros coming to this country and I think that Folks [sic] should be made an *example* [emphasis original] of what will happen to others who try to get away with murder." Jackson concluded with the appeal, "For the future's sake, and the sake of all decent citizens, and even the sake of the 'darkie' who might get such ideas, lets let the sentence go as the courts have ruled."[38]

Snell's response to Jackson showed he was not concerned about aligning himself with her vehemently racist sentiments. He simply responded with the same three-paragraph form letter with which he acknowledged most correspondents who petitioned against clemency. He thanked Jackson for her "kindness in writing to me," agreed the Folkes case was "quite parallel to the Layton case," and stressed prior actions of the circuit court, the state supreme court, and the Supreme Court of the United States, implying he was reluctant to interfere with those decisions. Finally, he closed with the salutation "thanks for your thoughtful letter."[39]

The governor's most thoughtful, personalized acknowledgments often went to correspondents who espoused the most aggressively racist and vindictive arguments in the governor's file. Harry O. Newton, secretary-treasurer of the Oregon and Washington division of the Travelers Protective Association of America, for example, asked, "Why should this negro be given any consideration other than the fair trial he had . . . and get by with it by merely be [sic] supported the rest of his life. Just consider your own daughter or mine. . . . Being a Native Texan and knowing the negro race probably better than any one else in Portland, I could not refrain from writing you this letter."[40] Harry Sturman of Portland opined, "Thanks to Mr. Kaiser, we are blessed with ten times too many of the black devils in Portland and between them and the Japs that will come back we are headed for a lot of trouble. . . .

If Folks [*sic*] gets away with it the niggars [*sic*] are going to be plenty cocky in Portland. . . . That is nigger style."[41] In response, Snell's acknowledgment letter began, "Friend Sturman: I appreciate your kindness in writing," and concluded, "Again, thanks for your thoughtful letter. Sincerely yours, [governor's signature]."[42]

Snell's private correspondents often combined racist arguments with antiunion or antiradical sentiments, suggesting they viewed the case as a test of the governor's resolve against worker radicalism and organized labor, as well as a test of his willingness to uphold a racialized standard of justice. Snell responded with friendly and supportive phrases in his response to a racist screed from Mr. L. H. O'Neal of Portland, who questioned how a "negro porter or cook" could afford to hire "[seven] Lawyers and have a bunch of ministers from the union to protect him from his guilt of one of our good United States Girls and a wife of one of good fighting men it is a Disgrace to the state of Oregon that we let a crime like this go with out just punishment."[43] Again, Snell thanked O'Neal for his "kindness in writing" and for his "thoughtful letter," restating his own conviction that the case was "quite parallel to the Layton case."[44] Likewise, in response to Portland resident Ormand Case, who argued, "too often, the guilty escape," and who offered the veiled threat that "in few states . . . would such an atrocious crime have caused less threats of mob violence," Snell signed a letter identical to the one he mailed O'Neal.[45] Case's letter, however, also suggested a public rationale Snell later worked into his own public statements and letters in which he bothered to explain his thinking: "You could so announce . . . that the governor's pardoning power is a grave public trust, to be used only when there is evidence of miscarriage of justice; that in this instance the proceedings have been reviewed and approved by both the state and the U.S. Supreme Courts; that you can find no evidence that justice has not been done and are therefore refusing to intervene in the orderly processes of law enforcement and justice."[46]

Case and others encouraged Snell to hide behind the pretense of raceless due process, while supporting an execution they themselves rationalized with expressions of vicious racism and veiled threats of lynch-mob "justice." On the same day he received the letter from Case, Snell also fielded a postcard from John W. Banholster of Coquille, representing the Elijah Association, to whom he responded with an acknowledgment letter identical to the one he mailed Case. Banholster's typewritten postcard, however, liberally deployed capital letters for emphasis and, instead of the diplomatic language with which Case framed his arguments, offered only a racist rant: "Regarding that BLACK OAF! That BLACK RASKEL [sic] of a KILLER: Robert Lee Folkes: ... This association dont [sic] want a grain of mercy shown this OAF."[47] Snell's response blandly thanked Banholster for his "kindness in writing," and for his "thoughtful letter."[48]

INVOKING AN OREGON DIFFERENCE: THE PRETENSE OF RACELESSNESS AND THE STRATEGY OF DEFERENCE

The myth of an "Oregon difference" and the pretense of racelessness permeated arguments from those who supported execution and from those who favored clemency. Critics of the execution were especially circumspect and deferential in their petitions to Snell, often assuring him they did not suspect racism motivated the sentence and emphasizing, instead, a raceless concern that the death penalty, once executed, was irreversible. They asked the governor to commute the sentence to life, not pardon the convicted man, and they noted the possibility that later evidence might emerge exonerating Folkes. Clergymen, as a group, composed one of the largest categories of petitioners, virtually all of them urging the governor to extend clemency, with the isolated exceptions of Reverend Theodore Smith of Calvary Baptist in Tigard and Reverend T. A. Edwards of St. Paul's Cathedral in Yakima. Smith and Edwards stand out as the only clergymen who wrote Snell before the scheduled execution to voice their opposition to clemency. Smith, writing on 22 December, accused Rossman of injecting "the racial issue" into the case with his argument that newspapers had prejudiced the jury pool with sensationalized coverage of the murder investigation. On the contrary, Smith argued, "I read, with great care, all details that were published in the daily newspapers and was gratified to find that *the racial issue was not raised whatsoever* [emphasis added]."[49] Snell replied with a form letter virtually identical to the one he mailed Banholster.[50]

Snell's bland acquiescence and expressions of sympathy and appreciation to those who petitioned him with overtly racist diatribes belie his repetitious assertion he had race-free reasons for avoiding involvement. Instead, he seemed to endorse a return to the reactionary racism and euphemistic language of "100-percent Americanism" that characterized his party's platform in the Klan-dominated elections of 1922, when the majority of representatives elected to the state legislature with Klan endorsements ran on the Republican Party ticket. Snell continued his practice of mailing friendly acknowledgments to people who sent him racist diatribes, such as Jno. R. Dix, who wrote the governor on the eve of the execution to ask, "How can you condescend to free the beast that murdered Mrs. Martha James in our state? The niggers in this state [California] are as brazen as a jackass in the act of cornering a mare. Damn 'em, I despise kinky headed, flat nosed, puffy liped [sic] niggers. Their sarcasm is beyond endurance. So! Governor, do your stuff and send this lone bred nigger to nigger Hell."[51] Snell delayed his response to Dix, a self-avowed "ex-Oregonian," until 9 January 1945, when his brief acknowledgment letter included a sentence blandly thanking "Dear Mr. Dixon" for his "letter regarding the Folkes case."[52]

Snell's approach apparently resonated with the only other clergyman who penned an argument opposing clemency, Reverend T. A. Edwards of Yakima, Washington, who emphasized family values, feminine virtue, and "sterling" Americanism as reasons for withholding clemency. In a statement laden with coded meanings at a time only fifteen years removed from the era of Klan dominance in Oregon politics and only eighteen years after Oregon deleted from its constitution the provision prohibiting African Americans from residing in the state, Edwards praised Martha James, "this fine married woman for her fidelity to chaste virtue . . . a good woman. She gave her life for her principles, and should this life have been in vain?" He also touted "our sterling American ancestry who were not found wanting in any part of the great United States . . . for controlling crime, as witness the code of the early pioneers even in Oregon." Edwards warned, however, that if Snell acted to extend clemency to Folkes, "the South will feel likewise that we in the North do not follow true American principles." He closed with assurances that "all men of fine American traditions will back you up in resisting any change in the judgment."[53]

Personal appeals and testimonials from a few close friends and Masonic associates clearly weighed more heavily in the balance for Snell than the sheer bulk of petitions asking him to extend clemency. Snell's exchange with Archie McMurdo of Heppner, three weeks after the execution, suggests the importance of lodge connections as factors more likely to influence the governor than reasoned argument. McMurdo, with offices in the Masonic Building in eastern Oregon (Heppner), addressed him as "Earl," cited their "many years of friendship," and praised Snell for his fortitude "in the face of such strong, organized pressure to try and keep a convicted criminal at large . . . when there appeared no other interest probably than financial."[54] The governor responded with the salutation "Dear Archie," thanked McMurdo for his "thoughtful letter, and the message of encouragement," reflected on the "great burden" of having to make such a "weighty decision," and expressed his appreciation for "your friendship."[55]

The file of petitions and replies in Snell's records indicate an influential network of privileged access that belied his public persona as a populist man of the people. Snell's letters, in their style and substance, demonstrate his disproportionate concern for the opinion of his lodge fellows on the matter of the Folkes case, as compared with other petitions from constituents and correspondents. In the same week the governor fielded the congratulatory letter from McMurdo, Snell also received an appreciative letter from another member of the Masonic brotherhood—Wilbur G. Brinson, father of Martha James. Brinson's letter extended his "thanks and appreciation for the fine spirit and steadfast manner in which you refused to stay the execution or commute the sentence." Observing that he had retained Sisemore's services in the aftermath of the trial, Brinson reported that the Klamath Falls DA and Weinrick had kept him informed of "the various interests supported and maintained by various groups in behalf of the interests of the colored race. It is generally their policy to fight to the last."[56]

Contrary to the assertions Brinson made to Snell, petitioners for clemency emphasized their concern the case involved a miscarriage of justice. Most petitioners in that category were less likely to cite racial grounds for their appeal than were those who urged the governor not to intervene in the scheduled execution. The groups to which Brinson apparently referred with the phrase "the interests of the colored race" were, moreover, a much more diverse group than Brinson's characterization might suggest. They included the NAACP and the Urban League, but they also included labor unions representing dining car workers and other trainmen, both Black and White, from across the western and midwestern United States. In addition, the petition file includes communications from church groups, lawyers, judges, and youth organizations. Petitions from all these and other groups, along with many individual appeals, urged the governor to show clemency. According to some reports, in addition to written petitions, several hundred people telephoned the governor's office with appeals for clemency during the holiday season bracketing Christmas and the New Year. The governor's file on the case includes no surviving record of who made those calls, or how they couched their arguments for or against clemency, but it does include over four hundred surviving records documenting the efforts of petitioners who submitted letters, signed group appeals, or sent telegrams asking the governor, in the words of Miss Purity Lamb of 2602 South Central Avenue in Los Angeles, to "Let Mercy Temper Oregon Justice."[57] Lamb, like virtually everyone else who wrote Snell asking mercy for Folkes, received a terse three-line form-letter response.[58] The governor signed these acknowledgments one day after he profusely thanked Banholster and Smith for their "thoughtful" and "kind" letters and assured them he viewed the Folkes case as essentially parallel to Layton's, who had been executed more than two weeks earlier.

A few Oregon-based petitioners who favored clemency and seemed most familiar with Snell couched their arguments in racist terms, apparently assuming that approach might find a friendly audience. Hal Moore, a Portlander whose letterhead indicated his profession as "Public Relations," and who self-identified as a "hard-headed newspaperman" and experienced crime reporter, typed a letter on 2 January 1945 that began "Dear Earl" and ended with the simple sign-off "Hal." Moore's first sentence read, "If I were governor I'll be damned if I could let that nigger Folkes be executed Friday." Snell tailored his response to Moore with instructions to his administrative assistant scrawled in the margins of the original, detailing things to add to the standard acknowledgment letter: "appreciate views etc—full consideration etc—trial in circuit court—appealed Supreme—then U.S. Supreme—Today another hearing/ State supreme Court/with appeal denied. Mighty difficult for me/Hal/to say courts are wrong. Shd like to see you one of these days."[59]

Snell commonly scrawled brief notes in the margins, as he did with Moore's petition, indicating to his administrative assistant which standard clauses to include in the acknowledgment, and these brief notes offer some insight into his thinking beyond the formalized response letters. The marginal comments Snell scrawled on Moore's original letter were more extensive and personalized than most others, which suggests he appreciated, or at least was not offended by, the tone "Hal" adopted. In the case of the Brewster letter, the governor's marginal comments suggest he dashed off instructions without much thought or attention to detail. He scrawled in the margins of Brewster's original: "wrote her before—so Thank you for your additional comments." In fact, Snell received three letters from the George E. Brewster household: one from George Brewster (20 December), one from Mrs. George Brewster (29 December), and one from Mary Jane Brewster (27 December)—three different people at the same address.[60] At the time he penned these comments in the margin of the 29 December letter, he had not yet answered Mary Jane Brewster's letter, but he had responded to George E. Brewster.[61]

Moore's apparent comfort with racist terminology when petitioning "Earl" in an otherwise crisply written and well-crafted typewritten letter suggests he understood the governor would not object to such language and, in fact, might likely sympathize with it. Moore went to great lengths to disassociate himself from any personal interest: "Please don't think I'm one of the nigger-loving whites, either, because I have no truck with what Franklin and Eleanor are doing to make these jigs a highly objectionable social factor in this country." Only after establishing his racist credentials did "Hal" offer his most substantive argument: "It's just that there's too much of what the courts call 'reasonable doubt' in this case. If he were PROVEN guilty I wouldn't mind helping him over the hump to nigger heaven—but not the way it shows to date."[62] Apart from the closing line, Snell's response followed the form Ormand Case suggested in his letter of 23 December 1944.[63]

The Brewsters, unlike Moore, tried to appeal to the governor on more intellectual grounds, but Snell brushed them off with abrupt stock phrases that suggest he did not even read their petitions. All three of their letters were typewritten, erudite, and well-crafted in terms of logic, syntax, and grammar, but they received only the standard three-line response letter. In the case of Mrs. Brewster, she received only a brief, one-line letter that falsely implied she had written a previous letter. Mary Jane Brewster's letter asserted that "real justice and fairness" to "all accused persons" was "one of the things our boys are fighting for in this war."[64] George Brewster's letter argued Folkes was "the victim of a deliberate legal frameup and was convicted of a crime which was committed by someone else." He described himself as "a member of the superior white race, a 12-time Red Cross Donor, member of the Coast Guard Reserve, and an employee of the Oregonian since 1917."[65] Snell responded to Brewster's page-long typewritten appeal with his standard three-line acknowledgment letter unadorned with any personalized notes.[66]

Class standing and ideology, more than race, divided those who favored clemency from those who advocated executing Folkes. Petitioners for Folkes had to tread carefully in the latter stages of the war, when the forces of reactionary racism mobilized a campaign to reverse wartime expediencies that opened some avenues for advancing civil rights. Petitioners who favored gubernatorial clemency cautiously phrased their appeals with more deference, formality, and dispassionate arguments than their opponents'. Although the majority of lawyers and judges who petitioned the governor overwhelmingly favored clemency, their carefully typed letters accounted for less than 0.3 percent of all petitioners who asked the governor, in letters, telegrams, or group petitions, to set aside or commute Folkes' sentence. Apart from telegrams, most petitioners, by far, mailed handwritten notes and letters. Of the 119 people who signed petitions or wrote letters or notes from Los Angeles asking Snell to grant clemency for Folkes, less than 9 percent (ten of 119) typed their appeal. The typed messages included petitions from more prominent organizational leaders of the civil rights community or from labor organizations: Thomas Griffith, president of the Los Angeles chapter of the NAACP; Floyd Covington, executive director of the Los Angeles chapter of the Urban League; Lovic Howell, district chairman of the Los Angeles chapter of the Protective Order of Dining Car Waiters; and Pollard, who offered his twenty-point letter as a "private citizen" but was also a prominent leader in Local 582 of the Dining Car Workers Union to which Folkes belonged. Of the other six typed letters, one was drafted by A. Wendell Ross, pastor of Pleasant Hill Baptist Church, and the other five were all written by women: Margaret Rakestraw, who identified herself as president of the Phys-Art-Lit-Mor Club; Grace Hamrick (who authored two different letters); Purity Lamb; and the officers of the Sojourner Truth Home. With few exceptions, petitions from Los Angeles, accounting for over a hundred petitioners, followed closely on the heels of an appeal from the Robert Folkes Defense Committee that the *California Eagle* published on 21 December 1944.

The timing of clemency petitions from Los Angeles suggests many of the people who wrote the governor considered Folkes a victim of racial injustice, even though their appeals carefully avoided any charge of racism. In appealing, deferentially, to the White governor of Oregon, advocates for clemency also adopted the pretense of racelessness in a self-conscious effort to avoid turning Snell against their cause in a fit of reactionary racism. The RFDC appeal that appeared in the *California Eagle* was a guest article printed in boldface directly beneath the editorial cartoon on the opinion page of the *Eagle* and headlined, "PUBLIC SUPPORT NEEDED TO SAVE FOLKES' LIFE." The article, apparently drafted by Pollard in cooperation with Clara Folkes, called upon "the people of the United States who are believers in justice" to make an "eleventh hour" appeal, writing or wiring Governor Earl Snell requesting a stay of execution and a commutation of sentence for Robert E. Lee Folkes. The article observed that Folkes "up to this day [21 December

1944] maintained his innocence for the crime," and it noted that since he was "convicted by a jury on which there was not a single Negro, it is the consensus of most Negro leaders throughout the country that the young dining car cook is a victim of circumstantial evidence which even in his case was not sufficient to warrant the death penalty. From the records of the court, it is the opinion of Negroes that the marine who played an active part in an[d] out of the Lower 13 compartment that ill-fated night in January 1943 was more than a mere 'material' witness in the case." The article then linked this appeal effort to the Scottsboro case and Sleepy Lagoon (zoot-suit) cases, noting, "If it were not for mass pressure . . . the true facts in [those cases] would never have come to light." The communiqué from the RFDC also referenced "the celebrated case of Tom Mooney, who was sentenced to die for a crime which he did not commit." Mooney, whose sentence was commuted as a result of such efforts, the article concluded, was eventually proved innocent.[67]

AN "OREGON DIFFERENCE": PRESENTING THE CASE FOR CLEMENCY AS A HUMANE OPTION

The myth of an "Oregon difference" clearly influenced the strategy the RFDC deployed in its effort to secure clemency from Snell, and most petitions favoring Folkes invoked the notion the people of Oregon were above the mindless racism petitioners linked with the Deep South. The RFDC clearly recognized the role race played in the arrest, interrogation, and verdict against Folkes, and that was a central feature of the campaign to rally a petitioning drive; however, most petitioners adopted a deferential tone and carefully avoided racially themed arguments. Advocates for clemency in Oregon struggled uphill against top-down reactionary racism, and they also struggled to push their message through the veneer of pretended racelessness and rhetorical fairness that muffled public statements and pronouncements of criminal justice officials in the state. Although rural jurors of Linn County passed judgment on Folkes, well-connected officials managed and manipulated the case they heard, and that pattern continued through the gubernatorial petitioning process. Opponents of clemency were mostly well connected and largely urban, even though many others who demanded Snell not interfere with the execution were apparently disaffected and obviously alienated people of lesser status or influence. For all his emphasis on personally answering every citizen who wrote to him, however, Snell clearly paid more attention to a small cadre of relatively prominent people who darkly warned of a looming race issue.

Recognizing that privileged confidants had back-channel access to Snell, RFDC supporters tried to counter those influences by making direct, face-to-face appeals to the governor, organizing meetings that included committees of prominent citizens affiliated with well-respected professional organizations. One day after the *Eagle* printed the committee's desperate appeal for a petitioning campaign, a delegation of seven lawyers and ministers met with Snell in Salem, asking him either to order a new trial or, failing that, to commute the sentence to life imprisonment. The United Press wire service report of that meeting the next day (23 December) observed that attorney William Palmer of Portland headed the group. Nels Peterson, president of the Civil Rights Committee of the Oregon Bar Association, told the governor during the meeting that Clara Folkes told him the confession introduced at trial "was not bona fide and that she had been unable to talk to him [Folkes] alone since he was arrested and brought to see her in what she described as a drunken condition." Other members of the delegation included Reverend George W. Halstead; John Sneddon, business manager of the Merchant Marine Cooks and Stewards Union; Reverend Browning C. Allen, minister of the Portland Bethel African Methodist Episcopal Church; Reverend George R. Cromley, of Woodburn First Presbyterian Church; and F. C. Salter, minister of Ardenwald Community Church.[68]

There is no evidence that the group presence the legal and clerical delegation mustered for its appeal had any more success than the individual petitions, cards, and letters the governor dismissed with his formulaic three-line acknowledgment. In the crucial weeks of the holiday season, between 23 December and 5 January 1945, the governor seldom varied how he worded that acknowledgment: "The matter to which you referred in your letter of [insert date] has been and will continue to receive careful consideration, study and consideration." Clippings from the Oregonian and other papers that published a news service report on the legal delegation to Snell (headlined, "Snell Listens to 'Lower 13' Slayer Pleas") made their way into the governor's official case file, where they accompanied a letter from Vancouver resident Mrs. E. Mabry to Snell (23 December 1944). According to the press release, "The governor promised serious and careful consideration of the arguments presented to him."[69] Nothing in the record indicates this was any more than lip service.

With time running out, Clara Folkes appealed to Snell on a personal level, emphasizing their common bond as parents with strong family values. Few who petitioned Snell for clemency in late December 1944 could say they had spoken with the governor personally within the previous month, and in that context, the governor's response to Clara Folkes was particularly revealing. As mother of the condemned man, Clara Folkes met with Snell, along with Lomax, Pollard, several local clergymen, and local leaders of the NAACP shortly before the scheduled execution. In mid-December 1944, she penned a handwritten two-page letter to Snell, asking him to intercede. In that letter, she referenced her son as "Robert E. Lee Folkes whom you know all about." Her words conveyed the sense that from her communications with Snell she was convinced he was not an unfeeling man: "I feel that you feel the same as I that my Boy is not Guilty theirfore [sic] we would not want to put an innocent person to death without the fact of his Guilt." She appealed to Snell as an empathetic man of good conscience, and she addressed him with respectful honorifics: "Now your Honor. You Realize this would Be Horriable [sic] on your—Conscience Should He die then later it is proven that He is not Guilty—But the one who paid for the crime is Dead could you Bring Him Back. And Restore Happiness again to His Mothers Breaking Heart?" Only after making these appeals to their common humanity did Clara Folkes offer the governor her written critique of the case against her son: "Dear Sir Know that 45 witness[es] could not verify Him as the guilty one." At that point, she reminded the governor he was accountable to a higher authority than his constituents: "Now sir Be Honest with God and your Self. Just How do you feel about this case knowing that if you'll be Honest with God your maker & your Self you would give this case a Just and serious thought & may God Bless you with all your undertakings. . . . Yours in Humble prayer that you'll have mercy on my Son Robert Folkes."[70]

Nothing in Clara Folkes' letter made any reference to the issue of race or the racial or cultural differences between the governor and her son. Instead, the mother appealed to the governor as a father who she had to believe cared about his children, and she emphasized their common humanity, not their differences. Snell's response to Clara Folkes, just two days after her letter, was a dismissive, passive rejection of that approach. The exchange of letters was only one element in an ongoing conversation that stretched across several months and was often mediated through lawyers and clergymen, but which included at least one face-to-face conversation. He could not have escaped recognizing this mother and her letter. Hers was a constant, composed presence in Lewelling's courtroom throughout the trial, where reporters frequently described her demeanor and appearance. By the time she met the governor, shortly before the execution, Clara Folkes was a well-recognized figure with a public persona of tragic suffering that rivaled that of the victim's father. That composed, tragic persona, however, belied her efforts, for nearly two years, to rally public and private support for her son, during which time she made countless public speaking appearances before church groups and civil rights organizations in California and Oregon. Snell, who confided to several correspondents that he wrestled mightily with the weighty decision of life or death for Layton and, by implication at least, also for Folkes, certainly must have known his response to Clara Folkes might shape how others in the civil rights community perceived his decision. His response to her heartfelt personal appeal, however, was pro forma: she received the same three-line letter he mailed others who petitioned for clemency, not even acknowledging he knew she was Folkes' mother.[71]

INVOKING THE OREGON DIFFERENCE: WILLIAM POLLARD AND THE LEGAL CASE FOR CLEMENCY

Snell's tactless dismissal of Clara Folkes and her desperate, deferential appeal to the governor's humanity galvanized more radical voices into an aggressive, direct assault on the verdict as a miscarriage of justice that was out of step with Oregon's mythic reputation as a progressive, forward-looking state. They included prominent voices such as McClendon, who leaned on arguments by seasoned activists such as Pollard. With Clara Folkes, Pollard was a prominent, ever-vigilant presence at the trial and a well-known labor organizer and leader who accompanied her to many public appearances as they worked together during the clemency campaign. A striking, serious-looking man of studious demeanor, Pollard was an articulate writer and labor union secretary with considerable experience facing down the pretended righteousness of White men who wielded indiscriminate power. His multipage letter, detailing twenty points of concern, framed the legal case for executive clemency, rejecting the formal reasoning of the state's highest court. Pollard argued the original trial was tainted because Albany was a virtually all-White town and the jury was drawn from an all-White pool of jurors, many of whom were avowedly prejudiced and openly admitted they could not give Folkes a fair trial. Pollard asserted he was "very active in the defense of Robert Folkes, only because I am thoroughly convinced that the evidence presented thus far has failed to implicate him in any instance." Noting he had "talked to thousands of people who feel that he is innocent," he argued prosecutors presented only circumstantial evidence insufficient to merit a conviction and, especially, a death penalty.

Moving beyond legal arguments, Pollard's letter challenged the militarized narrative that framed the case from the beginning, arguing the investigation was tainted with "war hysteria." That mind-set, he argued, "upset many fair-minded Americans." Wilson, far from being a military hero, Pollard asserted, was actually a questionable figure whose pending transport to the South Pacific on the eve of the murder was "not a military secret." Turning the militarization theme around and aiming it squarely at "the marine," Pollard noted many other "members of our armed forces" who had fulfilled their duty and actually reported on station in the South Pacific had generously contributed to the RFDC. He implied Wilson was a shirker, while the military men who supported Folkes were real heroes. More importantly, Pollard emphasized, "The testimony of the occupant of Upper 13, Marine Wilson, was contradictory throughout the trial." After detailing a number of ways Wilson's testimony conflicted with the sworn testimony of other prosecution witnesses, Pollard outlined a few of the marine's more questionable behaviors: he made sure he was fully clothed before he called for help, he sent Hughes the opposite direction from where he claimed he saw the murderer flee, he testified Folkes was perspiring while frying eggs on a stove he (Wilson) had previously testified was cold at the time, and he found a bloody towel hours after police did not.

Pollard went further than most petitioners in questioning the reasoning of police, prosecutors, and the court in their willingness to excuse Wilson's contradictory behavior while ignoring other evidence favoring Folkes. He noted prosecutors established no motive for the murder, failed to produce any murder weapon or witnesses linking Folkes with the murder or murder scene, and offered no fingerprint evidence or blood evidence. He emphasized Folkes never read nor signed the "alleged confessions or statements," that LAPD officers admitted supplying Folkes (a minor) with alcohol, and that "45 State's witnesses failed to involve Robert Folkes." In addition, Pollard emphasized Folkes' diligence in attending to his duties the morning after the murder: between the time someone attacked and killed James around 4:30 a.m. and the time a brakeman came into the diner for coffee before 5:05 a.m., Folkes prepared five gallons of coffee, baked six tins of muffins, cooked several pots of Cream of Wheat and oatmeal, and put five pies to bake in the oven. Over the remainder of the trip, Pollard noted, Folkes continued serving as second cook, preparing seven meals in two days "without any sign of nervousness."[72]

All this, Pollard concluded, more than met the standard of reasonable doubt and clearly did not meet the standard of evidence Oregonians expected in a case requiring the death penalty.

Pollard's letter followed closely the narrative laid out in the NAACP preface to the Rossman dissent, and it laid the foundation for the formal petition for executive clemency that Clara Folkes filed with Snell's office just three days after the governor's dismissive response to her private appeal. In that petition, speaking through her Portland-based attorney, L. Nicholas Granoff, Clara Folkes formally requested Snell commute her son's sentence to life imprisonment. The petition asserted Folkes "was not accorded a fair trial," in violation of his rights under the Fifth, Sixth, and Fourteenth Amendments of the US Constitution, and in violation of Sections Ten, Eleven, and Thirteen of the state constitution of Oregon. Granoff specifically referenced the Rossman dissent and detailed "various and divers irregularities" at the trial, all of which "operated to the violent prejudice of the accused . . . and otherwise effectively denied to him a fair trial." Granoff's petition, on behalf of his client, Clara Folkes, asked for a "formal hearing" to further discuss the petition directly with the governor.[73]

PUBLIC AUDIENCES AND LONGER-TERM IMPLICATIONS OF POLLARD'S LEGAL RATIONALE

Although most petitioners from Southern California addressed the governor in deferential tones and carefully tiptoed around the "race issue," Pollard's more radical approach directly confronted Snell with evidence of overt racial bias and prejudicial institutions, including court and police officials in Oregon, as well as jurors in Linn County. His reframing of the case amounted to an indictment of the state of Oregon in the court of public opinion, and that approach inspired other letter-writers to adopt a similarly direct, more challenging approach. Many who wrote Snell from Southern California in the last two weeks of December, with the execution looming in early January, mentioned Pollard's twenty-point letter to the governor, which the *Eagle* also published as a highlighted editorial for its South Central readers.

Pollard's open letter, in fact, jump-started a second wave of last-gasp petitioning from Los Angeles and other areas where it was republished in the Black press and in union newsletters. San Pedro resident W. B. Jones, for example, cited the "twenty points in the letter of Mr. William E. Pollard," offering his own four-page letter in tightly packed, well-formed handwriting.

Jones restated several of the points Pollard's letter addressed and then added, "There have been many Negroes to die for a crime that was commit [sic] by a white man and later the real murder is found after some other man's life have been taken. Who is guilty then?"[74] South Central resident Mildred Charleston likewise summarized details of the case as described in Pollard's letter, emphasizing Wilson's suspicious behavior aboard the train, and then she posed a rhetorical question: "Can't we let blame fall where it's due?" After reviewing some points of evidence from Pollard's letter that implicated Wilson, Charleston bluntly raised the issue most previous petitioners from Southern California scrupulously avoided: "Dear Governor, couldn't we just forget color prejudice just once in the favor of justice and just not presume Folkes is guilty just because he's colored and therefore must be guilty? . . . In this case I think you'll find Folkes the innocent one."[75]

SOUTH CENTRAL PETITIONERS: CLASS, DEFERENCE, AND THE MYTH OF AN "OREGON DIFFERENCE"

South Central petitioners who responded to Pollard's last-gasp appeal for an outpouring of support were relatively powerless people of lower economic and social status. Their petitions were more deferential and less grammatically correct than those of the many lawyers and prominent leaders who spoke out on behalf of Folkes, and their desperate pleas more directly challenged the pretense of racelessness. Few petitioners from Los Angeles who favored clemency could marshal the resources for a typewritten letter, and most managed only brief notes with short sentences in cramped, awkward handwriting on small scraps of paper or postcards. They mostly denied any motivation based on race solidarity, but they also found it difficult not to discuss the matter without reference to race. Mrs. C. Phillips, for example, emphasized at the start of her letter, "I am an old woman, and NOT of the Negro race." She linked her plea with militarized virtue, as the mother of "a son in the army, and I'd hate to think my son was being railroaded to Death to satisfy a Negro hating police officer." Her letter referenced patterns of police brutality and doping as common procedures that she had witnessed in her twenty-four years living in the Los Angeles area. Regarding Folkes and his interrogation in Los Angeles, she concluded, "This Negro was beaten and made to drink until his family thought he was doped." She asked Snell to grant clemency "for the sake of his mother."[76]

Los Angeles petitioners, as in the case of Phillips, most commonly sought legitimacy and moral authority by grounding their appeals in the virtues of motherhood, military service, and/or religious or moral rectitude. They less commonly referenced the racial concerns Phillips included in her appeal. Corporal R. L. Thompson, writing through a military mailbox at Fort McPherson, Georgia, for example, wrote a page-long, single-sentence, typewritten letter without punctuation to "the Governor of Oregon" on 28 December, emphasizing race was not his primary motivation in writing: "I am jus a solder that do hate death but I am in the war and have been for three years and haven been any kine of truble."[77]

Thompson's letter turned on its head the militarized ideal of virtuous self-sacrifice that prosecutors used to sanctify Wilson and to shield him from close scrutiny in the courtroom. Thompson, himself a soldier, stressed the wartime context of the murder and the meaning of the war as his primary reason for petitioning the governor for clemency. Writing in the vernacular of a person more accustomed to the sound of words than how they appear in written form, Thompson produced a typewritten stream-of-consciousness dissertation on the nature of justice in wartime. He observed, "I am not saying that he is not gultie but I do say please see if he is whin you think of all of htis you will see what I mean with all of the killing that is goning on and more to die and thin for you all to just kill A man without amy reason that is some thing to think of and we are fighting this war just as you all and we do want our men to get A fair chance at life. . . . I thaught that we was fighting for our country and its rights but if its rights is to kill just to see a A man die thin I don't want to do any thing but die my self." Finally, he suggested the decision undermined the war effort: "a thing lick this si why the nigro don't see what they are fighting for" and he agreed, "I am just about to think so my self," and then he closed his letter with the salutation "YOURS AS A SOLDER."[78]

Excluded from structures of power and privileged access in Oregon that worked against the RFDC, petitioners for Folkes laboriously gathered signatures in his home community, hoping to overcome in numbers what they lacked in status and authority. Most petitioners from Los Angeles added their signatures to group appeals. A simple petition, on blue-squared graph paper, addressed to "Hon Earl Snell—Gov State of Oregon," began with a brief statement: "We the undersigned respectively ask you to commute the death sentence of Robert Folkes to life imprisonment." Sixty-two people from South Central neighborhoods signed this simple petition. Signatures appeared in various hues of blue and black ink, and in pencils of differing hardness and shades, including one signature in red pencil. The two-page tattered petition showed signs of having been passed around from person to person, and most signatures included addresses from within one or two blocks of Central Avenue between 20th Street and 43rd Street.[79] This, and one other petition, accounted for eighty-four people from South Central who added their voices to the campaign to secure clemency for the young man who had grown up in their neighborhood and attended nearby schools before taking a job with the railroad. Although the list included many local civil rights leaders, including attorney Walter Gordon and local newspaperman Leon Washington, Charlotta Bass was conspicuous in her absence. Her name does not appear as a signatory, or as an independent petitioner, in any of the records included in Snell's file for this case, although the *Eagle* apparently prompted the late-December signature-gathering effort by printing the joint appeal from Pollard and Clara Folkes.

OREGONIANS FOR JUSTICE: CLASS DIFFERENCES IN THE APPEAL FOR CLEMENCY

Support for and against clemency among Oregonians who petitioned the governor broke down along surprisingly complex lines of class and educational accomplishment. By comparison with petitions from California, where over 91 percent of all petitioners who mailed notes or letters wrote them by hand, Oregonians who petitioned their governor were far more likely to use the more formal (and expensive), typewritten approach. Although a small number of prominent Oregonians wrote personal appeals urging Snell to stand firm against the petitioning drive to save Folkes, a larger number of Oregonians who urged him not to intervene were apparently less well educated and less likely to use modern technological innovations like typewriters, even for the formal task of petitioning the governor. Nevertheless, Oregonians were far more likely than petitioners from outside the state to mail typewritten letters, and over half of all Oregon petitioners (thirty-eight of the seventy-five who did not self-identify as lawyers, and all nineteen lawyers) submitted typed letters. Of the twenty-seven non-lawyers from Oregon who wrote to oppose clemency for Folkes, more than 74 percent (twenty of the twenty-seven) submitted handwritten notes. By comparison, of the forty-eight non-lawyers from Oregon who wrote the governor urging him to extend executive clemency to Folkes, only about 40 percent (nineteen of forty-eight) sent handwritten letters or notes.

The petitioning campaign provides some evidence of an emerging movement of activist leaders and followers in Oregon. Those who wrote longer letters—including Mrs. George E. Brewster, a Southeast Portland resident whose name also appeared as a contact on the inside cover of the NAACP pamphlet—sometimes presented arguments on behalf of larger groups of correspondents. Brewster, for example, began by describing her familiarity with the case, noting she had watched it "from the start" and that she discussed the case with "a number of attorneys" after 19 December 1944 and was convinced "several grave mistakes have been made." She argued "everyone on that train should have been under suspicion" and that officials should have searched "each person and piece of luggage" before releasing them from custody. She noted the Hearst publication *American Weekly*, which came as an insert in her Sunday *Oregonian*, falsely claimed police found the murder weapon in Folkes' suitcase, and that this misrepresentation was "widely published" and so warped public opinion against Folkes that a fair trial was virtually impossible. Finally, she concluded by questioning Wilson's past record and urging the governor to look into that aspect before deciding on whether to extend clemency.[80]

The idea of appealing directly to the governor in writing seemed to appeal more strongly to urban than to rural residents of Oregon, but a much larger and more diverse group appealed to the governor by telephone and telegraph. The overwhelming majority of Oregon petitioners who wrote letters to Snell (both for and against clemency) listed Portland as their place of residence, with Albany residents (five) and Salem residents (five) the most common among non-Portlanders. Oregonians from all over the state, however, submitted written petitions, including missives from Heppner, Roseburg, Gold Beach, Newberg, The Dalles, Coquille, Lebanon, Weston, Reedsport, Oregon City, Rainier, Rogue River, Wheeler, Tillamook, and Otis. Those who wrote to oppose the execution and those who petitioned to oppose clemency were represented from all around the state in relatively similar proportions. Three of the five letters from Albany opposed clemency, as did three of the five letters from Salem. Letter-writers from Otis, Oregon City, Roseburg, Lebanon, Tillamook, Coquille, Wheeler, Rogue River, and Heppner also were opposed to executive clemency. Small-town petitioners, however, also favored clemency (and opposed the death sentence), including the balance of petitioners from Albany and Salem, as well as writers from Rainier, Newberg, Oregon City, Reedsport, Weston, Lebanon, Coquille, and The Dalles. Apart from Portland, Salem, and Albany, no more than one person for each side (for or against clemency) wrote letters from any Oregon town. Apart from telephone calls, telegrams were among the most expensive methods of petitioning the governor, and virtually all who chose this method urged the governor to extend clemency to Folkes.

Despite the surge of last-gasp petitions that flooded the governor's office in the last weeks before the scheduled execution, perhaps the more important outcome was the fact that most Oregonians did not respond at all to the call for petitions to the governor. Although hundreds of people appealed for clemency, hundreds of thousands of Oregonians were content to let time run out for Robert E. Lee Folkes; they implicitly stood behind the decision of the trial court, the jury, and the state supreme court. A core group of civil rights activists from all over the state had mobilized into a coherent movement to oppose this application of the death penalty, but most Oregonians had not. Despite the myth of an "Oregon difference," Oregonians were largely indifferent to the fate of a young Black man in the winter of 1944–1945.

LETTERS FROM THE MID-VALLEY: AN UNDERCURRENT FOR CIVIL RIGHTS

Mid-Valley critics of the Folkes verdict were less numerous and therefore less obviously visible than civil rights activists in the Portland area, but given the small size of their home communities, they are no less significant as evidence that the case awakened a progressive mind-set with roots in both rural and urban Oregon. Many mid-Valley residents had the particular advantage of observing firsthand the miscarriage of justice in Lewelling's courtroom. Most correspondents from Portland cited the Rossman dissent, which apparently motivated them to write and from which they derived most of their substantive arguments about the case, but petitioners from Albany and Lebanon more often cited their own firsthand observation of the trial in Lewelling's courtroom when they petitioned the governor, asking that he extend clemency. Mrs. Paul Steidel, a farm wife from Albany, Oregon, and Mrs. Emma Densmore of Lebanon, for example, each sent the governor handwritten letters between Christmas and New Year's Day. Both women emphasized they personally attended the trial and argued the prosecution failed to supply sufficient proof for conviction.[81] Steidel, who noted, "I was at that trial from beginning," asserted, "There was no proof at all Folkes did it."[82] Steidel, who wrote on stationary headed "Even Tide Farm," indicated she was writing because she could not get the case off her mind: "That boy never killed that woman. . . . Please do not let them kill an innocent boy in Salem or Oregon." Joining her in that sentiment were other petitioners from more far-flung communities, including Mrs. G. Johnson of Coquille; the Reverend Florence River Jardine of Weston, Oregon; and Mrs. E. Mabry of Vancouver, Washington.[83]

Mabry's letter, a neatly typed, close-packed argument, constructed a narrative of the murder that accounted for the conflicting stories witnesses presented at trial, and her theory of the case emphasized the evidence pointed at the "bloodstained marine," who should have been a lead suspect but was inexplicably "used as a star witness against the young Negro."[84] The governor, Mabry argued, must recognize "many truths are not legal facts." The truth of segregation, Mabry argued, prevented defendants like Folkes from securing character witnesses that a White jury would respect. In closing, Mabry self-identified as a White person and warned the governor that if he allowed the execution to go forward, "that won't close the case; it will be left an open sore, past remedy. I think that the Folkes case will be a classic, and will have a place in history. I don't believe that this story has come to its close."[85] Mabry's example, and those of Densmore and Steidel, suggest that directly witnessing the trial experience awakened many Oregonians, rural as well as urban, to the reality that Oregon courts were tainted by forces of prejudice, and that experience motivated them to take action, adding their energy to an emerging movement for civil rights and opposition to the death penalty.

AN ORGANIZING LEGACY OF THE FOLKES CASE

Mabry's warning articulated a way of thinking about the Folkes case that connects it with an emerging self-consciousness about race prejudice in the Pacific Northwest at war's end. Executing Folkes would not discourage the people who found common cause protesting his sentence. Petitions from fourteen Oregon-based clergymen and group petitions from labor unions and benevolent organizations from Oregon and other states flooded the governor's mailbox after Christmas 1944. An unaffiliated group of Salem residents sent a three-page group petition listing sixty-three names, and a Portland-based social action committee representing the Congregational Conference of Oregon submitted a petition on behalf of its members. Another unaffiliated petition bearing the names and addresses of twenty-eight Portland-area youth also reached the governor, as did a handwritten petition from the Stockton, California, branch of the NAACP. Petitions favoring clemency were submitted by the Portland editor of the *Northwest Enterprise*, Mary M. Duncan; the managing editor of the Fort Worth, Texas, magazine the *Opinion*; the Fort Worth chapter of the Dining Car Employees Union; and the Oakland, California, local of the Dining Car Cooks and Waiters Union.[86] The case brought them together in a common cause that crossed state and local boundaries.

Beyond its immediate locale in Oregon and California, the RFDC campaign for clemency attracted attention from progressive labor unions and civil rights advocates across the country, but larger news about the latter stages of the war and planning for the postwar period mostly overwhelmed this smaller story. Petitioners from beyond Oregon sent telegrams in two waves: right after Christmas (26 December 1944), and one or two days before the scheduled execution (3–4 January 1945). These telegrams were mostly from dining car employee union affiliates, including locals from Oakland, California; Ogden, Utah; Kansas City, Missouri; Milwaukee, Wisconsin; Santa Fe, New Mexico; and Pittsburgh, Pennsylvania. Other unions representing dining car workers submitted letters from locals located in Fort Worth, Texas, and Oakland, California. The eleventh-hour telegrams that arrived on 3 or 4 January 1945 mostly came from ministers and pastors, including a joint telegram from three pastors in Pendleton, Oregon, who represented congregations affiliated with the Methodist, Christian, and Presbyterian denominations. A telegram from the director of the National Negro Council in Washington, DC, and several individual telegrams, all from the Portland metropolitan area, rounded out these last-minute appeals. All these wired petitions were very brief, and they simply urged the governor to intervene, sometimes offering the insight that a commutation of the sentence would allow further investigation to identify the "real murderer."

THE PRETENSE OF PROGRESS: STORIES OF BLACK SUCCESS THAT BURIED THE FOLKES APPEAL

Despite the proliferation of communiques from union locals that supported clemency, both the Black press and mainstream news outlets favored more positive stories about progress on the racial integration front over tragic stories with a possibly flawed protagonist. Leading progressive voices were uneasy over the possibility Folkes actually might be the flawed character police and prosecutors claimed he was. In an effort to set a more positive tone for the postwar transition, these news outlets favored happier stories with more uplifting messages, and Folkes paid the price for their pretense of progress. The gains of organized labor, for example, garnered far more attention in the Black press during December 1944 than the effort to save Folkes at that critical juncture. While individual and group petitioners inundated the governor's office with cards, letters, telegrams, and phone calls demanding clemency, official news outlets—even those geared toward progressive causes—focused on more upbeat issues. With the scheduled date for Folkes' execution looming only weeks away, the *Eagle* was preoccupied with Walter Gordon's role in organizing a defense for sixty-eight of the 136 Dining Car Workers Union members charged with conspiracy against the Union Pacific Railroad. The 21 December 1944 front page of the *Eagle* prominently featured photographs of "principals in U.P. Dining Car Waiters Case," and it featured positive labor union accomplishments on page six. The article cited the "leadership of General Chairman William E. Pollard and an able negotiating committee . . . who have worked for six months to complete negotiations to initiate a vacation plan for the workers they represent."[87] It made no mention of Pollard's role in the Folkes case, and although the RFDC's appeal on page twelve of the issue apparently encouraged a surge of petitions, the newspaper's regular coverage paid little attention to details of the case.

Even newspapers oriented toward a White readership in Oregon's mid-Valley emphasized heroic Black contributions to the war effort in the last days before the execution. The Albany newspaper, in late December and early January, paid only scant attention to the looming deadline, while it emphasized, in a series of articles on African American soldiers, the role of "American Negros" who heroically "pushed back in [resisting the] Nazi Counterattack" in the European theater of the war.[88] On 2 January 1945, however, the Albany paper included a very brief, inconspicuous article that noted "a group of Portland ministers and lawyers . . . presented clemency arguments to Gov. Earl Snell recently."[89] The next day, a longer article reported the OSSC had refused the petition that Granoff filed at the request of Clara Folkes.[90] One day later, on 4 January, the *Democrat-Herald* reported, in a prominent front-page headline: "Folkes' Last Hope Rests With Snell." Noting that the federal courts and the OSSC had denied Granoff's last-minute petitions for a writ of habeas corpus, an appeal to Snell was the only recourse remaining to Folkes. The report noted Snell had made no comment on the case, "despite visits from various delegations seeking to hold up the death sentence," and it portrayed Folkes as nonchalantly unconcerned "in the death cell at Salem."[91] On that same day, in Los Angeles, the *Eagle* reported that the NAACP had "spearheaded a spirited campaign to free [Folkes] because of the firm belief in his innocence," but the lead story for that issue focused on Gordon's defense

of UPRR dining car employees.[92] As Folkes braced for the death chamber in
Oregon, his home community seemed ready to move on.

KILLING FOLKES: A PASSIVE-VOICE EXECUTION AND THE "OREGON DIFFERENCE"

News reports of the 5 January 1945 execution resuscitated earlier narratives
regarding the setting and context of the murder, and they cast the entire investigation in passive-voice prose: no one had manipulated Folkes into confessing—things just happened. The Albany paper recapped the murder, claiming
it happened while the train was "speeding southbound," and that "suspicion
first centered on Mrs. James' husband, who was found to be missing from the
train . . . until it was discovered that he had taken the second section. There
were other potential suspects, including a marine private [Wilson] who was
discovered to have had blood on his clothes and who occupied the berth
above Mrs. James. Folkes was brought under suspicion and arrested when the
train reached Los Angeles. He was taken into custody by Los Angeles police,
and an alleged confession was obtained from him, but which he said he did
not sign. The 'confession' was entered as evidence at the trial and was the basis
of appeals to the higher courts."[93]

In the aftermath of the execution, newsmen and public officials returned
to the myth of an "Oregon difference": they argued that the criminal justice
system in Oregon worked as it was intended to work, and that the case demonstrated Oregon, unlike most southern states, followed professional standards
and equitable rules founded on the principle of racelessness. Oregonians,
it seems, could not see color in the courtroom. Snell ultimately refused to
intervene, delaying his announcement until after Folkes was already dead,
and he claimed special knowledge not in the public record: "I have before
me, evidence, information, and confesslors [sic] which convince me beyond
any question of doubt of the guilt of Robert Folkes in the slaying." Noting the
case was tried in circuit court, appealed to state and federal supreme courts,
and then a second time to state and federal courts, Snell concluded, "In view
of all circumstances involved, I do not see how I could possibly interfere."[94]
The Oregon criminal justice system, he concluded, had worked, and his role
was to affirm it worked by not acting. The system, not individual people, had
killed Folkes.

Once the man was dead, newspapers around the country suddenly took
an interest in the details of how he died, after largely ignoring the details of the

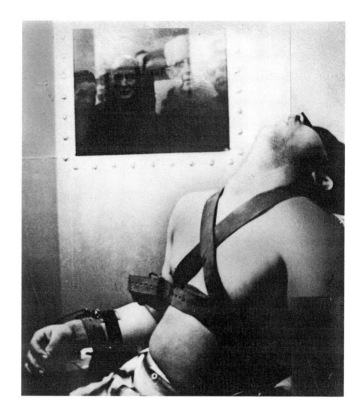

Robert Folkes in gas chamber 5 January 1945. Original print located in OSP case file, SPR collection, CSRM Library and Archives. Image courtesy the California State Railroad Museum.

appeal or even the Rossman dissent. According to news reports on the day of the execution, besides the twelve official witnesses listed on the Execution Notice that the OSP delivered to the Linn County clerk, more than eighty other people (including Weinrick and one member of the jury—reportedly a Scio resident) witnessed the execution in Salem.[95] Norfolk's *Virginian-Pilot* reported the execution the next day in a two-column story at the top of its back page, noting Folkes refused both "a customary heavy meal" and "a blindfold over his eyes." Folkes reportedly told newsmen as he entered the death chamber "that he was taking the walk 'because they had to convict someone—and it's easier to convict a Negro than a white person. But I am innocent,' he insisted." The story, which made no mention of a petition campaign, noted that Martha James' husband was killed "several months ago" in a plane crash near Pasco, Washington.[96]

The *California Eagle*, a weekly publication, dwelt on Folkes' demeanor and last words at a more detailed level than it ever managed to accomplish in reporting on the case or the appeal process. In an article that appeared six days after the execution, under a headline near the bottom of the first page that read "'Innocent' Says Folkes," the *Eagle* ran a short story on the execution next to an unrelated, upbeat photo and story describing a woman who gave birth to a miracle baby. The execution article emphasized that as Folkes' walked into the gas chamber "minus the usual blindfold," he called out, "So long to everybody" as the door closed, and he maintained to reporters, "'I have nothing to say except that I am innocent,' adding that he had been convicted because it was easier to convict a Negro than a white person." According to this report, "His mother remained with him until 10 p.m. the night before his execution." The *Eagle* seemed almost more sympathetic to the governor than to the condemned man. It reported that Snell was "besieged with petitions and phone calls," receiving "hundreds of phone calls" during the night preceding the execution, and said he (Snell) "did not sleep nor eat from the strain." Snell, by this account, said that he did not grant Folkes clemency "because of evidence 'which convinces me beyond any doubt of the guilt of Robert E. Folkes.'"[97] By this same report, Reverend C. H. Steinman, of Salem, spent part of the night with "the condemned youth," who, the reverend reportedly told newsmen, "maintained his innocence throughout their conversations." There was no last-minute confession to salve the conscience of those who ushered Folkes to the gas chamber. Immediately after that last sentence, the editor of the *Eagle* inserted a quotation from Browning: "Grow old along with me. The best is yet to be."

The Black press in Portland, Oregon, offered an exception to the general approach to the story elsewhere in the country, suggesting that it was a more traumatic and lasting issue that galvanized progressive forces in the state in ways that lingered on through the execution and after. Most newspapers buried the news of Folkes' execution beneath triumphalist portrayals of accomplished men and women of color in uniform in the following weeks,[98] but in Portland a labor dispute involving a Black shipyard worker, known locally as "the Anderson case," dominated front-page news in the *People's Observer*, which continued its linkage of the two stories, with a lengthy summary and analysis of the Folkes case on page two by "an interested local white citizen" who prepared the article for "the American Negro Press." A related article on page four reprinted coverage from the *Los Angeles Sentinel*, headlined, "Folkes Death Does not cinch Charges of Guilt," and an editorial on the same page quoted Folkes in the headline: "It's Easier to Convict a Negro."[99] The *Observer* also carried news of dining car workers' unions and awards but seemed relatively unimpressed with the supposed victory for Union Pacific dining car crews for which Charlotta Bass' *Eagle* credited Gordon during the same period.

The *People's Observer* editorial that appeared two weeks after the execution reconstructed a counter-narrative that placed the Folkes case squarely within the context of wartime social turmoil and economic transitions. Criticizing local leaders who ran Portland like "a big city operating on small-town ideas," McClendon argued that the transformative influence of war production caused those "prejudiced and provincial" people great "mental anguish" in their efforts to ensure that "the influx of Negroes" and also "migrant whites" who moved to Portland during the war "would find only a temporary economic existence." Toward that end, the *Observer's* editor opined, "they overlooked no opportunities to continue to inflict hardships on the Negro people."[100]

Outside observers, amid the clemency campaign, corroborated McClendon's observations regarding race prejudice in Portland. Associated Press accounts in mid-December 1944 reported that Reginald A. Johnson, a New York resident and field secretary for the National Urban League, following a visit to Portland, found "an unusual proportion of 'white only' restaurants . . . and other signs of discrimination." Warning that the situation would worsen after the war, Johnson urged national leaders to develop "housing for economic, not racial, groups; a fair system of layoffs in war industries; and . . . new peacetime industry."[101]

McClendon argued an old-guard African American population that he termed "the royal order of Portland's original Negro population" avoided involvement with "the in-migrant Negro worker" who arrived during the war. As a consequence, in-migrants suffered discrimination and abuse without support from the prewar African American community. Worse, McClendon claimed, "Negro renegades" (or "white folk lovers") collaborated with political and social efforts "that might tend to drive away the incoming Negro workers," providing cover for White reactionaries. These forces, he argued, were at work "in every detail" of the Robert E. Lee Folkes case. "Vicious whispering campaigns" defamed "all of the Negro people" and incensed White Oregonians "to a point bordering on mob hysteria." Most disturbingly, McClendon asserted, "even today, many Negroes are not conscious of their personal obligation to resist and protest the taking of this youth's life without his guilt being clearly established."[102]

McClendon saw in the Folkes case a concerted campaign waged by influential White people to send the message that the far Northwest would again be off-limits to Black people in the postwar era. It was Folkes' misfortune, McClendon argued, to be caught up in a scheme that was designed to "engender hatred in the hearts of all people against Negroes" and to "halt completely the westward migration of the Negro people." Linking the case with the formation of anti-Japanese organizations that mobilized during the latter stages of the war to oppose the return of relocatees to Oregon, and writing without access to the racist diatribes that opponents of clemency had actually mailed the governor, McClendon nonetheless deduced that White political leaders like Snell were under severe pressure to demonstrate their race solidarity in the Folkes case: "Any expression of fairness to Folkes and the Negro people would be construed to mean that they were incabable [sic] of protecting white supremacy concepts. This would be political suicide." McClendon closed on a dismal tone: "Many people view this portion of America as a locality where legal guarantees to minorities are strong and durable. Folkes' death is Oregon's refutation of this."[103] Oregon, McClendon argued, was not the Promised Land it pretended to be.

Virtually no other journalists, White or Black, followed McClendon's lead, and apart from brief accounts of Folkes' execution, the mainstream and advocacy press mostly abandoned the story as a closed case. News accounts of the execution mostly repeated brief summaries of false storylines laid down early in the investigation, noting that Folkes was "convicted of Oregon's most famous murder."[104]

McClendon, in the aftermath of the execution, was a lone voice who struggled to contextualize the significance of the Folkes case as evidence of the need for a concerted campaign to advance civil rights in the postwar era. In that sense, he defined a real "Oregon difference" in the case of Robert Folkes. Oregonians who had witnessed the case unfold could not pretend it was not about race, class, power, and access, and that provided a framework for continuing the fight against the death penalty into the postwar period. Beyond Oregon, the case had less significance. The Associated Press synopsis of the case was most remarkable for its virtually complete lack of context. The murder, by this account, took place without reference to the war, and with no backstory on anyone except for the sketchy information that Martha James was "a bride" from Norfolk, Virginia. It included nothing at all on her family, apart from the brief information about her military husband's death that fall, just a few months before the execution. It is a narrative so devoid of context that its detailed accounting, minute by minute, of Folkes' activities in the moments leading up to the execution, and its description of how he spent the previous night, served as a metaphor for the conduct of the investigation and the prosecution of the case through the trial and appeals process. It was a case in which obsession over details offered the pretense of due process without substantive attention to how and where the alleged "facts" emerged. In the process leading to arrest, conviction, and execution of the young man Robert E. Lee Folkes, an original, imagined narrative determined which facts gained credence before the jury and which simply vanished into the untold past. In Oregon, however, it left a legacy of mistrust regarding the death penalty and the system by which it was applied. Oregon's progressives emerged from the war with a renewed network of support that they owed, at least in part, to the trials of Robert E. Lee Folkes.

Conclusion
Folkes on the Death Train in Oregon

The Folkes case was never just about race—it was ultimately about the death penalty and, in the latter stages of the appeals process, it was more about seeking and organizing a humane alternative to reactionary forces of militarized authority and raw exercises of cynical power. Governor Snell's inaction in the Folkes case galvanized other Oregonians into action. A progressive coalition joined forces and refocused attention on the death penalty near the end of the war, linking the Folkes appeal with a resurgent civil rights movement in the state. Their belated effort to save Folkes fell short, but progressive leaders like McClendon and Pollard also made the Folkes case about more than one man—as a unionized Black trainman, he became a symbol of race and labor issues in Oregon industry during a period of growing concern about postwar readjustments. In response to concerted pressure from economic and social elites in and beyond Oregon, Snell pretended the matter was out of his hands and allowed other Oregon officials to execute Folkes. Killing Folkes accomplished two objectives for Snell and his supporters: it snuffed out an important organizational purpose for an emergent network of civil rights activists in Oregon, and it demonstrated the power and determination of reactionary forces to retain their control and authority into the postwar era. In constructing a challenge to the Folkes death sentence, however, McClendon and Pollard reconstructed a dramatic narrative for the postwar era that countered the moralizing simplicity of prewar and wartime melodramas that Weinrick and Sisemore had exploited to establish and assert control during the investigation and trial. The Folkes case began as a moralizing melodrama, but it ended as an experience of civil rights activism and organizational networking linking Oregon progressives more firmly into a broader regional and national movement.

The execution of Robert Folkes on 5 January 1945 was the end result of a long journey through the experience of wartime hysteria and militarization that profoundly shaped the postwar response to centralized forces of authority and control. In Oregon, between 1943 and 1945, local civil rights leaders were engaged in an organized campaign that challenged the morality of the death penalty in a case that linked their efforts to concerns about race, gender, class, and privileged access to power. The murder of Martha James, early in the war, raised the specter of chaotic, random violence at a time when authorities were desperately trying to craft a sense of orderly, purposeful action. The trial and sentencing of Robert Folkes in that case served a moralizing purpose, delineating clear lines of racialized evil, feminized virtue, and militarized, masculine authority. Prosecutors borrowed liberally from the stereotypical storylines of the true-crime detective novel that had gained popularity during the interwar years of the 1920s and 1930s—reporters, police investigators, and prosecutors fell back on the standard plot devices of that genre, beginning with early reports of the crime and continuing through the trial, sentencing, and appeals process.

Folkes, a self-confident product of the South Central neighborhoods of Los Angeles during the interwar era, apparently transgressed all the boundaries of deferential demeanor that White passengers expected of a Black trainman. His assertive personality as a self-confident Black workingman and card-carrying union man likely prompted his special treatment, and possibly torture, early in the murder investigation, at the hands of Southern Pacific railway detectives and the Los Angeles police, but he subsequently endured a drawn-out legal proceeding, not a vicious lynching. The multiweek trial balanced the expectations of the victim's family, from a state (Virginia) where lynchings were relatively common, against the ideals and pretensions of a state whose citizens espoused the conceit of an "Oregon difference"—a landscape of promise and new opportunities regardless of class or background.

In an adaptation to wartime militarization, authority figures assumed a more positive role in the Martha James murder case than was common in true-crime detective stories of the earlier interwar period. Before the war, crime reporters and novelists elevated the cool, detached, cynical detective to the status of a cultural icon, immortalizing the type in characters such as Ellery Queen, Perry Mason, and Sam Spade. In the James murder case,

OSP pathologist Beeman filled the role of the cool, detached detective, but with more organizational authority and an added aura of scientific method and precision. Beeman's more sinister role in either extracting or dictating questionable "confessions" in both the Folkes case and in the closely parallel Layton case during the early months of 1943 went largely unexamined in the courtroom record. In a bizarre twist, unexplained elements of the case, rather than raising questions about the validity of the charges, merely made the case seem more believable and closely parallel to the detective-novel genre. Brazil observes that the interwar years were a period in which Americans found irrationality and ambiguity the rule rather than the exception: "It is a world in which there are lots of loose ends, lots of things one does not or cannot know and at which one can only hazard guesses."[1] The story that police presented as if it were Folkes' confession played to that expectation of unexplained loose ends. The very fact that the evidence did not fit the charges against Folkes, consequently, may actually have worked against his defense. Jurors steeped in the traditions of interwar true-crime narratives expected nothing less.

TELLING STORIES: IMAGINING MURDER BEFORE AND AFTER FOLKES

Four years after the execution of Robert Folkes, an unknown assailant aboard the Southern Pacific Railroad's West Coast Limited crept into Lower Pullman Berth 5 in the early morning hours of 16 January 1949 and attacked Mrs. Opal Holmes as the train rolled through Lane County, Oregon. Holmes, a married mother of two and a resident of Richland, Washington, was travelling to visit family in Riverside, California, at the time of the attack. After she screamed, according to the AP press release that appeared in various newspapers across the country the next day, "she was aware of a man fleeing through the aisle, ripping berth curtains as he went," and the woman's screams awakened other passengers and alerted railway officials.[2] Southern Pacific investigators boarded the train at Klamath Falls, where they interrogated over three hundred passengers before releasing the train four hours later. As it continued its southward journey over the next twenty-four hours, they questioned a handful of suspects while en route to Los Angeles, but they ultimately made no arrests. Associated Press reports compared the 1949 Lower 5 rape with the 1943 Lower 13 murder on the same Southern Pacific route, observing that the 1943 victim, Martha James, "was found ravished and her throat cut." As in the case of the James murder, according to this report, Holmes, in the 1949 rape case, was no more able to identify her assailant than the earlier murder victim was. Southern Pacific special agent J. J. Finneran, who was a leading figure in the murder investigation in 1943, also led the 1949 investigative team during onboard interrogations that stretched from Klamath Falls to Los Angeles.[3]

According to some reports, Sergeant E. W. Tichenor of the Oregon State Police—the same Sergeant Tichenor involved in the 1943 investigation—informed newsmen that railway detectives detained six men for further questioning on the ride toward Los Angeles, and he grouped them by race and military affiliation: two Negroes, three sailors, and one soldier. Some reports noted that this group of six suspects included three "Mexicans,"[4] while others indicated that railway police whisked two sailors from the train into an interrogation room at Union Station in Los Angeles, where US Navy Shore Police and LAPD detectives briefly questioned them. Finneran's investigative team later told reporters that at least one of those sailors was in the same sleeping car as Holmes, and that earlier that evening, as she played cards with them in the club car, conversation "turned to a lively discussion of the 'murder in Lower 13' case." According to news reports, "this discussion took place in Oregon, some time before the attack."[5]

Stories about the past, as Mrs. Holmes tragically discovered that wintery night in 1949, powerfully shape how people think and act in the present. The tale of the Lower 13 murder, told and retold in police interrogation rooms, railcar bathrooms, newspaper reports, courtrooms, petitions, judicial opinions, and motivational pamphlets, also appeared in fictionalized and dramatized form, beginning in early 1943 and in various other accounts over the next seven decades. By the early twenty-first century, online memoirs and memorialized accounts emphasized the roles that various lawmen played in the investigation and asserted a linear narrative that represented as fact supposed "details" of the crime that clearly contradicted sworn testimony and other statements that police gathered in the early stages of the investigation.

STORIES UNEXPLORED: OF MOTIVE AND CIRCUMSTANCE UNKNOWN

While Folkes' 1943 murder trial and subsequent appeals process played out, another legal battle proceeded without notice in the wartime media, perhaps because it conflicted with the wartime narrative of manly stoicism that reporters constructed for the bereaved husband and father. Only four days after the murder, and one day after the LAPD extracted a supposed confession from

Folkes, Ensign Richard James filed a claim with J. A. Ormandy, claims agent at the Southern Pacific Company's Portland office (622 Pacific Building), for reimbursement on the ticket he had purchased for his wife, Martha James. Ormandy presented the claim for James in a 27 January 1943 letter to the Pullman Company's general passenger agent, J. J. Nolan. The GPA replied to Ormandy and copied his response to Mr. G. H. Gibney, enclosing a Pullman Company check in the amount of $2.80 for Claim No. 2187-R, made out to "Ensign Richard F. James, Nassawadox, Va." The amount, according to his note to Gibney, "represents the difference between the tourist berth rates Portland to Sacramento and Portland to Eugene."[6]

While James claimed the $2.80 refund for the unused portion of his murdered wife's ticket, his father-in-law, Wilbur Brinson, retained Sisemore as his personal attorney for the purpose of filing a $10,000 wrongful death claim with the Pullman Company. Shortly after the trial verdict, Sisemore, representing himself as the "attorney for Mr. W. G. Brinson," presented a claim to the Pullman Company "for the maximum amount allowed under our statute" for "damages arising out of the death of Martha Virginia Brinson James occurring January 23, 1943." Superintendent L. W. Snider informed Sisemore the next day (7 May) that he was submitting the claim "to our management in Chicago," and he forwarded it with a cover letter to H. S. Anderson, Chicago general manager for the Pullman Company.[7] Several weeks later, reality and fiction converged when a claims agent for the Southern Pacific Railroad, E. P. Stewart, called Snider with the news that Sisemore had also filed papers with him, suggesting that the two companies collaborate in settling the claim.[8] In communicating Stewart's information to Anderson, however, Snider also forwarded a copy of the Hearst publication *American Weekly*, a magazine that appeared as a Sunday insert in many newspapers, including the Sunday morning *Oregonian* of 23 May 1943.

The *American Weekly* for that week featured a dramatic rendering of the Lower 13 murder, under the heading "Actual Crime with All the Settings of Fiction," juxtaposing an imaginatively retouched version of Martha Brinson's college yearbook photo with a schematic drawing depicting Robert Folkes as a sinister-looking man with the large lips, protruding brow, and sullen expression of a stereotyped Black man in 1940s newspaper caricatures. The schematic showed Folkes in three circular cutouts at various locations in Car D and in the diner, with a dotted line depicting his alleged route to and from the murder scene. In the first scene, near the bottom of the page, a frowning

Folkes sat at a table in the diner drinking whiskey with other trainmen. From there, the dotted line led back to the kitchen, where a second scene showed Folkes, dressed in a dark overcoat and hat, testing the edge of a knife blade. In the third scene, near the middle of the page, Folkes carried the knife into Car D, to the sleeping woman, and then rushed back toward the diner, still holding the knife and still dressed in the overcoat and hat, while a porter looked on in horror. A newswire photo of Folkes, wearing a porkpie hat and dark suit coat, was set in a box just to the left of the schematic, forming a triangle between the drawing of the fleeing murderer and the sprawled form of the sleeping/murdered woman. Other photos, on the opposite side of the schematic, depicted a grieving Richard James in full dress uniform and a photo of Car D, on the siding in Klamath Falls, with a group of men standing near one of the entry doors.[9]

The image-conscious officials of the Pullman Company kept a close eye on the case throughout the early investigation and trial and into the post-trial phase of appeals and petitioning. Company correspondence and memos from this period (23 January 1943 through 5 January 1945) stressed the importance of clarifying, in public statements, the distinction between Pullman Company employees, such as sleeping car porters, and Southern Pacific Railroad employees, such as dining car waiters and cooks. The murder was a public relations disaster, but company watchdogs monitored the trial and execution of the young dining car cook in an effort to mitigate damage to the Pullman Company's image. The press adopted a nickname for the case—the Lower 13 murder—and referenced the murder car as "Tourist Car D," in terms that carefully avoided any reference to the more iconic "Pullman" name.

Whereas Pullman authorities were primarily concerned with how their company came off in the story, the *American Weekly* article was more concerned with fitting the story into the murder-mystery literary genre. The article that accompanied the schematic drawing introduced a dramatic overview of the crime with many inventive additions and then asked a rhetorical question: "All that remains is to assess Life's ability as a mystery story writer. How does it compare with Agatha Christie, Mary Roberts Rinehart and other standard authors in the field [?]" The author compared the story to Rinehart's "The Man in Lower 10," and to Christie's "The Mystery of the Blue Train." The article argued, however, that, with train traffic at an "all-time high and also in an all-time state of confusion . . . it was the extraordinary difficulties under which railroads are laboring today that set the stage for the crime." It related how Richard and Martha were separated by "Fate" and asserted, "Had they all been together, the crime would probably never have occurred, for it was Mrs. James' search for her husband that brought her to the murderer's attention."[10]

In constructing the narrative as a militarized murder mystery, reporters and investigators ignored other possible approaches to the case, including the one that People's Observer editor McClendon suggested in his postmortem to the case in the weeks following the execution. Rumors and suggestions for an alternative narrative abounded, but in an era of wartime censorship, none found their way into print. Petitioners seeking leniency from the governor suggested, in letters and cards, that the case closely resembled the Scottsboro case and other celebrated examples of racial scapegoating. Trial witnesses implied possible improprieties and racial mixing at the steward's party aboard the diner at Portland's Union Station, and several letter-writers and petitioners suggested that an outraged White racist (possibly even her new husband) may have killed Martha, or arranged to have her killed for fraternizing with Black trainmen. Investigators insinuated, in their questioning of Folkes and other trainmen, that the steward's party with "Navy fliers" may have included the Keatons and their friends, the James couple—both husbands being navy officers and pilots. The 1949 rape case indicates that suggestive banter at a club-car party may have escalated into a sexual assault later that night. The purported transcript of Wilson's interrogation, which prosecutors never disclosed to reporters or to the defense, but which survived in the files of railway investigators, corroborated claims attributed to Folkes, in his Albany statement, that a man in military uniform claiming to be her husband offered to pay someone on the dining car crew for a hit on Martha James.

FRAMING THE FOLKES CASE: POLICE MISCONDUCT AND CIVIL RIGHTS ABUSES

While all the alternative scenarios suggested above are problematic in that they lack sufficient proof, concrete evidence, or corroborating witnesses, they are no more outlandish in those characteristics than literary and legal claims that "the evidence" pointed to the second cook in the diner. Rossman, who carefully deconstructed the court's error in admitting the police transcripts as if they were actual statements or confessions, only touched on the internal contradictions of police testimony, and he addressed only a few of the instances where other witnesses directly contradicted their claims. Lomax suggested, at various points in the trial, more far-reaching concerns about police misconduct in Los Angeles, during the transfer from Los Angeles to Albany, and in Oregon, on the drive from Sweet Home to Albany and in the Albany courthouse and jail, but the mainstream press never followed up on those claims or linked them to other examples of police brutality in Los Angeles Central Jail or elsewhere. Even the alternative African American press in Los Angeles, Chicago, and Portland ignored that angle until after the Oregon State Supreme Court ruled on the case.

In the years following the Folkes case, detectives Tetrick and Rasmussen attracted notice in the *Los Angeles Times* for their involvement in police corruption and abuse of power scandals. Vernon Rasmussen resigned from the LAPD in February 1945,[11] amid allegations of corruption,[12] and took a position as chief of the Glendale police. In 1946, his name surfaced in connection with an investigation into Ku Klux Klan influence in the Los Angeles Police Department. Two other suspects were eventually sentenced to prison terms in that case, but Rasmussen escaped prosecution, and after a brief career as a Glendale city councilman, he died in summer 1948 amid further investigations into police corruption and scandal involving, among other suspects, the man who succeeded him in the Glendale Police Department.[13]

Edgar A. Tetrick, according to the Los Angeles Police Historical Society, served on the force from 17 March 1928 until 1 August 1950.[14] Tetrick was reportedly involved in the accidental shooting of a police cadet in 1932,[15] but his record of irresponsibly shooting a junior officer under suspicious circumstances did not prevent the LAPD from honoring him for "outstanding police work" only a few months later, in 1933.[16] On 21 January 1943 (just three days before Tetrick and Rasmussen took charge of Folkes at Central Jail), Tetrick was implicated in an inquiry during which Mrs. Maxine Beebe identified police sergeant Otto Schlinske as the man who administered the fatal kick during the beating death of her husband while in police custody at Central Jail the previous December.[17] In January 1944, Tetrick was involved in allegations that police wired an interrogation room with a dictograph and then introduced "ventriloquy" evidence implicating Isato (Jake) Stein in a murder case.[18] This raises questions about whether he and Rasmussen recorded or invented the supposed "statement" they attributed to Folkes.

Evidence of possible corruption and dishonesty by the two LAPD officers who produced the first statement implicating Folkes included accusations of bribery, murder, and planting evidence. While testifying in a murder case in Los Angeles in 1944, Tetrick admitted he accepted the "gift" of a wrist-watch from Amil Weller, who was at the time under arrest on suspicion of theft and murder.[19] In January 1945, Tetrick was involved in the "accidental" police shooting of Bernard Webb, a twenty-three-year-old man from E. 53rd Street, whom homicide detectives mistakenly identified as the second of "two Negro gunmen" involved in a service station holdup.[20] In April 1949, Tetrick was involved in bringing charges for burglary against three suspects *before* the burglary was actually reported and possibly before it actually occurred.[21] This record, compiled from scattered news accounts, bears out Rossman's legal opinion that the testimony of these two LAPD officers in the Folkes case was, at best, unreliable. None of this information, much of it readily available from wire service reports at the time of the trial and appeals process, made it into the narrative that newsmen constructed for the Folkes case.

FRAMING THE FOLKES CASE: NEWSMEN, IMAGINED IDENTITIES, AND POPULAR CULTURE

In constructing their stories about the crime, newsmen self-consciously drew on prewar traditions of the murder-mystery genre, and investigators subsequently sorted facts according to the logic of that initial narrative. Reporters could expect their readers would be familiar with the conventions of crime fiction, and breathless leads framed the breaking story in those terms. Prosecutors, likewise, could prepare the case along similar lines, while selecting for a jury they could expect to identify with their story. As Michael Ayers Trotti observed in a 2001 review essay, when particular acts of violence became public sensations by virtue of their harrowing impact, they drew crowds of onlookers at trial and prompted expanded news coverage and sensationalized pamphlets and books. As a result, such cases are particularly useful to historians for exploring and understanding the society in which those crimes occurred. In this sense, he argues, studies of these "sensational" crimes are "histories less of crime than of communities coming to terms with violence, telling stories about it, and finding rationales to explain and learn from it."[22]

The "whodunit" approach to the murder, as promoted in journalistic, subliterary, and legalistic narratives, divorced the investigation from context and focused it on imagined identities in the artificially constructed landscape of the railcar interior. Suspects and witnesses in that artificial landscape argued over minute details of timelines, lighting, and whether, in the darkened railcar, it was possible to discern color at all, or if everything blurred into the color of night. Jurors and judges credulously accepted narratives in which brown pin-striped suitcoats became blue or black or possibly even green overcoats without pattern. Pompadour hairdos morphed into hats and closely cropped kinky hair. Witnesses looking directly down from their bunks couldn't see people who other accounts indicated stood right next to their bunks, and they saw the green curtains as red, black, or blue overcoats or possibly only a shadow in the night—a darker shade of black in a darkened car that other witnesses described as well-lit. Railway records and Pullman Company employees corroborated defense claims that some passengers in the murder car, and virtually all passengers on other cars in that overcrowded train, completely escaped investigation, and many of them apparently left the train without providing legitimate names to investigating officials. The number of potential suspects with access to Car D and about whom virtually nothing appears in the historical record approaches nearly two hundred people.

Wilson's own military record, rumored at the time to include sexual assault and other violent offenses, never entered the trial record. The navy's judge advocate general records indicate that Lomax requested the marine's service record shortly after the trial, but that marine officials summarily denied the request, noting that it was "the invariable practice of the Navy Department" to decline such requests from defense attorneys, but that the department would "promptly furnish copies of papers or records in such cases upon call of the court."[23] In other words, only the court could request the records, not the defense attorney. There is no record in the case file, however, that Lewelling's court ever responded to such a request from defense attorneys for Folkes, nor is there any evidence that Lomax made such a request to the court.

CONVICTING FOLKES: RURAL JURORS AND METROPOLITAN SENSIBILITIES

Amid all of the uncertainties involving details taken out of context, inexperienced jurors and senior jurists alike abandoned the complexities of sworn testimony for the simplicity of imagined narratives. The murder of Martha Virginia Brinson James, like earlier, celebrated cases of beautiful women[24] trapped in a tragic web of circumstance and fate, resonated with a reading populace preoccupied and disoriented by the wartime mobilization and militarization of civil society. By the time Folkes walked into the killing chamber in January 1945, that context had shifted with the experience and progress of the war, with Allied success on all fronts, Germany nearing defeat, and Japan in full retreat and on the defensive. The paranoia and fear of the winter months of December 1942 through the months of the investigation, trial, and conviction in early 1943 gave way to the confidence and forward-looking gaze of the last year of the war, with anticipation of postwar readjustments and reconversion problems relating to labor and race. The letter-writing campaign to urge gubernatorial clemency or resolve focused more on matters of who would wield authority and how they would assert it in the postwar period. Prewar fascination with true-crime narratives faded into the background. Arguments about respect for the law, the courts, the public process, and the time and effort that professionals had already invested in apprehending, interrogating, and securing the conviction of the supposed perpetrator overwhelmed outraged claims that the process had been unfair or racially prejudiced. The prewar narrative, however, still framed the stories that people told to rationalize their arguments: even the staunchest advocates for clemency largely accepted the premise that Folkes had acted strangely and that he ultimately had admitted guilt, and that narrative structure remained the dominant storyline well into the postwar period.

REMEMBERING ROBERT E. LEE FOLKES:
MOVING ON AND FINDING MEANING

After the execution, the surviving principals in the case mostly faded into relative obscurity, but the story of the Lower 13 murder remained a potent narrative well into the future. Clara Leach Folkes virtually disappeared from the public record after January 1945, but for sketchy records in voter registration lists and in the obituaries that accompanied news of her son's death. Apart from cursory news stories, obituaries for Robert E. Lee Folkes are scarce. The most detailed version appeared in a Kansas City, Kansas, newspaper, and in St. Louis, where his mother's brother, Thurston Leach, lived[25] and apparently maintained contact with Clara Leach Folkes throughout the trial. These reports noted that the young cook's immediate family also included his brother, Eugene Folkes, and his sister, Shirley Ann Folkes. After funeral services at the Ivory Chapel of the People, in South Central Los Angeles, Robert E. Lee Folkes was buried the Saturday before 12 January 1945 in Evergreen Cemetery, near the corner of 1st and Lorena Streets in the East Los Angeles neighborhood of Boyle Heights. One of the oldest and largest cemeteries in the city, Evergreen was located on the site of a former potter's field. A locally prominent journalist and civil rights leader in South Central,

Leon Washington Jr., reportedly covered the final five dollars in costs for the burial,[26] indicating both the financial strain that the trial and appeals process had imposed on Clara Folkes and also the concern for her situation within the African American community that had become her adopted home.

Beyond the immediate family, others involved in the case also went on with lives that help place their roles during the trial into broader perspective. Wilbur Brinson and his wife, Grace, retired to their country club estate until she died in March 1969, and he lived for another eleven years, still putting in appearances in the downtown business district of Norfolk, Virginia, until his death in March 1980, when he was buried in the family plot, next to the graves of his wife and his first daughter, Martha. William Pollard continued as a labor leader into the 1950s, when his radical brand of labor activism fell into disfavor in a nation gripped in the anticommunist hysteria of the McCarthy period, and he is largely unrecognized in the local histories and reminiscences of the interwar and postwar communities of South Central Los Angeles. Sisemore retired from public service and entered private law practice shortly after the trial.

Within the decade, financial crises and corporate restructuring transformed passenger rail service in the United States. A consortium of railroads, including Southern Pacific, took over management of sleeping cars. This ended the reign of the Pullman Company in passenger car service, despite efforts by its corporate representatives to isolate the story of the murder from the corporate image of the Pullman Company—successfully rebranding it the "Lower 13 Murder," not the "Pullman Car Murder," and distinguishing between the sinister "dining car cook" (an employee of the Southern Pacific Railroad) and its own, steady, Pullman porters. Wilson lived on into the 1990s, eventually divorcing the woman he conveniently married during the trial and appeals process, but not before fathering several children. He died as an old man, stepping off a curb in downtown Dayton, Ohio, where a passing truck struck and killed him. The death penalty in Oregon outlived all these people—it died an unquiet death in 1964 only to be reborn twice in the next two decades. It lived on, in controversy.

DEATH IN OREGON: CAPITAL PUNISHMENT AND THE CONCEIT OF CRIMINAL JUSTICE

Oregon was a bellwether of sorts for shifting public attitudes about capital punishment throughout the twentieth century. It was an issue that shifted back and forth in popularity, through periods of anxiety and dislocation from familiar patterns. In the optimistic era preceding the First World War, Oregon had abolished the death penalty by a 1914 initiative petition resulting in a vote of 100,552 in favor of abolition and 100,395 opposed. Then, in the postwar era of antiradical hysteria, Oregon reinstated the death penalty in 1920 in a referendum vote that passed, 81,756 to 64,589, in a low-turn-out special election. The American League to Abolish Capital Punishment struggled to reverse the national conversation on this issue through the 1930s and 1940s, under the leadership of Clarence Darrow, but emerging theories of "scientific" criminal justice complicated their task with arguments that stressed the importance of authority and control to discourage "impulsive" behaviors. Those theories favored a more hard-nosed approach to following through with executions following a conviction, reversing earlier patterns of executive clemency. During this period, Oregon switched to the use of the gas chamber for state-ordered executions in 1937, on the argument that it was a more progressive and humane mechanism for killing. Oregon's governor Snell, who subscribed to those theories, authorized a flurry of executions at a time when other governors were rethinking that approach. Executions in the United States actually declined during the war, from a nationwide total of eighty-four in 1938 to an average of only thirty per year by the early 1950s. The Folkes case galvanized opponents of the death penalty and linked their efforts with a broader civil rights movement in the state. After nearly another two decades of agitation, in 1964 an Oregon referendum to abolish the death penalty secured 60 percent of the vote, passing 455,654 to 302,105 in a period of widespread international criticism of the use of the death penalty in the United States.[27] It was a temporary victory in a broader civil rights struggle that was less successful on other fronts, and Black trainmen suffered significant setbacks in both their home and "away" lives in those years.

Despite the notoriety of the case and the extensive coverage of the murder, investigation, trial, and eventually, the execution of Robert E. Lee Folkes, remarkably little about the executed man survives into the present. His mother and two surviving siblings lived on into the late twentieth century and, as of this writing, his sister is still living in Los Angeles. His brother, Eugene, died in the early 1970s, and his mother in the early 1980s. The case inspired a made-for-television documentary that aired on the History Channel in the late 1990s, and that showing apparently prompted Pierce James Mullaly to write *The Railroading of Robert E Lee Folkes: A True Mystery of Murder on Train Number 15*, published in 2006 through a small press in Bakersfield, California,

(Mullinahone Press). Mullaly's treatment, like the History Channel documentary, relied largely on newspaper accounts, Rossman's published opinion, and reports of the investigation that are stored with the Southern Pacific Railroad collection housed at the California State Railroad Museum and Library in Sacramento, California.

The actual trial record, which Mullaly apparently did not consult, survives only in the Oregon State Supreme Court case archive, which serendipitously retained the complete trial transcript, apart from some key omissions, as noted earlier in this study. The Linn County Circuit Court, in Albany, disposed of most of its records on this case, including the original trial transcript, considering it a closed matter.

The transcript retained in the Oregon State Supreme Court case archive includes a penciled notation that the daughter of one of the trainmen who testified at the trial entered, indicating her efforts to investigate a matter that haunted her father to his death. She apparently visited the state archives in the early 1970s after a few written inquiries to which archives staff had replied that she would need to plan a visit in order to personally explore the record. On arrival, she was confronted with a trial transcript that exceeded nine hundred pages in length. She apparently read the first few pages of the trial transcript, making minor marginal notes and markings to keep her place, and then skipped to the supposed "confession." At that point, all marginal marks cease, and she apparently stopped reading. There is no indication whether she ever returned after that brief visit. It is hard to believe that anything she had seen before throwing up her hands at the task before her could possibly have settled the harrowing uncertainty that her letters indicated her father had carried throughout his life and into the grave.

The sheer volume of the trial record apparently intimidated actual jurors at the trial, as well as the Oregon Supreme Court justices who considered the condemned man's final appeal. Like the trainman's daughter, the justices, jurors, and reporters mostly focused on the purported confession, which tells a compelling narrative closely adhering to the stereotypical script of the true-crime murder trial magazines and newspapers and the murder-detective pulp fiction stories of the interwar years. Archival records from the Newberry Library and from the California State Railroad Museum include documentation of the investigation that fills more than five archival file boxes, much of it calling into question even the courtroom testimony as reproduced in the trial transcript and, even more so, the narrative that court officers and

Folkes at defense table, Albany courtroom, during a break in proceedings. Versions of this image were published in the *Oregonian* and the *Oregon Journal* on 21 April and 23 April 1943. Image courtesy the Oregon Historical Society bh013298 and the *Oregonian*.

investigating officials attributed to Folkes. Jurors saw none of that material in written form and had no written record from the trial upon which they could rely during deliberations. All they had were their recollections of a chaotic trial, the closing arguments of the prosecutor and defense attorney, and the written "transcript" of narratives that the court told them were "confessions" that the defendant made to the police.

OREGON'S RURAL JURORS AND THE IMAGINED RURAL-URBAN DIVIDE

A jury comprising mostly middle-aged women of rural farming backgrounds considered the fragmentary testimony that a parade of mostly male witnesses presented in a packed courtroom filled with up to three hundred onlookers and one very small, slightly built young Black man. A courtroom photo shows Folkes looking small and alone at the front of the room at the defendant's table, staring into the camera flash, while ranks of White faces, looking grim and staring into his back, fill the frame behind him during a break in the trial. Voices of women from the train mostly failed to materialize at the trial, with only a few exceptions, even though they made up the majority of the passengers in the so-called murder car. Voices of authority in the courtroom were exclusively White and male, in the persons of the judge, prosecutors, defense attorneys, and even the jury foreman on a body mostly comprising women. Huddled in the ranks of mostly White onlookers, Clara Folkes and Jessie Wilson Folkes listened to stories that were mutually contradictory but were somehow believed in that setting. At the end of the trial, the mother sat alone, disbelieving, and then disappeared into the past. Her son's death is public record, but his birth is undocumented, and published accounts of his death carried no mention of his brother or sister, but for a single death notice that his family apparently purchased in the obituary section of the *Plaindealer*.

In the end, the story of Martha Brinson Virginia James, her murder, and the trial and execution of the man accused of that crime escapes resolution. Someone certainly killed the young woman on the train. Beyond that, nothing is certain. Most likely, the person who murdered Martha James was not Robert E. Lee Folkes, and the most probable alternative suspect was the man assigned to guard him at the Linn County jail on the top floor of the courthouse: Harold Wilson. Folkes, like everyone else aboard Train 15 on the night of 22 January 1943, experienced events that unfolded in linear progression from Portland to Klamath Falls, but the stories that each person told demonstrate more conclusively how people lived in different worlds in the same enclosed spaces on that train, depending on their race, gender, age, and class. Beyond these categories, each person lived and moved within the remembered contexts of the lives they had left behind for this accelerated passage through the winter landscape of a militarized Willamette Valley. After the murder, people remembered sounds, smells, textures, and even tastes from their time aboard that train, but their memories survived into the historical record mostly in fragmentary written form, or not at all.[28] Those written records focused mostly on what people saw and, to a lesser degree, what they heard aboard that train.

The most important details from that night, however, involved one person touching another person with force and violence, resulting in sounds that faded into a darkened interior landscape shrouded in muffling heavy curtains, swaying with the motion of the train as it clicked along the rails under blackout conditions through a snow-filled winter night. That interior landscape of constant mobility and distracting sounds was familiar only to trainmen and frequent travelers, while to most other passengers it was an exotic and transient experience filled with unfamiliar smells, disorienting motion, and unexpected, often frightening noises.

The voices most qualified to offer a trained, dispassionate account of events aboard that train were those least respected in the investigation and courtroom proceedings: African American men of military age who served in a low-status but draft-exempt position in a time of war. The voices in closest proximity to the murdered woman at the time of her death were those least likely to be heard in the courtroom: women and children trying to sleep in the surrounding berths. The voices most influential in the courtroom were those of men not even aboard the train that night—the forensic investigator, the Los Angeles police detectives, the special agents for the railroad and Pullman Company. The most privileged voices were those of uniformed military men who claimed authority beyond their experience, station, or rank and acted with confidence that their own credibility would not be questioned.

Jurors with backgrounds and lives rooted in the mid-Willamette Valley were ill-equipped to sort out the truth from these stories—not because of their rurality, but precisely because they were so well versed in the popular culture that drew together rural and urban Oregonians in a racist period of our recent past. The stories that most influenced the way jurors heard those voices were crafted more than two decades earlier, in the fertile imaginations of true-crime storytellers and novelists. Those stories, which a young man in a crisp uniform retold in a militarized and chaotic landscape of disoriented passengers and racialized trainmen, captured the imagination of investigators, prosecutors, and reporters, who then retold them to a credulous public, all across the United States, at a time when that public was struggling through a fearful stage of an overwhelming war. Those stories, more than anything else, transported Robert E. Lee Folkes from the familiar landscapes of a relatively integrated South Central Los Angeles to the hostile and racially exclusive terrain of Albany, Oregon, and ultimately, to the sterile gas chamber at the Oregon State Penitentiary, in Salem, Oregon. Robert E. Lee Folkes' final trip, to his family's cemetery plot in central Los Angeles, was on a train that he couldn't see. That part of the story never made it into any of the newspapers that told so many others about that man, as if his real identity—his home, his family, and their history—did not exist at all.

Acknowledgments

Right out of the gate, this project reconfirmed how much historians rely on the committed professionals and lay workers who make it possible for us to pursue our craft. My apologies, in advance, for anyone I unintentionally leave out of this account. At the start, manic and dogged research by my longtime friend, Derek J. Phillips, helped me zero in on this case. Without his initial burst of energy, it is unlikely I would have taken on this project. Staff at the Albany Public Library and Elizabeth Nielsen at OSU's Special Collections & Archives Research Center graciously facilitated my earliest research forays in local records and newspapers.

At the Oregon State Archives, David Wendell guided me through OSSC files and records, and Layne Sawyer helped me navigate governors' files, offering invaluable advice on next steps. At the Newberry Library and Archives, Autumn Mather saved me inestimable time and resources while helping me secure vital research materials. Rukshana Singh, at the Southern California Library for Social Studies and Research, was welcoming and supportive, facilitating efforts to understand the world of Robert Folkes' youth. Dace Taub, at the USC Library and Archives, helped locate images and materials relating to life in South Central. Max Millard, who transformed Thomas Fleming's reminiscences and oral narratives into online publications, helped me access those materials. Glynn Martin, of the LA Police Historical Society, was helpful on matters regarding the LAPD. Mark Mullan, at the National Archives, helped me with inquiries regarding Wilson's service record. In Sacramento, CSRM Archivist Kathryn Santos and Librarian Cara Randall guided me through the extensive SPRR collections on the case and related matters. In the Sargeant Memorial Room at Norfolk Main Library in Virginia, Robert B. Hitchings and W. Troy Valos provided invaluable support and advice that helped me understand the world of Martha James' youth and also connected me with Mel Frizzell, Special Collections Assistant, and Dr. Peter C. Steward, both of Old Dominion University. In Minnesota, Cottonwood County Historical Society director Linda Fransen provided context on Harold Wilson.

At the Oregon State University Press, from the earliest stages, Mary Braun was empathetic and encouraging but also posed challenging and pointed questions in memorably far-ranging conversations that were always thoughtful and inspiring. Susan Campbell's insightful and incisive editing is responsible for whatever grace survives on these pages, while I am naturally to blame for any remaining errors. It is impossible to sufficiently thank Susan for this level of attentiveness and encouragement. I was also fortunate the project came under the expert and steady guidance of Micki Reaman, who, with Tom Booth and Marty Brown, so patiently guided me through the editing, design, and production process. The list of people who helped me secure the images appearing in this work also includes Christy Karpinski, Jo Ellen McKillop Dickie, and John Powell of the Newberry Library; Tricia Gesner of the Associated Press; Abigail Cape of the Union Pacific Railroad Museum; Diana Banning of the Portland City Archives; Scott Rook of OHS; Drew Vattiat of the *Oregonian*; and David D. Perata of David Perata Studios.

At Western Oregon University, Jeanne Deane assisted with arranging travel and managing research grant funds from WOU's Faculty Development Committee and from the Social Science Division. Steve Scheck, as dean of Liberal Arts and Sciences, supported my sabbatical and funded requests for computing and research materials. My faculty colleagues in the History Department provided a stimulating intellectual environment, as did the many graduate students and undergraduates who enrolled in courses where we worked through theoretical works and case studies cited in this book.

Most of all, however, my daughter, Mitra Geier, saw me through turbulent times, supplying enthusiasm and positive energy when the subject and project threatened to drag me down. She knows firsthand how dangerous these shadows and ghosts from the past can be. In the end, I leaned most heavily on Keni Sturgeon, who knows all about my ghosts and yet agrees to spend her life with me. I still find that amazing.

Notes on Sources

Abbreviations in notes reference the following archival collections and records.

CSRML, SPR: California State Railroad Museum Library, Southern Pacific Railroad, MS 26, Railroad Law Enforcement Collection, Box 5.

OSA: Oregon State Archives, Salem, Oregon.

GCF: Earl Snell, Record Group #93A-18, Office of the Governor (Governor Snell), Parole Files, 1943–1947, Box 7, OSA.

PPCR: Pullman Palace Car Company Records, Folkes Case (Record Group 05/01/03, Box 5), Newberry Library and Archives.

LAPHS: Los Angeles Police Historical Society.

OSP: Oregon State Police witness statements are cited in the text and notes by last name and date—e.g., Aaron (10 February 1943)—and are located in Witness Statements, Oregon State Police Files, CSRML, SPR, MS 26, Railroad Law Enforcement Collection, Box 5. PPC agent Sheehan also forwarded OSP witness statements to his superiors at the Pullman Palace Car Company's home offices, and these are located in the Pullman Palace Car Company Records (PPCR), Folkes Case (Record Group 05/01/03, Box 5), Newberry Library and Archives. Sheehan's cover letters accompanying those various collections of statements provide more substantive context for the circumstances in which the OSP collected the statements.

Stone Report: W. H. Stone reported on the trial to SPRR executives; the text and notes cite those communications as Stone, Report (page). These records (titled "Trial of Robert E. Lee Folkes Held Albany, Ore.—April 7 TO 23 1943") are located in CSRML, SPR, MS 26, Railroad Law Enforcement Collection, Box 4.

Transcript: *State of Oregon v. Robert E. Lee Folkes*, Transcript of Testimony, Oregon State Supreme Court Case Files, Case No. 14865, Drawer No 9449, Oregon State Archives, Salem, Oregon. This is the official transcript from the Folkes trial as found in the Oregon State Supreme Court (OSSC) case files, along with other supporting documentation from the appeal process. Pagination in the transcript document is sequential, with prefixes D and X indicating direct and cross-examination (and RD and RX for redirect). Those portions of the transcript not directly referencing a witness on the stand include only the page number, without the X or D designation. Notes follow the protocol "Transcript, name of voice, X-###."

Layton Trial Transcript: The official trial transcript from the Layton trial is also located in the OSSC case files and follows a similar protocol for pagination at the OSA as other transcripts.

Train 15 Order of Line from Portland: In a 25 January 1943 letter to PPC executive F. R. Callahan, PPC field agent H. C. Lincoln listed the order of cars in Train 15 the night of the murder as follows (beginning with the first car in line behind the locomotive): Mail car SP 4096; Baggage car SP 6197; Baggage car SP 6425; Baggage car 7235; DH Diner SP 10001; DH Diner T&NO 913; DH Diner C&NW 6901; Coach SP 1801; Coach SP 2311; Coach SP 2170; Coach SP 2692; Coach SP 2332; Tourist car E 4003; Tourist car D 4001; SP Diner 10110; Juana 60; East Ascot 69; Lake Chaplin 61. These eighteen cars, plus the locomotive, made up the train on which Martha James was murdered. Regular Pullman cars were assigned names (Juana, East Ascot, Lake Chaplin) but were referenced in PPC communications by their designated numbers (Pullman cars 60, 69, and 61, respectively). Coach cars were also commonly known as chair cars. PPC, Lincoln to Callahan (25 January 1943).

Notes

PROLOGUE

1   The organization was formally known as the Dining Car Cooks and Waiters Union, but contemporary reporters more commonly referred to it with various shortened names, including Dining Car Employees Union and Dining Car Workers Union. It will be referenced in this work by the latter term.

INTRODUCTION

1   "Governor Kitzhaber Statement on Capital Punishment," *Oregonlive* (22 November 2011), http://media. oregonlive.com/pacific-northwest-news/ other/Microsoft%20Word%20%20 Final%20Final%20JK%20Statement%20 on%20the%20Death%20Penalty.pdf.

2   Between 1864 and 1903, by state law, death sentences in Oregon were administered only through county sheriffs. The Oregon legislature revised that law in 1903, making legal executions the responsibility of state officials at the Oregon State Penitentiary in Salem. Prior to 1864, state law made no provision for administering the death penalty. http:// www.oregon.gov/doc/PUBAFF/pages/ cap_punishment/history.aspx.

3   This is not to say that there were no illegal lynchings in Oregon, but a report compiled from Tuskegee Institute archives detailing known lynchings from across the United States from 1882 to 1968 found only thirteen states with fewer lynchings than Oregon, where only one of twenty-one reported lynchings targeted a Black man. America's Black Holocaust Museum, however, lists four victims of extralegal executions in Oregon from 1891 through 1914. http:// law2.umkc.edu/faculty/projects/ftrials/ shipp/lynchingsstate.html; http://www. abhmuseum.org/category/lynching-victims-memorial/oregon.

4   This discussion of state-sponsored executions does not detail executions by local jurisdictions before 1904. Local executions of Black men in Oregon were not common, but they were also not unknown. On 20 March 1885, for example, in what many critics considered a notorious miscarriage of justice, Joe Drake, a Black man, was convicted of murdering Dave Swartz and was hanged at the Marion County courthouse, despite widespread claims he was falsely convicted. http://www.salemhistory. net/people/criminals.htm.; http://www. oregon.gov/doc/GECO/docs/pdf/ exec_table.pdf.

5   Three tabloid news organs catered to an apparently insatiable public appetite for reality-based narratives and dramatized court proceedings elevating cases from mundane trials to news spectaculars: William Randolph Hearst's *New York Daily Mirror*, Bernard McFadden's *Evening Graphic* (along with his *True Confessions* and *True Story* magazines), and Robert McCormick's *New York Illustrated Daily News*. John R. Brazil, "Murder Trials, Murder, and Twenties America," *American Quarterly* 33:2 (Summer 1981), pp. 163–164, http:// www.jstor.org/stable/2712314, accessed 20 June 2008.

6   Brazil, pp. 166–167.

7   Brazil, p. 167.

8   Brazil, pp. 170–171.

9   Brazil, pp. 177–178.

10 Leon Litwack, "Hellhounds," in *Trouble in Mind: Black Southerners in the Age of Jim Crow* (New York: Alfred A. Knopf, 1998), pp. 281–325.

11 Litwack, p. 285.

12 Litwack, pp. 306–307.

13 Paul Fussel explores social implications of wartime militarization in *Wartime: Understanding and Behavior in the Second World War* (New York: Oxford University Press, 1989).

14 Erasmo Gamboa, *Mexican Labor and World War Two: Braceros in the Pacific Northwest, 1942–1947* (Austin: University of Texas Press, 1990), pp. 27–47.

15 *1956 Report of the Linn County, Oregon Farm and Home Outlook Conference* (Albany, OR: Albany Printing Co., March 1956), http://ir.library.oregonstate.edu/xmlui/bitstream/handle/1957/13862/Linn1956.pdf?sequence=1.

16 A useful study of the Scottsboro case is Dan T. Carter, *Scottsboro: A Tragedy of the American South*, revised edition (Baton Rouge: Louisiana State University Press, 1969, rev. 1979).

17 *Camp Adair: The Story of Camp Adair, Oregon*, Online Exhibits, Benton County Historical Society & Museums, http://www.bentoncountymuseum.org/exhibitions/camp_adair/.

18 Regarding shipyard labor issues in Portland and Los Angeles, see Alonzo Smith and Quintard Taylor, "Racial Discrimination in the Workplace: A Study of Two West Coast Cities during the 1940s," *Journal of Ethnic Studies* 8:1 (Spring 1980), pp. 35–54. Taylor also compares Seattle and Portland experiences during the Second World War in "The Great Migration: The Afro-American Communities of Seattle and Portland during the 1940s," *Arizona and the West* 23:2 (Summer 1981), pp. 109–126.

19 William G. Robbins, *Landscapes of Conflict: The Oregon Story, 1940–2000* (Seattle: University of Washington Press, 2004), pp. 8–13.

20 Beth Tompkins Bates, *Pullman Porters and the Rise of Protest Politics in Black America, 1925–1945* (Chapel Hill: University of North Carolina Press, 2001), pp. 18–25; Douglas Flamming, *Bound for Freedom: Black Los Angeles in Jim Crow America* (Berkeley: University of California Press, 2005), p. 301.

21 The *Portland People's Observer*, for example, included a series of observations on the "New Negro" and the "habits" of certain "types" that were holding back the race. *People's Observer* (31 July 1943).

22 Bates, pp. 151–154, 158–162.

23 Amy G. Richter explores this concept in *Home on the Rails: Women, the Railroad, and the Rise of Public Domesticity* (Chapel Hill: University of North Carolina Press, 2005).

24 Stephen Kern, *A Cultural History of Causality: Science, Murder Novels, and Systems of Thought* (Princeton, NJ: Princeton University Press, 2006), pp. 286–287.

25 Brazil, p. 179.

26 Brazil, pp. 182–183.

CHAPTER ONE

1   *Corvallis Gazette-Times* (23 January 1943).

2   *Gazette-Times* (23 January 1943).

3   *Gazette-Times* (23 January 1943).

4   *Albany Democrat-Herald* (23 January 1943).

5   *Democrat-Herald* (23 January 1943).

6   *Democrat-Herald* (23 January 1943).

7   *Oregon Daily Journal* (23 January 1943 and 24 January 1943); *Norfolk Virginian-Pilot* (1 September 1942).

8   Carlos Schwantes, *The Pacific Northwest: An Interpretive History*, revised and enlarged edition (Lincoln: University of Nebraska Press, 1996), p. 330.

9   Gordon Wright, *The Ordeal of Total War: 1939–1945* (New York: Harper and Row, 1968), pp. 167–188; James MacGregor Burns, *Roosevelt: The Soldier of Freedom, 1940–1945* (New York: Harcourt Brace Jovanovich, 1970), pp. 305–330.

10 *Oregon Daily Journal* (24 January 1943).

11 *Oregon Daily Journal* (24 January 1943).

12 *Oregon Daily Journal* (24 January 1943).

13 *Oregon Daily Journal* (24 January 1943).

14 *Oregonian* (24 January 1943).

15 *Oregonian* (24 January 1943).

16 *Washington Post* (24 January 1943); *Oregon Daily Journal* (24 January 1943); *Oregonian* (25 January 1943).

17 *Washington Post* (25 January 1943).

18 *Oregonian* (25 January 1943).

19 *Oregon Daily Journal* (24 January 1943).

20 *Oregonian* (25 January 1943).

21 *Gazette-Times* (23 January 1943).

22 *Oregon Daily Journal* (24 January 1943); *Washington Post* (24 January 1943).

23 *Oregonian* (25 January 1943); *Oregon Daily Journal* (25 January 1943).

24 *Democrat-Herald* (25 January 1943).

25 *Democrat-Herald* (25 January 1943).

26 *Washington Post* (25 January 1943); *Norfolk Virginian-Pilot* (25 January 1943).

27 *Democrat-Herald* (25 January 1943).

28 *Oregonian* (26 January 1943).

29 *Oregon Daily Journal* (26 January 1943).

30 *Oregon Daily Journal* (26 January 1943).

31 *Oregon Daily Journal* (26 January 1943).

32 A grand jury report on police brutality in the Los Angeles Central Jail made nationwide news just before the trial, documenting police beatings and deaths of detainees during the period Folkes was held in that facility (*Oregon Daily Journal*, 13 March 1943). Systematic brutality at Central Jail continued after the trial, as evidenced in the savage beating of a young "Negro Boy" held there later that year (*California Eagle*, 23 December 1943).

33 *Democrat-Herald* (26 January 1943).

34 *Virginian-Pilot* (26 January 1943).

35 See below for discussion of the Brinson family's status and connections in Norfolk, Virginia, society circles.

36 *Oregonian* (27 January 1943).

37 The *Gazette-Times* (27 January 1943) did briefly note that Folkes denied committing the murder.

38 *Gazette-Times* (27–28 January 1943).

39 *Democrat-Herald* (27 January 1943).

40 *Oregonian* (28 January 1943).

41 *Democrat-Herald* (28 January 1943).

42 *Virginian-Pilot* (27 January 1943).

43 *Democrat-Herald* (28 January 1943).

44 *Democrat-Herald* (23 January 1943); *Oregonian* (24 January 1943); *Washington Post* (24 January 1943); *Gazette-Times* (25 January 1943); *Oregon Daily Journal* (26 January 1943).

45 Thomas Fleming, who worked in the same division of SPRR, describes the career ladder for dining car cooks: "As the fourth cook on a dining car… they were supposed to be teaching you how to become a cook. Then you got promoted to third cook, second cook, and eventually chef." Thomas C. Fleming, "Chapter 40: Fourth Cook on a Railroad Diner," in *The Columbia Free Press: Speaking Truth to Power* (24 June 1998), http://www.freepress.org/fleming/flemng40.html.

46 Eddie Dooley's statement to Lieutenant Howard, Oregon State Police, at Union Station, Portland, Oregon (4 February 1943), pp. 1–8, CSRML, SPR; hereafter Dooley (4 February 1943).

CHAPTER TWO

1 Quintard Taylor considers the American West a flawed refuge for Black migrants: *In Search of the Racial Frontier: African Americans in the American West, 1528–1990* (New York: W.W. Norton & Company, 1994).

2 Taylor notes the Great Migration concentrated formerly rural Black southerners in urban centers, forging a Black "urban ethos" in northern cities. Taylor, *The Forging of a Black Community: Seattle's Central District from 1870 through the Civil Rights Era* (Seattle: University of Washington Press, 1994), pp. 5–7. Flamming (pp. 45–50) observes, however, that the Great Migration was more evident in northeastern cities, less so in the West. Los Angeles, he argues, experienced only a "Modest Migration," continuing prewar rates of Black population growth.

3 The all-Black Waiters Union, Local 17, and the Dining Car Cooks and Waiters Union, Local 582, were among the most prominent labor organizations in South Central, argues Flamming, p. 248.

4 Flamming, p. 68.

5 Death registers in Arkansas list a Robert Folkes, of Jack, Arkansas, deceased 3 February 1921. Official birth records for young Robert could not be located.

6 The Progressive Farmers and Household Union of America was a self-help organization championing "the moral, material, and intellectual interest of our race."

7 Nan Elizabeth Woodruff, "The Killing Fields," in *American Congo: The African American Freedom Struggle in the Delta* (Cambridge, MA: Harvard University Press, 2003), pp. 74–109.

8 Woodruff, "The Killing Fields."

9 All extant records list the father as "Robert Folkes, deceased," or simply "deceased."

10 Taylor, *Racial Frontier*, pp. 222–257, indicates that a major share of immigrants to western cities during the 1930s and 1940s arrived from four states: Arkansas, Louisiana, Texas, and Oklahoma.

11 *Index to Register of Voters*, Los Angeles City Precinct No. 540, Los Angeles County, CA, 1932, 14th Congressional District, 38th Senatorial District, 62nd Assembly District, 2nd Supervisorial District, p. 564; Ancestry.com, California Voter Registrations, 1900–

1968 (database online) (Provo, UT: The Generations Network, 2008). Original data: State of California, United States, Great Register of Voters (Sacramento: California State Library).

12 *Index to Register of Voters*, Precinct No. 548, Los Angeles County, CA, 1934. 14th Congressional District, 38th Senatorial District, 62nd Assembly District, 2nd Supervisorial District, p. 624.

13 *Index to Register of Voters*, Precinct No. 371, Los Angeles County, CA, 1936, p. 391.

14 *Index to Register of Voters*, Precinct No. 371, Los Angeles County, CA, 1938, page 793.

15 Robert Folkes Minor's Release form (18 December 1941) and Robert Folkes Personal Record (5 April 1942) for Hospital Department, Personnel file, CSRML, SPR, MS 26, Box 5, Folder 14.

16 Jessie Folkes testified she lived with Robert Folkes at that address beginning February 1941, suggesting Folkes maintained his official address with his mother at 1250 E. 20th Street while also living with Jessie.

17 Renamed Martin Luther King Jr. Boulevard in the 1980s.

18 William E. Pollard to Earl Snell (12 December 1944), and Clara Folkes to Earl Snell (17 December 1944), GCF, OSA; *Index to Register of Voters*, Precinct No. 373, Los Angeles County, CA, 1944, p. 426.

19 Kathy Peiss, *Zoot Suit* (Philadelphia: University of Pennsylvania Press, 2005), explores the emergence of the style as an expression of personal taste and resistance to authority.

20 Josh Sides, *L.A. City Limits: African American Los Angeles from the Great Depression to the Present* (Berkeley: University of California Press, 2003), pp. 50–51.

21 *California Eagle* (3 February 1943).

22 *California Eagle* (3 March 1943).

23 Peiss, pp. 33–34.

24 Peiss, pp. 37–38.

25 Peiss, pp. 44–45.

26 *California Eagle* publisher and editor Charlotta Bass devoted a special issue to the Sleepy Lagoon case (8 September 1943) and later termed the case an attempt by local government to "terrorize an entire racial group." Charlotta A. Bass, *Forty Years: Memoirs from the Pages of a Newspaper* (Los Angeles: Charlotta Bass, 1960), pp. 124–125.

27 Sides, pp. 48–50.

28 Dooley (4 February 1943), pp. 2–3.

29 For examples, see *Southern Pacific Bulletin* (June 1942–September 1945).

30 Dooley (4 February 1943), pp. 2–3; "Record of Employment for Robert Folkes, 18 December 1941 to January 25 1943," H. E. Lynch to H. A. Butler (30 January 1943), CSRML, SPR, MS 26.

31 Dooley (4 February 1943), pp. 3–4.

32 Dooley (4 February 1943), p. 6; Statement of Clermont Baker (7 February 1943), CSRML, SPR, MS 26; hereafter Baker (7 February 1943).

33 Fleming, "Chapter 40: Fourth Cook on a Railroad Diner."

34 Baker (7 February 1943), p. 4; Fleming, "Chapter 40: Fourth Cook on a Railroad Diner."

35 Baker (7 February 1943), p. 4.

36 Statement of William G. Aaron to OSP sergeant Thos. J. Sheridan at Milwaukie Office, Department of State Police, Portland, Oregon (10 February 1943), pp. 1–2, CSRML, SPR, MS 26.

37 Baker (7 February 1943), p. 1.

38 Baker (28 January 1943), p. 5.

39 "Down Central Avenue and Beyond," University of Southern California, Center for Scholarly Technology, 17 April 2005, http://www.researchchannel.org/prog/displayevent.aspx?rID=3373; "The Bar at the Club Alabam, Los Angeles, ca. 1941–1945," University of Southern California, Libraries, Record ID: scl-m0476.

40 "Down Central Avenue and Beyond."

41 "Down Central Avenue and Beyond"; Fleming, "Chapter 43: Racial Attitudes on the Railroad."

42 Bass, pp. 121–123; Sides, pp. 139–141.

43 Flamming, pp. 310–311.

44 Sides, pp. 45–46.

45 Sides, pp. 46–47.

46 Sides, pp. 46–48.

47 Bass, pp. 70–71.

48 Larry Tye, *Rising from the Rails: Pullman Porters and the Making of the Black Middle Class* (New York: Henry Holt and Company, 2004), pp. 194–195.

49 *Southern Pacific Bulletin* (June 1942), cover and p. 9.

50 *Southern Pacific Bulletin* (August 1942), p. 10.

51 *Southern Pacific Bulletin* (November 1942), pp. 5–6.

52 Bass, p. 84.

53 *Southern Pacific Bulletin* (November 1942), pp. 8–9.

54 *Southern Pacific Bulletin* (November 1942), pp. 10–11.

55 Bass, p. 84–85.

56 *Southern Pacific Bulletin* (December 1942), p. 1.

57 *Southern Pacific Bulletin* (January 1943), pp. 4–7, 10, 11.

58 *Southern Pacific Bulletin* (November 1941), [n.p.].

59 *Southern Pacific Bulletin* (January 1943), p. 15.

60 *Southern Pacific Bulletin* (January 1943), p. 19.

61 *Southern Pacific Bulletin* (December 1942), p. 6.

62 *Southern Pacific Bulletin* (December 1942), p. 8.

63 *Southern Pacific Bulletin* (December 1942), p. 11.

64 *Southern Pacific Bulletin* (December 1942, March 1943, May 1943, August 1943).

65 *Southern Pacific Bulletin* (March 1943), p. 13.

66 *Southern Pacific Bulletin* (June 1943), p. 17.

67 *Southern Pacific Bulletin* (July 1943), p. 24.

68 *Southern Pacific Bulletin* (August 1943), p. 13.

69 *Southern Pacific Bulletin* (September 1943), back cover.

70 *Southern Pacific Bulletin* (February 1944), p. 3. The article was headlined "Stretching a Point," with an accompanying graphic depicting two black-face cartoon figures in cook outfits stretching a "V 1" Ration Stamp over a plate of food. *Southern Pacific Bulletin* (November 1944), pp. 22, 24.

71 *Southern Pacific Bulletin* (February 1944), pp. 11, 21–22. Passenger volume for 1943 was reportedly 205 percent higher than in 1920, the all-time peak year for Southern Pacific prior to that time. *Southern Pacific Bulletin* (November 1944), p. 24.

72 *California Eagle* (8 January and 22 January 1943).

73 *California Eagle* (15 January 1943).

74 *California Eagle* (1 April 1943).

75 *California Eagle* (22 January 1943).

76 *Oregon Daily Journal* (7 April 1943).

77 *Democrat-Herald* (7 April 1943).

78 *Oregon Daily Journal* (18 April 1943).

79 *Democrat-Herald* (23 April 1943).

80 *California Eagle* (8 July 1943).

81 Bass, p. 72.

CHAPTER THREE

1 Statement of William H. Banks (25 January 1943), OSP Files, CSRML, SPR, MS 26, Box 5; hereafter Banks (25 January 1943).

2 Banks (25 January 1943), p. 1.

3 Banks (25 January 1943), pp. 2–6.

4 Banks (25 January 1943), p. 6.

5 Banks (25 January 1943), p. 2.

6 Banks (25 January 1943), p. 4.

7 Banks (25 January 1943), p. 7.

8 Banks (25 January 1943), p. 3.

9 Banks (25 January 1943), p. 2.

10 Banks (25 January 1943), p. 4.

11 Banks (25 January 1943), p. 4.

12 Enell (25 January 1943), pp. 1–3, OSP Files, CSRML, SPR.

13 Photo caption with photo no. 4, Joseph Beeman Reports, CSRML, SPR, MS 26, Box 4, Folder 9.

14 Harold R. Wilson Statement on board S.P. Train No. 15 (23 January 1943), p. 1, OSP Files, CSRML, SPR, MS 26, Box 5, Folder 9; hereafter Wilson (23 January 1943).

15 Wilson (23 January 1943), p. 1.

16 Wilson (23 January 1943), pp. 2–3.

17 Special Agent Frederick A. Taylor to D. O'Connell (29 January 1943), OSP Files, CSRML, SPR, MS 26; hereafter Taylor to D. O'Connell (29 January 1943); Officer reports on the conduct of the investigation, Beeman File, CSRML, SPR, Box 5, Folder 1; Banich to D. O'Connell (31 January 1943).

18 Taylor to D. O'Connell (29 January 1943).

19 Taylor to D. O'Connell (29 January 1943).

20 Patricia Cline Cohen, in *The Murder of Helen Jewett: The Life and Death of a Prostitute in Nineteenth-Century New York* (New York: Alfred A. Knopf, 1998), explores this staple of the true-crime genre, examining a celebrated murder mystery from the time Poe innovated the approach.

21 Taylor to D. O'Connell (29 January 1943).

22 Taylor to D. O'Connell (29 January 1943).

23 Taylor to D. O'Connell (29 January 1943).

24 Taylor to D. O'Connell (29 January 1943).

25 Taylor to D. O'Connell (29 January 1943).

26 Taylor to D. O'Connell (29 January 1943).

27 Taylor to D. O'Connell (29 January 1943).

28 The conductor held Train 15 at Dunsmuir while Banich took a call from the Klamath County sheriff's office, Banich to D. O'Connell (31 January 1943), OSP Files, CSRML, SPR, MS 26; hereafter Banich to D. O'Connell (31 January 1943).

29 Wilson (23 January 1943), pp. 2–3.

30 Robert Folkes statement (signed) to John Huber on board Train 15 (23 January 1943), CSRML, SPR, MS 26; hereafter Robert Folkes statement (signed) (23 January 1943).

31 Taylor to D. O'Connell (29 January 1943).

32 Taylor to D. O'Connell (29 January 1943).

33 R. M. Kelso was chief watertender, US Navy, from El Cajon, California, about six feet two inches tall, fifty-one years old at the time of these events. Statement of R. M. Kelso to John Huber (23 January 1943); Banich to D. O'Connell (2 February 1943), CSRML, SPR, MS 26.

34 Banich to D. O'Connell (31 January 1943).

35 Banich to D. O'Connell (31 January 1943).

36 Statement of R. M. Kelso to John Huber (23 January 1943), hereafter Kelso (23 January 1943); Banich to D. O'Connell (2 February 1943).

37 Banich to D. O'Connell (31 January 1943).

38 Robert Folkes statement (23 January 1943).

39 Robert Folkes statement (signed) to John Huber (23 January 1943).

40 Robert Folkes statement (signed) to George Banich on board Train 15 (24 January 1943); hereafter Robert Folkes statement (signed) (24 January 1943).

41 Kelso (23 January 1943).

42 Statement of H. M. Hughes (23 January 1943), CSRML, SPR.

43 Statement of Corporal William W. Van Dyke (23 January 1943), CSRML, SPR.

44 Dorothy Van Dyke, for example, was first interviewed at her home in San Jose on 27 March 1943 by an SPRR investigator. Green's report of that interview to Weinrick included the observation that she stated she had not been interviewed prior to his visit. Raymond S. Green to Mr. D. O'Connell (27 March 1943), CSRML, SPR, MS 26.

45 Statement of Maxine S. Flieder (23 January 1943), witnessed by George Banich, CSRML, SPR.

46 Statement of Mrs. Davis Chamberlin (23 January 1943), witnessed by John Huber, CSRML, SPR.

47 Statement of Mrs. W. H. Donnelly (23 January 1943), CSRML, SPR.

48 Statement of Mrs. Alton Bailey (25 March 1943), witnessed by R. L. Boone, CSRML, SPR.

CHAPTER FOUR

1 *State of Oregon v. Robert E. Lee Folkes.* Transcript of Testimony, Oregon State Supreme Court Case Files, Oregon State Archives, Salem, Oregon (hereafter Transcript), pp. 428, 555. The train arrived in Los Angeles at 8:20 a.m. on 25 January 1943. Transcript, Tetrick D-428, Tetrick X-555.

2 Apparently this was Arthur Stein, who left the Southern Pacific shortly after the murder and was at Camp Wolters, in Texas, when investigators tracked him down in preparation for trial.

3 Statement of Benjamin Russell Johnson (2 February 1943), OSP Files, CSRML, SPR, MS 26.

4 Based on the following documents, all from OSP Files, CSRML, SPR, MS 26: Statement of Clermont Baker (7 February 1943); Statement of Sterling Bolton (8 February 1943); Statement of Edward Ralph Smith (7 February 1943); Statement of Ralph Hamilton Hickman (7 February 1943); Statement of Elmer Devereaux (4 February 1943); Statement of Booker T. Johnson (4 February 1943); Statement of John Logan (4 February 1943); Statement of Elmer White (4 February 1943); Statement of Elmer White (1 February 1943). Hereafter cited by the person's last name and date of their statement.

5 Logan (4 February 1943).

6 Statement of Charles Greenman (1 February 1943), CSRML, SPR.

7 White (4 February 1943).

8 White (4 February 1943); White (1 February 1943).

9 Baker (7 February 1943).

10 Smith (7 February 1943).

11 Devereaux (4 February 1943).

12 Smith (7 February 1943).

13 White (4 February 1943); White (1 February 1943).

14 Hickman (7 February 1943).

15 Johnson (4 February 1943).

16 Logan (4 February 1943).

17 Greenman (1 February 1943).

18 In his earlier statement (1 February 1943), Greenman stated that White joined the party for a few minutes, but in his second statement (4 February 1943), he claimed White spoke with him only after the party.

19 Greenman (4 February 1943); Greenman (1 February 1943).

20 Sheehan to Gibney (2 February 1943), PPCR.

21 L. W. Snider to Mr. L. R. Armstrong (11 February 1943), PPCR.

22 Sheehan to Gibney (2 February 1943), PPCR.

23 Designation in a job considered "vital to the war effort" sometimes prevented railroad workers from quitting their jobs to take other, more lucrative jobs that were

opening up in war industries. Tye, pp. 194–195.

24 In the aftermath of the murder, Sheehan reported that Albany locals had complained to company officials that their Pullman porters were lazy and shiftless, and failed to provide sufficient security aboard their cars.

25 D. O'Connell to Mr. C. F. Donatin (9 February 1943), PPCR.

26 *Gazette-Times* (27 January 1943 and 29 January 1943); *Oregonian* (28 January 1943); *Oregon Daily Journal* (28 January 1943); *Democrat-Herald* (27 January 1943, 28 January 1943, 29 January 1943, 1 February 1943); Sheehan to Gibney (13 February 1943), PPCR.

27 Sheehan to Gibney (13 February 1943 and 18 February 1943), PPCR.

28 Sheehan to Gibney (18 February 1943), PPCR.

29 Sheehan to J. J. Hodges (26 February 1943); Hodges to Sheehan (8 March 1943); both PPCR.

30 Sheehan to Gibney (26 February 1943), PPCR.

31 Sheehan to Gibney (26 February 1943), PPCR.

32 C. M. Fitzgerald to L. W. Snider (11 March 1943), PPCR.

33 Sheehan to Gibney (19 March 1943); Sheehan to Gibney (20 March 1943); H. C. Lincoln to F. R. Callahan (20 March 1943); Gibney to Sheehan (25 March 1943); all in PPCR.

34 Sheehan to Gibney (20 March 1943), PPCR.

35 Snider to Gibney (31 March 1943), PPCR.

36 Sheehan to Gibney (31 March 1943); Sheehan to Weinrick (1 April 1943); Weinrick to Sheehan (30 March 1943); Weinrick to D. O'Connell (30 March 1943); all in PPCR.

37 Sheehan to Gibney (7 April 1943), PPCR.

38 Sheehan to G. H. Bigney [sic] (8 April 1943); Sheehan to G. H. Gibney (7 April 1943); both in PPCR.

39 Sheehan to Gibney (7 April 1943), PPCR.

40 Sheehan to Gibney (7 April 1943), PPCR.

41 Sheehan to Gibney (7 April 1943), PPCR.

42 Sheehan to Gibney (7 April 1943), PPCR.

43 Sheehan to Gibney (7 April 1943), PPCR.

44 Sheehan to Gibney (7 April 1943), PPCR.

45 Sheehan to Gibney (11 April 1943), PPCR.

46 Sheehan to Gibney (11 April 1943), PPCR.

47 Sheehan to Gibney (11 April 1943), PPCR.

48 Sheehan to Gibney (15 April 1943), PPCR.

49 Sheehan to Gibney (15 April 1943), PPCR.

50 Sheehan to Gibney (17 April 1943), PPCR.

51 Sheehan to Gibney (19 April 1943), PPCR.

52 Sheehan to Gibney (19 April 1943), PPCR.

53 *California Eagle* (8 January 1943).

54 Sheehan to Gibney (20 April 1943), PPCR.

55 *Los Angeles Sentinel* (28 January 1943).

56 *Los Angeles Sentinel* (28 January 1943).

57 *Los Angeles Sentinel* (28 January 1943).

58 *Los Angeles Sentinel* (28 January 1943).

59 *Los Angeles Sentinel* (28 January 1943).

60 Of particular note, the death of Stanley Beebe while in custody at Central Jail led to the indictment of several members of the Los Angeles police (Transcript, Tetrick X-463, X-464). Tetrick denied that any of the officers who interrogated Folkes were involved in the death of Beebe, who had died in custody the previous month, but before Lomax could ask if he knew whether any of the officers who handled Folkes at Central Jail were involved in handling Beebe, Judge Lewelling interrupted and declared, "We are not going to try the police force of Los Angeles in this court" (X-464). Lomax, during his cross-examination, suggested that someone at Central Jail said to Folkes, "All we need is some rope and a tree and we'll fix you up right" (X-465); *Oregon Daily Journal* (13 March 1943); Sides, pp. 136–137.

61 The first statement was later introduced at trial as Defense Exhibit 2, while prosecutors introduced the second statement as State's Exhibit K. *State of Oregon v. Robert E. Lee Folkes.* They subsequently referred to them as the Bechtel Statement and the Lyman Statement, respectively. Transcript, pp. 683–688; Bechtel Statement (26 January 1943); Lyman Statement (27 January 1943).

62 These were likely her husband, Richard James, and the Keatons. Thos. J. Sheridan, Officer's Report (25 January 1943), OSP Files, CSRML, SPR, MS 21, Box 5, Folder 8.

63 *California Eagle* (5 October 1944).

64 Transcript, pp. 545–546.

65 Transcript, p. 604.
66 Lomax then asked if prosecutors had any other statements purportedly made by Folkes. Weinrick evaded the question by asking "Taken at Los Angeles?" Lomax responded, "Correct." Weinrick answered "No." Later, he introduced a lengthy "statement" that Folkes allegedly made in Albany, after he was transported there from Los Angeles. Transcript, pp. 605–606.
67 Transcript, pp. 794–797.
68 *Democrat-Herald* (26 January 1943); Transcript, pp. 801–802.
69 Transcript, p. 800.
70 Transcript, pp. 598–600.
71 Transcript, pp. 649–650.
72 *Virginian-Pilot* (27 January 1943).
73 Transcript, pp. 649–650; Lyman Statement, pp. 1–2.
74 Lyman Statement, pp. 1–2.
75 Lyman Statement, p. 2.
76 Lyman Statement, p. 3.
77 Lyman Statement, p. 4.

CHAPTER FIVE

1 See Justice Rossman's dissent, as discussed in later chapters.
2 The Klan presence in Oregon is well documented in works that include Lawrence Saalfeld, *Forces of Prejudice in Oregon, 1920–25* (Portland: Archdiocesan Historical Commission, 1984); Eckard Toy, "The Ku Klux Klan in Oregon," in *Experiences in a Promised Land: Essays in Pacific Northwest History,* edited by G. Thomas Edwards and Carlos A. Schwantes (Seattle: University of Washington Press, 1986); and a volume by the Oregon Northwest Black Pioneers, with an emphasis on the state capital of Salem and surrounding areas, *Perseverance: A History of African Americans in Oregon's Marion and Polk Counties* (Salem: Oregon Northwest Black Pioneers, 2011). Election results and ballot measures relating to exclusion and suffrage are summarized in the *Oregon Blue Book: Almanac and Fact Book, 2013–2014* (Salem, Oregon: Office of the Secretary of State, 2013), pp. 295–297.
3 Senate Bill 40, Oregon Laws, 1943 (Chapter 75), p. 81. Approved by governor 18 February 1943, filed in office of the secretary of state 19 February 1943.
4 *Democrat-Herald* (1 March 1943).
5 Transcript, p. 3.
6 *Oregon Daily Journal* (7 April 1943). There is no surviving transcript of the process of selection of jurors. It is not included in the trial transcript filed with the appeal to the OSSC, and there are no surviving transcripts from the case at the Linn County courthouse. Transcript, p. 3.
7 *Oregonian* (8 April 1943).
8 *Democrat-Herald* (8 April 1943).
9 *Oregonian* (8 April 1943).
10 *Democrat-Herald* (8 April 1943).
11 *Oregonian* (9 April 1943). Hometowns of the jurors (women all listed as "Mrs."): Albany area—three (two women, one man); Harrisburg area—one woman; Lyons area—two women; Shedd area— one woman; Brownsville area—one woman; Tangent area—one woman; Lebanon area—one man (plus one woman alternate); Scio area—one man; Sweet Home area—one man.
     Women: Edith Elkins (Albany, farm wife), Lola Junkins (Harrisburg/Albany, housewife), Clara Horner (Lyons, housewife), Lena Swank (Albany, housewife), Beatrice Hiatt (Lyons, housewife), Clara Sprenger (Shedd, farm wife), Nannie L. Isom (Brownsville, housewife), Lottie Hense (Tangent, housewife).
     Men: John Brown (Lebanon, paper mill worker), John Densmore Jr. (Scio, mill and grain elevator operator), Asa Smith (Sweet Home, farmer), and Lee Doerfler (Albany, plywood worker). Alternate juror: Veda Whetstone (Lebanon, housewife); *Oregon Daily Journal* (9 April 1943), p. 6. In a separate reference to the jury, in an article about the judge's instructions to jurors just before they began their deliberations, one newspaper editor described them as "mostly farm folk." *Gazette-Times* (21 April 1943).
12 The *Journal* published a photo of the twelve jurors and one alternate. *Oregon Daily Journal* (21 April 1943).
13 Recent works that discuss Edgar Allan Poe and Arthur Conan Doyle in relation to the "closed room" murder-mystery genre include Amy Gilman Srebnick, *The Mysterious Death of Mary Rogers: Sex and Culture in Nineteenth Century New York* (New York: Oxford University Press, 1995); Daniel Stashower, *The Beautiful Cigar Girl: Mary Rogers, Edgar Allan Poe, and the Invention of Murder* (New York: Dutton, 2006); Eric H. Monkkonen, *Murder in New York City* (Berkeley: University of California Press, 2001); and Karen Haltunen, *Murder Most Foul: The Killer and the American Gothic Imagination* (Cambridge, MA: Harvard University Press, 1998).

14 Southern Pacific Railroad representative W. H. Stone compiled a daily digest of the trial for his employer, which, together with other news reports, details courtroom proceedings more completely than the official record that Lewelling allowed in the trial transcript. W. H. Stone, "Trial of Robert E. Lee Folkes" report (7 April–23 April 1943) to Mr. D. O'Connell (hereafter Stone, Report); Transcript, pp. 5–9.

15 Stone, Report, pp. 1–2; *Oregonian* (9 April 1943); *Democrat-Herald* (9 April 1943); Transcript, pp. 10–14.

16 Stone, Report, pp. 1–3; *Oregonian* (9 April 1943), p. 3.

17 Transcript, p. 15.

18 *Oregonian* (9 April 1943); *Oregon Daily Journal* (9 April 1943).

19 1940 Census Population Report, p. 989. As of the 1940 census, the Albany population was 5,654 and Lebanon's was 2,729, while all other towns in Linn County had fewer than 2,000 people—the minimum for designation as an "urban" center. The census lumped most towns in with rural districts to arrive at population figures for each district that, with few exceptions, numbered fewer than 1,000 people each. The total population for the county in 1940 was 30,485. 1940 Census Population Report, p. 1024. Nearly half the population of the county that year was classified as "rural farm" (14,110). The median years of schooling for Portland residents, by contrast, was over ten, according to the same census (p. 1044).

20 *Oregon Daily Journal* (9 April 1943).

21 Stone, Report, p. 2.

22 *Oregon Daily Journal* (9 April 1943); Trial Transcript, p. 20.

23 Stone, Report, p. 3; *Democrat-Herald* (9 April 1943).

24 Transcript, Wilson, X-181.

25 Transcript, Bryant, D-89–91, D-96.

26 Transcript, Bryant, X-106.

27 Transcript, Bryant, X-107.

28 Transcript, Hoffert, D-109.

29 Transcript, Reynolds, D-111, D-112.

30 Transcript, Chamberlin, D-115–117.

31 Transcript, Chamberlin, X-123.

32 Transcript, Chamberlin, D-118.

33 Transcript, Chamberlin, X-123–125.

34 Transcript, Chamberlin, D-119.

35 Stone, Report, pp. 9–10.

36 Transcript, Wilson, D-130.

37 Transcript, Wilson, D-132, D-133.

38 Transcript, Wilson, D-133.

39 Transcript, Wilson, D-135, D-136.

40 Transcript, Wilson, D-137–140.

41 Transcript, Wilson, D-138, X-186.

42 Transcript, Wilson, D-147, D-148.

43 Transcript, Wilson, D-149, D-150.

44 Transcript, Wilson, D-151.

45 Transcript, Wilson, D-151.

46 Transcript, Wilson, D-156, D-157.

47 Transcript, Wilson, D-164–168.

48 See, for example, Transcript, Wilson, X-176.

49 Transcript, Wilson, X-179.

50 Transcript, Wilson, X-181, X-182.

51 Transcript, Wilson, X-186, X-187.

52 Transcript, Wilson, X-190, X-191.

53 Transcript, Wilson, X-195.

54 Transcript, Wilson, X-200–203.

55 Transcript, Norton, D-231, D-232.

56 Transcript, Norton, D-233.

57 Transcript, Norton, X-242.

58 Transcript, Norton, D-236, D-237.

59 Transcript, Norton, X-253, X-254.

60 Transcript, Norton, X-257.

61 Transcript, Wasserman, D-274.

62 Transcript, Wasserman, D-276.

63 Transcript, Wasserman, D-276, D-277.

64 Stone, Report, p. 13.

65 Transcript, Wasserman, X-280.

66 Transcript, Kelso, D-304, X-305, X-306.

67 Stone, Report, p. 15.

68 Stone, Report, pp. 15–17.

69 Stone, Report, p. 17.

70 Transcript, Hughes, D-314–319.

71 Transcript, Hughes, D-322, X-345.

72 Transcript, Hughes, X-342.

73 Transcript, Hughes, RD-362.

74 Transcript, Hughes, RD-364.

75 Transcript, Champlin, D-373.

76 Transcript, Tetrick, D-434.

77 Transcript, Rasmussen, D-478.

78 Transcript, Rasmussen, D-479.

79 Transcript, Tetrick, X-461, X-462.

80 Transcript, pp. 497–498.

81 Transcript, p. 508.

82 Transcript, Tetrick, D-537.

83 Transcript, Shelton, D-608.

84 Transcript Shelton, X-609–611.

85 Transcript, Shelton, X-609–612.

86 Transcript, p. 735.

87 Transcript, Tetrick, D-737, D-738.

88 Transcript, Shaw, D-749–751.

89 Transcript, Shaw, RD-753–754.

90 Transcript, Shaw, RD-755–RX-757.

91 Transcript, Sibley, D-764, X-766.

92 Transcript, Scurry, D-769.

93 Transcript, Scurry, D-770.

94 Transcript, Greenman, D-783, X-784.
95 Transcript, p. 803.
96 Transcript, p. 804.
97 Transcript, Houston, D-805.
98 Transcript, p. 815.
99 Transcript, pp. 816–823.
100 Transcript, pp. 824–826.
101 Stone, Report, pp. 43–44.

CHAPTER SIX

1 *Oregon Daily Journal* (23 April 1943).
2 *Democrat-Herald* (23 April 1943); *Virginian-Pilot* (23 April 1943).
3 *Oregon Daily Journal* (23 April 1943).
4 William H. Harris, *The Harder We Run: Black Workers since the Civil War* (New York: Oxford University Press, 1982), pp. 114–117.
5 Harris, p. 118.
6 See, for example, the *People's Observer* (29 June 1943).
7 Elizabeth McLagan, *A Peculiar Paradise: A History of Blacks in Oregon, 1788–1940* (Portland, OR: The Georgian Press, 1980), pp. 173–174.
8 *People's Observer* (29 June 1943).
9 McLagan, pp. 175–177.
10 *People's Observer* (29 June 1943).
11 The *Gazette-Times*, for example, completely ignored the case, with no apparent coverage between the time Lewelling sentenced Folkes to death and the date scheduled for the execution.
12 *People's Observer* (29 June 1943).
13 *People's Observer* (29 June 1943).
14 *People's Observer* (29 June 1943).
15 *People's Observer* (8 July 1943).
16 *People's Observer* (31 July 1943).
17 *People's Observer* (31 July 1943).
18 *People's Observer* (18 August 1943).
19 *California Eagle* (2 September 1943).
20 *People's Observer* (21 September 1943).
21 *People's Observer* (20 October 1943).
22 Linn County DA Harlow Weinrick, according to notations on the transcript and in a certification letter from the Linn Count court clerk, I. M. Russell, filed a certified copy with the Oregon Supreme Court on 13 October 1943. Weinrick also certified "Transcript Service" on 22 November 1943. The clerk for the OSSC acknowledged receipt of the transcript, including a bill of exceptions (the basis for appeal by the defense), with two volumes of testimony, exhibits, and judgement roll, in a letter to the Linn County clerk on 24 November 1943. Between May and November, Lomax repeatedly petitioned the circuit court, seeking an extension for filing an appeal due to delays by the prosecutor's office in preparing and delivering to defense attorneys the complete trial transcript, which the defense required in order to prepare the appellant's brief with the court.
23 Page numbers refer to the Transcript.
24 *Norfolk Journal and Guide* (1 May 1943).
25 *Democrat-Herald* (15 May 1943).
26 *California Eagle* (20 May 1943).
27 *California Eagle* (27 May 1943).
28 *California Eagle* (27 May 1943).
29 *California Eagle* (10 June 1943).
30 Bill of Exceptions, *State v. Folkes*, 12 pp. Filed 24 November 1943, Supreme Court, State of Oregon, Case No. 14865, Drawer No. 9449, OSA.
31 *California Eagle* (27 January 1944).
32 *Democrat-Herald* (21 June 1944), p. 1.
33 Brand, *State v. Folkes* (174 Or. July '44, *Oregon Reports*, OSSC), pp. 571–572; hereafter opinions as [justice's name], *State v. Folkes*.
34 Oral Arguments, *State of Oregon, Respondent, v. Robert E. Lee Folkes, Appellant*, 1 March 1944, Oregon State Supreme Court Case File, Case No. 14865, Drawer No. 9449, OSA.
35 Oral Arguments, p. 2.
36 Oral Arguments, p. 3.
37 Oral Arguments, p. 10.
38 Oral Arguments, p. 14.
39 Brand, *State v. Folkes*, pp. 572–573.
40 Brand, *State v. Folkes*, p. 575.
41 Brand, *State v. Folkes*, p. 577.
42 Brand, *State v. Folkes*, p. 576.
43 Brand, *State v. Folkes*, p. 578.
44 Brand, *State v. Folkes*, p. 579.
45 Brand, *State v. Folkes*, p. 585.
46 Brand, *State v. Folkes*, p. 586.
47 Sheldon Goldman, *Constitutional Law and Supreme Court Decisionmaking: Cases and Essays* (New York: Harper and Row, 1982), p. 331.
48 Brand, *State v. Folkes*, p. 588.
49 Brand, *State v. Folkes*, pp. 591–593.
50 Brand, *State v. Folkes*, p. 593.
51 Brand, *State v. Folkes*, p. 597.
52 Brand, *State v. Folkes*, pp. 608–611.
53 Brand, *State v. Folkes*, pp. 611–616.
54 Brand, *State v. Folkes*, p. 616.
55 Brand, *State v. Folkes*, pp. 618–620.
56 Belt, *State v. Folkes*, p. 622.
57 Lusk, *State v. Folkes*, pp. 622–636.

58 Lusk, *State v. Folkes*, p. 630.

59 Lusk, *State v. Folkes*, p. 630.

60 Lusk, *State v. Folkes*, p. 631.

61 Rossman, *State v. Folkes*, p. 668.

62 *Democrat-Herald* (17 July 1944).

63 *California Eagle* (22 June 1944).

64 *California Eagle* (22 June 1944).

65 *California Eagle* (3 August 1944).

66 *People's Observer* (7 August 1944).

67 *Virginian-Pilot* (30 September 1944); *California Eagle* (5 October 1944); *Democrat-Herald* (20 November 1944).

68 *Democrat-Herald* (10 February 1943).

69 *Oregon Daily Journal* (26 April 1943).

70 *Democrat-Herald* (18 and 29 December 1944).

71 *People's Observer* (30 November 1944). The actual title for this pamphlet was *The FACTS in the Robert Folkes Case*, but it was referenced in McClendon's newspaper with this shorter name. Hereafter, all references to this pamphlet will go by the correct, full name as it appeared on the cover of the document.

CHAPTER SEVEN

1 Robbins explores one side of this notion of a uniquely Oregon spirit of constructive optimism and hopes for a progressive postwar spirit in *Landscapes of Conflict*, pp. xvii–xxi, 15–30. David Peterson del Mar focuses more on experiences with race, ethnicity, and gender in relation to the influx of new residents and policies of exclusion and control during the war with an emphasis on the notion of Oregon exceptionalism in *Oregon's Promise: An Interpretive History* (Corvallis: Oregon State University Press, 2003), pp. 198–209.

2 *People's Observer* (18 January 1945).

3 Governor's Clemency Files (December 1944–January 1945), OSA (hereafter GCF, OSA).

4 Biographical Files, State of Oregon Law Library.

5 Biographical Files, State of Oregon Law Library.

6 *The FACTS in the Robert Folkes Case* (Portland, OR: NAACP, Portland Branch, [Fall 1944]), p. 2.

7 William R. Long, *A Tortured History: The Story of Capital Punishment in Oregon* (Eugene: Oregon Criminal Defense Lawyers Association, 1999), pp. 5–15.

8 *The FACTS in the Robert Folkes Case*, p. 3

9 *The FACTS in the Robert Folkes Case*, p. 4.

10 *California Eagle* (30 November 1944).

11 Layton Trial Transcript, Layton-D-353, Oregon State Supreme Court Case Files, OSA.

12 *State v. Layton* (174 Or. May '44), p. 232.

13 *State v. Layton* (174 Or. May '44), pp. 232–233.

14 In a subsequent letter on the eve of Layton's execution, psychiatrist Herman A. Dickel wrote to Snell, certifying his professional opinion that the defendant exhibited "extremely limited mental capacity," which he described as "a mental age of nine years . . . or an IQ of 65." Dickel to Snell (2 December 1944), GCF, OSA.

15 Harry G. Hoy to Snell (30 October 1944 and 2 December 1944), GCF, OSA.

16 Hoy to Snell (3 November 1944), GCF, OSA.

17 Rossman, *State v. Folkes*, p. 636.

18 *State v. Folkes*, pp. 638–639.

19 Rossman, *State v. Folkes*, p. 643.

20 Rossman, *State v. Folkes*, p. 648.

21 Rossman, *State v. Folkes*, pp. 652–654.

22 Rossman, *State v. Folkes*, pp. 654–655.

23 Rossman, *State v. Folkes*, p. 657.

24 Rossman, *State v. Folkes*, p. 658.

25 Rossman, *State v. Folkes*, pp. 658–659.

26 Rossman, *State v. Folkes*, pp. 662–663.

27 Rossman, *State v. Folkes*, p. 663.

28 Rossman, *State v. Folkes*, p. 664–665.

29 Rossman, *State v. Folkes*, p. 666.

30 Snell to Mrs. Paul Steidel (26 December 1944), GCF, OSA.

31 Snell to Ormand Case (26 December 1944), GCF, OSA.

32 Snell to Browning C. Allen (7 December 1944), GCF, OSA.

33 Darden to Snell (21 December 1944), GCF, OSA.

34 Unattributed note, GCF, OSA.

35 Nunn to Snell (15 December 1944), GCF, OSA.

36 Sims to Snell (19 December 1944), GCF, OSA.

37 Swopes to Snell (21 December 1944), GCF, OSA.

38 Jackson to Snell (20 December 1944), GCF, OSA.

39 Snell to Jackson (22 December 1944), GCF, OSA.

40 Newton to Snell (21 December 1944), GCF, OSA.

41 Sturman to Snell (28 December 1944), GCF, OSA.

42 Snell to Sturman (2 January 1944), GCF, OSA.

43 O'Neal to Snell (23 December 1944), GCF, OSA.

44 Snell to O'Neal (2 January 1944), GCF, OSA.

45 Case to Snell (23 December 1944); Snell to Case (26 December 1944); both in GCF, OSA.

46 Case to Snell (23 December 1944), GCF, OSA.

47 Banholster to Snell (22 December 1944), GCF, OSA.

48 Snell to Banholster (26 December 1944), GCF, OSA.

49 Smith to Snell (22 December 1944), GCF, OSA.

50 Snell to Smith (26 December 1944), GCF, OSA.

51 Jno. R. Dix to Snell (3 Jan 1945), GCF, OSA.

52 Snell to Dix (9 January 1945), GCF, OSA.

53 Edwards to Snell (27 December 1944), GCF, OSA.

54 McMurdo to Snell (17 January 1945), GCF, OSA.

55 Snell to McMurdo (20 January 1945), GCF, OSA.

56 Brinson to Snell (22 January 1945), GCF, OSA.

57 Lamb to Snell (25 January 1945), GCF, OSA.

58 Snell to Lamb (27 December 1944), GCF, OSA.

59 Moore to Snell (2 January 1945), GCF, OSA.

60 Mrs. George E. Brewster to Snell (29 December 1944); George E. Brewster to Snell (20 December 1944); Mary Jane Brewster to Snell (27 December 1944); all in GCF, OSA.

61 Snell to George E. Brewster (22 December 1944), GCF, OSA.

62 Moore to Snell (2 January 1945), GCF, OSA.

63 Snell to Moore (4 January 1945), GCF, OSA.

64 Mary Jane Brewster to Snell (27 December 1944), GCF, OSA.

65 George Brewster to Snell (20 December 1944), GCF, OSA.

66 Snell to Brewster (21 December 1944), GCF, OSA.

67 *California Eagle* (21 December 1944).

68 *Oregonian* (23 December 1944); Mrs. E. Mabry to Snell (23 December 1944), GCF, OSA.

69 Snell to Mabry (26 December 1944), GCF, OSA.

70 Clara Folkes to Snell (17 December 1944), GCF, OSA.

71 Snell to Folkes (19 December 1944), GCF, OSA.

72 Pollard also raised the issue of why police detained Funches in the Albany jail until just days before the trial began, "and he has not been heard from since." William E. Pollard to Snell (12 December 1944), GCF, OSA.

73 Clara Folkes to Snell (27 December 1944), GCF, OSA.

74 Jones to Snell (27 December 1944), GCF, OSA.

75 Charleston to Snell (22 December 1944), GCF, OSA.

76 C. Phillips to Snell (29 December 1944), GCF, OSA.

77 Thompson to Snell (28 December 1944), GCF, OSA.

78 Thompson to Snell (28 December 1944), GCF, OSA.

79 Thompson to Snell (28 December 1944), GCF, OSA.

80 Brewster to Snell (29 December 1944), GCF, OSA.

81 Densmore to Snell (1 January 1945); Steidel to Snell (26 December 1945); both in GCF, OSA.

82 Steidel to Snell (1 January 1945), GCF, OSA.

83 Johnson to Snell (27 December 1945); Jardine to Snell (19 December 1944); Mabry to Snell (23 December 1944); all in GCF, OSA.

84 Mabry to Snell (23 December 1944), GCF, OSA.

85 Mabry to Snell (23 December 1944), GCF, OSA.

86 Earl Snell (December 1944–January 1945), GCF, OSA.

87 *California Eagle* (21 December 1944).

88 *Democrat-Herald* (28 December 1944).

89 *Democrat-Herald* (2 January 1945).

90 *Democrat-Herald* (3 January 1945).

91 *Democrat-Herald* (4 January 1945).

92 *California Eagle* (4 January 1945).

93 *Democrat-Herald* (5 January 1945).

94 *Democrat-Herald* (5 January 1945).

95 *Democrat-Herald* (6 January 1945).

96 *Virginian-Pilot* (6 January 1945).

97 *California Eagle* (11 January 1945).

98 The *Virginian-Pilot* (13 January 1945), for example, published photos of Alma M. Jackson of Richmond, reportedly "the first Negro woman to be commissioned by the Public Health Service" and assigned to Liberia. On the same page, a photo of

Second Lieutenant Johny Birdsong, of Dallas, Texas, showed the (clearly Black) army officer leading, reportedly, "the first combat patrol across the Arno river."

99   *People's Observer* (18 January 1945).

100 *People's Observer* (18 January 1945).

101 *Klamath Falls (OR) Herald and News* (14 December 1944).

102 *People's Observer* (18 January 1945).

103 *People's Observer* (18 January 1945).

104 *Herald and News* (5 January 1945).

CONCLUSION

1   Brazil, pp. 170–171.

2   *Walla Walla (WA) Union Bulletin* (17 January 1949).

3   *Coshocton (OH) Tribune* (17 January 1949).

4   *Valley (Harlingen, TX) Morning Star* (16 January 1949).

5   *Ogden (UT) Standard Examiner* (1 January 1949).

6   J. A. Ormandy to J. J. Nolan (27 January 1943); Nolan to Ormandy (4 February 1943); Pullman Company check # RB 3-756 (Claim No. 2187-R) (3 February 1943); all in PPCR.

7   L. Orth Sisemore to L. W. Snider, Superintendent Pullman Company, Union Pacific, Portland, OR (6 May 1943); F. R. Callahan to J. M. Carry (10 May 1943); Snider to Anderson (7 May 1943); all in PPCR.

8   Snider to Anderson (27 May 1943), PPCR.

9   Snider to Anderson (25 May 1943); *American Weekly* (23 May 1943); both in PPCR.

10 *American Weekly* (23 May 1943).

11 *LA Times* (13 February 1945).

12 *LA Times* (1 March 1945).

13 *LA Times* (16 October 1946, 12 June 1946, 28 March 1947, 12 August 1948, 11 September 1948, 8 April 1948, 27 July 1949, 4 August 1949, 16 March 1946).

14 Communication from Glynn Martin, LAPHS (16 April 2007).

15 *LA Times* (11 May 1932).

16 *LA Times* (15 February 1933).

17 *LA Times* (1 March 1945).

18 *LA Times* (13 January 1944).

19 *LA Times* (22 February 1944).

20 *LA Times* (21 January 1943).

21 *LA Times* (6 April 1949).

22 Michael Ayers Trotti, "The Lure of the Sensational Murder," *Journal of Social History* (Winter 2001), p. 429.

23 Leroy L. Lomax to Adjutant and Inspector Division, Marine Corps, Washington, DC (telegram, 4 May 1943); Joseph H. McDowell, Captain, US Marine Corps to Leroy L. Lomax (8 May 1943); both in JAG CORR, 1942–44 A6-6(2) May 1943, Box 4, RG125, Stack 550, Row 69, Compartment 7, Shelf 7, National Archives and Records Administration (NARA).

24 Studies that have explored the ways in which popular culture frames and transforms the narrative within which a broader populace discovers and learns about such cases include Cohen, *Murder of Helen Jewett*; Suzanne Lebsock, *A Murder in Virginia: Southern Justice on Trial* (New York: W.W. Norton & Company, 2003); and Haltunen, *Murder Most Foul*.

25 Communications from Eric Foster to author (5 July 2010 and 15 July 2010).

26 "Robert Folkes Executed, Buried," *Kansas City (KS) Plaindealer* (26 January 1945); "Cook Dies for Killing in 'Lower 13' Case: Youth Goes to Gas Chamber Denying Guilt," *Plaindealer* (12 January 1945).

27 Stuart Banner, *The Death Penalty: An American History* (Cambridge, MA: Harvard University Press, 2002), pp. 199–200, 221–222, 244; Bill Bradbury, *Oregon Blue Book, 2003–2004* (Salem: Oregon Secretary of State, 2003), pp. 296–316.

28 Mark M. Smith, in *Sensing the Past: Seeing, Hearing, Smelling, Tasting, and Touching in History* (Berkeley: University of California Press, 2007), argues historians overemphasize sight and undervalue other senses as causal factors in history because they rely mostly on textual sources.

Index

away life: as struggle for control, 160; of trainmen in Portland, 160

The FACTS in the Robert Folkes Case: Brewster family role in, 319; NAACP support for, 280; publication of, 280

Aaron, William G. (SPRR chef): as Folkes' mentor, 105; as SPRR chef, 104; cooking crew of, 104–105; replacement of, 105

Adler, George (Dr.): as Klamath County coroner, 64; collection of evidence by, 138, 139; role in investigation, 64, 138, 139

Albany, Oregon: Black trainmen in, 169, 170, 178; Folkes statement at, 236; Porter Hughes in, 178, 179, 180; race relations in, 169, 170, 179, 180; Stone report and, 179, 180

Albany Motel, 178

Albany statement, 236. *See also* Miller statement

American Federation of Labor, 117

American Weekly: depiction of Folkes case in, 335, 336; Pullman company and, 335, 336

Annual Sermon of the Dining Car Employees Union, 118. *See also* DCWU

anticommunism, 301, 302

antiunionism, 303, 304

appeals process: challenges to, 247; news coverage about, 246, 262; racialized understandings of, 262; strategies of, 247; wartime context of, 246

Arkansas: Delta–area pogroms in, 79; Folkes family and, 9, 10, 79

Bailey, Alton (Mrs.): time estimates of, 151; witness statements by, 151, 152, 153

Baker, Clermont (SPRR chef): as Aaron's replacement, 105, 106; at Medley, 163, 164; inexperience of, 105, 106; interactions with Folkes, 163, 164

Ball, Bernice, 138, 139

Banich, George (SPRR investigator), 133, 134

Banks, William: as train conductor, 121; closed–room scenario and, 211, 212; interrogation of, 122; investigation by, 121, 122; murder timeline estimates of, 122; suspects Wilson, 123, 124; testimony of, 211, 212

Bass, Charlotta, 254, 258. *See also California Eagle*

Bechtel statement: as defense exhibit, 239, 240; contradictions of, 297; discovery of, 235, 236; prosecution discounting of, 193, 194; Tetrick's actions and, 297; value to defense of, 193, 194

bedside confession, 191

Beeman, Joseph (Dr.): as source of news leaks, 58; confessions and, 289, 290; forensic laboratory of, 40–42; investigative role of, 28; professional status of, 40–42; rape euphemisms by, 58; role as OSP interrogator, 236, 237; role in Layton case, 289, 290

Black exclusion clause (Oregon Constitution), 11, 201, 202

Black fugitive rumors, 52, 53

Black middle class, 36: Black trainmen and, 37; Clara Folkes and, 89; voting habits of, 89

Black trainmen: as mainstays of Black middle class, 37; courtroom status of, 36; deferential demeanor of, 333; discrimination against, 36; interrogations of, 63, 163; racialized roles of, 333; turnaround time in Portland of, 161, 162; Union Station (Portland) and, 161, 162

Boilermakers and Shipbuilders Union: Portland Local No. 72 of, 248, 452, 253; racist leadership of, 252, 253; segregated locals of, 254, 255

Bolton, Sterling (SPRR waiter), 163

bracero program, 33

Brand opinion: errors of, 268; Folkes case and, 267. *See also* OSSC

Bremerton, WA, 8, 9

Brewster family, 319

Brinson, Grace, 342
Brinson, Wilbur: social standing of, 56, 57; political connections of, 70, 71; wrongful death claims by, 335; Sisemore retained by, 335; death of, 342; as father of Martha James, 342
Bronzeville, 108. See also South Central
Brotherhood of Sleeping Car Porters, 10, 34, 37, 38. See also BSCP
BSCP: Hughes and, 172, 173; PPC and, 172, 173
Bryant, J.A.: as Pullman conductor, 212, 213; grand jury testimony of, 170, 171; witness statements and, 213

California Eagle: criticizes rural southern immigrants, 91, 92; editor of, 91, 92; Folkes family and, 79, 80; progressive leadership of, 91, 92; promotion of militarized identities in, 92; RFDC appeal in, 309, 310; South Central and, 79, 80. See also Bass, Charlotta
Camp Adair, 33, 35: Albany hotels and, 172; Folkes trial and, 172
capital punishment: gender and, 204; juror selection and, 204; Oregon history of, 342, 343. See also death penalty
Car D: conditions in, 45–49; demographics of passengers in, 46–47. See also Car D
Casablanca, 54–55
Cayton, Revels: CIO and, 117; William Pollard and, 117
Central Jail (L.A.), 68: coerced confessions at, 84; conditions at, 186, 187; Folkes experiences at, 186, 187, 195, 196, 338, 339; interrogation tactics at, 273, 274; LAPD scandals and, 234; murdered prisoners at, 84, 234; OSSC deliberations at, 273, 274; Preston Jones beating at, 276–277; systematic abuses at, 338, 339; torture of prisoners at, 195, 196
Chamberlin, Davis (Mrs.): courtroom testimony by, 214, 215; description of murder scene by, 215, 216; vagueness of, 215, 216; witness statements by, 151, 152
Champlin, C.W. "Champ": as lead SPRR investigator, 64; investigation by, 133, 134; testimony of, 228, 229
crime scene: management of, 125; multiagency investigation of, 125
circumstantial evidence: and gender bias, 204; and juror selection, 204
civil rights: 1944 presidential election and, 275, 276; activists at Folkes trial, 202, 203; as context for appeal, 247, 248; Folkes execution and, 328, 329; in Portland, 14; McClendon's editorial and, 328, 329; OSSC decision and, 275, 276

class difference: clemency petitions and, 316; deference and, 316; investigators and, 140, 141
clemency campaign: access to Snell and, 308; advocates for, 298, 299; arguments of, 298; basis for, 298; deferential appeals and, 308; Earl Snell (Gov.) and, 287, 288; effectiveness of, 299, 300; FBI sting operation and, 288, 289; labor radicalism and, 288, 289; NAACP and, 277; national reach of, 306–308; racial identity and, 306–308; racialized context of, 287, 288; RFDC and, 277; Snell's response to, 299–300, 307–308; strategies of, 298, 299
closed–room scenario: as pretense by investigators, 135–138; compromised handling of, 140–141; murder–mystery genre and, 135–136; prosecution arguments and, 207–208; SPRR investigators and, 137–138; uncounted passengers and, 140–141
Clow, James J. (Rev.): challenges Folkes verdict, 249; criticism of police by, 249; Portland civil rights community and, 248–249; Portland Council of Churches and, 248–249; Portland NAACP and, 248–249
collective bargaining: DCWU wage proposals and, 111–112; Dining car workers and, 111–112; William Pollard and, 111–112. See also Dining Car Workers Union
collusion: of Linn County prosecutor (Weinrick) with SPRR and PPC, 169–171, 174–175, 180–181; of SPRR and PPC officials, 181–182
Combined Negro Churches of Los Angeles, 259–260
Commissary (Portland), 164–165
common–law marriage: Folkes family and, 88–89; middle class respectability and, 94
concealing evidence: Linn County District Attorney (Weinrick) and, 180–181; PPC and SPRR officials, 181–182
confession: admissibility of, 28–29; as in Lyman statement (Los Angeles statement), 196–197; as in Miller statement (Albany statement), 200; claims of, 235–236; Brand's definitions of, 268; contradictions of, 189–190, 197–198; defense challenges to, 193–194; embellishments of, 182–183; fictional nature of, 266–267; Folkes denial of, 189–190; inadmissibility of, 268, 292–293, 295; incomplete nature of, 197–198; LAPD claims of, 182–183; LAPD detectives and, 235–236; mentions steward's party, 196–197; OSSC pretense about, 266–267; prosecution claims of, 182–183; prejudicial nature of, 292–293, 295; timing of, 68
Conner, Ralph, 224

counter-clemency campaign: effectiveness of, 300; racist components of, 305; Snell's response to, 300–301, 305
court error, 268–269
courtroom galleries, 202–203
crime scene, 122
crimewave theories, 42–43
criminal deviance: as sociological theory, 42; Lower 13 case and, 46–47
criminal justice: John Dewey and, 41; theories of, 41–42

Darden, Colgate (Gov.): connections with Brinson family, 71; opposes clemency, 300–301; pressures Snell, 71, 195–196, 199, 300–301
dark overcoat: 221–222
death penalty: abolition of, 343; and race, 14–15, 21–22; Folkes sentencing and, 244; gas chamber and, 343; morality of, 293–294, 296; Oregon history of, 20, 22, 343–344; repeal of, 343–344; Snell's use of, 343
defense worker designation, 89–90
Democratic Socialist Party: Clara Folkes and, 89–90; South Central voters and, 85–86, 89
Devereaux, Elmer (SPRR waiter): as military recruit, 116; at Medley, 164; steward's party and, 164–165
dining car 10110: juror tour of, 207–208; staging for trial of, 173–174, 207–208
dining car chefs, 104–105
dining car cooks, 10–11: away life in Portland of, 11; checkered pants and, 104; daily routine of, 98–99; skills required of, 101–102; uniforms of, 89–90, 104; wartime speedup and, 101–103
Dining Car Division (SPRR), 40
dining car kitchens: crew cohesion in, 104, 126, 127; working conditions in, 104, 220
dining car stewards, 126–127
dining car waiters, 10–12
dining car waiters case (Union Pacific Railroad), 323–324
dining car workers: car-loading duties of, 103–104; commissary interactions of, 103–104; community among, 167–168; functional work units of, 105–106; leave time routines of, 161–162; living conditions of, 100–101; racial differences of, 62–63, 162; sleeping berth arrangements for, 100–102; strategies of resistance by, 160–161; surveillance of, 62–63, 104, 126–127; uniforms of, 104; working conditions of, 96–97
Dining Car Workers Union, 10, 25: contract negotiations of, 111–112, 117–118; Local 582 of, 114, 117–118, 309; Local 465 of,

117; organizing principles of, 96; South Central Headquarters of, 88–89; wartime priorities of, 182; RFDC and, 276
directed verdict: circuit court judge refusal of, 213; defense motion for, 212
discovery phase: defense access and, 212–213, 241–242; stonewalling defense during, 174–175
Donnelly, R. G. (Mrs.), 151–152
Dooley, Eddie (SPRR cook), 75–76
Dooley's overcoat: Folkes' reference to, 188; loaned to Folkes, 75–76; police confiscate, 186
due process rights: 303–304

education: Folkes family and, 86–87; South Central and, 86
Elaine Schoolhouse Massacre (Arkansas), 83–84
Elijah Association (Oregon), 303–304
employment record (Folkes), 86–87
Enell, Arthur (SPRR brakeman), 128–129
Eugene, Oregon, 126
execution, 14: news reports of, 324–325; wartime context of, 331–332; witnesses of, 325–326
Executive Order 8802: effectiveness of, 247–248; FEPC and, 38, 247–248. See also Fair Employment Practices Committee
Executive Order 9346, 248
executive clemency petition, 315
exoticization of murder victim, 52–53, 56–57, 60–61

Fair Employment Practices Committee, 38–39, 247–248; Folkes case and, 254. See also Executive Order 8802
Federal Bureau of Investigation (FBI), 134
Finneran, J. J. (SPRR investigator), 334
Flieder, Maxine, 151–152
Folkes case: appeal process and, 261–262; labor unrest and, 252; racialized reporting of, 252, 257–258
Folkes, Clara [Leach], 14: activism of, 313; Arkansas residence of, 83; as single mother, 84–85; Black middle class and, 89; church involvement of, 88–89; courtroom demeanor of, 312–313; experience in Albany of, 179–180; family of, 341–343; letter to Snell, 311–313; migration of, 83–85; NAACP support for, 279; occupations of, 85–86, 88; political affiliations of, 85–86; reaction to verdict, 245; Porter Hughes and, 179–180; RFDC and, 250–251; speaking tour of, 279, 313; travel to Oregon by, 279
Folkes, Eugene, 341–343

Folkes, Jessie Taylor Wilson: describes alleged "confession," 184–186; experience in Albany of, 179–180; family of, 186–187; home life of, 75; residence of, 88–89, 186–187; testimony of, 296

Folkes, Robert (Sr.), 83–85

Folkes, Robert E. Lee, 9: appearance of, 67–70, 73–74, 141, 159, 194–195; arrest in Los Angeles, 65–67; as union member, 16; background of, 77–78, 332; bedside confession of, 187; blames conviction on prejudice, 192–193; Central Jail (LA) experience of, 184–186; childhood of, 81–83; confession of, 69–71, 73–74, 121; cooperation of, 145–146; coworkers and, 75–76; denies role in murder, 144–145, 192–193; employment record of, 81–82, 85–87; family of, 15; home life of, 75–76; interrogations of, 121, 141–142; introverted personality of, 31; LAPD interrogations of, 157–159; kitchen activity of, 219–220; LAPD treatment of, 184–186, 194–195; last hours of, 326–327; misspelled name of, 69; obituaries of, 341–342, 346; Portland activities of 157–159; racialized identity of, 32, 69; raincoat of, 75–76; self-presentation of, 80, 332; serves steward's party, 167–168; signed statements of, 144–146; SPRR uniform of, 159; stereotyping of, 32; stocking dining car, 167–168; trial of, 155–156; work schedule of, 97–98; workplace demeanor of, 168–169; work ethic of, 80–82, 102–103

Folkes, Shirley Ann, 341–343

"Food Fights for Freedom," 116

forced labor, 170–171, 177–178

form letters (from Snell), 302

Funches, John: as early suspect, 12, 58, 136; as SPRR waiter, 136; detention of, 58, 64; photos of, 64,

gender: exclusion of witnesses by, 151–153; investigators and, 49–50, 137–138; investigative biases and, 137–138; suspects and, 49–50; witnesses categorized by, 137–138; witness testimony and, 214–215

gendered roles: dining car workers and, 111; in South Central neighborhoods, 86; racial categories and, 111, 113–114

genteel space, 39–40

geographic mobility, 85–87

Gordon, Walter L., 105–106

grand jury proceedings, 170–172

Granoff, L. Nicholas, 315

Great Migration, 10–12: Folkes family and, 79, 84–85

Greenman, Charles (SPRR steward), 162–163

Guadalcanal, 54–55, 278–279

Haefner, Ruth (NAACP Portland), 250–251

Hale, R.H., 179

Hardle, James B. (Major): as Marine Corps liaison, 68–69; role in Folkes' interrogation, 194–195

Harrisburg, Oregon, 49–50

Helena Jail murders (Arkansas), 83–84

Henderson, J. Raymond (Rev.): Baptists Union in L.A. and, 258; RFDC fundraising and, 259; Lenza Smith case and, 259

Hildebrand, Ruth, 290

Hill, T. Arnold, 37–38

Hoffert, Harold, 213

Holmes case, 334–335: Lower 13 case and, 333

Howard, R.C. (OSP officer): Layton "confession" and, 289–290; OSP interrogations and, 236–237

Hughes, Harry McKinley (Pullman porter), 124–125, 147–148; as combative witness, 229–230; discovery of murder by, 223–230; describes Wilson's appearance, 230–231; Folkes family and, 179–180; grand jury testimony of, 170–171; housing in Albany and, 175–176; questions stenographer's accuracy, 230–231; racialized identity of, 229–230; testimony of, 228–230; timeline estimates of, 230–231; worker resistance and, 176–177

inadmissible evidence, 261

instructions to jury, 242–243

interagency investigative team, 134–135

interstate networks, 258–259

James, Harry Mapp, 56–57

James, Martha Virginia Brinson "Marti," 7: appearance at murder scene, 66, 124, 125, 218; media image of, 66, 328–329, 340–341; murder of, 12, 45–46, 49–50, 328–329, 340–341

James, Richard Floyd, 8: as suspect, 12; claims unused ticket refund, 335; claims wife's body, 134; college career of, 57; death of, 277–278, 328–329; marriage to Martha Virginia Brinson, 57; social status of, 65–66; told of wife's murder, 134; travel arrangements of, 60

Japanese exclusion, 32–33

Jefferson High School: racial integration and, 106; South Central community and, 75

Jim Crow system, 263–264

Johnson, Booker T.: Portland night life and, 166; as dining car waiter, 165

Johnson, Russell, 164–165

judicial error, 294

juror deliberations, 211: duration of, 243–244; Lleweling's instructions and, 244

juror selection: and death penalty, 203–205; and
gender, 13–14, 26, 203–204; and
occupational bias 204–205; and racial bias,
204–205
jury verdict, 244–245

Kaiser shipyards, 11, 36
Keaton, G. E.: as Mr. Zinni, 163; marine status
of, 61; steward's party involvement of, 62;
with wife, 62
Kelso, R. M.: militarized privilege and, 143,
148–149; reluctant testimony of, 210, 228–
229; role in LA "confession" of, 188–189;
witnesses abuses, 142–144
Kitzhaber, John, 19–20
KKK: 100-percent Americanism and, 304–305;
Oregon legacies of, 200–201; Rossman and,
285; Walter Pierce and, 285
Klamath Falls, Oregon, 8: interrogations at,
63–64; investigation at, 134
Ku Klux Klan. See KKK

labor: management of, 111–112, 181–182;
organizing of, 79–80, 88–89, 94, 248–249;
rural ideal of, 209
labor relations: in wartime industries, 11; Folkes
case and, 253–254; SPRR and, 88–89
Lane County coroner, 125
LAPD (Los Angeles Police Department): abuses
in Lenza Smith case, 259; arrest of Folkes by,
156; Central Jail inquiry and, 234;
interrogation procedures of, 183–184, 234;
scandals involving, 234; transcripts of
interrogations by, 190–191
Layton case: as Snell's rationale, 301; clemency
campaign for, 290; comparisons with Folkes
case, 269–270; differences from Folkes case,
291–292; OSP interrogations and, 289–290;
OSSC ruling and, 289–290
Layton, Richard: execution of, 289–290;
statement at sentencing by, 290–291
Lebanon, Oregon, 33
Linn County: as site of murder, 49; farm tenancy
rates in, 33; urban places in, 33–34
Llewelling, L. Guy: as circuit court judge, 221–
222; as trial judge, 221–222; courtroom
demeanor of, 221–222; hearsay ruling of,
231–232; ruling allowing Lyman and Miller
statements, 232–234
Logan, John C.: as dining car waiter, 162–163,
165; steward's party and, 166
Lomax, Leroy: conspiracy claims of, 208–210;
list of exceptions by, 260–261; opening
arguments of, 208
Los Angeles Police Department. See LAPD
Lower 13 case, 29–30; initial stories about, 46–
47; moralizing narratives of, 55–56. See also
Folkes case

Lyman statement: inaccuracies of, 194–195,
271; in OSSC deliberations, 265–266;
introduction of, 235; role of alchohol in,
195–196
Lyman, Nancy: as LAPD stenographer, 232
233; coaching of, 235–236; contradictions
of, 235–236; testimony of, 195–196, 235–
236
lynching, 21, 29–30, 43–44, 302

March on Washington Movement, 34. See also
MOWM
masculinity, 30: rural values and, 205–208;
urban values and, 205–206
Masonic Order, 20, 305–306
McClendon, William H.: as editor of People's
Observer, 248–251; clemency appeals and,
283; criticizes police methods, 252; criticizes
White press, 251–252; Folkes case and,
248–249, 252, 283, 327–328; on Black
passivity, 327–328; on White supremacists,
327–328. See also People's Observer
McNabb v. United States, 270
Medley Hotel: as Black trainmen's refuge, 99–
100, 158, 162–163; People's Observer
distributed at, 251
Mendenhall Grocery, 106
militarization: and train travel, 12–13, 15;
clemency appeals and, 317–318; Folkes case
and, 260; implications for Robert Folkes,
92–93; of investigation, 68–69, 149–150,
153; of news reports, 51–52; regional
context of, 23; of SPRR, 48, 112–115; South
Central and, 113; urban implications of,
32–33; Wilson's testimony and, 217–218;
witness believability and, 59–60
Miller statement: inaccuracies of, 269–271; in
OSSC deliberations, 265–266; OSP
stenographer and, 237. See also Albany
statement
Miller, Kathleen: as courtroom reporter, 255; as
OSP stenographer, 237; transcript delays by,
255–256
Moore v. Dempsey (1923): coerced confessions
and, 84–85; SCOTUS ruling on, 84
MOWM, 37–38. See also March on Washington
Movement
murder: discovery of, 48–49, 148; method of,
189–190; reports of, 50–51
murder scene: as observed by Banks, 123–124;
description of, 151–152; lighting at, 218–
219; location of, 218–219
murder timeline: Folkes' LA "confession" and,
188–189; William Banks' estimates about,
122–124
murder weapon: 57–58

NAACP, 14; in Oregon, 78; in South Central, 107; Los Angeles local, 106–107, 117–118, 309–310; national office of, 280; supports RFDC, 192–193, 280

National Association for the Advancement of Colored People. See NAACP

Navy (United States), 51, 61

Negro Shipyard Organization for Victory (Portland), 253

Negro Victory Committee (Los Angeles), 118

Norfolk Journal and Guide, 258

Norfolk, Virginia, 8, 53–54

Norton, Eugene W.: military identity of, 49, 225–226; testimony of, 123–124, 224; witness statements by, 49

O'Connell, O. (SPRR executive), 133–134

Okie migration, 107

Oregon Bar Association, 284

Oregon State Grange, 278–279

Oregon State Penitentiary: death row at, 251; transport of Folkes to, 244

Oregon State Police: forensic pathology lab, 28, 42; Joseph Beeman and, 28, 40–42, 58, 236–237, 289–290

Oregon State Supreme Court. See OSSC

OSP. See Oregon State Police

OSSC, 14: Folkes case and, 255; oral arguments before, 262–263

OSSC decision (in Folkes case): Brand opinion and, 264–265; news reports of, 297–298; racialized understanding of, 262–263, 297–298

Oyster House (Portland), 163

People's Observer: conflict with Snell of, 286–287; Folkes case and, 248–251; McClendon as editor of, 248–249; report on Folkes execution in, 326–327. See also McClendon, William H.

PFHUA. See Progressive Farmers and Household Union of America

physical abuse, 142–143

Pierce, Walter: Albany speech of, 278–279; race–baiting by, 278–279

pin–striped suit: Harold Wilson and, 119; morphing of, 221; murderer described wearing, 136; search for, 136

PPC. See Pullman Palace Car Company

police misconduct: Folkes interrogations and, 338–339; LAPD and, 316, 338–339

Pollard, William E. appearance in Albany of, 80; as labor organizer, 25; California Eagle and, 117–118; Clara Folkes and, 192–193; clemency petition by, 283, 309; Dining Car Workers and, 323–324; DCWU Local 582 and, 88–89; labor activism of, 342; letter to

Snell from, 313–314; moral framework of, 283; outlines prosecution's flaws, 314; physical description of, 313–314; reaction to verdict of, 245–246; RFDC and, 192–193, 250–251; urban identity of, 209–210; "war hysteria" claim, 314. See also Dining Car Workers Union, RFDC

Portland, Oregon, 8, 11: demographics of, 37–38; trainmen's "away" lives in, 157; wartime growth of, 54

premeditation: as pre-requisite for death penalty, 242; Llewelling's definition of, 243

Progressive Farmers and Household Union of America, 83–84

public-private collusion, 134–135

Pullman Palace Car Company (PPC), 40; company investigators of, 90–91, 169–170; public relations concerns of, 336–337

Pullman porters: excluded from Albany hotels, 175–176; nicknamed "George," 153; questioning of, 140–141; racialized identities of, 153

Pullman sleeping car, 9, 12

race relations: in Albany, 169–170; in Portland, 169–170; labor unrest and, 249–250; rural-urban relations and, 249–250

racelessness: as cover for racist appeals, 301, 304; as denial of difference, 301; as Snell's public posture, 301, 324; Clara Folkes' appeal and, 312; pretense of, 265–266, 309–310, 324

racial exclusion: in Albany, 170–172; in Albany hotels, 155–156; in Portland, 78–79; wartime patterns of, 282

racial mixing: 167–168

racialization: of Folkes, 24; of Folkes' OSSC appeal, 262; of railroad workers, of suspect lists, 51–52, 59–60, 128; selection of evidence and, 69–70; war propaganda and, 32–33

racialized bias: as basis for clemency petitions, 321–322; of investigators, 149–150,153

rail travel: SPRR profits from, 113–114; wartime surge of 114–115

Randolph, A. Philip, 10, 37, 38. See also MOWM

rape: allegations of, 12, 272–273; as alleged in OSSC opinions, 272–273; as motive for murder, 12, 32, 68; euphemisms for, 32

Rasmussen, Vernon: as LAPD captain, 233; believability of, 233–234; LAPD career of, 273; postwar record of, 338–339; role in Folkes interrogations of, 233–234

RFDC, 259–260: CIO Anti-Discrimination Committee support for, 259–260; civil rights activists and, 248–249, 284, 322–323; Clara Folkes and, 276–277, 280; clemency campaign of, 286, 297–298, 322–323;

NAACP support for, 280, 286, 323–324; Negro Victory Committee support for, 259–260; origins of, 192–193, 248; OSSC appeal and, 255–256; OSSC ruling and, 297–298; Pollard and, 117–118, 314–315; Portland labor movement and, 248; progressive leadership and, 323–324

Robert Folkes Defense Committee. *See* RFDC

Rossman, George: background of, 284–286; civil rights activism and, 282; dissenting opinion of, 274–277, 282; on death penalty standards, 292–293; professional credentials of, 284–286

rural-urban networks: 32–33, 155–156, 249–250

rural-urban relations: 319–320, 345–347

second cook: duties of, 99–100, 314; Folkes' morning routine as, 314

segregated housing, 178

self-incrimination, 271

Shaw, N. L. (Pullman porter): grand jury testimony of, 170–171; signed statements of, 181–182; travels to Albany by, 170–171; trial testimony of, 181–182

Sheehan, M. K.: as district claims agent, 170; Pullman porters and, 170–171; reports from Albany by, 171

Sisemore, L. Orth (Klamath Falls D.A.): assistance to Weinrick by, 41–42; depositions by, 137–138; personal background of, 41–42; post-war career of, 342; role in investigation by, 134–135

sleep deprivation tactic, 143–145

Snell, Earl (Gov.): communications with Colgate Darden, 71; death penalty views of, 20, 275–276; election of, 11–12, 200–201; pressures Weinrick, 71; relations with NAACP (Portland local); responses to petitioners, 299–300; response to Clara Folkes, 313

South Central "Station," 108

South Central Los Angeles, 10–11: clergy of, 258–259; community centers in, 75; community experience of, 79, 107–108; Folkes family and, 79; racial conflict in, 109–110; wartime migrants in, 91–92; wartime reputation of, 107–108

South Central petitioners: Charlotta Bass and, 318–319; class difference and, 315–317

Southern Pacific Railroad, 10–11, 39–40, 79–80: employment opportunities with, 60, 86–87; Folkes family and, 86–87; labor policies of, 96–97; Los Angeles Station of, 106; military transport role of, 95–96; South Central Commissary of, 75, 103–104; South Central presence of, 79–80; South Central "station" of, 10. *See also* SPRR

SPRR (Southern Pacific Railroad): dining car division, 109–110; hiring practices of, 109–110; investigators, 102–104, 160–161, 133–135, 179–180; labor management practices of, 110–111; war bonds drive of, 110–111, 114; workers, 95–96

SPRR detectives: interrogation methods of, 143–145; leadership of, 133–134; role in investigation, 62–63; surveillance of dining crews by, 103–104, 160–161; worker-control concerns of, 160–161

SPRR dining car division: car-stocking work of, 164–165; militarization of, 95–97; racialized jobs of, 109–111

St. Turubius Catholic Church (South Central LA), 88–89

Stalingrad, 54–56

states' rights argument: OSSC ruling and, 270; Brand opinion and, 272

steward's party, 8: Keaton and James couples at, 62; murder motives and, 337–338; racial mixing at, 62, 159, 337–338

Stone, William: as SPRR agent, 208–209; trial report of, 179–180, 208–209

subpoenaing witnesses: labor management methods and, 175–177; racial differences and, 174–175

surprise witnesses: gender of, 214–215, 226; perjury of, 225–226; prosecutor coaching of, 225–226; racial identity of, 224–225, 227; youth of, 226

Tangent, Oregon: as location of murder, 52, 56–57; management of train at, 122–123

Taylor, Frederick A.: as SPRR investigator, 133–135; investigative priorities of, 136–138

Tetrick, Edgar A.: as LAPD detective, 189–190, 273, 338–339; Folkes' statements and, 233; record of, 338–339; role in alleged corruption, 338–339; role in Folkes interrogation, 189–190, 299

The Facts in the Robert Folkes Case: introductory essay of, 287–288; NAACP and, 287–288; publication of, 286

Tichenor, E. W. (OSP officer), 334

timeline estimates, 147–148

torture: third degree and, 232–233; trial court hearing on, 232–233

Tourist Car 4001: as murder scene, 127–128; conditions in, 45; re-staging in Albany of, 173–174. *See also* Car D

transcriptions: errors of, 231; incomplete nature of, 239, 242

trial jurors, 202

trial transcript: delayed preparation of, 261–262; disposition of, 344; inconsistencies of, 256–257; OSSC deliberations and, 263; OSSC records and, 344 true-crime literature: as model for prosecution's case, 21, 119–120, 332, 336; criminal justice and, 42–43; influence on jury of, 27–28; militarization of, 27–28; moralizing purpose of, 119–120; plot devices of, 332, 336

Union Pacific Railroad, 289–290
Union Station (Portland), 8–9: as focus of Black community, 78–79; commissary at, 164–165; military transfers through, 54; stocking dining car at, 164–165
Union Station (Los Angeles), 10
University of Virginia, 57
Urban League, 309–310
urbanization, 33

Van Dyke, William: contradicts Wilson, 151–153; location in Car D of, 150–151; militarized identity of, 59, 151–153; observes bloodied Wilson, 151–152; statements of, 150–151
Vanport City, 36–37
voter registration trends, 85–86

war bride, 8, 12
war hysteria, 283–284
War Relocation Authority, 33: Japanese removal and, 202
wartime profiteering, 166–167
wartime speedup, 97–98
wartime travel, 48
Washington, Leon: as community activist, 342; as Folkes' in-law, 318, 342; as reporter with the Los Angeles Sentinel, 186–187
Wasserman, Marjorie: as "surprise" witness, 224–225; racial identity of, 227–228; testimony of, 226–227; vagueness of, 224–228; youth of, 224–225
Weinrick, Harlow "Whitey," 41–42: collusion with PPC of, 169–170; collusion with SPRR of, 169–170; on motives of murderer, 67–68; political pressures on, 70; transcript editing and, 255–256
West Coast Limited (SPRR), 60
White backlash: 277–278
White, Elmer (SPRR waiter), 163
White, Walter: FEPC and, 37–38; meeting with Clara Folkes, 280; NAACP and, 37–38; supports RFDC, 280
William and Mary College: 56–57
Wilson, Harold, 9, 11–12: actions of, 215–216; adaptability of, 129–130; Albany statement of, 192; as material witness, 58; behavior at murder scene, 127–128; behavior in Seattle of, 191–192; changing stories of, 216–217, 220; characteristics of, 131–132; charismatic appeal of, 129–131; contradictory

statements of, 71, 73–74, 127–130; credibility of, 223–224; criminal record of, 22, 217–218; death of, 342; demeanor of, 131–132; description of crime scene by, 58–59, 132–134; description of murderer by, 58–59, 131–132; detention of, 22, 58, 64; encounters with James couple by, 192; harassment of Doris Price by, 191–192; interrogated by Banks, 126; interrogations of, 129–132, 192; militarized identity of, 119–120, 129–131; military persona of, 30–31; military record of, 340; Minnesota origins of, 72–73; misrepresentations of, 71; photos of, 64; popularized image of, 52; postwar career of, 342; sexual assault and, 217–218; stories of, 119–120, 126; testimony of, 215–217
Wister, Owen, 43
witness tampering, 216–217
witnesses: management of, 211–212; suppression of, 241–242
women: death penalty views of, 203; descriptions of murder scene by, 151–152; exclusion as witnesses of, 137–138; Oregon juries and, 203
Women of the Jury, 7
work: Folkes' record of, 87, 210; SPRR uniforms for, 89–90; virtues of, 210
worker control, 160–161
worker flight: as response to Folkes trial, 114–116; SPRR concerns about, 160–161; SPRR dining car division and, 113–114, 116
worker radicalism, 303–304
working conditions: SPRR dining car workers and, 75, 87–88; in SPRR dining cars, 156, 160–161

Zinni, Mr. and Mrs.: as pseudonyms, 162–163; as guests at steward's party, 162–163
zoot suit: origins of, 93–94; racial conflict and, 94–95; Robert Folkes' style and, 89–90; wartime regulation of, 93–94